Virtue, Rules, and Justice

Acknowledgments

Sources

1. Initially published as "Kant" in *The Routledge Companion to Ethics*, ed. John Skorupski (New York: Routledge, 2010), 156–67.
2. "Kantian Normative Ethics," in *The Oxford Handbook of Ethical Theory,* ed. David Copp (Oxford: Oxford University Press, 2006), 480–514. Reprinted by permission.
3. "Kantian Constructivism as Normative Ethics," *Oxford Studies in Normative Ethics*, ed. Mark Timmons (Oxford: Oxford University Press, 2011), 26–50. Reprinted by permission.
4. "Finding Value in Nature," *Environmental Values* 15/3 (2006).
5. "Kant on Weakness of Will," slightly revised, initially published in *Weakness of Will from Plato to the Present*, ed. Tobias Hoffmann (Washington, DC: Catholic University of America Press, 2008), 210–30.
6. "Kantian Virtue and 'Virtue Ethics'," *Kant's Ethics of Virtue*, ed. Monika Betzler (Berlin: Walter de Gruyter, 2008), 29–60.
7. "Kant's *Tugendlehre* as Normative Ethics," in *Kant's Metaphysics of Morals: A Critical Guide*, ed. Lara Denis (Cambridge: Cambridge University Press, 2010), 234–55.
8. "The Dignity of Persons: Kant, Problems, and a Proposal," initially published in German as "Die Würde der Person: Kant, Probleme und ein Vorschlag," trans. Joachim Schulte, in Ralf Stoecker (ed.), *Menschenwürde: Annäherung an einen Begriff* (Vienna: öbv&hpt, 2003), 153–73.
9. "Assessing Moral Rules: Utilitarian and Kantian Perspectives," in *Normativity, Philosophical Issues (A Supplement to Nous)*, 15 (2005), ed. Ernest Sosa and Enrique Villanueva, 158–78.
10. "The Importance of Moral Rules and Principles," The Annual Lindlay Lecture, 2006 (Kansas: Department of Philosophy, University of Kansas, 2007).
11. "Moral Construction as a Task: Sources and Limits," *Social Philosophy and Policy* 25/1 (2008), 214–36.
12. "Questions about Kant's Opposition to Revolution," *Journal of Value Inquiry* 36/2–3 (2002), 283–96.
13. "Treating Criminals as Ends in Themselves," *Jahrbuch für Recht und Ethik/ Annual Review of Law and Ethics* 11 (2003), 17–36.

14. "Kant and Humanitarian Interventions," *Nous Supplement: Philosophical Perspectives* 23 (2009), 221–40.
15. "Moral Responsibilities of Bystanders," *Journal of Social Philosophy*, 41/1 (2010), 28–39.

While writing these essays I have received help and support from many sources. Financial support was given by the University of North Carolina at Chapel Hill and the Kenan Foundation. The faculty and students in the philosophy department here provided a philosophical community that demonstrates that pursuit of excellence is compatible with an encouraging collegiality. I have had the opportunity of sharing in seminars with Bernard Boxill, Douglas MacLean, and Susan Wolf; and other colleagues have been helpful in many ways. Over the years I have had wonderful encouragement from former graduate students, and I continue to learn from their work and appreciate their good-spirited approach to philosophical discussion. At recent workshops on topics relevant to this volume, along with colleagues Jan and Bernie Boxill, these included Macalester Bell, Samuel Bruton, Andrew Cohen, Andrew Courtwright, Adam Cureton, Richard Dean, Jeffrey Downard, Carl Ficarotta, Tamra Frei, Sarah Holtman, Andrew Johnson, Robert Johnson, Sean McKeever, Cynthia Stark, Karen Stohr, Brian Thomas, and Yolanda Wilson. I am also grateful for the contributions of other participants—Kimberley Brownlee, Lara Denis, Samuel Kerstein, Oliver Sensen, David Sussman, and Mark Timmons. As acknowledged in the notes to several chapters, I have benefited from comments of faculty and students when I discussed my work at various universities and conferences. My debt to many other Kant scholars is perhaps too obvious to need mention but too great to fully acknowledge. These especially include Marcia Baron, Sharon Byrd, Stephen Engstrom, Paul Guyer, Barbara Herman, Joachim Hruska, Christine Korsgaard, Onora O'Neill, Thomas Pogge, Andrews Reath, Arthur Ripstein, Helga Varden, Allen Wood, and Arnulf Zweig.

Adam Cureton served as my research assistant for several years while completing his doctorate at UNC. His resourcefulness, technical savvy, and editorial skills have been incredibly helpful, and, even more, my work has been enriched by his insightful comments in our long philosophical conversations. Later Kiran Bhardwaj also helped and prepared the index.

My sons, Tom and Kenneth, wisely realized that two generations of philosophers was enough, but I am pleased that their interest in my work persists despite their quite different professions.

Most of all, I am grateful to Robin for making it possible for me to do philosophical work while also enjoying family and friends. Her extraordinary generosity, intelligence, energy, and efficiency are well known even if too infrequently acknowledged. As a medical social worker she takes care of elderly patients, as she did for my father until he died at 97. Her patients and I know what he meant when he called her a "guardian angel."

Contents

General Introduction

The essays presented in fifteen chapters here are about Immanuel Kant's moral theory and ethics from a broadly Kantian perspective. A primary aim has been to interpret, explain, and extend Kant's ideas in ways that highlight their relevance to contemporary ethics. Kant's writings on ethics are complex, comprehensive, and challenging, and they have been the subject of excellent work by many Kant scholars and Kantian theorists. By continuing my efforts to explain and engage critically with Kant's work, I have tried not only to make his ideas more accessible but also to extend some of them. My underlying interest has always been in the philosophical questions that I find in Kant's work. Accordingly, although I often summarize and interpret Kant's views as I understand them, I also go beyond historical scholarship with a view to developing a broadly Kantian theory drawn from some of his ideas. At different points in these chapters I mean to describe Kant's view, propose an interpretation, or draw critically from Kant to develop a modified but broadly Kantian position. These are different aims, and I hope that it is sufficiently clear which is intended in each context.

As will become evident, my focus is primarily on normative moral and political theory and potential applications rather than on metaethical foundations. The topics here are wide-ranging but are divided into four parts, according to their main purpose and themes. To preview (with numbers that correspond to chapters): Under "Basic Themes" the first three chapters (1) introduce briefly the major aspects of Kant's ethics, (2) explain various ways his formulations of the supreme moral principle have been interpreted, and (3) sketch a "constructivist" reading of Kantian *normative* ethics distinct from the Kantian constructivisms of O'Neill and Rawls. Under the heading "Virtue," the next four chapters (4) discuss whether it might be a virtue to regard the natural environment as intrinsically valuable, (5) address puzzles about moral weakness in Kant's ethics, (6) contrast ideas of virtue in Kant's ethics and in "virtue ethics," (7) comment on duties to oneself, second-order duties, and moral motivation in Kant's Doctrine of Virtue. In the section on "Moral Rules" the four chapters (8) propose human dignity as primarily a guiding value for a system of norms rather than a self-standing test for isolated cases, (9) contrast Kantian and rule-utilitarian perspectives on moral rules, (10) highlight the importance and limits of specific rules and basic principles in the Kantian framework by contrast with moral particularism, and (11) distinguish often-conflated questions about moral relativism and objectivity and outline a Kantian position on two central issues. Drawing from previous chapters, under the heading "Practical Questions" the next three chapters show how, at least if partially critical of Kant's official theory of law, a broadly Kantian theory might revisit questions about (12) revolution, (13) prison reform, and (14) forcible interventions in other countries for humanitarian purposes. The final chapter (15) develops some implications of Kant's Doctrine of Virtue for the responsibility of bystanders to oppression.

The chapters were written originally as self-standing discussions, intended to be clear and mostly understandable without special background, but always with an eye to how they might make up a coherent collection. They may be read separately, depending on the reader's interests and prior familiarity with Kantian theory, but different aspects of Kant's systematic thought and of my broadly Kantian framework emerge gradually as the chapters progress from topic to topic. Each was initially addressed to a different audience, but most are meant to be accessible to advanced students and serious general readers as well as professional philosophers.

What is distinctive about these essays? First, many topics addressed here are rarely discussed by Kantians, and some are relatively neglected by philosophers generally. For a long time attention was focused primarily on Kant's claims about the role of reason in ethics, the relation among the formulas of the Categorical Imperative, and their application to particular controversial cases. Until recently Kant's ideas of virtue and justice in his later writings were rarely examined closely or appreciated as Kant's fuller development of moral theory beyond the familiar *Groundwork for the Metaphysics of Morals*. Initially puzzling features about Kant's theory remain surprisingly underexamined: for example, how can it explain weakness of will, what can it say about negligent non-intentional wrongdoing, and what role can it give to actual socially supported moral codes (as distinct from laws of the state)? Although Kant's famous examples in the *Groundwork* and his notorious late essay on lying to a murderer are often cited, the full resources of Kantian theory have not been brought to bear on pressing contemporary issues of justice and public morality, for example the mistreatment of criminals and terrorist suspects, the limits of state sovereignty, and the responsibility of ordinary citizens in an unjust world. My essays are meant to open up or advance discussion of these practical issues from a critical Kantian perspective, but obviously more discussion is needed.

Second, by contrast to many who study or occasionally refer to Kant, my aims and method are neither those of pure historical scholarship nor of entirely text-independent philosophical investigation. I respect, admire, and rely on Kant scholars whose close and literal study of texts contributes to our understanding. I also respect, admire, and learn from moral philosophers whose independent thinking takes us outside the theoretical frameworks of the past. I am convinced, however, that there is also value (as well as danger) in trying to combine the best in both approaches. The danger is that ties to a historical tradition may prevent us from giving due regard to good objections and alternatives, but the potential value is that we can make critical use of the good efforts of our predecessors, building on the best while respectfully dissenting from opinions that we find inapplicable or untenable now. My work is not unique, of course, in its attempt to combine historical understanding and philosophical investigation. For example, Marcia Baron, Stephen Engstrom, Paul Guyer, Barbara Herman, Christine Korsgaard, Onora O'Neill, John Rawls, Andrews Reath, and Allen Wood all combine philosophical and historical interests, giving more or less priority to one or the other in their various works. On substantive matters beyond methodology, however, my understanding of Kant and my proposed development of a broadly Kantian framework differ from others' in significant ways, and the next three points (labeled third, fourth, and fifth below) indicate some areas in which there are differences.

Third, many Kantians attribute to Kant, with apparent approval, a strong "guise of the good" thesis. Loosely expressed, this is the claim that whenever one acts intentionally or for reasons, one takes it to be *good* to act this way. In other words, one is always acting with the *belief* (or assumption) that one's act is good or, metaphorically, one *sees* what one is doing *as* good. There are stronger and weaker versions of this idea. At the weaker extreme Hobbes claimed that there is nothing good in itself or in nature, what is good always being relative to a person's desires.[1] We do not desire things because they are good, but instead we merely call things good because we desire them. We act as we most strongly desire at the time, and so we naturally regard our acts as good *relative to our desires* at the moment. An extremely strong version of the thesis says that whenever one acts intentionally (or for reasons) one takes one's act to be *universally and objectively good to do all things considered*. In other words, one believes or assumes that one's act is fully justified from the point of view of everyone. Assuming a Kantian account of moral wrongdoing, this would apparently imply that it is impossible to do intentionally what one knows to be morally wrong, contrary to common sense that says we (too) often act from moral weakness or even defiance of moral constraints in ways we correctly see as bad and wrong to do. Now these issues are complex and the relevant passages in Kant's texts are many, and so here I merely note that it appears to me that Kantians in recent years tend to veer dangerously close to implausibly strong versions of the guise of the good thesis when they interpret and draw from Kant's texts.[2] Critics have often charged that passages in the *Groundwork* imply that to act freely is to act in accord with the moral law, raising the question of how we can be responsible for our (unfree) wrongdoing. More recent interpretations of Kant are more subtle than the simple reading that prompted this charge, but they still raise questions about the possibility of intentional wrongdoing. For example, if the will is nothing but practical reason and every maxim is implicitly willed in the "form" of universality, then it seems that our *will is* always for the good and wrongdoing must be simply due to mistakes resulting from flawed use of our rational capacities.[3]

A key question here is how to interpret Kant's claim that the moral law is the principle of rational persons with autonomy of the will. Some apparently take this to mean that every intentional choice (or "willing") is ultimately guided by the moral law, implying that all bad acts are somehow

---

[1] Hobbes held that in a state of nature we call things good relative to our own desires, but in a civil state by agreement we count the Sovereign's will as determining what is good in cases of conflict, *Leviathan*, pt. I, ch. 6, para. 7.

[2] It is hard to generalize with appropriate caution over so many commentators, but attributing a strong guise of the good thesis to Kant seems to play an important role in the work of Stephen Engstrom, Christine Korsgaard, Andrews Reath, and Tamar Schapiro. I comment on Reath's version in "Legislating the Moral Law and Taking One's Choices to be Good," Hill (2008c), 97–106, and on Engstrom's version in "Practical Reason, the Moral Law and Choice" (Hill, 2012, forthcoming).

[3] See Engstrom (2009), chs. 4–6.

presented because they are more self-contained, accessible by topic, and suitable for nonspecialists than they would otherwise be. The disadvantages of this mode of presentation are that I needed to repeat the outline of some core ideas, such as the Kantian legislative perspective, in several chapters and needed to fill gaps with many back references to my previous papers. In present form the essays reveal my exploratory, often ambivalent, but hopeful attitude about Kant's moral and political theory, which is also expressed in the subtitle "Kantian *Aspirations*." The essays, I think, demonstrate my conviction that in ethics theoretical and practical questions are mutually interdependent and also that work on Kant's ethics and broadly Kantian ethics remains incomplete but promising. I owe whatever merit there may be in these essays mostly to others, but I own the defects.

I. Basic Themes

1. Kant's Ethical Theory: an Overview (2010)

This introductory chapter presents a concise summary of major themes in Kant's moral philosophy, broadly conceived. Topics include Kant's a priori method for basic questions, the special features of moral judgments, the formulations of the Categorical Imperative, justice and the moral obligation to obey the law, and ethics and religion.

2. Kantian Normative Ethics (2006)

Kant's formulations of the Categorical Imperative express basic requirements to universalize our maxims, respect humanity as an end in itself, and conform to the more specific moral principles that we do or would will as rational persons with autonomy. Kantians disagree about the interpretation and relative importance of these various formulations, but most now agree that, although they provide no algorithms, the formulations can be helpful in guiding moral deliberation and judgment. In this chapter I explain the basic features of the formulations, review different interpretations, and note various problems that each formulation raises. I review briefly ideas of Alan Donagan, Barbara Herman, Christine Korsgaard, Onora O'Neill, H. J. Paton, Thomas Pogge, John Rawls, and Allen Wood. A primary aim is to call attention to the different ways in which contemporary Kantians have attempted to develop Kant's normative ethics.

A secondary aim is to show how Kantian ethics, under different interpretations, addresses the questions when and why we are morally required
to help others. Kant's theory is justly famous for its insistence that pursuit of
happiness, for oneself and others, is constrained by moral requirements of
justice and respect for human dignity. Kant also argues, however, that it is
categorically imperative for us to make it our maxim to promote the
happiness of others. It is currently a matter of controversy how much
latitude this requirement is supposed to leave us to pursue non-obligatory
projects of our own. Focusing on beneficence to illustrate various contemporary developments in Kantian ethical theory helps to bring out similarities
and differences among them and may reveal some relative strengths and
weaknesses.

3. Kantian Constructivism as Normative Ethics (2011)

What would Kantian constructivism be like as a normative (not metaethical)
theory that focused on ethical, not political questions? First I review
conceptions of the normative/metaethical distinction, general features of
constructivism, and the versions of Kantian constructivism described by
Rawls, O'Neill, and my earlier papers. Then I highlight features of the
normative ethical theory that Kant developed in his late work, the Doctrine
of Virtue (The Metaphysics of Morals, Part II), proposing that this can be
viewed as a normative ethical theory with constructivist features separable
from the more ambitious metaethical claims in the prominent Kantian
constructivisms of Rawls and O'Neill. When interpreted in this way the
Doctrine of Virtue fits well with the constructivist normative theory that
earlier I drew from Kant's later formulations of the Categorical Imperative
in the Groundwork. Finally, I respond to some of O'Neill's objections to
Rawls's constructivisms that would apply as well to my project.

II. Virtue

4. Finding Value in Nature (2006)

In a previous paper[9] I argued that those who despoil the natural environment
often express objectionable attitudes rooted in ignorance, self-importance,

---

[9]   Hill (1983).

and patterns of aesthetic insensitivity that, if not themselves vices, give evidence of deficiency in the natural bases of human excellences, such as proper humility, gratitude, and aesthetic appreciation. My main point was that in order to show that environmental ethics is not all about rights and welfare it is not necessary to presuppose that natural phenomena have intrinsic value in a metaphysical sense.

Now, supposing there is a broader human virtue we might call appreciation of the good, I consider whether this could be manifested by appreciating aspects of nature as good in themselves. Those who are already committed to intrinsic value as a metaphysical property should have no objection to this idea, but they typically regard the value of nature as prior to and totally independent of human capacities for appreciation. In my view the relation is not so simple and one-directional. Values are not natural or nonnatural properties that we perceive as pre-existing in a nonhuman world, but they are also not simply things we create or mere reflections of our subjective tastes. The philosophical challenge is to explain, without metaphysical obscurity or undue anthropocentrism, how and why it is good to value certain natural phenomena for their own sakes and to recognize and respond appropriately to the value they have, in a sense, independently of human rights and welfare. The explanation, I suggest, requires sensitivity to distinctions, reflected in ordinary language, between desiring and valuing, between valuing something and regarding it as valuable, and between regarding something as valuable for various purposes and regarding it as valuable in itself.

5. Kant on Weakness of Will (2008)

Here I review the background in Kant's moral psychology, suggest how weakness of will might be understood in Kant's theory, and comment on the implications for moral responsibility. In brief, my proposal is this. For Kant, weakness of will is not a physical incapacity or disability but contrasts with virtue understood as developed strength of will to do our duty despite obstacles. The will is not literally a force, strong or weak, but is conceived as either law-giving practical reason (*Wille*) or choice to act on a maxim (*Willkür*). Morally weak persons, I suggest, choose to act on particular maxims in conflict with both practical reason and their general maxim to act as they should. Our general life-governing maxims, like laws of the state, may be weak in content (vague and indeterminate) or willed weakly (with little provision for implementation). Moral weakness mitigates culpability without excusing. Contrary to some interpretations, weak-willed bad acts are, in an important sense, freely chosen and not necessarily failed efforts to act well. How this is possible, in Kant's view, cannot be explained empirically or metaphysically.

6. Kantian Virtue and "Virtue Ethics" (2008)

This chapter explores similarities and differences between Kant's ideas about moral virtue and various ideas associated with virtue ethics. I try to identify some misconceptions of Kant's ethics and highlight features that may be overlooked. Drawing from the essay of the previous chapter, I highlight Kant's distinctive understanding of virtue as moral strength. Finally I comment on the apparent differences between Kant's theory and some views associated with "virtue ethics" regarding (A) the need for moral rules, (B) sensitivity to particular contexts, (C) morally good motivation, and (D) the standard for right action.

Kant treats *virtue* as a kind of strength of the will to do what is right. Virtue is more than having good intentions, and we need to develop it over time. We have a duty to try to develop virtue, but we are also responsible if, lacking sufficient virtue, we do wrong through weakness of will. We have particular virtues insofar as our will to fulfill various specific duties is strong, but it is not the implications of Kant's position for particular virtues (and vices) of character that is most interesting. Apart from that, Kant's ideas raise questions about moral responsibility and strength and weakness of will that present special problems of understanding, even though (arguably) in some respects Kant's ideas reflect familiar common-sense views.

7. Kant's Tugendlehre as Normative Ethics (2010)

This chapter reviews, highlights, and raises questions about themes in Kant's Doctrine of Virtue, Part II of *The Metaphysics of Morals*. In a wide-ranging discussion it comments briefly on the topics: (1) how Kant's normative ethics relates to science, metaphysics, metaethics, and philosophy of law, (2) how Kant's first principles relate to more specific moral principles and judgments, (3) how Kant's idea of duties to oneself compares to contemporary conceptions, (4) how Kant addresses the problems of moral negligence, self-deception, and weakness, and (5) how to understand the role of the motive of duty in a virtuous life. The chapter emphasizes the constraints of law and justice on virtue, the moral (if not epistemological) priority of the first principles of ethics, and the irrelevance of many contemporary objections to Kant's conception of duties to oneself. The chapter also highlights Kant's important second-order principles regarding due care in deliberation, self-scrutiny to expose excuses, and development of strength of will to resist temptations. The morally necessary motive of duty is interpreted, not as an extra duty added on each particular duty, but as the basic choice to maintain a pervasive attitude that puts moral responsibility before self-interest.

III. Moral Rules and Principles

8. The Dignity of Persons: Kant, Problems, and a Proposal (2003)

What is it to treat someone as a person with dignity? There are no doubt some descriptive criteria for "treating a person as a person," but the idea of dignity implies something more. Drawing from Wittgenstein's famous duck-rabbit example, we might try to interpret "*seeing* someone *as* a person" in a more expressivist fashion. Though perhaps promising, this leaves open important ethical questions. I turn, then, to Kant, who made the idea of dignity a centerpiece in his moral theory. After a review of basic features of Kant's idea, I express doubts about aspects of the interpretations proposed by some other commentators, notably David Cummiskey, Alan Donagan, and Marcus Singer. Kant's idea of dignity raises two important problems of application. The first is that it apparently generates conflicts of duty. The second is that, although it offers an appealing contrast to consequentialism, it imposes such severe constraints that its practical implications are often counterintuitive. In particular, it seems to require strict conformity to moral principles that are appropriate for most conditions even when extraordinary circumstances make it reasonable to make exceptions. Arguably these problems are more manageable, however, if we use the idea of the dignity of persons at a second-order level of moral deliberation rather than case by case.

To pursue this suggestion, I develop further my previous ideas about humanity as an end in itself and incorporate them into a fuller account of the deliberative standpoint suggested by Kant's ideal of moral legislation in a kingdom of ends. This is a framework for articulating and assessing mid-level moral principles, addressing conflicts among them, and considering possible exceptions. It is an expansion of my previous work and a basis for the later chapters here on practical issues.

9. *Assessing Moral Rules: Utilitarian and Kantian Perspectives (2005)*

This chapter compares and contrasts rule-utilitarian and Kantian thinking about what moral rules should be accepted and what exceptions they should allow. We do not, and may never, know just what particular rules would maximize expected aggregate utility, and the relevant Kantian perspective is not a fully determinate decision procedure. So assessment by reference to putative counterexamples is unpromising. Nevertheless, I give four considerations for thinking that the Kantian *way of assessing moral rules* is more plausible than the rule-utilitarian way. The fundamental problem, I argue, is that rule-utilitarianism gives an inadequate account of *relevant moral reasons* even if it does not clearly lead to counterintuitive conclusions. Promoting utility (the general welfare, preference satisfaction, etc.) is not the only reason for moral permissions and requirements, for why certain commitments are morally worthy, and for why facts about the past matter. To have a right and moral permission to pursue one's own projects in certain contexts, for example, it is not necessary that general adoption of a system of rules allowing it would maximize utility. Kantians and rule-utilitarians will no doubt agree that one should not in general commit murder to prevent a comparable murder, but arguably this is not *simply* a matter of the utility of accepting moral codes permitting or forbidding it. Further, we may question whether it is *morally worthy* to commit oneself to any set of rules *solely because* they are utility maximizing. Finally, although rule-utilitarianism can be expected to favor moral codes with some backward-looking requirements regarding fidelity, reparations, gratitude, and just deserts, we may doubt that their moral force stems entirely from forward-looking estimates of their effects on aggregate welfare.

10. The Importance of Moral Rules and Principles (2006)

Here I describe elements of the broadly Kantian conception of *why* certain rules are important, review some common objections, and consider these questions: (1) Is it morally important to have shared moral *rules* about specific types of problem, rules that are distinct from laws of the state and yet not merely heuristic guides? (2) If there are such morally important rules, does their moral authority or the justifiability of particular moral judgments depend on more fundamental moral standards that can be expressed in the form of *principles*? (3) If there are such fundamental moral principles, what sort of framework do they provide for deliberation about the content of moral rules, their limits, and the priorities among them? (4) If principles and rules are important, how can we respond to common objections to their use and abuse in philosophy and in ordinary decision-making? My answers, not surprisingly, are affirmative: (1) we need specific moral rules; (2) justification presupposes more general principles, as illustrated in a Kantian account of practical reason; (3) one sort of deliberative framework can be drawn from Kant's basic moral principles; (4) common objections show the limits but not the unimportance of moral rules. All these issues are controversial. My aim is not to settle the disputes but to sketch a view of moral rules and principles worth taking seriously.

In the discussion I propose a reconstruction of Kant's view of reasons and rational principles, distinguishing the pattern for hypothetical imperatives from the pattern for moral (categorical) imperatives, and asking where in these patterns are the "reasons" for action? Then I comment briefly on the familiar objections: (1) rules are no substitute for good judgment; (2) rule-worship is irrational; (3) morality is not all about social rules; and (4) moral thinking is not all about systems of possible rules.

11. Moral Construction as a Task: Sources and Limits (2008)

Initially written for a conference on "objectivity" and "relativism" in ethics, this chapter distinguishes six different questions that fall under these general headings, and it comments briefly on Kant's position regarding them. Then the chapter sketches a broadly Kantian position on two of the questions.

First, how can basic moral principles guide and constrain deliberation about more specific moral principles? Regarding this, I review Kant's ideal of legislation in a moral commonwealth, interpreted as a deliberative procedure different from those commonly (and perhaps more literally) attributed to Kant. This ideal, which is explained further and used in other chapters, is presented as a constructivist procedure for normative ethics that, unlike metaethical constructivisms, presupposes and makes use of basic moral values associated with the idea of humanity as an end in itself. The proposed legislative perspective is like contractualism in assuming legislators' rational self-regard and willingness to reciprocate, but the Kantian perspective differs from contractualism in important respects.

Second, how can a theory's basic standards be defended? In response to this question, two Kantian strategies for vindicating basic principles are briefly described. Setting the stage for these strategies were Kant's arguments that all previous moral theories were mistaken, and these arguments remain relevant to contemporary moral theories. Beyond this, the strategies in question are, first, to argue analytically that the basic principles are presupposed in common moral concepts and, second, to appeal to each person's consciousness of what practical reason demands when duty conflicts with self-interest. These strategies of defense invite comparison with Rawls's method of reflective equilibrium.

Practical Questions

12. Questions about Kant's Opposition to Revolution (2002)

Kant's denial of a right to revolution is famous, but he was an ardent supporter of the spirit of the French Revolution. He acknowledged cases of conscientious refusal and passive resistance, and unlike Hobbes, thought standards of justice should apply to rulers; but he argued against any right to overthrow a bad legal system governed by a tyrant. In a spirit critical of Kant but trying to understand his underlying thoughts, I take up these questions: How could Kant consistently express enthusiasm for the French Revolution while denying a right to revolution? Does Kant have adequate arguments against a legal right to rebel against a tyrant? Do his arguments support his view that overthrowing the supreme legal authority is always morally wrong? Do the reasons implicit in his formulations of the Categorical

Imperative, which ground his endorsement of passive resistance, justify revolution in certain conditions, despite what he himself concluded?

13. Treating Criminals as Ends in Themselves (2003)

First, I consider how the idea of humanity as an end might guide policies regarding the *manner* in which punishment is carried out insofar as this is independent of Kant's official principles of law and justice. Those principles addressed the central questions about punishment: who should be punished, how much, by what means, and why? Kant's official principles of punishment include a standard for the appropriate *amount* of punishment for various offenses, but they do not determine every aspect of how criminals are to be treated. Even if we provisionally assume that those principles are justifiable, then, we can usefully ask whether ethical considerations urge us to seek reforms in the manner in which just punishments are carried out.

Second, setting aside the provisional acceptance of Kant's official principles of punishment, I consider the *implications of the humanity formula* regarding those same questions of punishment: who should be punished, how much, by what means, and why? What I propose here is an admittedly un-Kantian thought experiment. Suppose that we were to reject or disregard Kant's own theory of just punishment and yet accept my reconstruction of his humanity formula: what sort of practice of punishment, if any, would we as conscientious individuals advocate and support? Would the humanity formula, applied in this context, provide presumptive reasons for urging reforms for our current practices?

Third, I consider the discrepancy between the results of the last section and some of Kant's official principles of punishment. Arguably, the humanity formula, applied independently of Kant's official theory of justice, would endorse policies in conflict with aspects of that official theory. The conflict calls into question his official principles of punishment and the special distinction between law and ethics on which the principles rest. Unless these can be adequately justified on independent grounds, the ideals encapsulated in the humanity formula would require modification of those official principles.

14. Kant and Humanitarian Intervention (2009)

This chapter sketches a Kantian deliberative perspective, the moral presumption in favor of humanitarian interventions, relevant practical considerations, and Kant's apparently inflexible opposition to any forcible intervention in the governance or constitution of another state. The critical questions then are: (1) Does a government's responsibility to its citizens prohibit intervention primarily for the sake of citizens of other countries? (2) Does the case for humanitarian intervention depend on illegitimate ideas about the right to punish or forfeiture of the right to govern? (3) Does forceful intervention in the governance of another state necessarily violate the rights of the citizens of that state? At issue are relations among ethics, law, and international relations.

I argue that (1) Kant's ethics rightly indicates that there is a presumption in favor of humanitarian interventions in some cases, (2) he wisely points to grounds for caution, avoiding punitive motives, and respecting the reasonable will of the citizens in other states, but (3) in the arguments reviewed here Kant did not provide adequate reasons for an absolute prohibition of humanitarian interventions in all cases.

15. *Moral Responsibilities of Bystanders (2010)*

My aim here is, first, to frame my question about the responsibility to resist oppression, second, to describe briefly three second-order responsibilities especially pertinent to "by-standers," third, to note some connections to often overlooked aspects of Kant's ethics, and, finally, to suggest briefly how we might see neglect of these responsibilities as failures to respect both oneself and others. My main question here is not about what specifically to do in various contexts of oppression. It is instead a prior question about certain forward-looking moral responsibilities of those who may be or become bystanders in oppressive conditions. The three special responsibilities are second-order responsibilities to exercise *due care* in deliberation, to *scrutinize one's motives* for remaining passive, and to try to *develop virtue* conceived as strength of will to do what is right despite obstacles. The three responsibilities are drawn from Kant's later writings on ethics and religion, where Kant seems to take more seriously the problem that many moral failures are due to negligence rather than intentional wrongdoing. By neglect of the special second-order duties we contribute to the ongoing oppression of others, but we also fail to respect ourselves properly insofar as we do not do what we can to implement our basic moral commitments.

Note: bracketed numbers in citations of Kant's works refer to the volume and page of the standard Prussian Academy edition, *Kant's gesammelte Schriften*, ed. Königlich Preußischen Akademie der Wissenschaften (Berlin, 1902–). The *Critique of Pure Reason* is cited by A/B pagination.

I
Basic Themes

1

Kant's Ethical Theory: An Overview

Kant's writings on ethics followed his monumental *Critique of Pure Reason* (1781). There he tried to show that all previous metaphysical theories failed because they did not begin with a critical assessment of the powers of reason. His own critical study attempted to revolutionize metaphysics and synthesize the best from rationalist and empiricist traditions. A major conclusion relevant to ethics was that theoretical reason cannot prove the existence of God, immortality, or freedom of the will, though it leaves room for faith. In his later ethical writings he argued that nevertheless from *practical* reason we can establish the supreme principle of morality and the freedom of choice that it presupposes. At least, he argued, these can be shown to be valid for purposes of deliberation and action. These are major themes of his classic *Groundwork for the Metaphysics of Morals* (1785). Here he also defends his a priori method for the foundations of ethics, draws a sharp contrast between moral and nonmoral "ought" judgments, and articulates several versions of the supreme moral principle. Shortly after, in his *Critique of Practical Reason* (1788), he reaffirms his previous conclusions but modifies his argument. Here he also offers moral reasons for faith that God exists and hope for immortality, but not as a basis or motive for morality. Later Kant published *The Metaphysics of Morals* (1797–8), which (in Part I) presents his theory of law and justice and (in Part II) explains how his ethical principles apply to recurrent moral issues. Contemporary philosophers have interpreted Kant's ethical writings in many different ways. This chapter simply highlights some of the main themes, inviting readers to explore them further for themselves.

A Priori Method for Basic Questions

When addressing the most fundamental questions, Kant argues, moral philosophy should be "pure" and not based on empirical generalizations. For example, the validity of its basic principle should not depend on how altruistic or selfish human beings are naturally inclined to be. In Kant's view, pure moral philosophy aims first to discover the most basic and comprehensive moral principle inherent in ordinary thought about moral duty and morally worthy actions. This requires what he called an *analytic* mode of argument, which is a matter of examining our concepts carefully to see what further ideas they presuppose. The conclusion of such arguments is always conditional. For example, in *Groundwork* II, Kant argues *not* that the supreme moral principle (which he calls "the Categorical Imperative") is rationally binding for us, but only that *in believing* that we have genuine moral duties *we are necessarily committed* to the Categorical Imperative as a rationally imperative moral principle.

Pure moral philosophy also aims to determine whether or not conformity to the basic moral principle is necessarily *rational*, and this is not a question that can be settled by empirical studies of how people actually behave. Even polls about what people *say is rational* would be inconclusive because the claim that violations of moral requirements are contrary to reason is a *normative* claim. It is a claim about what in fact we have *good and sufficient reason* to do, which is more than a prediction about what most people would say if asked. To establish that the basic moral principle is rationally binding, Kant says, requires a different type of argument, one that proceeds *synthetically*. This is what he attempts in the notoriously dense reasoning in *Groundwork* III. Here the question is not about what is *presupposed* by our common moral beliefs but about whether we have sufficient reason to regard those beliefs as true. Both questions, in Kant's view, call for an a priori method. *Groundwork* II uses an a priori analytical argument to show that our moral beliefs presuppose that moral requirements are rational, but *Groundwork* III uses a different ("synthetical") a priori procedure to show that this presupposition is not an illusion.

None of this implies, however, that ethics is completely independent of empirical facts. Most obviously, we cannot make judgments about what we ought to do on a particular occasion without some information about the situation. Even general principles of the sort Kant presents in *The Metaphysics of Morals* depend on at least general facts about the human condition. Kant does defend the controversial claim that some principles (for example, the prohibition of lying) are binding regardless of the particular circumstances, but he acknowledges that the application of other principles (for example, those regarding giving aid, developing one's talents, and even retributive punishment) may vary with the situation. When moral philosophy focuses on empirical facts, such as the conditions that facilitate moral education, he calls it *moral anthropology*.

The Special Features of Moral Judgments

In Kant's view, it is crucial to distinguish between morality and prudence. Too often, in theory and in practice, we confuse moral reasons with self-serving reasons. Philosophers mistakenly urge us to be moral as a means to happiness, and in daily life we make exceptions of ourselves by treating our strong self-regarding desires as excuses. At the heart of Kant's moral theory is his explanation of the contrast between moral and nonmoral "ought" judgments. The former express (or are based on) *categorical imperatives* whereas the latter express (or are based on) *hypothetical imperatives*. All imperatives (in Kant's sense) have two features: they are (at least conditionally) *rational* to follow and they are *expressed in terms appropriate for those who can follow them but might not* ("ought," "should," "must," "Do it!"). *Categorical* imperatives are said to be unconditionally necessary "commands" of reason that prescribe an act as good in itself. They express the idea that we (rationally) must do as prescribed whether or not it will contribute to our happiness or serve the particular ends we happen to have. *Hypothetical* imperatives, by contrast, are "counsels of prudence" or "rules of skill" that prescribe an act as (conditionally) good to do if or because it serves as a means to our happiness or particular ends we happen to have. Strictly speaking, Kant argues, there is only one Categorical Imperative—the most basic principle of rational morality (to be discussed shortly)—but he also used the term for strict requirements that are based on this basic principle.

Characteristic examples of specific categorical imperatives, in Kant's view, include "One must not make false promises," "Do not treat anyone as worthless," and "Adopt the happiness of others as an end." The idea is that failing to conform to these moral principles is contrary to reason ("irrational" or "unreasonable," we might say) and, in Kant's view, this is not because these failures would make us unhappy or unable to achieve what we want. Examples of hypothetical imperatives might include "One ought to floss one's teeth if one aims to avoid gum disease," "Work out harder!" (assuming you aim to be successful in sports), "Since you want to be happy, you should avoid dwelling on past troubles," and "Save something for a rainy day!" (where the implicit reason is that you will be unhappy otherwise). The idea in these cases is that it is one's particular aim or general concern to be happy that explains why it is rationally necessary to act as the hypothetical imperatives prescribe—unless there is a compelling (perhaps moral) reason not to.

Why are certain facts reasons to act and others are not? Kant treats facts as reasons insofar as they would fit appropriately into a pattern of reasoning governed by a general principle of rational choice. In the case of hypothetical imperatives the general principle seems to be something like this: You ought, if you aim for a certain end, to take the necessary means to it—or else give up the end. This principle picks out certain facts as reasons to act—or at least to modify one's plans. For example, it identifies as reasons the (joint) facts that you aim to be successful at sports and exercising harder is needed to accomplish that goal. These reasons do not make the exercise absolutely mandatory, of course, because you may have good reason to give up your plan to succeed at sports. Our natural desire for happiness (lasting contentment and achieving our desire-based ends) cannot be altogether given up, Kant thought, but we can choose not to pursue happiness as our end on particular occasions when there is sufficient reason (for example, a moral imperative) to choose otherwise. In addition, Kant reminds us, how we conceive of our happiness is vague and our understanding of how to achieve it is uncertain. Prudence, then, only gives us conditionally rational "counsels," not strict "commands," which are only given by categorical imperatives.

When we turn to categorical imperatives, what is the rational principle that identifies compelling reasons to act? Kant thinks that there must be such a principle and it must be a basic Categorical Imperative in the strictest sense—an absolutely unconditional and nonderivative rational principle. His thought is that the existence of particular moral requirements, which we all recognize, presupposes that there is such a principle. How else, for example, could it be (as he assumed) that there are unconditional commands of reason not to make false promises for profit, to commit murder for revenge, or to ignore the welfare of others? The main aims of the *Groundwork* were to articulate and vindicate our reliance on this presupposed rational principle, the Categorical Imperative.

Universal Law Formulas of the Categorical Imperative

Given Kant's a priori methodology and arguments so far, this supreme moral principle must have compelling credentials as a necessary form or standard that should shape all rational deliberation and choice about practical matters. Too often rationalist theologians and philosophers had uncritically declared their substantive moral dictates to be the voice of reason, but the aim of Kant's critical philosophy was to expose false pretensions in such claims to rational authority and, when possible, to vindicate the proper use of practical reason. The supreme moral principle, however, must also be plausible as a standard presupposed in common moral thought, for example, in our general understanding of the differences between duty and self-interest and in our ability to distinguish right from wrong in particular cases. Because the Categorical Imperative must be the supreme principle of practical reason as well as of morality, we should not be surprised, even if initially disappointed, to find that what it prescribes is essentially that we fully respect the development and exercise of the powers of practical reason in each person. The formulations of this requirement vary as analysis reveals its more specific meaning.

The most general idea Kant is working with here is that good (moral and rational) choice is constrained and guided by the necessity "to conform to universal law." "Universal law" here is by definition a necessary requirement of reason that guides the conduct of any fully rational agent and, in imperative form, is an inherent standard unavoidably recognized by all imperfectly rational human beings. So assuming that there are universal laws, the imperative "Conform to universal law" in this sense should be uncontroversial. In two controversial moves, however, Kant argues that from this basic idea we may infer his famous *formula of universal law*:

(FUL): *Act only on that maxim by which you can at the same time will that it should become universal law.*   (Kant (1785), 4: 421)

This is followed immediately by a variation, the *formula of a universal law of nature*:

(FULN): *Act as though the maxim of your action were to become by your will a universal law of nature.*   (Ibid.)

Kant illustrates the use of FULN, and so (indirectly) FUL, with four examples: suicide to escape a troublesome life, borrowing money with a lying promise to ease financial problems, not doing anything to develop one's useful talents, and refusing to give any help to others in trouble. Agents can determine the wrongness of these acts and omissions, Kant argues, by using FULN to test the *maxim* (intention or policy) on which they propose to act.

Scholars differ on how exactly these formulas are supposed to guide moral deliberation. It is clear, however, that any application must begin by identifying the maxim of a proposed act. This is meant to be an honest articulation of what one intends to do and why: for example, "I intend to do this (e.g. borrow money that I know I cannot repay) for a certain purpose (e.g. to pay for an expensive holiday) because I care more for my pleasure than the rights and interests of the lender." Problems arise because there may be several different ways of expressing the maxim, but in any case the next step is to try to conceive of the maxim as a universal law (or law of nature). This has been variously interpreted as a teleological law, a psychological law, or a law of permission: that is, we are to conceive a possible world in which one's purposeful act *fits into a system of natural purposes*, a world where everyone *does act on* the maxim, or a world where anyone *may* do so. Maxims that cannot without contradiction be conceived as universal laws in the appropriate sense are deemed wrong to act on. Some maxims, however, can be *conceived* as universal laws but not *willed* as universal laws. Kant's examples are neglecting one's talents and refusing to give aid to those in dire need. Acting on these maxims too is deemed wrong, though Kant calls the duties to develop one's talents and help those in need "imperfect duties" by contrast to "perfect duties" such as not to make lying promises.

Kant's followers and critics have long debated whether proper application of FUL and FULN really leads to moral judgments that are correct and compatible with common understanding. Many scholars now doubt that it is important to Kant's basic moral theory that these formulas function as explicit decision-guides regarding particular cases. As Kant sometimes suggests, they may serve as heuristic aids to help us see more clearly that what we propose to do is contrary to principles we already accept and apply to others. Because we are tempted to make illegitimate exceptions for ourselves, reflecting on a world where everyone does (or may) act as we intend can help to expose our self-deceiving excuses. Another idea is that the formulas (with later formulations of the Categorical Imperative) provide a framework or perspective for thinking about very general moral principles rather than deciding particular cases. These would be, for example, the ethical principles of the sort Kant proposes in *The Metaphysics of Morals*: "Do not violate the (legal) rights of others," "Respect every human being as a person," "Seek your own natural and moral perfection," and "Promote the happiness of others."

Regarding the importance of examples, Kant repeatedly insists that the basic moral principle cannot be identified or established as rational by appeal to examples, but he also expresses confidence that ordinary people have a basic knowledge of right and wrong that implicitly relies on the ideas expressed in his formulations of Categorical Imperative. For this reason Kant suggests that careful use of his formulas in moral judgment would "clarify" and "strongly confirm" his claims about the supreme moral principle (Kant (2002), 194 [4: 392]).

The Formula of Humanity as an End in Itself

The universal law formulas are concerned with the "form" of moral maxims, but Kant's next formulation of the Categorical Imperative concerns their "matter" or "end." He states this *formula of humanity as an end* thus:

(FHE): *Act in such a way that you treat humanity, whether in your own person or in any other person, always at the same time as an end, never merely as a means.*

(Kant (2002), 230 [4: 429])

The idea of expressing the essential features of morality in terms of means and ends was not original to Kant but he used it in a way that contrasts with many traditional moral theories. These "teleological" theories tried to describe the ideal end or goal of a moral life and viewed specific virtues and constraints as necessary means to achieve that goal (and sometimes as constitutive elements presupposed in the goal itself). For Kant, rational nature ("humanity") in each person is an *end in itself* in a special sense, not as a goal to be achieved but as a status to be respected. It limits the legitimate pursuit of personal and social ends, Kant argues, by prohibiting the use of certain means (for example, lying promises and revolution) and also by requiring us to adopt and pursue certain moral ends (the perfection of oneself and the happiness of others).

Specific interpretations of this formula vary. For example, some understand FHE as just a different way of expressing the same requirement as the universal law formulas, that is, a maxim is permissible only if it can be willed consistently as universal law by anyone, whether on the "giving" or "receiving" end of a transaction. For example, the maxim of a lying promise would have to be rationally acceptable, not only to the deceiver, but also to the person deceived. Often the formula of humanity is assumed to be an intuitive guide to be used case by case, ruling out proposed acts that seem not to respect each person as a rational agent. A more formal reading treats the formula as an abstract requirement to honor the rational ("law-making") will in each person, as later understood through the formula of autonomy and the formula of the kingdom of ends. Any principle's alleged exceptions need to be ultimately justifiable from a perspective that takes appropriate account of the rational will of every person, especially those who are harmed or thwarted in their pursuits for the sake of others. In discussing ethical duties in *The Metaphysics of Morals*, Kant seems to appeal to a more substantive standard, suggesting that to treat humanity as an end implies strong (though not always absolute) presumptions in favor of preserving, developing, exercising, and honoring rational capacities in oneself and others.

The Formulas of Autonomy and the Kingdom of Ends

From the previous formulations, Kant says, a third one follows. This *formula of autonomy* is expressed in several ways, including:

(FA): . . . *the supreme condition of the will's harmony with universal practical reason is the Idea of the will of every rational being as a will that legislates universal law . . . [; and] every human will is a will that enacts universal laws in all its maxims . . .*

(Kant (2002), 232–3 [4: 431–2])

This formula of autonomy, Kant says, leads to the "very fruitful concept" of a kingdom (or commonwealth) of ends, and he uses this concept to re-express the idea of autonomy in a variation often understood as a separate principle—the *formula of a kingdom of ends*. Kant expresses this as follows:

(FKE): *A rational being must always regard himself as lawgiving in a kingdom of ends made possible through freedom of the will . . . [and] [a]ll maxims which stem from autonomous lawgiving are to harmonize with a possible kingdom of ends and a kingdom of nature . . .*

(Ibid. [4: 434–6])

FKE, like FULN and FHE, is supposed to express the supreme principle in a manner "closer to intuition (by means of a certain analogy) and thus nearer to feeling" (ibid. [4: 436]). In the *Groundwork* Kant suggests that for purposes of judgment we should rely primarily on FUL or FA (ibid. [4: 436–7]), but in *The Metaphysics of Morals* he appeals most often to the idea of humanity as an end in itself (FHE).

Interpretations vary but the basic analogy is with an ideal commonwealth in which all members legislate the laws and are subject to them. The members of a kingdom of ends are conceived, in abstraction from personal differences, as rational agents with private ends and as ends in themselves who autonomously legislate universal laws (ibid. [4: 433 ff.]). The "laws" here are ethical principles rather than enforceable state laws, and the law-makers are not influenced by biases and irrationalities as state legislators often are. The analogy with the laws of a commonwealth suggests that the legislators do not legislate the supreme moral principle itself—the constitution, as it were, specifies the basic framework under which they make laws. Rather, they adopt more specific moral principles while being guided and constrained by ideas inherent in the supreme principle (autonomy, rationality, universality, and the dignity of legislators as ends in themselves). If this reading is correct, when Kant says without explicit qualification that we are *subject only to laws we give ourselves* (ibid. [4: 432]), then the "laws" here refer to the more specific universal ethical principles that we "legislate" with the authority, guidance, and constraints of the basic "law" of practical reason and morality (the Categorical Imperative). The basic law must be self-imposed in a different sense, for example by being authoritative for us because it is the fundamental principle of our own shared practical reason, not because of "alien causes," natural sentiments, alleged intuitions, or even divine commands. Kant does not develop FKE further or propose examples to show how it might be applied to practical issues. Instead, his treatment of specific ethical principles in *The Metaphysics of Morals* mostly appeals to FHE. In addition, some passages suggest that members are conceived as making the laws, not together in a common legislative session (as the analogy suggests), but simply by always choosing in practice to act only on maxims that they can will as universal laws in the sense of FUL.

Freedom and Arguments for the Categorical Imperative

The most difficult and controversial aspects of Kant's writings on ethics are his treatments of freedom of the will and how they figure in his defense of his claims about the Categorical Imperative. The main theses for which he argues in *Groundwork* I and II and the *Critique of Practical Reason* are: (1) he has identified the basic, comprehensive principle implicit in common moral thought, and it is expressed in FUL and equivalent formulas; and (2) common morality *presupposes* that this basic principle is the one and only Categorical Imperative in the strict sense. To be the Categorical Imperative in the strict sense a principle must be a universal and necessary principle of practical reason and not a particular hypothetical imperative or the general requirement of coherence among one's ends and means (the Hypothetical Imperative). What Kant needs to show, then, is that common morality relies on the principle expressed in his formulas and that the principle is an unconditionally rational requirement. Kant argues analytically for the first claim in *Groundwork* I and II, trying step by step to reveal FUL as implicit in the ideas of a good will and duty. Passing over details, the main steps are these: Common morality accepts that only a good will could be good without qualification, or worth preserving in all situations. We express a good will when our ("morally worthy") acts are both in accord with duty and done out of duty. So the essence of the basic principle of a good will is not that it must bring about desirable consequences, or even aim to do so, but that we must do what is morally required by maintaining an attitude of respect for the (moral/rational) law. By analyzing the essential motive or attitude of a good will, the argument is supposed to reveal that *the basic principle of a good will is "Conform to universal law"* and from this Kant infers FUL.

In *Groundwork* II Kant tries to draw out the presuppositions of the common idea of duty, and the mains steps can be paraphrased as follows. By contrast to what we ought to do for prudential or pragmatic reasons, a moral duty is what we ought to do for compelling reasons not based upon our personal aims and desire to be happy. We could have duties, understood this way, only if they are backed by a fundamental principle of reason that identifies these compelling reasons without appealing to prudence or rationally optional aims. In other words, duty must be based on a Categorical Imperative in the strict sense. From the concept of a Categorical Imperative, Kant argues, the only principle that could qualify is (to paraphrase): *it is rationally necessary to conform to universal law.* From this (again) Kant infers (with little explanation) that FUL is the Categorical Imperative.

These arguments, Kant dramatically points out, leave open the theoretical possibility that morality might be an illusion. They only reveal what common morality presupposes, not what is necessarily rational to accept. In *Groundwork* III Kant confronts this challenge, arguing that the presupposition that the supreme moral principle is unconditionally rational is valid for all purposes of deliberation and choice. As rational agents, Kant argues, we "cannot act except under the Idea of freedom" (2002 [4: 448]). This is an essential aspect of the standpoint of practice. In deliberation, choice, and acting for reasons we take our wills to be free in a negative sense—able to cause events "independently of alien causes determining it" (ibid. [4: 446]). Negative freedom, however, is inseparable from positive freedom or autonomy, "the property that a will has of being a law to itself" (ibid. [4: 447]). In order to make sense of the idea that we can act for reasons independently of our inclinations and sentiments, we must suppose that we can govern ourselves by standards inherent in our nature as rational agents. And, again assuming negative freedom, these rational standards must give us prescriptions that are not relative to our inclinations and sentiments. In sum, when we act as rational agents we necessarily take ourselves to have autonomy of the will, and *Groundwork* II is supposed to show that the

Categorical Imperative is the standard of rational agents *if* they have autonomy of the will. The upshot is that in taking a practical standpoint we
inevitably and rationally take ourselves to be subject to the Categorical
Imperative.

In Kant's view, freedom of will is an Idea that we must use in practical
thinking but we cannot comprehend. Theoretical reason, empirical and
speculative, can neither prove nor disprove that we have such freedom.
Arguments in the *Critique of Pure Reason* are supposed to show that all
empirical phenomena are subject to natural laws of cause and effect, but
Kant held that the idea of free will presupposed by morality cannot be
defined empirically or explained by natural laws. He embraced the apparent
consequence, however obscure, that we must think of moral agents as
"free" members of an "intelligible world" to which our spatial and temporal
concepts do not apply. Perhaps few philosophers today follow Kant's
thinking this far, but his idea of autonomy has inspired some to develop
and use related concepts.

Justice and the Moral Obligation to Obey the Law

Our moral choices are inevitably made in a context that includes a particular
legal system and complex international relations. We can conceive of a
"state of nature" but this remains a mere idea for most practical purposes. In
Part I of *The Metaphysics of Morals* Kant presents his theory of law and justice,
and earlier in *Perpetual Peace* (1795) he offers recommendations for international justice and global peace. Exactly how Kant's moral theory is related to
his theory of law and justice remains controversial, but some points seem
clear. For example, Kant's theory of law and justice is a part of his official
(published) "metaphysics of morals," and he held that it is an "indirect
ethical duty" to obey the law. An exception, rarely mentioned, is that one
should not do anything "intrinsically immoral" even if ordered to do so by
the government in power. Law makes determinate rights of property,
contracts, and status, and its officials have a juridical (and so indirectly
ethical) duty to enforce the law justly. They must not, for example, use
punishment simply as a means to promote general welfare. Thus even if the
Categorical Imperative of the *Groundwork* is only meant as the appropriate

standard for individual choices, and not for institutions, the requirements of law and justice are inevitably relevant to individual ethical decisions.

Law and justice, according to Kant, are concerned with the "external freedom" and enforceable rights of persons, not moral motivation. The "universal principle of right" (or justice) is a "postulate" similar in some respects to the universal law formula of the Categorical Imperative (FUL). This principle of right says: "Any action is right if it can coexist with everyone's freedom in accordance with a universal law, or if on its maxim the freedom of choice of each can coexist with everyone's freedom in accordance with a universal law" (Kant (1996a), [6: 231]). A corollary of the principle, Kant says, is that coercion to serve as a "hindering of a hindrance to freedom" is consistent with right (ibid.). He assumes a fundamental right to freedom, equality, and independence, and develops from this an account of "private law" which includes rights of property, contract, and status. Anyone in a state of nature, Kant argues, would have a duty to join and maintain a system of "public" law necessary for "a juridical condition." This is not because of the brutality or inconveniences of a state of nature emphasized by Hobbes and Locke, but because "rightful" or just relations among persons are impossible without an authoritative way to settle disputes. Full justice, Kant argues, requires republican government with separation of powers, abolition of hereditary political privilege, and freedom to criticize the government. Full republican justice, however, is only a standard for gradual reform, for we must obey the law even in very imperfect (even "despotical") legal systems. Scholars have argued, however, that "rogue states," such as Nazi Germany, fail to meet even Kant's minimum conditions for being a legitimate legal order that is owed obedience.

Regarding international justice Kant argues that, although a world government would be ideal in some respects, a voluntary federation of sovereign states would be the best hope for peace, at least in a world of diverse cultures and languages. States should recognize a cosmopolitan right of noncitizens to trade and visit peacefully, and they should not exploit indigenous peoples.

Ethics and Religion

Ethics is concerned directly with the question "What ought I to do?" but Kant also addresses the question "What can I hope for?" This belongs primarily to his philosophy of religion, but it deserves mention here because his answer depends on his ethical theory.

Kant argues that knowledge of right and wrong is not based on religion, but to the contrary our moral knowledge provides the only basis for religious faith. In the *Critique of Practical Reason* Kant presents moral arguments for belief in God and immortality even though the *Critique of Pure Reason* established that we cannot strictly prove or even understand these "Ideas" beyond all possible experience. Religion cannot provide the basis for moral knowledge because in order to identify as morally authoritative any supernatural power or even any supposed exemplar of perfection (such as Jesus) we would already need to have an understanding of right and wrong. The moral arguments for faith are based on two prior moral ideas: that we must seek virtue independently of happiness and that the highest good (to be hoped for) would be perfect virtue combined with well-deserved happiness. In his late work *Religion within the Boundaries of Mere Reason* (1793), Kant argues that morality also provides the limits of a rationally acceptable religious faith. We should see moral duty *as if* commanded by God, but certain doctrines are ruled out as contrary to morality: for example, extreme doctrines of innate and incorrigible human depravity (as opposed to a willful *propensity* to evil), divine cruelty and partiality, and the efficacy of prayer for material rewards. The kingdom of ends discussed earlier has a Godlike "head" that has unlimited powers but, like a traditional political sovereign, is not *subject* to laws made by others. The head wills the same rational laws as the members do, however, and is not *subject* to the will of others just because it is independent and has no needs. The most basic principles for any rational being, human or divine, are essentially the same, although they become imperative for human beings who are finite and imperfectly rational.

2

Kantian Normative Ethics

Kant is often studied for his contribution to debates that today might be classified as metaethical,[1] but my concern here is with questions of normative ethics. In particular, I want to focus on how certain basic normative questions are addressed by Kant and various contemporary Kantians who interpret and extend Kant's theory. The main questions are familiar ones: Are there many basic moral principles or only one? How are we to articulate and interpret the basic principle or principles? How do they, or does it, function as an action-guide for particular moral problems? Are the basic Kantian principles really (as Kant thought) the norms underlying common moral judgments?

My discussion will be wide-ranging, but still limited in several ways. Kant's ethical writings are open to different interpretations, and the literature devoted to interpreting and extending his ideas is vast, diverse, and of mixed quality. Although I draw from several prominent contemporary Kantians, I cannot survey all the good literature in this area. When illustrating the action-guiding use of Kant's basic principles, I limit my discussion by concentrating primarily on cases of beneficence and mutual aid rather than addressing a full range of moral problems. Because I review many different interpretations, my description and illustration of each, including the ones that I find most promising, must be quite brief. My primary aim is to call

---

[1] For example, are moral judgments based on reason or sentiment? What does it mean to say that something *ought* to be done? What distinguishes moral from nonmoral "ought" claims? Do moral predicates refer to properties that are objective and real? Are they empirically accessible natural properties or constructs of some kind? The terms we use in our contemporary discussions are often different from Kant's, but Kant clearly had positions and arguments that are relevant to these issues. Some may doubt that metaethical and normative questions can be separated and answered independently, but I will proceed as if they can be usefully addressed, at least to some extent, as separate matters. My project, then, is to survey Kantian answers to the normative questions, leaving aside for now questions about how these are related to other issues.

attention to a variety of different ways in which contemporary Kantians are attempting to develop Kant's normative ethics. I hope that this will encourage further investigation and development of the views only sketched here.

A secondary aim is to illustrate these different developments by relating them to a particular task that any normative ethical theory needs to address. This is to determine, at least in broad terms, when and why we are morally required to help others. Kant's theory is justly famous for its insistence that pursuit of happiness, for both oneself and others, is constrained by moral requirements of justice and respect for human dignity. Kant also insists, however, that it is categorically imperative for us to make it our maxim to promote the happiness of others. It is currently a matter of controversy how much latitude this requirement is supposed to leave us to pursue non-obligatory projects of our own.[2] Focusing on beneficence to illustrate various contemporary developments in Kantian ethical theory should bring out similarities and differences among them. It may also reveal some of their relative strengths and weaknesses.

Willing Maxims as Universal Laws

The Formulas of Universal Law

Kant's interpreters have most often taken as his primary action-guiding principle the first formulation of the Categorical Imperative, the formula

---

[2] My discussion of beneficence here, though inevitably sketchy, may help in a small way to fill a gap in my previous accounts of the duty of beneficence in Kantian ethics. See Hill (2002), chs. 3, 5, 7. The last of these essays, "Meeting Needs and Doing Favors," addresses the recent controversy over whether this duty to promote others' happiness should be interpreted as a very stringent ("rigoristic" or "robust") requirement or as a quite limited ("minimal" or "anemic") requirement. Following H. J. Paton and Mary Gregor, I argued earlier that the duty to promote the happiness of others, at least as presented in Kant's fullest account of it in *The Metaphysics of Morals* (1996a), is a minimal requirement. David Cummiskey and, to some extent, Marcia Baron have argued that the requirement is more stringent. My contention is that, unsurprisingly, we find a modest beneficence requirement in *The Metaphysics of Morals,* for that work is supposed to describe duties in the most general way appropriate for all human conditions. A modest general requirement makes good moral sense, however, only if there is a plausible way to argue from basic principles that in various special circumstances helping others is not optional. By using beneficence as my example when I survey applications of Kant's basic moral principle, I can show various ways in which Kantians can argue from the Categorical Imperative to this conclusion. These arguments may help to fill the gap in my previous defense of the minimal interpretation of the general principle of beneficence, for, if successful, they would supplement Kant's minimal general principle with Kantian grounds for judging that, in many cases, giving aid to others is strictly required. See Baron (1995) and Cummiskey (1996).

of universal law. The initial expression of this in *Groundwork* I is: "I ought never to act in such a way *that I could not also will that my maxim should become a universal law*" (Kant (2002), 203 [4: 402]).[3] Kant's first formula of the Categorical Imperative in *Groundwork* II is commonly thought to express the same idea: "Act only on that maxim by which you can at the same time will that it should become a universal law" (ibid. 222 [4: 421]). Kant then offers a variant of the formula: "Act as though the maxim of your action were to become by your will a universal law of nature" (ibid. 222 [4: 421]). Following tradition, we can label the first two quotations as expressions of the *formula of universal law* (FUL) and the third as an expression of the *formula of a universal law of nature* (FULN). Kant repeats these formulas with variations in wording throughout his ethical writings.[4]

All these are supposed to express the only principle that can be, in the strictest sense, a "categorical imperative," and so it is called a formulation of *the Categorical Imperative* (ibid. 214 [4: 413]). This implies that it expresses in the form of an imperative an unconditional basic requirement of practical reason. An *imperative*, in Kant's technical terminology, expresses an objective principle as a *constraint* on imperfectly rational persons. An *objective principle* is one that any *fully rational* person would follow—but human beings (who are imperfectly rational) might not (ibid. 214 [4: 401]). Kant later states several other formulas of the Categorical Imperative, but he claims that these are simply different ways of expressing fundamentally the same principle—the supreme principle of morality (ibid. 237 [4: 436]). He sometimes refers to more specific moral principles as "categorical imperatives." This may cause confusion, because he says explicitly that there can only be one categorical imperative (ibid. 222 [4: 421]). We can understand his view as consistent if we take the Categorical Imperative, expressed in various formulas, as the only imperative that is categorical *in a strict sense* but then add that more specific moral principles can be called "categorical imperatives" *in an extended sense* if they are derived from the Categorical Imperative and hold without exception.

Commentators differ significantly about how Kant's formulas are supposed to work as action-guides, but some points seem clear enough.

---

[3] Numbers in brackets refer to the corresponding volume and page numbers in the standard Prussian Academy edition.

[4] Wood (1999), 363–5 plausibly suggests that some of Kant's statements that are commonly taken to be versions of FUL are in fact expressions of his later formula of autonomy.

First, to determine whether a proposed act would be right, we must identify "the maxim" of the act. Maxims are "subjective principles" on which we act (ibid. 202 n. [4: 401 n.]).[5] The fullest statements of them describe the act, its purpose, and the underlying reason (at least as the agent understands these).[6] They can be expressed as policy statements with the form "In conditions C, I shall do X in order to E from the motive M." They may be very general, such as "I shall always do what best serves my own interests," or quite specific, such as "When in need and aware that I cannot repay loans, I shall borrow money anyway with a (false) promise to repay."[7] Some maxims are morally bad, some are good, and many are morally indifferent. Kant offers the universal law formulas as a way of testing whether acting on our proposed maxim would be wrong.[8] Of course, it may actually be rare that we have in mind an explicitly articulated maxim when we act. If, however, we sincerely question whether a proposed act would be morally permissible, we can reflect on what we are about to do, and why, and from this try to construct the relevant maxim to test by the universal law formulas. How exactly this should be done remains a problem, but certain guidelines seem implicit in the aim to deliberate conscientiously. For example, our maxim can only refer to facts of which we are aware, and it should reflect honestly our beliefs about what is morally relevant in the situation. Apart from this, it should not include details that are irrelevant to our policy, purpose, and reasons for acting as we propose to do.[9] If our first

[5]   Later Kant restricts the term to the "material principles" that agents act on, i.e. principles based on their (nonrational) desires. See Kant, *Critique of Practical Reason* (1997*b*), 17–19 [5: 19–22].

[6]   Kant's own examples are not uniform in structure. They usually describe the act and indicate its purpose but only sometimes state a separate reason or motive. In Kant's suicide example ((2002), 223 [4: 422]), the act is suicide, the purpose to end pain (when life promises no more compensating pleasures), and the underlying reason or motive is "self-love."

[7]   O'Neill (1989), 84, makes a case that the maxims that should be tested are "underlying principles or intentions by which we guide and control our more specific intentions." This suggestion that they express our more general, fundamental life commitments is in line with Kant's suggestion in *Critique of Practical Reason* that all nonmoral maxims fall under "the general principle of self-love or one's happiness" (O'Neill (1989), 84; Kant (1997*b*), 19 [5: 22]). Kant himself does, however, use the universal law formulas to test examples that are more specific.

[8]   Here I set aside controversies about whether FUL proposes a test for maxims different from that proposed in FULN.

[9]   The reason for the first point is that, for purposes of her deliberation, the maxim must reflect the agent's understanding of what she is doing (and why). (Kant often suggests that we cannot know with certainty what maxims we were really acting on in the past, but in deliberating about what to do next we must assume that we will act on whatever maxim that we adopt after due reflection.) The second point stems from the fact that the very purpose of trying to articulate our maxims is to determine for ourselves whether it is morally all right to act as we are inclined to. It would defeat our purpose to work with a

attempts to articulate our maxim fail the test, it may be that, on honest reflection, we can rephrase the maxim in a way that more aptly describes what we propose to do, our purpose, our reasons, and the limits of the policy that we mean to endorse.[10] Since the practical purpose of the formula is to guide conscientious deliberation about whether it is permissible to act as we are inclined to do, it would be both dishonest and self-defeating to try to rig the statement of our maxim so that Kant's tests will "justify" what we really believe is wrong. Philosophers sympathetic to Kant's project also may be suspected of rigging maxims in a dishonest and self-serving way if, *whenever* faced with counterexamples, they keep redescribing the maxim until Kant's texts yield the intuitive result that they want. If that is necessary, the formula is not really serving as a decision guide.

Second, Kant distinguishes between two kinds of maxim that fail the test posed in the universal law formulas. Some maxims cannot be *conceived* as universal law[11] without contradiction; others can be, but cannot be consistently *willed* as universal law. Thus, in effect, our maxims must meet two requirements. The first is that we must be able to *conceive* our maxim as a

---

phony maxim that not even we ourselves see as accurately reflecting what we intend to do, our reasons, and factors we count as morally relevant. Suppose you plan to gain political power to serve your ethnic community but you know that taking the necessary means will harm many innocent people. A maxim that omitted reference to the fact that your act would harm innocent people would not be the morally appropriate one to test. (This fact should turn out to be salient anyway, when you try to conceive and will the world where everyone acts on your *unqualified* maxim to take the available means to help your ethnic community.) If the third point were ignored, the reasons we could will certain maxims as universal law might have nothing to do with their moral status. For example, one might (mistakenly) argue that because irrelevant details make unwelcome recurrences of the case unlikely, you might will as universal law the maxim "To convenience myself, I shall tell a lie to a bald, skinny, diabetic man on a Tuesday night with a full moon." If we dishonestly include morally irrelevant detail or omit salient moral considerations, the universal law tests are likely to give morally inappropriate results. However, the apparent need to make judgments of moral relevance before applying the universal law tests poses a problem for those who think that the tests are sufficient by themselves to determine right and wrong. Herman (1993) addresses this problem at length.

[10] The sort of limits I have in mind may be expressed, for example, in the maxim "I will refuse a government order to do something (such as to bear false witness in court) *if what was ordered was contrary to an already established perfect ethical duty* " This is a qualification or limit that Kant acknowledged ((1996a), 98 [6: 322], 136–7 [6: 371]; (1998b), 153 n. [6: 154 n.]). Despite what Kant himself thought, it seems only reasonable that the maxim of a person who wants to help an innocent friend escape from a murderer might be "I will tell a lie *if it is told to someone who is threatening the life of an innocent person and if it is the only way, as far as I can tell, to prevent a murder.*"

[11] That is, cannot be conceived as either a universal law or as a universal law of nature (if that is different). For present purposes, I am setting aside the question whether the formulas offer two tests or only one.

universal law without contradiction. If we cannot, then it is wrong to act on the maxim. If we can conceive our maxim as a universal law without contradiction, we must then still ask whether we can *will* our maxim as a universal law. Maxims that satisfy both requirements are supposed to be permissible to act on; those that fail either requirement are supposed to be wrong to act on. In the *Groundwork*, Kant gives two examples of maxims that fail the first test and two examples of maxims that fail the second test.[12]

Third, although Kant presents these requirements as tests of the *permissibility* of acting on a proposed maxim, they could lead us to the conclusion that we have a positive *duty* to act in certain ways. If we wonder whether it is also our duty to act on a given permissible maxim, then we must consider what our maxim would be if we chose to do otherwise. If we could not consistently conceive and will that alternative maxim as a universal law, then it is wrong to act on the alternative maxim. Whenever it is wrong to act on the only alternative to a permissible maxim, it is a positive duty to act on the permissible maxim. There may, of course, be many alternatives, but at least we can say that it is a positive duty to act on the initial permissible maxim, unless at least one of the alternatives can be conceived and willed as a universal law. Consider, for example, a maxim to aid persons in distress, at least when one can at little cost to oneself or others.[13] Presumably, this can be conceived and willed as a universal law, and so it is permissible to act on this maxim. When confronted with a particular case, we need to consider what our maxim would be if we did not act on this maxim to help the distressed person. There are obviously many other things we could do instead, but presumably the maxims we would be acting on if we did not help would need to make reference to the morally salient fact that we would be refusing to help someone in distress even though we could easily aid the

---

[12] Kant suggests that failure to pass the first (contradiction in conception) test indicates a violation of strict or "perfect" duty. Maxims that fail the second (contradiction in willing) test are bad maxims that we should not act on, but the general principles that we would violate by doing so are principles of "imperfect" duty. These require us, for example, to adopt the maxims to promote as ends the happiness of others and our own perfection. It is strictly a duty to adopt these maxims, but what we must do toward the prescribed ends is not specified in a determinate way.

[13] The maxim as stated here is perhaps too simple and unqualified to be reasonably willed as a law for all circumstances. We may, for example, have conflicting obligations; others may be better positioned to provide the aid; etc. For now, I set aside such complications. For any explicit maxim, there will presumably be background conditions implicitly understood. Any attempt to defend the universal law formulas as satisfactory determinants of right and wrong would have to confront the problems these implicit background assumptions raise.

person without harm to ourselves or others.[14] If these alternative maxims cannot be conceived and willed as universal laws, then not to give aid in the circumstances would be wrong, and so giving aid would be a positive duty.

Questions of Interpretation

This is not the place to try to evaluate all interpretations with regard to either their fidelity to texts or their plausibility as moral standards, but here are a few of the variations on Kant's theme.

A preliminary question concerns the relation between FUL and FULN. Do both of these offer procedures for testing the morality of maxims? If so, do they propose exactly the same test or different ones? On one reading, the more abstract FUL is not a practical action-guide by itself but expresses an idea that can be applied to human conditions only when "universal law" is replaced with the more specific concept "universal laws of nature."[15] On another reading, FULN simply specifies what was implicitly intended in FUL, and so the two formulas offer exactly the same test for maxims. A third possibility is that the FUL and FULN offer slightly different tests. In one version, FUL is concerned with *laws of freedom,* while FULN is concerned with *teleological laws of nature.* Thus the first asks us whether we can will that everyone freely choose to act on our maxims, and the second asks us whether we could consistently conceive and will our maxims as teleological laws in a harmonious system of natural purposes.[16] A more promising

---

[14] Suppose, instead, in considering not aiding accident victims (even though only I am available to help them), I describe my proposed maxim merely as "To save time, I will not make stops on my drives to work." Because this omits the morally salient fact that not stopping now may result in the death of innocent persons, the maxim may seem quite innocent, that is, one that we can conceive and will as universal law. Nevertheless, it seems clear that it would be wrong not to aid the injured persons. (Arguably, if the maxim I stated is intended as an inflexible policy, we should be able to see that it cannot be reasonably willed as a universal law, despite its innocent look; for, if we reflected carefully, we should be able to anticipate emergencies that will require exceptions.).

[15] In favor of this interpretation is the fact that in the *Critique of Practical Reason* Kant suggests that the universal law formula can only be applied through a "typic," the idea of a natural order, that mediates between the abstract moral law and our concrete situation ((1997*b*), 59–60 [5: 69–70]). In addition, Kant's examples in the *Groundwork* all refer to laws of nature. Some evidence to the contrary is that Kant does not refer to laws of nature in the formula that (in his review of formulas (2002), 237 [4: 436–7]) he says is best to use in moral assessment. In addition, Kant sometimes gives examples that suggest that the relevant question is whether we can conceive and will our maxim as one that it is permissible for everyone to act on (ibid. 204 [4: 403]).

[16] See Paton (1958), chs. 14, 15. Under FUL, Paton says, we ask whether "we can will our maxim as an instance of a principle valid for all rational beings and not merely adopted arbitrarily for ourselves" (p. 146). With FULN, by contrast, "we put ourselves imaginatively in the position of the Creator and

variation, in my view, is this: FUL asks us whether we can consistently conceive and will our maxim as *permissible* for everyone to act on,[17] and FULN asks us whether we can consistently conceive and (if we had the power) will that, as if by a law of nature, everyone adopts and acts on the maxim.[18]

Other questions arise about what might, in a relevant sense, prevent us from conceiving a maxim as a law, or law of nature, for everyone. Most obviously, if everyone's acting (or being permitted to act) on a given maxim is logically impossible, then the maxim cannot be conceived as a universal law in the relevant sense. Kant's examples, however, suggest that they be ruled out if, *assuming some general background facts* about the human condition, it is logically impossible for everyone to act on them.[19] On another interpretation, they are excluded if it is logically impossible for a harmonious system of nature to include everyone's acting in the manner *and for the purpose* indicated in the maxim.[20] A more promising suggestion, perhaps, is that maxims cannot be conceived as universal laws (or laws of nature) if it is logically impossible to will simultaneously the following set of intentions: (1) to act on the maxim, (2) to bring it about (if one had the power) that everyone else act on the maxim, and (3) the normal foreseeable consequences of everyone's acting on the maxim.[21] This is a particular version of the idea that we cannot conceive of a maxim without contradiction if the maxim "would be self-defeating if universalized: [Our] action would

suppose that we are making a world of nature [i.e. a system of natural purposes] of which we are a part" (p. 146).

[17] An example of this type of interpretation is developed by Pogge (1998).

[18] We must try to conceive everyone adopting the maxim and acting on it *in conditions where it is applicable*. The conditions should be given in the maxim, which has the form "In conditions C, I shall do X . . ." Presumably, when we conceive a maxim as a *universal law of nature*, we assume that some appropriate conditions will occur and so the maxim will be acted on. Otherwise, a maxim would pass the first test if, though no one could act on it, everyone could "adopt it" (perhaps in the form "In C, I shall X if I can"). To understand the test that way would undermine Kant's most persuasive example, that of a lying promise to repay a loan (Kant (2002), 223 [4: 422]).

[19] Brandt (1959), 27–35, among others, noted this. An example would be the fact that people would generally remember those who did not repay loans and would be reluctant to trust those persons again.

[20] Paton (1958), 146–56.

[21] See Nell (1975). In this early work, she maintains that one who wills a maxim thereby, if rational, wills the normal foreseeable consequences of what she wills. For example, if I will for everyone to adopt and act on my maxim to rob a bank for personal enrichment, then, if rational, I thereby also will the normal foreseeable consequence that bank security will become prohibitively tight. To will this, of course, is inconsistent with my original intention to enrich myself by bank robbery. I express some doubts about whether this account is satisfactory in my review *of Acting on Principle* (Hill, 1979).

become ineffectual for [our] purpose if everyone [tried to] use it for that purpose" (Korsgaard (1996b), 78).

There are also different ways of understanding the relevant impossibility of *willing* maxims that can be conceived as universal laws. I cannot review them all, but here is a sample. The least plausible, but all too common, idea is simply *being unwilling, for any reason, to choose* that our maxim be adopted by everyone. If, for example, racial bigots, because of their prejudice, would not be willing for everyone to work for racial equality, then they could argue that by Kant's principle they would be wrong to do so. Even worse, they could argue that because they are willing for everyone to adhere to their policy of strict racial segregation, it is morally permissible for them to pursue it.[22] Equally but less obviously implausible is the assumption that *any contingent inability* (in our nature or circumstances) to will our maxims as universal law means that we would be wrong to act on them. Especially when we consider rather specific maxims, this would mean that all sorts of morally irrelevant factors would rule out actions that are quite innocent. If there were not enough of some trivial commercial product for everyone to buy it, the test would apparently show that it is wrong for anyone to buy the product. If, because of dizziness, some people cannot climb high ladders, it would seem that no one should.

Now, by reformulating the maxims and adding ad hoc stipulations to the test, we might circumvent these and other particular counterexamples; but arguably the interpretation in question is mistaken in principle. What should be relevant under the universal law tests is whether we can *rationally* endorse a maxim as a universal law.[23] The fact that not everyone *can* act in certain ways is often no reason for others to refrain, and all sorts of morally irrelevant quirks and prejudices may determine whether we are willing to endorse policies for everyone. What we need to consider is whether

---

[22] Their argument would assume that the universal law formulas provide a sufficient, not merely necessary, condition of moral rightness. Wood (1999), 76–110, for one, argues that they do not provide such a criterion and were not meant to.

[23] The term "rationally" has apparently acquired a narrower sense in our times than Kant's sense, which arguably encompasses more broadly what we might prefer to call "reasonable." Thus, in my view, Kant's test should be construed as about what we can rationally *and reasonably* endorse as universal policies. Adding the term suggests, not inappropriately in my view, that the reasons relevant to whether we can will maxims as universal law are not restricted to logical inconsistency and formally incompatible intentions. However, it would be contrary to the structure of Kant's moral theory simply to rely on intuition unrelated to any version of the Categorical Imperative for the standards of what can be reasonably willed as universal law.

endorsing our maxims as universal laws is *contrary to reason* in some relevant way.[24] Obviously, maxims that cannot be *conceived* as universal laws without contradiction cannot be *rationally willed* as universal law, but beyond this, the relevant standards of rational willing are more controversial. A standard of logical consistency and coherence among one's intentions is unlikely to be sufficient by itself to generate appropriate results from the universal law tests. In a Kantian theory, however, these standards should not be intuitive moral norms that have no basis at all in Kant's moral theory, at least if we accept the common view that all other moral norms are derivative, in some sense, from Kant's basic moral principles.[25] In applying Kant's formulas, however, we should be able to rely on whatever specific moral norms we have already confirmed, or could confirm (on Kantian grounds) as rational requirements.[26]

Readers will need to assess the various interpretations for themselves, but a particularly important further controversy should be mentioned. In assessing whether we can *reasonably* will our maxims as universal laws, can we rely on the other formulas of the Categorical Imperative? To try to do so would be useless if, as some think, the later formulas add nothing new and action-guiding beyond what the universal law formulas say.[27] If, however, as others claim, the later formulas articulate basic moral standards apart from (or at least not explicit in) the universal law formulas, then they would provide resources for arguments that certain maxims cannot be reasonably

---

[24] Although as human beings we do not always "will" what we would if perfectly rational, Kant identifies our "will" with certain practical capacities we have as rational beings. He repeatedly says that acting on maxims that we cannot will as universal law implies "contradiction" or "conflict" in the will that would be absent if we were more fully rational.

[25] For example, to argue that it is unreasonable to will a certain policy as universal law because that would undermine certain traditional values, we must independently show (by Kantian principles) that we ought to preserve those traditional values. Most contemporary Kantians seem to accept that all other moral norms must be "derived," at least in a broad sense, from the Categorical Imperative and noncontroversial principles of instrumental rationality, but one could treat Kant's principles merely as a framework of general moral considerations that constrain all other moral considerations but need to be supplemented by them. We would naturally wonder, of course, what is the source of these other moral considerations, why we should accept them, and whether disagreements about them can be resolved.

[26] Kant himself suggests that in ordinary cases we come to our moral problem already having a stock of relevant moral beliefs, and if so, what reflection on the universal law formulas may do is simply to highlight the discrepancy between these general beliefs (that we readily apply to others) and our own proposed action (Kant (2002), 224–5 [4: 424]). Here, asking whether we can will our maxims as universal laws is a way of considering whether our proposed act fits ideas that we already have about what everyone may, and may not, do. Clearly, there is a "contradiction in the will" of someone who, without good reason, makes herself an exception to general principles that she accepts as reasonable.

[27] Singer (1961), 235, for example, argues this.

willed as universal laws. For example, if we exclude the later formulas, a rich miser who abhors charity for anyone might argue that he can will his maxim of refusing to help the needy as a universal law because he is prepared to die before accepting charity. If, however, we accept as a rational requirement that we treat humanity in each person as an end-in-itself, then arguably the miser could not reasonably endorse his "no charity" policy as a universal law.[28] Kantians take different positions on whether later formulas can supplement the universal law formulas, depending on their different inter-pretations of the textual evidence regarding Kant's intentions and their philosophical judgment as to what makes most sense.

Illustration: Helping Others in Distress

Kant's project in the *Groundwork* and *Critique of Practical Reason*, where the formula of universal law figures prominently, was not primarily to explain and illustrate how to apply his formulas to particular problems. In both works, and especially the latter, more attention is devoted to discovering and defending the basic presuppositions of the use of practical reason— finding its constitutive principles and their relation to freedom of the will (in several senses). *The Metaphysics of Morals* is the work where Kant turns explicitly to the task of working out intermediate principles for guiding ethical judgment in various areas of human life, and here the universal law formulas play a more modest role. In fact the idea of humanity as an end-in-itself is what Kant's arguments most often appeal to. Nevertheless, in the *Groundwork* Kant expresses great confidence that the universal law formulas can serve as guide to moral judgment, enabling us to distinguish right from wrong in every case (Kant (2002), 204–6 [4: 403–4], 224–6 [4: 424–5]). Moreover, he suggests that, although ordinary people can become confused, they implicitly respect and rely on the universal law formulas as a standard (ibid. 204–7 [4: 403–4]; (1997*b*), 7 n. [5: 8 n.]). Not surprisingly, not all readers have shared Kant's confidence in the formulas as an action-guide. For centuries now, critics have pointed out problems in applying them, and Kant's supporters have developed subtle defenses of his basic idea beyond anything that we can find explicitly in Kant's texts.

---

[28] Herman, as we shall see, has an argument against the miser that does not rely on the humanity formula, but I am not convinced that contemporary Kantians should follow her in this.

Let us consider how the universal law formulas might guide our moral reflection about helping others. First, we must acknowledge that many ways of helping others are morally impermissible. Justice, respect for others, and certain "perfect duties to oneself" set limits to what we may do to aid and promote the happiness of others. These constraints call for justification, by either the universal law formulas or later formulas, but let us assume for now that these restrictions can be justified. The general question is, if we fulfill our duties of justice, respect, and so on, what more must we do for others? To apply the universal law tests, we must look at the problem initially from the point of view of a particular agent in a particular context. Suppose, then, you are inclined to refuse an appeal to give to famine relief, but you wonder if this is morally permissible. The first thing to consider is what maxim honestly and accurately reflects what you propose to do. Cases will vary, but suppose you are inclined not to help anyone beyond what justice demands, though you could easily make a gift that would help to relieve someone's distress (Kant (2002), 224–5 [4: 424–5]). Your maxim might be, "From self-interest I will always refuse to help others in need except when they have a right to my aid, even though I could easily help without significant harm to myself or others." Presumably, you can consistently conceive a world in which everyone adopts and acts on this maxim. If everyone did so, however-er, and you should fall into dire need, by your policy others would help you only if you could demand help as a matter of justice (your rights). This, in most cases, would be contrary to your self-interest, and, by hypothesis, your purpose in adopting your maxim was to advance your self-interest. So willing that everyone adopt and act on your maxim would be willing a situation incompatible with your aim in adopting your maxim. You cannot rationally will both, and so, it seems, you would be wrong to act on your maxim.

Suppose now that you are an unusually wealthy, secure, independence-loving miser. You might object to the previous argument, saying that you would prefer to die rather than accept aid from others. Then, you might argue, you can consistently act on your personal preferences (expressed in your maxim) while also willing your maxim for yourself *and everyone else*, for in this case your purpose in adopting your maxim was to satisfy a personal preference that you *and everyone else* refuse to give to charity. To meet this objection, one might argue that you cannot *rationally* choose that you would forgo the means to your survival if you should happen to fall into dire need.[29] Arguably, the issue here is not the odds of your falling into dire need but rather what you can rationally will for the *possible* circumstance in which it happens, whatever the odds against it. As a *rational* person, one might argue, you necessarily value your existence as a rational agent over inclination-based preferences, and therefore you must treat the means to your survival as having a value of higher priority than your disinclination to accept charity. If so, it would be contrary to reason to will your maxim as one for everyone to follow. The upshot is that it is wrong for you to act on your maxim; and so unless you can honestly say that your refusal to give aid is based on some other, morally acceptable ground, you have a positive duty to give aid on the occasion in question. Furthermore, assuming you will have normal opportunities and abilities in the future, arguably you can ensure that you will not act on your impermissible maxim (or similar bad maxims) in the future only if you make it your principle generally to help others in need when you can at little cost to yourself or others.[30] None of this implies, however, that you must try to maximize happiness or to work for the happiness of others *whenever you have no conflicting duties.*[31]

Problems and Doubts

The most persistent worry about Kant's universal law formulas is that they often seem to lead to intuitively unacceptable conclusions. They apparently condemn some maxims that we regard as innocent and fail to condemn maxims that we regard as immoral. Frequently, revising the description of the maxim leads to more acceptable results, but there seems no principled way to tell before applying the tests what the "correct" description should be.[32] Even if we can always find some apt maxim description that allows us

---

[29] Here I follow roughly Herman's line of argument ((1984), 577–602).

[30] Kant holds that it is a duty to adopt the maxim, not merely to aid those in distress, but more generally to promote the (permissible) ends of others. Regarding how much one must do to promote others' happiness, and when and to whom one must do it, however, the duty is not determinate. Beneficence is a "wide, imperfect" duty.

[31] The latter implausibly stringent principle is a little-noticed consequence of Ross's famous system ((1930), ch. 2) of "prima facie duties," at least as long you think of your own happiness as *yours* rather than thinking of it impartially as merely the good of some person. Cummiskey (1996), esp. chs. 5, 6, argues that Kant is committed to a slightly weaker, but still incredibly stringent, principle of beneficence, namely that, absent other duties, we must maximize the general good (including happiness and rational development), taking all persons (including yourself as one) into account.

[32] Earlier I mentioned a few guidelines for constructing a maxim that may help to set aside certain counterexamples, but I doubt that, even if supplemented with other suggestions, such guidelines are sufficient.

to reach common-sense conclusions, we are not really being guided by the formulas if we need to rely on our understanding of the right conclusion in order to find the best statement of the maxim. Even if the tests appropriately show that acting on certain maxims is *wrong* and acting on others is *permissible*, they can generate a *positive duty* to do something only indirectly by showing that it is wrong not to do it. Since there are usually many ways of *not doing* something, we would need to identify and test all the many maxims that we might follow if we did not do as the alleged positive duty would prescribe. Defenders of Kant's universal law formulas have devised many subtle supplements to these as maxim-testing procedures, but argu-ably the proposals are merely ad hoc devices to patch up a flawed procedure or else they amount to an admission that the universal law formulas alone are not sufficient for determining particular moral requirements.

Another recurrent concern about treating the universal law formulas as the sole, or primary, moral action-guide is that the recommended test procedure, by itself, seems not to reflect what is most central to moral deliberation. As many Kantians now admit, or at least suspect, that even if the universal law formulas can flag certain maxims as morally wrong, they do not adequately explain *why* acting on those maxims is wrong. What is wrong with slavery, for example, is not adequately explained by saying that it is impossible for everyone to act on the maxim of a would-be slave-owner. It may be that those who rob banks and commit murder cannot consistently will both their maxim and that everyone act on that maxim, but this inconsistency seems at best only part of the story why such acts are wrong. Although Kant's formulas do not work well as precise decision procedures for particular moral cases, they should at least reflect, in a general way, essential features of a Kantian moral perspective for thinking about particular problems. Taken by themselves, the universal law formulas seem inadequate for this purpose. Arguably, Kant himself thought that the full import of the moral law becomes clear only when all the formulas are fully taken into account.

Treating Humanity as an End-in-Itself

The Formula of Humanity

Kant's next formulation of the Categorical Imperative is this: "*Act in such a way that you treat humanity, whether in your own person or in any other person, always at the same time as an end, never merely as a means"* (Kant (2002), 229–30 [4: 429]).[33] He elaborates this formula in various ways. He says both that *persons are* ends-in-themselves and that *humanity, or rational nature*, in persons is an end-in-itself.[34] An *end*, in Kant's broad sense, is "what serves the will as the objective ground of its self-determining"; that is, it gives us a *reason* to do or refrain from doing various things (ibid. 228 [4: 427]). Ordinarily we think of an end as something we aim to achieve or promote, but Kant says that an end-in-itself in his sense is a "self-sufficient" or independently existing end, rather than an end to be produced (ibid. 238 [4: 437]). An end-in-itself is necessarily an end for every rational being: that is, its existence is an objective reason for doing or refraining from certain acts, independently of our inclinations. To value rational persons as ends, we must not use them for ends that, in some sense, they cannot share (ibid. 230–1 [4: 430]). Kant adds that persons, conceived as members of a king-dom of ends, have a *dignity*, which is grounded in their *autonomy* of will (ibid. 234–7 [4: 434–6]).[35] Dignity is an "unconditional and incomparable worth," above all *price* and "without equivalent." Thus dignity is a value that is independent of a person's social status and utility, and it is not to be exchanged for anything with merely conditional value.[36] Negatively, it is a value against which we must never act; and yet, positively, we take the

---

[33] To derive this more general duty from universal law formulas, it seems that we would need to show that unless we adopted a maxim of promoting the (permissible) ends of others, we would act on some maxims that we cannot will as universal law.

[34] Kant apparently treated these expressions as equivalent, but it may matter which expression is taken as primary. Kant frequently contrasts our humanity (or rational nature) with our animality, as different aspects of our nature as human beings. In his *Religion within the Boundaries of Mere Reason* (1998b), he contrasts our animality with both our personality (or moral predisposition) and our humanity (other features of rational agency). Earlier I argued that we should understand the expression "treat rational nature in persons as an end in itself" simply as saying more specifically what is meant by "treat persons as ends in themselves." It would be a mistake, however, to equate these with a command to do whatever promotes the greatest possible development and use of reason, for Kant is clear that an end-in-itself is not an end in the sense of a goal or something to be produced. See Hill (1980).

[35] Not all commentators agree about whether the autonomy that grounds human dignity is our capacity and disposition to morality (i.e. giving ourselves moral laws as standards) or the actual realization of this capacity (i.e. willing always to conform to the moral law). Most commentators favor the former interpretation, but some passages suggest the latter. See Dean (1996), 266–88.

[36] Since dignity is "above price," it obviously cannot be legitimately exchanged or sacrificed for commodities or pleasures; but, apparently, though less obviously, Kant means that dignity has no "equivalent" even among other things with dignity. Thus, insofar as persons have dignity, they have an incalculable value that prohibits justifying one violation of human dignity by the thought that it would prevent two or more similar violations. This does not necessarily imply, however, that when we cannot save everyone's life in an emergency it would be wrong to do what would save more rather than fewer lives. I discuss this problem in my (1992c).

conception of humanity as an end-in-itself fully to heart only if we try to make the (permissible) ends of others our own (ibid. 230–1 [4: 430], 237–8 [4: 437–8]).[37]

Questions of Interpretation

The humanity formula, like the previous ones, has been interpreted in a variety of ways. One question is whether the formula has any independent action-guiding content. Obviously, it would not if the test for our treating humanity as an end were simply that we could will the maxim of such treatment as universal law.[38] Similarly, if the formula meant no more than "Respect persons' rights and give them moral consideration due to human beings," then it would obviously give no guidance unless supplemented with an independent account of rights and due consideration. Some commentators maintain that the formula offers nothing substantial beyond the formula of universal law.[39] Others take the humanity formula to be Kant's basic action-guiding principle, the first principle of morals from which all duties are derivable.[40] Most commentators, however, take an intermediate position, granting that the humanity formula at least adds significantly to our understanding of Kant's basic criteria or procedures for deciding what is right.[41]

[37] There is an often-noted tension between these passages, because the first tells us that ends-in-themselves are to be conceived only negatively, while the second prescribes a "positive agreement" with the idea.

[38] See Singer (1961).

[39] See ibid. 235. See also Wolff (1973), 176.

[40] This is the position of Donagan (1977), 57–74. Donagan, however, does not claim that the first principle is self-evident or indubitable. In a rational ethical theory principles can be presented in hierarchical form, representing more specific principles as deductive conclusions from more abstract and comprehensive higher-level principles; but, in considering reasons to accept the system, we may have initially more confidence in the more specific intermediate principles. Thus we may treat the fact that the "first principle" leads to just these principles, and not to conclusions we find unacceptable, as some confirmation that the first principle, as stated, is correct. See Donagan (1993). Wood gives the humanity formula a crucial "grounding" role in his interpretation of Kant's basic ethical theory, but does not give it as exclusive a role as Donagan does. See Wood (1999), 111–55.

[41] There is a variety of possible views of this sort. For example, one may think that the humanity formula only makes explicit what was presupposed in the formula of universal law, thus helping to clarify or interpret it. One may think that they are independent principles that are at best practically equivalent, in that they yield the same conclusions about cases. Or one may think that these two formulas each express certain aspects of a more comprehensive principle that is expressed in a later formula (or must be constructed from all the formulas). The latter is more or less the position I propose as a reconstruction, but not strict interpretation, of Kant's views.

Some accounts focus on whether our *purposes can be shared* by those affected by our acts;[42] but others take the key to be a relatively substantive idea of *human dignity*[43] and still others construe the formula as primarily an imperative to *respect persons*.[44] The apparent differences here are no doubt to some extent matters of emphasis, but some not entirely.

More specifically, the first line of interpretation draws heavily from Kant's claim that we must treat ends-in-themselves as "beings who must themselves be able to share in" our end in acting (Kant (2002), 230 [4: 430]). The point, surely, is not that we may do something to others only if they actually share our purpose in doing it, for (as Kant suggests) on this basis a criminal could object to the just sentence a judge imposes. The idea, instead, may be that, before acting in ways that seriously affect others, we must look at our proposed act and purpose from the point of view of a reasonable recipient. We should not act as we propose if the recipient of our act *could not* will for us so to act, that is, could not endorse our so acting without contravening (presupposed) appropriate rational standards for endorsing others' treatment of oneself. On this reading, both the universal law formulas and the humanity formulas ask us, in effect, to assess whether a person could (reasonably, by some appropriate standard) endorse a maxim as a general policy. The universal law formulas focus attention on the perspective of a reasonable agent; the humanity formula directs us to the perspective of a reasonable recipient; but neither sort of reflection is simply about our actual preferences, as agents or recipients.[45]

The second type of interpretation treats the main point of the humanity formula to be an attribution of a special value (*dignity*) to *humanity*, or *rational*

---

[42] See O'Neill (1989), 137–40.

[43] This was the theme of my early essay "Humanity as an End in Itself" (1980). Cummiskey (1996) also begins from an interpretation of the humanity formula based on the idea that to be an end-in-itself is to have dignity, as opposed to price.

[44] Donagan's (1977) account treats the formula as a principle of respect, but in *The Metaphysics of Morals* (1996a), Kant's discussion of respect for others is concerned only with certain aspects of morality (contrasted with beneficence, gratitude, etc.), not as a comprehensive moral guide. Similarly, Kant seems to treat self-respect as a more specific requirement than the Categorical Imperative, though one could argue that all duties to oneself are "really" requirements of self-respect.

[45] Although for purposes of developing Kantian ethics I suggest that an alternative interpretation in terms of dignity is more promising, I think that the account proposed here has some merit, at least as an interpretation of Kant's remark that ends must be valued *as able to share our end*. In "Donagan's Kant" (1993), I suggest this leads to a "thin" reading of the humanity formula, in contrast with an earlier "thick" reading that emphasized the incomparable value of rational agency. See my *Respect, Pluralism, Justice: Kantian Perspectives* (2000), 148–51.

nature in human beings. When dignity is treated as a substantive value, this means placing a high priority (above "price") on the preservation, development, exercise, and honoring of our rational capacities.[46] One radical version of this idea treats dignity simply as a high-priority value in a "Kantian consequentialism" devoted to maximizing value.[47] More traditional readings treat dignity as a status of inviolability, not a value that can be quantified and weighed, but a worth to be respected, esteemed, and honored in all our actions. In one version, discussed hereafter, the reasons for acting based on the idea of human dignity are *expressive reasons*, concerned with what our acts *say* and *mean*.[48]

In *The Theory of Morality*, Alan Donagan develops the idea that the humanity formula is a comprehensive principle of respect for persons. Donagan ((1977), 58–9) dismisses Kant's universal law formula as a nonsubstantive requirement of impartiality: that is, for a moral system legitimately to treat something as permissible for some persons and not others, there must be "a reasonable ground" in differences between the two groups or their circumstances. The highest moral principle, he maintains, is his version of the humanity formula: "[I]t is impermissible not to respect every human being, oneself or any other, as a rational creature" (ibid. 66). Although granting that judgment is needed to determine specifically what such respect requires, Donagan argues we have enough common understanding of the phrase "respect...as rational" that, without appeal to independent moral principles, we can see that the formula condemns some acts and requires others. In fact, Donagan develops a system of fairly specific moral principles that, he claims, can be derived from the fundamental principle of respect. These draw from Kant's *Metaphysics of Morals*, but modify it considerably.[49] The principles express quite stringent requirements regarding promise-keeping, truth-telling, suicide, murder, use of force, development of talents, beneficence, and various institutional obligations. These principles contain qualifications within them but are not

---

[46] e.g. Hill, "Humanity as an End in Itself" (1980).

[47] See Cummiskey (1996).

[48] See Wood (1999), 141. I turn to Wood's view shortly. See also Korsgaard (1996a), 106–32, esp. 275. Both Korsgaard and Wood emphasize our value-conferring status as beings who rationally set ends for ourselves.

[49] For example, Donagan's principle regarding lying is this: "Even for a good end, it is impermissible for anybody, in conditions of free communications between responsible persons, to express an opinion that he does not hold" ((1977), 89).

merely prima facie duties. To treat human beings with due respect, we must strictly comply with all the principles. Even to promote a very good end, we must never use means that violate the principles. We may, however, find ourselves in a moral dilemma because of previous wrongdoing, and then, though we will be acting wrongly no matter what we do, we must do the lesser of evils ((1977), 143–9; (1984), 291–309; (1993), 7–21). The human-ity formula, Donagan argues, sharply opposes the consequentialist doctrine of negative responsibility: that is, the idea that we are just as responsible for not preventing bad outcomes as for bringing them about directly through our actions. In fact, regarding Bernard Williams's famous story, Donagan thought it absolutely wrong for Jim to kill one innocent Indian to prevent Pedro from killing nineteen others.[50] Allen Wood also understands the humanity formula as a principle of respect, though Wood holds that all Kant's formulas should be taken together as a system. He agrees with Donagan that the humanity formula serves a crucial guide for moral judg-ment and that it is superior, in several ways, to the universal law formulas.[51] Like Donagan, Wood also thinks that some specific act-guiding principles can be derived deductively from the humanity formula when it is under-stood as a principle of respect for human dignity. We need intermediate premises specifying what it is to respect dignity in different contexts, but he argues that these are empirical and hermeneutical premises, not independent moral principles (Wood (1999), 154). Since the basic requirement is always to respect humanity in persons, we need intermediate premises specifying the *meaning* expressed by acts in various circumstances. The premises needed in Kant's arguments against suicide and false promises, for example, say that, for various reasons, suicide expresses disrespect for humanity in oneself and making false promises expresses disrespect for another person. Typically, we express disrespect, not by altogether ignoring the dignity of other persons, but by considering our own worth superior to others' or by valuing things of mere *price* above human *dignity*. In Wood's view, there are no algorithms or decision procedures for interpreting the expressive meaning of acts, but we can give reasons for our judgments about this. Kant's humanity formula was not intended to resolve all moral problems directly but to provide a

---

[50] See Williams (1973), 77–155.

[51] For example, the humanity formula can ground positive duties, express the basic value that "grounds" our moral judgments, and is not liable to generate the bizarre, counterintuitive results that the universal law formulas may yield when maxims are described in certain ways.

"correct framework" for deliberating about and discussing moral problems (ibid. 154–5).

Illustration Regarding Helping Others

Donagan's treatment of beneficence is typical of his Kantian theory. If we respect persons as rational creatures, we will "take satisfaction in their achieving the well-being they seek, and will further their efforts" as far as we prudently can. So "it is impermissible not to promote the well-being of others by actions in themselves permissible, inasmuch as we can do so without proportionate inconvenience" (Donagan (1977), 85). The ground is not that they deserve it, but that to refuse would be to fail to have respect for them as rational creatures. Proper respect, in Donagan's view, requires us to promote the well-being or "human flourishing" of others,[52] especially those who, for various reasons, cannot help themselves.[53] Two qualifications are important: it is wrong to promote others' well-being by means that are disrespectful of any rational person, and to promote others' well-being by sacrificing equal or greater goods for ourselves is not required but supererogatory (p. 86). Beneficence, based on respect, also requires "preventing what might harm others or frustrate their permissible projects, and abstaining from actions that would foreseeably elicit responses by which others would be injured" (ibid. 85). In general, we are required to make it our policy to promote permissible ends of others when there is no disproportionate inconvenience; but in those cases where only we can help another in serious need, without disproportionate sacrifice, then helping that person is morally mandatory.

Wood's treatment of beneficence is similar in some respects, but emphasizes the *meaning expressed* by helping or not helping others. In his view, "the reason that we should help others in need is that we thereby *exhibit* proper esteem for their worth as rational beings" ((1999), 149, emphasis added). Because of this, he argues, "rugged individualists" who want no one to be charitable cannot rationally will this as a universal policy, because this would entail willing that others "show contempt" for their humanity if they should

---

[52] Kant says that we have a duty to promote the *happiness* of others, and he typically understands happiness as a subjective idea of lasting contentment or realizing all one's desire-based ends (not the same idea as the classic idea of human flourishing). I discuss the contrast in Hill (1999a).

[53] Donagan (1977), 85, includes persons orphaned, grieving, injured, chronically ill, blind, deaf, senile, etc.

fall into dire need (ibid. 150). Presumably, not helping others in many circumstances would not show contempt for them, and so the duty to aid others is limited in various ways. Only when not helping is disrespectful of their humanity is it morally mandatory, and this is a matter of interpretation.

Problems and Doubts

Disputes about which interpretations best explain Kant's texts may be endless. For present purposes, I want merely to call attention to a few potential problems in different ways of developing and relying on Kant's humanity formula.

First, and perhaps most obviously, the formula presents an ideal that is important and inspiring but far from a determinate, precise decision procedure. Virtually all commentators acknowledge this to some extent, but some (e.g. Donagan) may have more confidence than warranted in our ability to agree on what specifically "respecting a person as rational" implies for a wide range of cases. This becomes more of a problem the more the humanity formula is taken to be a self-standing guide to decision-making in all particular cases or by itself a fully determinate first premise for justifying strict moral rules.

Second, if we treat the humanity formula, as Donagan and others do, as primarily about relatively simple, self-contained interpersonal exchanges, we risk missing relevant moral considerations that arise from the larger context. What seems on the surface to be a disrespectful way to treat one person (e.g. telling a lie) may have ramifications regarding others that could justify it from a perspective that is concerned with how best to express equal respect for all persons. From that perspective, even the person deceived might approve the general policy that would allow exceptions to the duty of truth-telling for that occasion. Exclusive focus on what is intuitively respectful in the narrower context of person-to-person interactions leads readily to apparent dilemmas in which, so far as we can tell, all our options are forbidden.[54] Arguably, however, we can make progress on some of these problems if we treat the humanity formula as an evaluative attitude mandated first and foremost for our deliberations about general moral principles and policies in the light of the many complex factors that may be relevant.[55]

[54] See Hill (1993), 46–9.
[55] This idea is proposed and illustrated in Hill (1992c).

Third, the more the humanity formula is understood to express substantive, "thick," and controversial values, the harder will be the task of arguing convincingly that everyone, despite cultural and individual differences, has good reasons to accept it. Sometimes, of course, it is hard to convince everyone of propositions that are nevertheless true and backed by good reasons, and so a strong burden of proof is not the same as disproof. Nevertheless, arguably, both Donagan's stringent nonconsequentialist "Kantian" rules and Cummiskey's "Kantian" consequentialism present the humanity formula as essentially committed to (opposite) sides of some issues about which reasonable persons disagree. For example, even with its (Kant-inspired) value priorities, Cummiskey's Kantian consequentialism seems open to the familiar objection that there are conflicts between justice and what promotes the best consequences. Similarly, Donagan's (relatively) inflexible principles apparently would require, in certain emergency situations, refusal to protect lives and other Kantian values by extraordinary means that reasonable persons might rightly (but reluctantly) approve. Donagan more nearly captures Kant's own particular moral beliefs, but these are not necessarily implicit in the humanity formula or correctly derivable from it. Both substantive theories have the burden of defending *why* some apparently reasonable common moral judgments are wrong.

Finally, apart from this, there is philosophical reason, as well as textual evidence, for treating Kant's supreme moral principle (in all its versions) as describing an essential framework for moral deliberation and discussion rather than as an independent and determinate guide, as some have assumed.[56] In a world of tragic cultural and individual conflicts, moral philosophy needs to articulate a point of view from which, despite substantial differences, human beings can work together toward reasonable, mutually acceptable principles and policies. This purpose is defeated if a theory *too readily* renders judgment on a wide range of controversial moral issues. This is not to say that a moral theory should not in the end sharply condemn certain conventional moralities. The point is that moral theorists should be careful not unduly to allow their own strong moral convictions about particular issues to shape their ideas about what is essential to a moral point of view. If, as Kant thought, morality concerns what reasonable

---

[56] This suggestion is developed further in the next section and in Hill (1992*a*), chs. 2, 10, 11, and (2000), chs. 2, 4, 8.

persons can accept, despite diversities, then accounts of the basics of morality should leave room for diversity and reasonable disagreement regarding many particular situations.

A Kantian Legislative Perspective

The Formulas of Autonomy and a Kingdom of Ends

Kant's next two formulas are closely related. In fact, Kant did not even distinguish them in his review of formulas. The first, commonly called the formula of autonomy, is initially characterized as "the Idea of *the will of every rational being as a will that legislates universal law*" (Kant (2002), 232 [4: 431]). The point, evidently, is that we must *always act in ways compatible* with this idea. The context makes clear that Kant conceives the rational law-giving in question as not motivated by inclinations and desires. There are some differences of interpretation among commentators, especially as the abstract formula of autonomy is reexpressed through the somewhat fuller idea of a kingdom of ends (ibid. 233–4 [4: 433]). The following points, however, seem fairly clear.

The independence of desires and inclinations that the formula attributes to rational lawmakers is not a total lack of motivating dispositions. It would be absurd to think of them as legislating while "caring" about nothing. All rational agents have ends; this is inherent in the very idea of a rational agent. In addition to whatever (rationally) contingent ends they may have as individuals, rational agents as such are (allegedly) disposed to acknowledge a rationally necessary ("objective") end-in-itself, which is "humanity" or "rational nature." In Kant's view, unlike Hume's, reason is not "inert." Kant holds that "pure reason can be practical:" that is, rational agents as such, independently of contingent inclinations, are supposed to be necessarily committed to basic noninstrumental, action-guiding principles, expressed in the formulas of the Categorical Imperative. The values inherent in this commitment can be a motivating factor, independently of our desire-based ends.[57]

---

[57] In the kingdom of ends, the lawmakers are conceived as having a system of personal ends, even though in thinking of the kingdom we "abstract" from their content. Having ends that one sets oneself is a necessary feature of being a rational agent, though these ends can vary among different kinds of rational

In addition, although Kant's claim that there can be rational law-giving not motivated by inclinations is controversial, it does not imply the process takes place in complete *ignorance* of human inclinations. Rational agents with autonomy are lawmakers in some respects like ideal secular or divine legislators, though their "laws" are not legal requirements backed by threats of punishment but rather moral principles endorsed for themselves (as well as for others). Rational legislators of universal laws do not choose their laws as a means to satisfying their own special inclinations, but, at some stage, they must take into account the conditions under which the laws will be applied. All the formulas of the Categorical Imperative are supposed to express basic objective principles the rationality of which does not depend on contingent human conditions, but none can be applied to particular human situations without some knowledge of that situation and general facts about our world. Many particular facts may prove to be irrelevant to a given judgment, but the formulas cannot guide us to any particular judgment until we consider the context of application.

Rational lawmakers are supposed to give themselves laws as rational wills with *autonomy*. This implies that they are committed to standards of rational choice beyond hypothetical imperatives. They do not merely acknowledge the rationality of taking necessary means to their desired ends; they have overriding rational standards of the form "One ought to do X, and not just because it promotes one's desire-based ends." They have the capacity and predisposition to act on principles that are not based on their desires as individuals. Further, all such principles are ultimately grounded in rational requirements (expressed in the Categorical Imperative) that are independent of all rationally contingent features of human nature. Human moral agents, being imperfectly rational, do not always live up to these principles that express their autonomy of will, but inevitably, Kant thought, they at least implicitly acknowledge the principles as standards that should override any conflicting claims of inclination. In extremely immoral persons, this

---

beings (e.g. human and nonhuman) and among individuals of the same kind. This has implications about the motivations of the rational legislators, even when (as if behind a "veil") they abstract from the content of their ends. For example, they would tend to favor whatever promotes everyone's ends and frustrates no one's, and whatever establishes conditions under which all can effectively pursue their ends. Because, as members of the kingdom of ends, they regard the humanity of each member as an end-in-itself, then they have a general motivational stance that will encourage promoting others' ends but rule out certain kinds of ends as unworthy.

acknowledgment may be more evident in their pangs of conscience than in any resolution to reform; but if some people lack it completely, this (in Kant's view) would indicate that either they lack the capacity for practical reason or (like very young children) they have not developed it.[58]

The idea of autonomy implies further that the legislators' laws are, in a sense, *self-imposed*. We need to distinguish here the basic principles that are constitutive of rational agency from the more specific "laws" that the rational legislators are supposed to give to themselves. The former presumably include the other forms of the Categorical Imperative, the Hypothetical Imperative, and any other principles necessary for rationally consistent and coherent choice. The latter are the more specific moral principles that, given appropriate facts, rational legislators (who are committed to those basic standards) would adopt for specified (e.g. human) conditions. (The *Groundwork* is primarily devoted to the basic principles, and *The Metaphysics of Morals* to intermediate level principles or "laws" for human conditions.) We cannot coherently think of the rational legislators as "making" and "giving themselves" the basic rational standards that constitute their rationality. Nevertheless, their autonomy implies that they *identify* themselves with these constitutive standards rather than seeing them as externally imposed and alien. When their reasoning according to these standards leads to a particular judgment, then they regard it as the result of their own judgment. The more specific "laws" that the legislators make can be understood as *given to themselves by themselves* in a further sense that is represented in the idea of a kingdom of ends. Here for good reasons, all rational legislators endorse the same general laws for everyone, and they are subject only to laws that they all endorse as legislators. In a sense, then, they

---

[58] Kant's belief, or perhaps faith, that virtually all competent adult human beings implicitly acknowledge his noninstrumental moral principles may be hard to sustain in our times, but it can be seen at least as a morally reasonable working presumption in the absence of compelling evidence regarding particular cases. In addition, we may see Kant as offering a model of rational agency (with related conceptions of "reasons," "reasonable," etc.) that (arguably) is presupposed in common thought, and this can be valuable, even if not every member of our species turns out to satisfy its criteria for being a "rational agent." Kant's claim that *rational* agents at least implicitly acknowledge his basic moral principles, I take it, is a substantive normative thesis, not an empirical hypothesis and not a proposition "analytically" true by virtue of the ordinary meaning of the word "rational" (or a special meaning that Kant stipulates). Contrary to some influential Kant scholars, I think that Kant's primary argument for his thesis is that *common moral consciousness* (especially the idea of "duty") *presupposes* that we are practically rational agents who, as such, acknowledge his basic principles. This, of course, is not an argument that would move anyone who lacked the sort of moral consciousness that Kant took for granted.

legislate for themselves rather than seeing laws as given to them by nature, tradition, or divine command.[59]

Kant does not give examples to show how the formula of autonomy might be applied. Instead, he develops its core idea into a *second* formula expanding the idea of autonomy, the kingdom-of-ends formula. This appears in his review of the formulas as a "complete determination of all maxims": "*All maxims which stem from autonomous lawgiving are to harmonize with a possible kingdom of ends as with a kingdom of nature*" (Kant (2002), 237 [4: 436]). A kingdom of ends is "a systematic union of different rational beings under common laws" (ibid. 234 [4: 433]). It is an ideal analogue of a political state or commonwealth in which rational members make all the laws to which they are subject. The members have "private ends," but in conceiving of the kingdom of ends we "abstract" from their content as well as from other "personal differences" among the members (ibid.). The kingdom has a nominal sovereign or head that makes the same laws without being subject to them. Because the sovereign (a "holy will") lacks needs and inclinations that might interfere with rational choice, the laws of the kingdom do not appear as *imperatives* or *obligations* for the sovereign (ibid. 240 [4: 439]).[60] Other (human) members are subject to obligation because, though subject to contrary inclinations, they too are committed to the same rational principles. The sovereign is conceived as having "unlimited resources adequate to his will." It may help to motivate us, Kant thought, to think of the kingdom of ends and the kingdom of nature as united under this same sovereign (ibid. 234–5 [4: 434], 239–40 [4: 439]). The kingdom of ends, Kant says, would become actual if everyone always followed its laws, but we are still obligated to follow the laws of a possible kingdom of ends in our world, where obviously not everyone does so (ibid. 238–9 [4: 438]).

---

[59] The kingdom of ends is said to have a "head" or "sovereign" who apparently legislates the same laws for the same reasons as the members. The head is not "bound" by the laws, presumably because, lacking in all needs and inclinations, the head is never tempted to deviate from rational principles. As Kant earlier says of a "holy will," the language of imperatives, necessitation, and "ought" is inappropriate when there is no possibility of misconduct.

[60] The "sovereign" or head (*Oberhaupt*) of the kingdom is technically like a state sovereign as traditionally conceived, in that the sovereign makes laws but is not *bound* by them, *subject* to them, or under *obligation* to follow them. This does not mean, however, that the sovereign may, or even can, act contrary to the laws that all members, including the sovereign, legislate. The point is that the sovereign, a "holy will," necessarily does whatever is rational by the sovereign's own nature, and so talk of the sovereign's obligations is out of place. Importantly, the members would legislate the same laws (because they are rational) and have the same obligations even if there were no sovereign.

Interpretative Issues

There are a number of questions about how to interpret these formulas. For example, how are they related to the preceding formulas? In his review of formulas, Kant suggests that the universal law formula is the best to use in judging maxims. The later formulas help to provide "access" to the moral law by bringing it "closer to intuition" and "feeling" (Kant (2002), 236–8 [4: 436–7]). He also suggests, however, that the kingdom-of-ends formula combines ideas in the preceding ones and so provides the most "complete determination" of moral requirements on maxims (ibid. 237 [4: 436]).[61] The former suggests that the main function of the kingdom-of-ends formula is to inspire and motivate us, but the latter suggests that it gives Kant's fullest characterization of the moral requirements on maxims and so, presumably, our most comprehensive action-guide.

Again, are we to think of all moral agents as members of the kingdom, or only those who show themselves worthy of it by acting morally? At one point, Kant suggests that the possible kingdom would become actual only if we all did our duty; but later he suggests that it would become a "true reality" only if God were sovereign of both nature and the kingdom of ends, thereby ensuring that the permissible ends of the virtuous would be fulfilled (ibid. 238–40 [4: 438–9]). For practical purposes, however, what matters is *what we as rational members would legislate,* not whether we think of ourselves and others as actually or merely possibly belonging to the kingdom of ends.

The most important interpretative question, especially for later development of Kantian ethics, concerns how the members in the kingdom make their laws. Kant's political metaphors suggest an ideal legislature in which all citizens are free and rational legislators and (except for the sovereign) bound by the laws that they make. As legislators, they share the same rational

---

[61] The text is ambiguous at several relevant points. For example, it is not clear whether Kant means that "each of [the three main formulas] by itself uniting the other two within it" (Kant (2002), 236–7 [4: 436]) or "one of them by itself containing a combination of the other two" (Kant (1964), 103 [4: 436]). If the latter were right, the one that combines the others would clearly be the kingdom-of-ends formula. Again, after Kant says that "[a]ll maxims have . . . a form, . . . a matter, . . . and a complete determination," it is not entirely clear whether the subsequent expressions of the moral law are meant as characterizations of the form, matter, and complete determination of the moral law (the *maxim* of a good will) or requirements regarding the form, matter, and complete determination of ordinary maxims of action (Kant (2002), 237 [4: 436]).

dispositions and values (e.g. humanity as an end-in-itself). Since the model abstracts from their personal differences and the content of their private ends, the laws that one legislator would endorse are just the same as the laws that each other would endorse. Nonetheless, the picture is that of joint legislation by and for all members. Their agreement results, as it were, from the fact that they acknowledge the same reasons and cannot be sidetracked by private concerns not shared or recognized by others. Here "abstracting" from differences functions, rather like Rawls's ((1971), 11, 17, 188–223) "veil of ignorance," to guarantee impartiality at the highest level of moral deliberation. On this reading, the kingdom-of-ends formula would tell us always to conform to those laws that we would make as members of this ideal moral legislature. The legislature would differ in significant ways from real legislatures. For example, the legislators do not make coercive laws backed by sanctions; their jurisdiction includes (at least initially) all rational agents;[62] the legislators are not bound by independent obligations or subject to external pressures; they never legislate irrationally; and so on.

Some passages, however, suggest a different picture. Here we imagine a possible world in which everyone conforms to the universal law formula, acting only on maxims that they can will as universal law. The outcome, we are to suppose, would be a harmonious system of ends, with no one being treated as a mere means and everyone having a chance to pursue permissible ends without undue interference. Since there is no legislature in this picture, arguably there is no need to ignore personal differences to ensure impartiality. The "laws" of the kingdom would be identified as individuals tested their maxims and found that certain ones could not be willed as universal law. "Never kill people for profit," for example, would be a law if no one could will a proposed maxim of killing for profit as a universal law. This interpretation allows the universal law formula to do the work of moral assessment, leaving for the kingdom-of-ends formula the role of an inspiring idea of the outcome if we all would do our part.[63]

---

[62] A reasonable extension of Kant's idea, I think, would have to view its application as proceeding in several stages, in a way to be explained later. At the first stage, we would imagine all rational agents legislating for all rational agents and so not tailoring their principles for any local circumstances.

[63] Wolff (1973), 183, for one, endorses this interpretation.

A Legislative Model for Deliberation about Moral Rules

On close examination, the texts remain ambiguous, and they leave many questions open. On the last interpretation, however, the kingdom of ends offers no new practical guide to deliberation and it inherits all the problems of applying the universal law formulas. Arguably, however, by construing the kingdom of ends instead as an idealized model of moral legislation and then extending this idea, we can take Kantian ethics (broadly conceived) in a different, and perhaps more promising direction. The inspiration for the project comes from John Rawls's theory of justice, although Rawls himself interprets Kant rather differently.[64]

The project presupposes that we can distinguish fundamental Kantian values from less basic rules and principles concerned with particular areas of the moral life. From the former, drawn primarily from versions of the Categorical Imperative, we would try to construct a conception of the perspective from which we should reflect about more specific rules and principles, how to articulate them, what qualifications they should contain, and so on. We would think of more basic values as constituting, for purposes of the theory, the essentials of an ideal point of view for trying to work out with others what moral demands and limits should be included in our principles concerned, for example, with obedience to the law, property rights, just punishment, gratitude, beneficence, respect, and friendship. It should not be assumed, of course, that we need specific principles or rules for all areas of life. Working toward common, well-defined standards is important in some areas; but in others, we may do better simply to approach problems with a good attitude and sensitivity to the context. In addition, the principles, if any, that we can justify as reasonable independently of historical context may be few and indeterminate in ways that leave much room for interpretation and judgment. In any case, despite what Kant himself thought, the best we can do may be to use the basic deliberative perspective to work on problems that arise in the more circumscribed

---

[64] The primary similarity to note between Kant and Rawls here is in the "constructivist" structure of the theories. There are other significant similarities, of course, but there are also very substantial and important differences. I have discussed the proposed legislative model, its relation to Rawls's work, and the problems it raises in several essays, and only a few basic points will be sketched here. See Hill (1992a), chs. 3, 4, 11, and (2000), chs. 2, 4, 8.

conditions in which we now live.[65] Reasonable principles for familiar circumstances may be applicable more generally, but extending them is impossible unless we understand the other contexts well enough to see that there are no relevant differences.

Although we might expect that actual people who take up the deliberative perspective could agree on some general principles that rather directly reflect their constitutive values, we cannot expect that they would always agree. Agreement on fundamental values does not ensure unanimity on how these can be best implemented in various situations. Differences in judgment and in understanding of background facts are bound to result in disagreements on particular moral issues. The legislative perspective may still be useful, however, as a standard for conscientious action. That is, we can think of conscientious action as doing whatever, after due deliberation and dialogue with others, we judge should be required by principles adopted from the legislative perspective. We would need to consider what we would recommend for universal approval if we were debating the matter from the legislative perspective. Then, as conscientious persons, we should follow this, keeping in mind that others may reasonably disagree.

The Kantian legislative perspective suggested by the kingdom-of-ends formula combines ideas from Kant's other formulas. First, as legislators, we deliberate by assessing whether we can reasonably endorse various general policies, considered as principles for everyone. Thus we must move beyond the narrower point of view that we take when first inclined to act in a certain way and consider how things would be if we endorsed moral principles permitting everyone to act that way. In doing so we need not identify precisely "the maxim" of each act, but instead can systematically review sets of permissive, prohibitive, and obligatory principles together. Although our maxim might be described in any of several ways, our act will be wrong if, under any description, it is incompatible with the principles that we would endorse from the legislative perspective.

---

[65] This is not to say that we take our moral standards from our historical circumstances. The point is that in using our basic standards to reach particular conclusions, we need to take into account the facts about our historical condition, at least insofar as they are relevant under those basic standards. We should not assume at the outset that we know the scope of the principles we can justify from basic values, how much they are open to exception, and even whether they are general enough to be useful guides. This is part of what would need to be worked out.

Second, legislators who acknowledge each other as ends-in-themselves would have to deliberate with the constraints and values, whatever these may be, inherent in the idea of humanity as an end-in-itself. Because the legislators have "private ends" but "abstract from differences," they must generally favor conditions that further the members' ends, but their law-making should not be influenced by partiality for their own ends in particular. In addition, arguably, the value of humanity as an end motivates them to place a high priority on members' survival, development, and opportunities to live as rational agents. More abstractly, the value of humanity is reflected in their unwillingness to engage in conduct that they could not, from the legislative perspective, justify to other members. This motivating disposition to treat humanity in each person as an end would be considered not merely a contingent desire but rather a disposition inherent in rational nature.

Third, the idea of autonomy is reflected in the stipulation that the legislators are subject to no laws or principles other than those they them-selves rationally endorse. They do not endorse principles merely because tradition, the state, or God sanctions them. They endorse some fundamental rational constraints and values, such as humanity as an end, simply because these express their nature as rational persons. They endorse more specific moral principles, such as beneficence and fidelity, because these principles prescribe conduct that expresses, secures, or promotes their basic values in the context of our complex empirical world. The idea of autonomy is also reflected in the stipulation that, when deliberating, legislators set aside inappropriate partiality toward their own special ends. Further, valuing other persons as (at least potentially) autonomous colegislators of the moral standards that govern our mutual relations has implications regarding specifically how we are to respect them as persons.

Illustration: Meeting Needs and Doing Favors

The Kantian legislative perspective sketched here is obviously not yet an adequate normative ethical theory, much less a complete one. Let us, however, overlook for now remaining gaps and problems and return, instead, to the example of beneficence. From a Kantian legislative perspec-tive, how might we think about grounds and limits of our obligation to help others? Let us consider what general duty we should attribute to everyone, acknowledging that special circumstances are likely to call for more or less than any general principles can anticipate.[66]

Consider several candidates regarding the general obligation to help others in need. (1) We should always help those in need when we can, whether they have a right to it or not. (2) Helping others in need is morally optional, except when they have a right to demand it. (3) We should help others with basic needs, at least when their need is great and the cost to us is proportionately small. As legislators concerned to work out a reasonable system of moral principles, we might at once see that all the principles need to be qualified by adding (a) *except that helping is generally wrong when their need is for resources to complete immoral projects* and (b) *except that it is wrong when we can only help by immoral means.* "Immoral" here would have to be determined by other, higher-priority principles that the legislators have adopted. On further reflection, we might see that what others need to survive, develop, and thrive as rational autonomous agents (i.e. "basic needs") should take priority over what they need to accomplish projects based only on personal preference. This seems implicit in valuing rational nature as an end-in-itself, at least on substantive interpretations. Especially within the first category, it seems that the greater the need, other things equal, the more reason to help. Given this, we might realize that the same priority applies equally well to the agent's own needs. Thus we should not in general disregard our urgent basic needs merely to help others in minor, optional projects. Thus the first candidate (1), even amended with (a) and (b), would be unacceptable, because it ignores the agent's own needs and potential differences in the kind and degree of need. If amended to take these factors into account, (1) would look more like (3).

We cannot evaluate (2) properly without first deciding what help persons can demand as their right. This would have to be a prior issue to take up from the legislative perspective, but let us assume for now that familiar intuitions about this are right. In general, since rights are enforceable claims, presumably moral legislators would want to express and promote their values not only by assigning individual rights but also by adopting principles that call upon conscientious persons to do more for others than they can

---

[66] I discuss this question in more detail in "Meeting Needs and Doing Favors," in Hill (2002), ch. 7.

demand by right.[67] If so, candidate principle (2) would be unacceptable. It implies that, beyond doing what we can rightfully be coerced to do, we may do as we please, ignoring all the needs of others, no matter how great these are and no matter how little it would cost us to help. If everyone, even everyone so inclined, were to act that way, then the prospects of everyone to live a full life as a rational, autonomous person would be diminished. Secure, wealthy individuals might calculate that they are likely to be better off under (2) than (3), but they could not justify that idea to others, or themselves, if they took up the legislative point of view that abstracts from personal differences and views humanity in each person as an end.

The third candidate (3), by contrast, seems quite promising. If this principle (at least) is endorsed, then, given the uncertainties of human life, the prospects of every representative person are better in ways that matter to rational legislators. The main question about (3) is whether it is too minimal a requirement, and so needs to be supplemented with further principles regarding helping.

Two supplements, at least, seem to be appropriate from the legislative perspective. First, because (3) addresses only cases where we could help others whose needs are great and basic to rational, autonomous living, we need some general principle about helping others whose needs are not as urgent and fundamental. We need to consider helping others in their personal projects: for example, doing favors rather than attempting to meet basic needs. As before, legislators will want to qualify any principle in this area by ruling out helping others in their immoral projects or by using immoral means, where immorality is defined by incompatibility with higher-priority principles, already endorsed. Consider three candidate principles concerning helping others where great basic needs are not involved: (4) Help others whenever you can, unless fulfilling some other duty. (5) Helping others is entirely optional, assuming that you fulfill your other duties. (6) Make it an end of yours that others realize their (permissible) ends; and so, to some significant extent, contribute to others' (permissible) ends as well as your own.

A problem with (4) is that it fails to acknowledge the importance, from the legislative perspective, of the agent's own personal ends. To be sure, (4)

---

[67] This, in any case, is how Kant views wide imperfect duties, such as beneficence, in *The Metaphysics of Morals* (1996a).

implies that others should help the helper, and so the helper's ends are not totally ignored. However, (4) also unreasonably implies that, other duties aside, each person should help to promote others' ends, irrespective of the cost to the person's own projects. Thus everyone would have to sacrifice their very important projects whenever they could permissibly help someone else on a relatively minor project. The principle must at least be adjusted to require only sacrificing opportunities to promote one's own projects when, all considered, helping others instead would contribute proportionately more to others' equally or more highly valued projects. Even amended this way, (4) is still a far more demanding requirement than most people could accept. Unless we are working to satisfy other duties, it requires us to drop whatever we are doing whenever an opportunity presents itself to work on another person's personal project, provided only the other person cares slightly more about his or her project than we care about ours. A readiness to do so might seem saintly, in some respects, but, given the limits of human nature, it seems more than could reasonably be expected of everyone. In addition, being constantly "on call" to help others who are not in urgent or vital need would make it difficult, if not impossible, to structure a life with meaningful personal projects of one's own, which is something that presumably rational autonomous agents would value.

Given that rational agents necessarily set themselves and pursue ends, candidate principle (5) arguably expresses an attitude incompatible with valuing rational agency in each person as an end-in-itself. It implies that we may ignore the (permissible) projects of others, no matter how much the others care about them and no matter how insignificant the inconvenience of helping would be to ourselves. If everyone, or even those so inclined, always acted in this way, everyone's prospects, considered from the legislative perspective, would be worse than if they adopted candidate principle (6). Some fortunately situated individuals might prosper, but legislators respecting humanity in each person equally would not cater to their special advantages. Arguably they would acknowledge the worth of all as rational, autonomous persons by requiring everyone to aid others in personal projects, to some significant extent, but leaving a wide latitude for choice (apart from the requirement regarding basic needs) as to when, how, and exactly how much to help. Principle (6) is just this sort of requirement, for it tells us to include it among our important ends that others also fulfill their (permissible) personal ends.

From the Kantian perspective, persons have a status of "unconditional and incomparable worth" that is acknowledged in practice by conforming to the "laws" to which they all, as rational and autonomous legislators, would agree. They are "equal," in that they have the same status under the moral law, no one being intrinsically more important than any other, and each person being inviolable in ways determined by the principles everyone mutually endorses. This equal standing under the moral law is quite different from the sort of equality that classic utilitarians prescribe. Equality for them is equal consideration (or "weight") for equal pleasures and pains, no matter whose they are. That idea is not part of the Kantian picture, and, as is often noted, following it could lead to exploiting and oppressing a few for the greater pleasure of many. Kantian legislators are not utility-maximizing legislators but are constrained by their acknowledgment of a worth of individual persons that cannot be quantified, weighed, or traded for "more" value. The specific implications of this idea still need to be worked out, but it clearly implies that Kantian legislators do not have the authority to prescribe *whatever* is predicted to produce a maximum quantity of some comparable and conditional value, such as pleasure, satisfaction, and the like. Further, rejecting the idea that they must measure, compare, and produce the greatest quantity of happiness, Kantian legislators need not even require the qualified principle "You must always help others whenever other duties allow and others would gain more happiness than you would lose by helping." By contrast, the more indeterminate principle (6) expresses respect for all persons by valuing their (permissible) ends without so restrictively dictating precisely when and how much time and energy to devote to helping others, beyond the requirement regarding basic needs (3).

Remaining Problems

These last comments are meant merely to illustrate how reflection on a Kantian legislative perspective might proceed. Further considerations are no doubt relevant, and in any case the legislative perspective has not been defined fully enough to permit more than rather loose, informal argument. In addition, my discussion has concerned only the general principle of beneficence, not special requirements in specific circumstances. All attempts to reconstruct Kant's basic normative standard must work out remaining problems and address various objections. The proposed idea of a Kantian legislative perspective is obviously no exception. For example, we need to consider further the importance and limits of rules and principles for a moral life. The appropriate degree and kind of "abstracting from personal differences" needs to be clarified, especially as this may vary with the context and scope of the problem to be addressed. Different ways of understanding the central value of humanity as an end-in-itself need to be clarified and assessed. Any other presupposed standards of "rational" and "reasonable" willing need to be articulated explicitly. Special problems are raised when we try to use and adjust principles for different social and economic conditions. If we insist on quite simple, inflexible principles appropriate for an idealized world, we may unreasonably ignore morally relevant differences between those conditions and the real world. If we bend and adjust principles too readily to accommodate special circumstances, there would be no point in having principles. It would be madness to insist that the consequences of adopting a principle never matter, but it must be clear how and within what limits reflection on consequences is appropriate from a Kantian legislative perspective. We also need to address suspicions that trying to construct principles from an ideal perspective complicates moral judgment needlessly and alienates us from our more particular moral perspective in daily life.[68] Much can be said in response to these problems, but whether the problems ultimately undermine the promise of this approach to Kantian normative theory remains to be seen.

---

[68] I discuss these and some other objections in Hill (2000), esp. ch. 2, and (2002), ch. 3.

3

Kantian Constructivism as Normative Ethics

[W]e cannot learn philosophy; for where is it, who is in possession of it, and how shall we recognize it? We can only learn to philosophize, that is, to exercise the talent of reason, in accordance with its universal principles, on certain actually existing attempts at philosophy, always, however, reserving the right of reason to investigate, to confirm, or to reject these principles in their very sources.

Immanuel Kant, *Critique of Pure Reason*, B 866

So we learn moral and political philosophy, and indeed any other part of philosophy by studying the exemplars—those noted figures who have made cherished attempts—and we try to learn from them, and if we are lucky to find a way to go beyond them.

John Rawls, *Lectures on the History of Political Philosophy*, p. xiv

Prologue

These passages reveal the attitude that Kant and Rawls had toward their exemplars in the history of philosophy. The attitude is deeply respectful but also modestly ambitious about the prospects of "going beyond" their work in ways appropriate for one's own projects and times. Kant and Rawls are both philosophical exemplars for me, regardless of ways in which they may disagree with each other and I with them. For many years I have thought, and occasionally proposed, that a promising kind of *normative* ethical theory

This chapter was initially presented as a keynote address for the First Annual Workshop in Normative Ethics in Tucson, Arizona, in January 2010.

can be drawn from Kant and Rawls by combining some of their ideas in a way appropriate for a somewhat different project. With some hesitation, I call this *Kantian constructivism as a normative ethical theory*. This is not the "Kantian constructivism" as interpreted by Onora O'Neill, Christine Korsgaard, or John Rawls. Their versions include at least negative metaethical claims, and they tend to focus primarily on Kant's first ("universal law") formulations of the Categorical Imperative. My proposal, instead, is to think of Kantian constructivism as a *normative* ethical theory that relies heavily on Kant's later formulations.

For several reasons the time seems right to explore alternatives to the more familiar normative ethical theories. My impression is that normative ethical theory is not as flourishing in contemporary philosophy as it could be. One reason, I suspect, is that the most familiar types of theory—the kinds that are summarized in textbooks—have been worked over for many years without any general consensus emerging. *Utilitarianism*, for example, strikes many as initially implausible, and after decades of development, criticism, refinement, subtle progress has been made but the core idea remains controversial. Interpretations of *Kant's universal law formulas* have also undergone cycles of criticism, refinement, and more criticism, and apparently most Kantians now abandon Kant's boldest claims about its adequacy as a moral decision guide. So-called *ethical egoism* appears to be a nonstarter, at least as a theory of morality, and I suspect textbooks now include it just for contrast with other theories. *Rossian pluralism* has some appeal as a default position, but even beginning students tend to be dissatisfied with leaving so much unexplained and indeterminate. Now advocates of "*virtue ethics*" propose to identify the common problem with other modern theories and then, with the help of Aristotle, offer a new approach. But too often their emphasis is more on what they reject than on developing their alternative as a normative theory. Dissatisfaction with all normative theories may be compounded when attempts to "apply" the theories to hard, real-world problems prove less fruitful than expected.

The lesson to draw, some say, is to abandon *normative* ethical *theory* and to stick to metaethics in moral philosophy and then just to expressing our personal commitments in the rest of life. Going even further, some followers of Wittgenstein believe we should abandon the effort to construct philosophical *theories* of all kinds. For those still content to theorize in *metaethics*, the temptation to abandon *normative ethical theory* may be reinforced by metaethical thinking dominated by certain forms of intuitionism and expressivism that seem to leave little need for theorizing within the realm of the normative. At least the simpler forms of intuitionism and expressivism allow adherents to enjoy comparing and contrasting their moral judgments about hypothetical scenarios, case by case, without relying on or looking for any general normative ethical theory.

I am not yet ready to give up on normative ethical theory, but my dissatisfaction with the currently available theories leads me to hope that more satisfactory theories can be developed. For example, various aspects of the work of Kant and Rawls provide the materials for a kind of constructivist *moral* thinking that does not try to replace or compete with metaethical theories such as rational intuitionism, naturalistic reductionism, and expressivism.

Rawls himself has provided models for at least two kinds of constructivism. First, his Dewey Lectures entitled "Kantian Constructivism in Moral Theory" lay out a relatively "comprehensive" moral theory that contrasts with the rational intuitionist idea that moral judgments are based on "perception" of an independent moral order (Rawls (1999*b*) and (1996)).[1] Then in *Political Liberalism*, taking a sharp turn away from comprehensive moral theories, Rawls (1996) introduced his special "political constructivism." This addressed normative political questions, starting from familiar normative assumptions, but the theory was restricted to a "political conception" of principles of justice for the basic structure of democratic societies. Several Kantians have since called their theories "constructivist," but both they and their critics apparently assume that constructivism is meant to deny moral realism as commonly understood in metaethics. A question that interests me, however, is: "What would constructivism be like if it were designed for ethical, not just political questions, if it remained (as far as possible) metaethically noncommittal, and if it drew appropriately from both Kant and Rawls?"

My aims here are to characterize the kind of theory I have in mind, to point to aspects of Kant's ethics as a possible example of it, and to address briefly some concerns about it. The label "constructivist" can be misleading,

---

[1] For Rawls's sense of "comprehensive" see his (1996), 13, 174. Theories can be more or less "comprehensive" in different ways. For example, they can cover more or fewer of the branches of ethics (justice, responsibility, virtue, etc.), but they can also be committed to more or fewer metaphysical and metaethical doctrines. As I use the term here, *comprehensive* theories include significant metaethical commitments. Normative ethical theory per se is not comprehensive in this sense.

and I do not insist on using it for Kantian normative ethics; but I want at least to suggest ways in which the procedures and assumptions of Kantian norma-tive ethics can be considered analogous to (though distinct from) certain core aspects of what Rawls initially introduced as Kantian constructivism.

My plan, more specifically, is this: First, I comment on the general idea of normative ethical theory and distinguish different conceptions of how *normative ethics* is related to *metaethics*. Second, I review general features of *constructivism* and briefly sketch several versions of *Kantian* constructivism. Third, I propose that to understand Kant's systematic normative ethical theory we must look beyond Kant's familiar *Groundwork for the Metaphysics of Morals*, to his later Doctrine of Virtue (Part II of *The Metaphysics of Morals*), and I highlight some main features of the normative theory he develops there. Fourth, I consider briefly how Kant's Doctrine of Virtue can be viewed as presenting a *normative* ethical theory that has constructivist fea-tures that are separable from the more ambitious metaethical claims in the prominent Kantian constructivisms of Rawls and O'Neill.[2] On my constru-al the Doctrine of Virtue fits well with my previous proposal of a "con-structivist" normative theory drawn from Kant's later formulations of the Categorical Imperative in the *Groundwork for the Metaphysics of Morals*. Finally, I respond to some of O'Neill's objections to Rawls's constructi-visms that would apply as well to my project. My remarks will be quite general and wide-ranging, but I hope appropriate for the occasion.

What is Normative Ethical Theory?

We can distinguish between the general idea of normative ethical theory and particular conceptions of it and its relation to metaethics. Here is a brief history, leaving aside details and qualifications.

The general concept of normative ethical theory. The distinction between *norma-tive ethics* and *metaethics* was not common, at least not pervasive and explicit, in moral philosophy before the twentieth century. The intuitionists G. E.

---

[2] The occasion for selecting Rawls and O'Neill to compare on Kantian constructivism was a conference on "Ethics and Politics Beyond Borders" at the British Academy in honor of O'Neill upon her retirement as its president. Thanks are due for helpful comments of philosophers there, at the First Annual Normative Ethics Workshop in Tucson, at the University of Northern Arizona, and the University of California, Riverside, and especially to Adam Cureton for long talks about these issues.

Moore and W. D. Ross and emotivists A. J. Ayer and C. L. Stevenson distinguished their studies of moral language from substantive moral claims about what is good to pursue and what we ought to do. With more subtle linguistic analysis, R. M. Hare and other prescriptivists continued to insist on the distinction between analytical/descriptive claims on the one hand and evaluative/prescriptive claims on the other. William Frankena, Richard Brandt, and no doubt others made prominent, at least in the United States, a distinction between metaethics and normative ethical *theory* (as distinct from specific moral judgments and the domain now often called "applied ethics"). Both metaethics and normative ethical theory were regarded as branches of the discipline of philosophy that are, in a sense, *about* what is worth pursuing, what we ought to do, and the basis of such judgments. Normative ethical theory was supposed to articulate, explain, and rank (if possible) the most general moral principles on which particular moral judgments depend. Meta-ethics, in contrast, was supposed to say what moral terms mean, whether there are moral facts, what sort of facts they could be, how they could be known, and what relation they have to psychology, biology, and physics. A central question of metaethics was whether any moral principles could be "deeply justified" (or undermined) by metaphysics, science, or analysis of language. There was a distinction, then, between the (normative) attempt to justify a moral judgment by the general principles of a normative ethical theory and the (metaethical) attempt to vindicate the judgment, or the theory, by metaphysical, scientific, or linguistic investigations.

This general concept of normative ethical theory leaves wide room for different conceptions of its procedures, content, and relation to metaethics.

Normative ethics as applied metaethics. A common view was that metaethics was to be done first and independently of substantive moral claims, and then this dictated how to proceed in normative ethics. Moore, for example, allegedly found through conceptual investigation that "good in itself" is "unanalyzable" and our "duty" is to do whatever would bring about the (intrinsically) best possible universe.[3] Normative theory, he concluded, must be utilitarian: the right thing to do is determined by the intrinsic value of the long-term consequences of each option. Because of his healthy skepticism about our ability to estimate long-term consequences, however, he

---

[3] This was the view in *Principia Ethica*, but later in *Ethics* he held it was not by definition but a synthetic truth that our duty is to bring about the most intrinsic good.

recommended normally just following conventional common-sense morality. *Naturalistic* theorists, in Moore's broad sense, analyzed moral terms as referring to descriptive properties, empirical or metaphysical, and so the task of normative ethics for such theorists was to investigate which acts have those properties. Neither naturalistic nor "nonnaturalistic" metaethical theories (such as Moore's) actually have to be consequentialist in normative ethics but they typically hold that what makes acts right or wrong is determined by facts independent of procedures of judging or constructing.

Normative ethics as plumping. Emotivism, prescriptivism, and (more generally) expressivism are metaethical theories that do not dictate determinative criteria or procedures for normative ethical judgment.[4] This freedom in normative ethics, however, makes it tempting to abandon normative ethical *theorizing.*[5] Individuals are to make moral judgments according to norms they adopt, and can revise, without prior *determinative* guidance or restriction from metaethical analysis. An expressivist might say, prescriptively, "As a person, plump for humane causes; but as a philosopher, stick to science, logic, and linguistic analysis." An expressivist can, however, endorse the first principles of traditional normative ethical theories or other complex systems of norms.

Normative ethical theory as self-standing or nonderivative.[6] Under the previous conceptions of normative ethics it is either plumping for norms or carrying out the instructions determined by prior metaethical investigations. Although Rawls was cautious in expressing its relation to metaethics, his early work represents an alternative conception of normative ethics. The general idea is this: set aside metaethical controversies, and start with a filtered set of particular moral judgments. A normative ethical theorist attempts to find, or (in a sense) construct, a set of general principles or a framework that makes sense of such judgments insofar as they are (relatively) informed, stable, made under conditions generally favorable for ("objective") judgments, and coherent with other persons' judgments filtered in

---

[4] Theories of these "noncognitivist" or broadly "expressivist" types vary in how restrictive they take moral language to be. R. M. Hare, for example, did not claim that utilitarianism follows from his universal prescriptivism, but he held that the use of moral language commits speakers in ways such that, given human nature, normally they cannot consistently reject utilitarianism (Hare, 1981).

[5] See Gibbard e.g. (1990).

[6] I add "or nonderivative" because, on this view, normative ethical theory can be developed according to theoretical ideals not derived from metaethics even if some think such normative theories must still be "standing" on metaphysical grounds or can be made to "fall" when metaethics or science undermines them.

this way. This is a process Rawls (1999a) called "looking for an *explication* of the considered judgments of competent moral judges."

Normative ethical theory can add several layers of complexity without thereby becoming derivative from metaethics. For example, in *A Theory of Justice* and *Political Liberalism*, Rawls relies on both a constructivist procedure and wide reflective equilibrium in developing his principles of justice.[7] In *A Theory of Justice* he uses commonly accepted values of freedom and equality, without further grounding, in building up his "original position," and in *Political Liberalism* even more explicitly he starts from normative ideals of Western democratic cultures without claiming that they are independently grounded. These methods for normative theory work from common (or relatively less controversial) normative assumptions to conclusions about contested (or more controversial) issues. Their use leaves open further (metaethical) questions about the reality of moral properties, the sense in which ethical claims are true (or not), and the linguistic force of normative words and sentences.[8] To do normative theory nonderivatively, one need not deny (or affirm) that further questions matter in a more comprehensive philosophical enterprise. Trying to understand better the basic content and structure of considered moral judgments can be important for many reasons. These include improving our understanding of ourselves and our culture and knowing what is at issue when we ask how our sense of morality relates to science, remote cultures, and various ideas of reality and truth. Metaethical intuitionists may treat the fact that certain principles are supported nonderivatively by these methods as evidence for their truth. Others may regard it as providing objectivity and justification of a different kind.

Varieties of Kantian Constructivism

The general idea of ethical constructivism. The term "constructivism" has a use in mathematics, but the comparison with ethics may not be particularly

---

[7] In *Political Liberalism* he appeals to the idea of an overlapping consensus of reasonable comprehensive doctrines on his principles conceived only as "political" in a sense implying that it does not claim to represent moral truth and reality to compete with, for example, theological systems. Here he is seeking wide reflective equilibrium on a normative political theory.

[8] In *A Theory of Justice* Rawls seems ambivalent on the relation between metaethics and his theory of justice, but he clearly wanted to bypass the methods of linguistic analysis that dominated metaethics at the time.

instructive.[9] The basic constructivist idea for ethics is to regard first-order moral principles as (at least *provisionally*) valid or justifiable for the intended domain just in case and *because* they would be endorsed by all members of an appropriately defined initial choice situation.[10] I emphasize the word "because" here to indicate that the constructivist does not merely treat principles as valid if and only if they would be endorsed from the initial choice position, but says that within the theory and by its methods there is no ground for asserting the principles as valid (for the intended domain) that is entirely independent of the constructivist procedure. What makes the theory *constructivist*, as I understand this, is not that it purports to avoid ontological commitments but that it makes use of a "procedure of construction" to identify and (in some sense) support principles of the sort we are looking for.[11]

This general idea of ethical constructivism does not settle whether or not the procedures of construction together with relevant facts *under*determine moral judgments, thereby leaving room for creatively "constructing" different and equally valid normative systems for the same domain. Critics may deplore the apparent indeterminacy of the idea that morality is a construct of human reason, but constructivists can differ about how much indeterminacy there is. The metaphor of "construction" (as O'Neill notes) implies a plan, materials, and agents who do the constructing, but not necessarily that there is always just one building that could result from proper construction. A constructivist theorist (as Rawls suggests) may need to interpret creatively our indeterminate familiar values, thereby meeting certain criteria that allow more than one interpretation. A constructivist could, however, believe that "in principle" the procedures and

---

[9] This was apparently T. M. Scanlon's conclusion, after reviewing points of comparison at a conference at the University of California, Riverside, in 1997; but see Rawls (1996), 102.

[10] I say "provisionally" because in Rawls's theories any derivation of principles from the relevant choice situation ("original position") is potentially revisable as we seek wide reflective equilibrium through critical review of our starting points, factual assumptions, etc. Under Rawls's reflective equilibrium method there can be confirmation (or revision) of the principles endorsed from the original position if they can be shown to reflect (or not) the pre-theoretical "considered judgment of competent judges."

[11] We can distinguish between two ideas of "support": (1) supporting a normative principle by showing it is required by basic and comprehensive *normative* ethical standards, from (2) supporting the principle by showing that it, or the standards from which it derives, are somehow more deeply grounded (e.g. in scientific facts or metaphysical reality) or shown to be true or justified by a coherentist epistemology (e.g. relying on a method of reflective equilibrium).

relevant facts determine completely the answers to all moral questions, even if the best available constructs are incomplete.

Constructivism that is broadly *Kantian* can take many forms. Here is a very brief sketch of three versions.

Rawls's Kantian constructivism. To review, in his Dewey Lectures Rawls (1999*b*) presented a *Kantian* constructivist theory to be contrasted with rational intuitionism. He interpreted rational intuitionism as a comprehensive moral theory committed to the reality of a moral order independent of our judgments and procedures of construction, and he presented Kantian constructivism as an alternative framework for ethical thought that denied or avoided such ontological commitments. In *Political Liberalism* Rawls contrasts his own (normative) political constructivism with Kantian constructivism, which he describes as a more comprehensive moral theory. The procedures of construction in the two types of constructivism, however, are structurally similar: the relevant principles of justice are whatever principles would be chosen by parties in an "original position" to govern relations among them, where the parties, the original position, and the context of application are appropriately specified.

The most striking feature of Rawls's Kantian constructivism, in my view, was not its stance toward metaphysical realism but its attempt to identify and support relevant moral principles by a procedure of construction together with certain conceptions of persons and society.[12] This is what I take to be the distinctive feature of any *broadly* Kantian constructivism. Although Rawls regarded principles of justice as the result of construction, the relevant background ideas of persons, society, and the initial choice situation reflect normative values.[13] The aim of construction is not to derive principles from value-free premises but to work out the implications

---

[12] "What distinguishes the Kantian form of constructivism is essentially this: it specifies a particular conception of the person as an element in a reasonable procedure of construction, the outcome of which determines the content of the first principles of justice. Expressed another way: this kind of view sets up a certain procedure of construction which answers to certain reasonable requirements, and within this procedure persons characterized as rational agents of construction specify, through their agreements, the first principles of justice," Rawls (1999*b*), 304.

[13] When the inevitable Euthyphro dilemma is posed, the constructivist should deny that the principles are arbitrarily constructed and instead readily affirm that value assumptions are represented in (or "built-into") the procedure of construction and related ideas. To the objection that this makes construction procedure redundant, the Rawlsian answer is that the resulting principles of justice are drawn from a complex combination of factors (the choice situation, the conceptions of persons and society, etc.) and not assumed as principles, for example known or believed by the parties to the original position.

regarding controversial questions from a combination of less controversial values. Rawls's several constructivist procedures are designed to answer (relatively) well-defined questions for a specified context. They concern the principles of justice for the basic structures of well-ordered societies, but the restricted focus on justice is not essential to Kantian constructivism as I understand it. Also, even though Rawls's Kantian constructivism and his political constructivism differ in their scope and ambition to represent moral truth, they are both *broadly* Kantian constructivisms, in my view, because they use procedures of construction and associated conceptions of persons and society that are akin to Kant's in some respects.

O'Neill's Kantian constructivism. In several works, most prominently in *Constructions of Reason*, Onora O'Neill presents her understanding of Kantian constructivism, distinguishes it from Rawls's, and raises objections to Rawls's theory of justice.[14] O'Neill emphasizes that at the core of Kant's critical method was the rejection of arbitrary authority. Drawing from Kant's first *Critique*, she argues that critical use of reason restricts the scope of legitimate metaphysics as well as that of claims based on empirical science. Even the use of reason in these critical projects, O'Neill says, must be "vindicated" in a recursive, public, and never fully completed process. She argues that "realism," "foundationalism," and traditional "rationalism" in ethics cannot survive reason's critique of their authority to assert their starting points. The fundamental principle of reason that can be vindicated, in her view, is Kant's Categorical Imperative to act only on maxims through which one can at the same time will that they be universal law. She argues that this is a basic principle of thought as well as action.[15] The implied procedure of construction for ethics, though difficult to interpret, is simple to state: maxims are to be rejected as morally unworthy or wrong to act on if they *cannot* be consistently and publicly communicated, made intelligible, and shared by everyone. The procedure, she argues, is only a negative test but it generates strong presumptive prohibitions of coercive force, polemical debate, deception, disrespect, and indifference to the welfare of others. These general principles are then to be used to develop or construct more specific ideas of individual virtue and just institutions, as appropriate to various contexts. These principles and the Kantian constructivist procedure

---

[14] See also O'Neill (1975), (1996), (2000), (2003a), and (2003b).
[15] O'Neill (1989), 26–7, 45–7.

are the basis for O'Neill's extensive later work on global aid, toleration, trust, and other practical issues.

My constructivist reading of Kant's kingdom of ends. In several previous essays I have sketched a reconstruction of Kant's idea of an inclusive commonwealth ("kingdom") united by common moral laws or principles.[16] The members are conceived as both lawmakers and subjects. They each have their own set of ends but in legislating they abstract from personal differences. They legislate as rational and autonomous, and so they make only laws they can justify to each other. As legislators they respect humanity in each person as an end in itself, and so they are guided and constrained by all the values and precepts inherent in this fundamental ideal. As a formulation of the Categorical Imperative, the principle tells us always to act in accord with the principles of a possible kingdom of ends. Various supplementary ideas are needed to bring this abstract model down to real-world conditions where, for example, local conditions vary and people are often partisan, weak, corrupt, and divided. For the most part we should expect that only very general and defeasible principles can be justified as universal. These would need to be applied to various historical circumstances in light of more specific information. The ideal is to find well-grounded principles that all reasonable, autonomous people would endorse; but because disagreements in applying principles are to be expected, as a practical matter the best we can do is to take ideas here as a guide for conscientious judgment and choice rather than as a sure path to moral truth. Among the advantages of this way of construing Kantian normative ethics, I argue, is that it turns our attention from individual maxims, considered case by case, to systems of interrelated principles.

Kant's Doctrine of Virtue

Rawls and O'Neill had ambitions for Kantian constructivism that extended beyond normative ethics. Where in Kant's writings are we likely to find his own version of normative ethical theory? We might look first, as I have

---

[16] The main idea, admittedly an extension and modification of Kant's explicit views, is described briefly in Hill (1992*a*), ch. 11, and developed further in Hill (2000), chs. 2, 4, and 8. Some objections to the use of the idea of hypothetical agreement in the legislative model are discussed in Hill (2002), ch. 3. There is further discussion in Hill (2003), 17–36, (2006), and (2008*b*), 214–36.

done, to his *Groundwork for the Metaphysics of Morals*, sections I and II. Here Kant starts with ideas (allegedly) implicit in common moral judgments and then argues to formulations of the supreme moral principle that are presupposed by them. His examples are just brief illustrations to foreshadow his later discussion in *The Metaphysics of Morals*. The main point of the first two sections is to argue that common moral understanding *presupposes* an identifiable supreme moral principle and a certain idea of persons. The method is (broadly) analytical, the supreme principle is the Categorical Imperative (expressed in several forms), and persons are conceived as rational and free (in several senses). Kant's starting point is not an investigation into how our moral judgments about particular cases tend to converge. He begins instead by attributing certain formal assumptions to ordinary thought—the special value of a good will and the idea of duty as categorically imperative. Then he argues that these ideas presuppose that his formulas express the supreme moral principle and that this principle would be affirmed by rational agents who have autonomy of the will.

We should hesitate to force classic works into contemporary categories, especially when they are as variously interpreted as Kant's *Groundwork*. The argument of its first two chapters, for example, could perhaps be seen as a metaethical analysis of moral concepts. *Groundwork* III, then, could be seen as metaethical inquiry into the ultimate rational or metaphysical justification for the use of such concepts. An alternative, and perhaps more compelling, interpretation would see Kant's whole enterprise in the *Groundwork* as practical, not metaphysical, moving systematically from normative starting points to normative conclusions. Interpretation here is difficult, but there are also other reasons to look beyond the *Groundwork* to find Kant's best analogue to our familiar normative ethical theories.

Kant's most extensive and mature presentation of his system of ethical principles is his Doctrine of Virtue, which is Part II of *The Metaphysics of Morals*. There are several features to highlight here because they reflect Kant's mature ethical thought and are suggestive for contemporary normative constructivism.[17]

(1) The Doctrine of Virtue presents a system of ethical principles with a complex structure that relies on substantive values as well as formal principles,

---

[17] For further discussion, see Denis (2010), and Timmons (2002).

proposes a partial ranking of principles, and takes into account different contexts of application.[18] Its categories include strict requirements for actions and attitudes, but also obligatory ends to be adopted with considerable latitude in how, when, and to what extent we pursue them. Kant divides duties, not always convincingly, into duties to oneself and duties to others, perfect and imperfect duties, negative and positive. A basic pervasive requirement is to accept the priority of duty over self-love when these conflict. The system of ethical principles is distinct from principles for coercive legal systems, but the ethical system includes both a requirement to obey legitimate laws of the state and also restrictions on what state authorities can legitimately command. The ethical principles are not all first-order requirements about how to act and what ends to adopt. They also include second-order obligations of due care, self-scrutiny, and character development in response to human liabilities to negligence, self-deception, and moral weakness. Virtue (and "the virtues"), the role of feelings, and moral education are discussed, though too briefly. In sum, the Doctrine of Virtue presents ethics, whether constructed, perceived, or merely endorsed, as a complex, structured network of interrelated norms responsive to persistent human problems, not just the result of individuals testing their day-to-day maxims, case by case, by a simple decision procedure.

(2) In *The Metaphysics of Morals* Kant presents his theory of law, rights, and justice (*Rechtlehre*) before his ethical principles for individuals (*Tugendlehre*). The relationship is controversial, but a few points should be mentioned. First, both parts belong to morality in a broad sense. The principles of law and justice include a fundamental human right to freedom, rights of property and contracts, principles of just punishment, and international relations. Second, these broadly moral concerns provide background limits on what ethical principles for individuals can demand as well as adding a strong presumption that the laws of a reasonably just legal order are to be obeyed. Third, a system of coercive laws is presupposed as a necessary condition for the full range of normal moral obligations. Laws are needed to interpret the general ideas of justice, define their applications, and institute ways to adjudicate conflicting claims. Laws are also needed to

---

[18] The distinction between "formal" and "substantive" (and "form" and "matter") is relative and dependent on context. To say that for Kant there are substantive values inherent in *humanity as an end in itself* does not mean that these are contingent, empirical, and variable.

curb violence and provide assurance that others will accept basic limits on their behavior. Fourth, some *specific* ethical obligations we have in normal times may be suspended or transformed under conditions of anarchy, war, and rule by lawless rogue regimes. How, when, and why normal obligations are changed are questions that belong to the broadly moral perspective governing both law and personal ethics.

(3) The philosopher's perspective in trying to construct or describe a reasonable system of ethical principles is not the same as the perspective of individuals trying to do what they should in everyday life. No one can avoid the everyday perspective, of course, and the philosopher's perspective should be accessible to anyone. The point is not about expertise but about what we are looking for. For everyday decision-making we look for ethical considerations relevant to the particular case at hand. From the philosopher's perspective we are looking for a whole system of ethical principles, whether constructed or not, in which the parts fit together coherently and express our most fundamental values. For everyday purposes we primarily need to internalize moral norms and apply them, but for moral philosophy we need to think through how our moral standards and our particular judgments might form a consistent and coherent whole.

(4) The main guiding standard in the Doctrine of Virtue is that humanity, or "the human being as such," is the basic end that everyone must adopt.[19] Rather than prescribing specific actions, *ethics* (in the narrow sense relevant here) basically prescribes *ends*.[20] The first principle has elements of both the universal law formula and the humanity formula of the *Groundwork*.

The supreme principle of the doctrine of virtue is: act in accordance with a maxim of *ends* that it can be a universal law for everyone to have.—In accordance with this principle a human being is an end for himself as well as for others, and it is not

---

[19] Kant says in his "deduction of the supreme principle" that this end is a duty because it is "the one and only basic end that *can be, and so is, willed by pure practical reason*" ((1996a), 157 [6: 395]). A background idea here is that willing by *pure* practical reason *alone*, one necessarily wills all and only fundamental principles for which there is sufficient reason a priori. From this special abstract perspective (a priori willing of all and only what reason requires), if one *can* rationally endorse a certain basic principle, then one does. It is a further question why humanity is the *only* end that can be willed from this perspective.

[20] Kant seems to use two different ideas or senses of an *end*. Perfection and happiness are ends of a kind that can be developed and promoted to various degrees, but, as in the *Groundwork*, humanity (or "the human being as such") as an end seems to be in part a status or value, ascribed by reason, to be respected and honored in various ways rather than itself an end literally to be promoted (like the happiness of others) or increased (like the degree of perfection of our natural and moral powers).

enough that he is not authorized to use either himself or others merely as means (since he could still be indifferent to them); it is in itself his duty to make man as such his end.   (Kant (1996*a*), 157 [6: 395])

On this basis, presumably, Kant proposes that the two main "ends that are duties" are the perfection of oneself and the happiness of others (ibid. 159–62 [6: 385–7]).

As in the *Groundwork*, the relation between willing universal law and treating humanity as an end is open to different interpretations. Kant does not give foundational arguments in the Doctrine of Virtue but simply begins with its first principle, and then proceeds to rely primarily on arguments that appeal to the idea of humanity as an *end* in a broad sense that evidently implies "something that ought to be appropriately treasured, respected, protected, and perfected." The meaning of "humanity" and "the human being as such" is indeterminate at first but is revealed in his arguments throughout the Doctrine of Virtue, especially in the duties to oneself and duties of respect for others. Details of scholarship aside, the important point for now is that as moral philosophers constructing or looking for a system of ethical principles we are not to be guided merely by the requirement that they must be universal, that is, for or "sharable by" everyone in the specified contexts. We must find or work out the system of principles that, taken together and given the human condition, best respects and furthers a basic end or value.[21]

(5) The normative ethical theory of the Doctrine of Virtue, then, appears to be structurally analogous to rule-utilitarianism but governed by a different set of values. We can think of a rule-utilitarian philosopher as trying to find a consistent and coherent set of rules the general adoption of which best serves the utilitarian aim of maximum happiness, satisfaction, or whatever.[22] Similarly, Kant lays out what he takes to be a consistent and coherent set of ethical principles such that, given human conditions, their universal adoption best respects the ideal of humanity as an end. Here what is to be willed as universal laws are not the personal maxims of individuals

---

[21] Contrary to O'Neill, I take "humanity as an end" to be a more substantive ("thicker") normative concept than is expressed by the universal law formula.

[22] This is the kind of theory defended in Hooker (2000), though Hooker is more broadly "consequentialist" than "utilitarian." See also Brandt (1979), 286–300.

but mid-level principles regarding lying, servility, self-abuse, due-care, self-scrutiny, conscience, self-improvement, respect for others, beneficence, gratitude, friendship, and (indirectly) being law-abiding and promoting our own happiness.[23] The idea of humanity as an end does not serve here as a simple norm to be applied case by case but a guiding idea behind a complex set of norms responsive to real-world problems of different kinds.

Although Kant does not explicitly invoke a "veil of ignorance," the general principles of his system are supposed to be rational for all human beings regardless of cultural and individual differences. Moreover, the search or construction is governed by an abstract end ("humanity") that determines what is relevant. These two factors require that the attitude of the moral theorist who tries to construct or lay out a system of moral principles must be impartial in ways analogous to the attitude of *ideal* state lawmakers who are subject to the laws they make, try to make only laws justifiable to all citizens, respect equality under the law, and make laws exclusively from a set of constitutionally prescribed values.

(6) Many of Kant's arguments in the Doctrine of Virtue make use of the idea of nature's purposes. This was no doubt a part of Kant's own thinking that would appeal to readers of his time, and *The Metaphysics of Morals* was supposed to be more accessible than the *Groundwork* and *Critiques*. He argued that the idea of nature as a teleological system had a regulative role for science and a practical role for ethics. Nevertheless, the claim that an end is "natural" cannot be a foundational moral claim. Kant's first principles are meant to be necessary principles of practical reason applied to the general human condition. Underlying his familiar teleological language is the conviction that practical reason endorses the aims and dispositions that are said to be natural ends. In Kant's teleological framework, the ultimate reason why we *ought* to seek a certain end is not that it is *nature's purpose* for us in an independent, morally neutral sense. To the contrary, I think, the deep rationale for thinking of an end as nature's purpose for us is in large part the prior underlying belief that that there are compelling reasons for us as human beings to pursue it.

---

[23] Most of Kant's arguments for these principles appeal in one way or another to the idea of humanity as an end, but beneficence (or mutual aid) is a notable exception ((1996a), 202 [6: 453]).

Constructivist Features of the Doctrine of Virtue

Kant does not explicitly describe the Doctrine of Virtue as a "constructivist" theory, and we should not exaggerate the affinities between contemporary and historical theories. Nevertheless, the Doctrine of Virtue has several features that invite a constructivist interpretation and point toward a possible Kantian constructivism in normative ethics.

First, the guiding standard for the Doctrine of Virtue can be interpreted as *a procedure of construction*. The first principle of the Doctrine of Virtue ((1996a), 157 [6: 395]) is in effect the Categorical Imperative as applicable to the task of laying out a system of ethical principles suitable for all human beings. Drawing from the *Groundwork* (2002), it combines ideas from the universal law formula and humanity formula, just as the kingdom of ends formula was supposed to do. How these ideas are combined and applied remains controversial, but at least on my interpretation and O'Neill's, these formulas prescribe conformity to procedures of construction that disallow or affirm more specific principles. That is, the basic action-guiding standard has the form, "Always conform to those principles, whatever they are, that result from the proper application of the procedure [e.g. a universalizability test or moral legislation from the perspective of rational autonomous members of a kingdom of ends]." The basic principles articulate the fundamental standard, but it is a further question how the principles and ideas presupposed by them can be defended.

Second, the basic procedures of construction presuppose and make use of a Kantian *conception of a person*. O'Neill thinks that applying the universal law formula should make use of only a relatively thin Kantian idea of persons, whereas on my reading the basic standard for guiding the selection of principles in the Doctrine of Virtue makes essential use of a relatively thick normative conception of "the human being as such" or "humanity" in us. My earlier reconstruction of the kingdom of ends formula also makes use of this thick conception. In all these interpretations human persons are conceived as rational, free, and equal in special senses. Kant's conception of persons, in my view, includes what Rawls called "the two moral powers," and more.

Third, in the Doctrine of Virtue, as in Rawls's constructivisms, the guiding standard or procedure of construction relies on a basic Kantian *conception of society* or, in other words, all persons united by their common laws, principles, and moral ends. This conception is implicit in what Kant took the task of developing a metaphysics of morals to be, that is, to identify or construct, from a common moral perspective, action-guiding ethical principles applicable to all human persons. Similarly, the kingdom of ends formula concerns principles for "a systematic union of rational beings through shared objective laws" (Kant (2002), 234 [4: 433]).

Fourth, although the Doctrine of Virtue does not explicitly refer to what Rawls calls "agents of construction," it implicitly provides different but compatible answers to the question "who constructs the principles?" The appropriate response depends on the level at which the question is asked. At the deepest theoretical (beyond normative ethics) level, the question is "who or what *makes* the moral principles valid?" In other words, by virtue of what are the principles necessarily rational and so categorically imperative for us? Kant implies that the validity of specific principles is determined by "pure practical reason," which then must be, metaphorically, "the ultimate builder" if there is one. The point is just that the principles are supposed to be what fully rational noninstrumental thinking by anyone would prescribe.

At another level, the initial question may be asking who has the job and prerogative to use the procedure of construction to develop and present publicly a system of valid ethical principles. Regarding the most general principles, Kant's implicit answer is that it is the job of moral philosophers to try to develop and articulate the system for others but this is not the special prerogative of any particular individual. Even if Kant was confident that he himself had successfully completed the task with his Doctrine of Virtue, he held that the theories of philosophers are always subject to challenge in public discussion. Anyone can in principle take up the role of a moral philosopher. In developing or criticizing a proposed system of principles, Kant assumed, a moral philosopher should be trying to work out a system of general principles through appropriate rational thinking, but he is not by his efforts inventing the principles or conferring validity on them. The most general principles, however, can apply to various circumstances in different ways. Working out specific ways to implement them requires practical knowledge, judgment, and creativity, which anyone may have and philosophers often lack.

These features of Kant's Doctrine of Virtue fit and supplement my idea of a Kantian perspective on moral rules, discussed in other essays. The proposal is that features drawn from both Kant and Rawls can form a constructivist theory for normative ethics. From Rawls we get models for constructivist thinking, from Kant central human values, and from both appreciation of thinking systematically. Rawls shows how constructivist procedures can be designed for limited ethical or political questions, Kant inspires us to extend our thinking to a fuller range of ethical questions, and both in their later years encouraged moral thinking beyond our borders.

My purpose here has not been to defend Kantian constructivism, but to encourage further thinking about this approach to normative ethical theory. I conclude with comments on objections that are raised by O'Neill.

Responses to Some Objections

Both Rawls's broadly Kantian constructivisms and my proposal for normative ethics, quite apart from (specified or missing) details, may seem to invite certain objections.[24] These objections, as posed by O'Neill, fall under three headings: (A) Rawlsian constructivisms are not Kant's and so they are only misleadingly called "Kantian." (B) Rawls's constructivist procedures argue from what ideal agents *would* endorse, but the only defensible constructivist procedure, Kant's formula of universal law, is concerned only with what real agents *can* endorse ("share," "communicate," and find "intelligible"). (C) Rawls's constructivist procedures, and therefore their results, presuppose ideals that are arbitrary. To respond briefly:

(A) *Not really Kant's.* The objection that a "Kantian constructivist" theory is not really Kant's does not cut very deep unless the theory was offered as such. An author can change the title, if necessary, or just note the differences and move on. Rawls says explicitly that his Kantian constructivism is not Kant's,[25] and although I mean to draw more closely from Kant's texts than Rawls does, my constructivist proposals are admittedly to some extent reconstructions and extensions of his ideas. Although not a substitute for close textual scholarship, calling attention to affinities between our

---

[24] My comments here draw from a fuller discussion of O'Neill and Rawls in Hill (2011).

[25] This comment concerns Rawls's ideas in "Kantian Constructivism" (Rawls, 1999b) and *Political Liberalism* (Rawls, 1996). In his *Lectures on the History of Moral Philosophy* (Rawls, 2000) and "Themes in Kant's Moral Philosophy" (Rawls 1999d) he tries to give an interpretation closer to Kant's texts and dominant ideas.

proposals and historical exemplars can be helpful. Looking at a text through new lenses can reveal significant patterns even if they distort some details. This seems especially true when the texts, like Kant's, are complex and richly packed with many different strands of thought. This, in any case, is how I regard my earlier proposal that we look at Kant's idea of legislation in a "kingdom of ends" as a constructivist procedure that avoids many familiar problems of application that plague the formula of universal law. In the same spirit, I have suggested here that Kant's Doctrine of Virtue provides further elements for contemporary constructivist theorizing.

(B) *"Could," not "would."* Both Rawls's Kantian constructivism and my hybrid version require us to think about what we, or our more ideal representatives, *would* endorse (choose, or legislate) under specified hypothetical conditions. O'Neill rightly points out that Kant's universal law formula asks us instead to think about what we *can* will as universal law. Her objection here is partly that Rawls is not faithful to Kant's texts, but she also objects to Rawls's use of idealizing and simplifying assumptions in his theory.[26] This is not the place to assess these specific complaints to Rawls's theory, though I think they are sometimes misguided. My worry is about a general rejection of moral arguments from hypothetical agreement. Here are just two brief comments for now.

First, the value of such arguments depends on the details—*who* would agree to *what* under *what* conditions, and *why*, and *what* is supposed to follow? No doubt theories can draw useless, even dangerous, conclusions from what idealized persons would agree to under unreal hypothetical situations. As they say, "garbage in, garbage out." O'Neill might say of Rawls instead, "fiction in, fiction out," but the strategy of arguing from hypothetical agreement can be useful and does not have to be misleading. What a normative constructivist should aim for, I think, is something more like "ideals (of moral deliberation) in, ideal (norms) out." Metaphors aside, the aim is to bring together, into a hypothetical choice situation, ideals of moral deliberation, relevant facts and options, breadth of vision, and focus on fundamental values, so that we can treat as justifiable (for various specified contexts) the norms that would be endorsed from this point of view. The process is a way of orienting moral thought, not a decision procedure for

[26] See O'Neill (2003*a*), 353, 359.

cranking out a fixed list of rules. And as Kant says of his "kingdom of ends" formula, apart from its value for guiding judgment, it can help to bring the idea of morality "closer to feeling and intuition" ((2002), 237 [6: 436–7]).

My second comment about O'Neill's complaint is this. Her alternative constructivist procedure just asks, "*Can* everyone consent to share my maxim?" Other familiar problems aside, it is hard to see how this avoids the need for appeal to hypothetical agreement. What actual people can or cannot consent to share is often a matter of ignorance, inconsistency, short-sightedness, and oppressive circumstances. So what matters at the deepest theoretical level is what they, hypothetically, *could* consent to share *if* they were adequately informed, consistent, uncoerced, and aware of the consequences of everyone having the same policies as they do. Besides, it matters *why* they could or could not consent to share maxims when adequately consistent and informed. From a moral point of view there are good reasons why no one *could rationally* accept certain maxims as shared and why anyone would be irrational not to share others. Kant apparently thought that the ideal of humanity as an end provides such reasons for anyone. If so, there is more to morality than being informed and consistently universalizing one's maxims. Individuals *cannot* will certain maxims as universal law because adopting them conflicts with general principles that they and others would endorse if free, informed, consistent, and fully respectful of humanity as an end.

(C) *Arbitrary starting points?* O'Neill objects that Rawls's constructivist procedures, and therefore their results, rely on arbitrary starting assumptions. There is obviously nothing formally objectionable about conditional arguments if the conclusions are appropriately qualified. If constructivists acknowledge the dependence of their conclusions on the values that they initially stipulate, then the problem, if any, must lie elsewhere. For example, conditional arguments can be useless when they merely draw out the implications of starting assumptions that are plainly false, incredible, or of no practical interest. Starting assumptions are "arbitrary" when there is no reason, practical or theoretical, to make them. Drawing out the practical implications of widely accepted value assumptions, however, can be illuminating and practically important, and so not arbitrary in *that* sense. Few, including O'Neill, would charge that Rawls most basic starting points— such as the general ideals of freedom, equality, and public justifiability—are plainly false, incredible, or of no practical significance. Apparently, then, O'Neill's objection is either to specific features of Rawls's constructivism or else reflects a broad metaethical concern that even its fundamental ideas are "arbitrary" because "not vindicated by reason."

Specific features of any constructivist proposal, of course, can be contested and need to be reviewed as objections arise. O'Neill's broader concern about arbitrariness, however, rests on her belief that the basic principle of reason is Kant's universal law formula. In her view, as I understand it, only this negative principle and the general prohibitions derived from it can be vindicated by reason, and even vindicating the rational use of this fundamental principle is an unending recursive task. In effect, then, any starting points in moral argument would be "arbitrary" in her strong sense if they are not ultimately "vindicated" by this principle. Despite its Kantian credentials, whether this principle, its claim to be the ultimate rational standard, and its application are defensible remains at least as controversial as many of the constructivist starting points that it might rule out.

In any case, I share Rawls's view that we should not assume that our current starting points are fixed and uncontestable, but our thinking about theoretical and practical matters must start somewhere. We should take our assumptions as provisional and subject to revision under further critique, and, as O'Neill and Rawls agree, whether they can be justified must emerge over time in "public" accessible discourse. To make progress we need to make proposals, drawing provisionally from ideas that open discussions give us some good reason to rely on more than others. One may hope that these can ultimately be vindicated in O'Neill's strong sense, but even if skeptical of success in that project we must stand somewhere and need to work out the implications of our stance. The metaphor appropriate for moral and political theories is not a ship permanently "anchored" or fixed in place by its working assumptions,[27] but rather a ship we choose to anchor for now with provisional assumptions in order to review the theoretical ship's problems and potential, and propose repairs and improvements, so that it may better serve its purpose and everyone affected. Investigation may convince us that the ship needs to be scrapped and replaced, maybe even that we can live better without ships, or without visions of ultimate anchoring.

---

[27] See O'Neill (2003a), 359.

II
Virtue

4

Finding Value in Nature

This chapter explores the idea that a proper valuing of natural environments is essential to (and not just a natural basis for) a broader human virtue that might be called "appreciation of the good." This kind of valuing may enable us to explain, without any commitment to a metaphysics of intrinsic values, how and why it is good to value certain natural phenomena for their own sakes. The chapter concludes by responding to the objection that such an approach is excessively human-centered.

Background and Aim

In an earlier paper, "Ideals of Human Excellence and Preserving Natural Environments," I argued against the assumption that the only factors morally relevant to environmental problems are human rights and welfare.[1] This assumption seems less common now, but there is no general agreement on what the best alternative is. My concern was not only with environmental ethics. Some of the same narrowness of vision, I thought, affected philosophical ethics in general. In short, ethics is *not all about* human rights and welfare. A key question that opens the way to broader reflection is, "What sort of person would do that?" This calls for thinking about attitudes, understanding, and sensibility more often discussed under the ethics of virtue than in theories of rights and costs and benefits. Apart from concerns about the natural environment, our attitudes and the acts that express these attitudes are often objectionable even though they violate no one's rights

---

[1] Hill (1983). This has been reprinted in several anthologies, including Hill (1991). The follow-up essay reprinted here was initially presented at a workshop on environmental ethics at Princeton University's Center for Human Values, in May 2005. I thank Dale Jamison, the organizer, and other participants for their comments.

and harm no one—or at least they are not objectionable solely because they violate rights or cause harm. Arguably what is objectionable in some cases is not that rights are violated or welfare is diminished. The ungrateful heir who spits on his grandmother's grave after the genuine mourners have left expresses an attitude that seems bad independently of rights, benefits, and harms. Similarly, I argued, those who despoil the natural environment often express objectionable attitudes rooted in ignorance, self-importance, and patterns of aesthetic insensitivity that, if not themselves vices, give evidence of deficiency in the natural bases of human excellences, such as proper humility, gratitude, and aesthetic appreciation.

My argument appealed to common understandings of human virtues and vices that are often ignored in the rights and welfare literature, but it would not satisfy those who want an ethics and value theory that can support good environmental policies without relying on assumptions about human relations and attitudes. Insofar as it appealed to ideals of human excellence and attitudes, my main argument made no appeal to the intrinsic value of nature, or nonhuman animals, or ecosystems, at least as "intrinsic value" is often construed.[2] Although skeptical of uncritical talk of "intrinsic values," I also believe strongly that the wrongness of most objectionable acts and attitudes is overdetermined. It is usually a mistake to say that *the* reason that something is morally objectionable is such and such (just one thing). So whether there are other, less human-centered, reasons against the environmental practices I discussed is another issue left open by my argument. My main point was that arguments from the intrinsic value of nature are *not necessary* to show the inadequacy of theories that appeal solely to human rights and welfare. Whether such arguments are tenable and provide additional support for the same conclusion is a further question. Many familiar objections to an ethics exclusively focused on human rights and welfare appeal to the idea of animal rights or the intrinsic badness of pain in any sentient beings. Other arguments turn on the value of species or ecosystems. My earlier essay set these aside, not because they are unimportant but because I thought that, for my limited purposes, they were unnecessary. Even broadening the discussion to include "animal rights" arguably fails to capture the full

---

[2] The term "intrinsic value" has been interpreted in different ways. As should become clear, my skepticism about its use applies primarily to interpretations, such as G. E. Moore's, that treat intrinsic value as a simple, nonnatural metaphysical property. This is a special philosophical usage, not inherent in the common understanding of "good in itself" or "valuable for its own sake."

range of values that are important to environmentalists and lovers of nature. My concern was to explore possible connections between attitudes toward the natural environment and familiar human virtues, such as humility, gratitude, and aesthetic sensibility. The question raised, about strip-mining, logging old redwood groves, and replacing gardens with asphalt, was not "Whose rights and interests were violated?" but "What sort of person would do that?" My suggestion in the end was that those who regard *only* human rights and welfare as reasons not to destroy the natural environment seem to lack the natural basis of the virtues of proper humility, gratitude, and aesthetic appreciation.[3] My conclusion was limited, but implied that, barring special explanation, we can expect that virtuous persons will value nature for its own sake[4]—at least they will not regard the natural environment merely as a means to human welfare or as something whose treatment is constrained only by human rights, for example property rights. My aim in that essay, frankly, was to capture some important environmental values without resorting to certain familiar ideas that I find unpromising, such as Native American animism, religious mysticism, and metaphysical realism about values inherent in nature.

So much for background. Now I want to explore the idea that a proper valuing of natural environments is essential to (and not just a natural basis for) a broader human virtue that we might call "appreciation of the good." Those who are already committed to the value of nature, or various aspects of it, as a metaphysical fact should have no objection to this idea, but they are likely to insist that the value of nature is prior to and totally independent of human capacities for appreciation. In my view the relation is not so simple and unidirectional. Values are not natural (or "nonnatural") properties that we happen to "see" as preexisting in a nonhuman world, but they

---

[3] By "natural basis" for a virtue I mean a pervasive human disposition, not primarily the product of particular social and cultural influences, that is not itself a morally excellent or praiseworthy trait but is a background tendency necessary to (or usually important for) the development of a morally excellent or praiseworthy trait. For example, in Hill (1983) I conjectured that a natural basis for proper humility is a tendency to care about animals and things independently of their utility (p. 220) and a natural basis for gratitude is a disposition to cherish for their own sakes things that give us joy (p. 224). Whether these conjectures are correct is, of course, an empirical question.

[4] It is important to note here, and later, that "valuing something for its own sake" is not the same as "believing that something is intrinsically valuable." This is especially evident if the latter is interpreted as the belief that the thing in question has a metaphysical property ("intrinsic value") that exists independently of relations to anything else. "Valuing for its own sake" is an attitude about the thing in question, not a belief about its intrinsic properties or even its relation to other actual or potential valuers.

are also not simply things we create or mere reflections of our subjective tastes. To understand all this is a major philosophical challenge, but, if successful, we would have gone beyond the aim and conclusion of my previous essay. That is, we would understand, without metaphysical obscurity or undue anthropocentrism, how and why it is good *to value* certain natural phenomena *for their own sakes* and to recognize and respond appropriately to *the value they have*, in a sense, independently of human rights and welfare.

The Common Experience of Finding Value in Nature and its Interpretation

Poets and novelists often express what many of us find difficult to put into words when we appreciate the beauty, variety, order, complexity, and awesomeness of aspects of the natural world. But when thinking about the redwood groves, the Carlsbad caverns, and the interplay of living things in an unspoiled forest, most of us could say not only that we *want* to see them, but that we *value* them, value them *for their own sakes*, not just for their utility or as sources of aesthetic delight. Moreover, if challenged, we might add that we do not think this is just a matter of taste or fashion: they *are* *valuable*, and *would be* even if everyone were to become so crassly materialistic and self-absorbed that they cared about them only for the profit, comfort, and passing pleasures that they get from them. If human beings were to disappear from the earth tomorrow, many of us would still count it as a bad thing, a further misfortune or calamity, that the earth be reduced to a lifeless, smoldering rock. This is no doubt due largely (and for some entirely) to a concern for nonhuman animals, but it is not obvious that even sentient animal life is all that we care about apart from its utility.

Some philosophers want to explain this attitude as a commitment to a metaphysics of independently existing intrinsic values that I find obscure and unhelpful. As before, however, I want to explore alternatives. Following my previous strategy, I want to consider a certain human excellence, or virtue, that seems to have implications regarding our treatment of the environment. But this time the virtue in question itself requires us to consider the idea of intrinsic value, the very topic that earlier I tried to avoid. The virtue that I have in mind now, broadly speaking, is a *manifest readiness to appreciate the good* in all sorts of things, and not just as an instrument or resource for something else. Although this does not appear on every philosopher's list of moral virtues, arguably it is widely (and rightly) recognized as a human virtue or excellence, an admirable trait of character. The basic idea is simple enough. There seems something important missing in those who persistently ignore, cynically dismiss, or remain coldly indifferent to the vast range of things that are sources of joy, inspiration, and value for others, and potentially for themselves. Obviously such people are more liable than most to behave in ways that mistreat, hurt, and dampen the spirits of others, but, even apart from that, arguably their systematic lack of appreciation is a defect of character, at least a falling short of an ideal. We may hesitate to label this strictly a *moral* vice, comparable to cruelty, dishonesty, and injustice, but we commonly treat the opposite trait as an aspect of an ideal person—that is, their openness to find and respond to value in a wide diversity of people, things, and experiences.

Most readers would probably concede the general idea that it is an admirable trait *to appreciate what is good*, but they would understandably require some qualifications in a fuller account of the virtue. We should appreciate what is good, *at least in appropriate contexts*. For example, we expect that a virtuous person, in most familiar circumstances, will value love and respect among friends, acts of courage and kindness, innocent pleasures of children at play, and so on. Perhaps we should appreciate *these* things in all contexts, but we do not suppose that in all circumstances a good person will value and take pleasure in everything that is *generally* good. This is partly because such things are often only provisionally good and become worthless or bad in special circumstances. Empathy and pleasure, for example, seem generally good, but not in someone engaged in sadistic torture. Even if these or other good things retain *some* value in all contexts, a virtuous person would not necessarily value and take pleasure in them in every case. There are good things of many kinds, some important and some trivial, and how ideally we would respond to them varies with many factors. For example, it is doubtful that a more virtuous Khrushchev would have tempered his public condemnation of Stalin by noting appreciatively that he often played nicely with his daughter. Also, we need not regard someone as a worse person because she channeled all her energies into one grand artistic or political project, remaining indifferent in the process to values that could be found in current TV comedies, stamp collecting, and poker tournaments. These complications, however, are not our present concern.

What is more controversial is whether the virtue of appreciating the good has any special application to our attitudes about the natural environment. It will be readily admitted, of course, that human life and pleasure are generally good things and so it matters that pretty scenes cause innocent pleasure and air pollution kills people. The deeper controversy is about whether values in nature are independent of such effects on human welfare and rights. Are there such values, and, if so, how are we to understand them? This is an important question in itself, but it is also crucial to exploration of connections between human virtues and our treatment of the environment. Specifically, does the general virtue of appreciating the good in appropriate contexts imply that we should value aspects of the nonhuman natural world independently of their utility and effects on our welfare? The answer seems to depend on whether we should think that those aspects of nature *are* good and valuable for their own sakes.[5] If so, a virtuous person should appreciate them; if not, appreciation would be optional, a matter of choice and not an issue of human excellence or virtue. For me the issue turns on whether we can plausibly affirm that aspects of nature are valuable in themselves, in an appropriate sense, without buying into a metaphysics that construes "intrinsic values" as independently existing natural (or "nonnatural") properties of things.

I turn in the next section to the large issue of how we might understand *appreciating the value of aspects of nature for their own sakes* without making dubious metaphysical commitments. This is a large topic, but it is necessary to address it here, even if briefly, in order to round out my suggestion that the virtue of *appreciating the good in appropriate contexts* has significant implications for our treatment of the natural environment.

---

[5] This is a point at which approaching environmental issues from a perspective on human virtues seems to require, rather than provide a way of avoiding, discussion of intrinsic value. My suggestion, however, is that practical judgments that aspects of nature are "intrinsically valuable," when understood in the ordinary sense relevant to real environmental debates, do not presuppose the metaphysical realist conceptions of intrinsic value that I have been trying to avoid. For present purposes I am not distinguishing "being intrinsically valuable," "having intrinsic value," and "being *valuable* for its own sake," though all of these, I assume, go beyond "being *valued* for its own sake."

Desiring, Valuing, and Appreciating Value: Is Metaphysics of Intrinsic Value Necessary?

Desiring vs. Valuing

As many philosophers have noted, desiring and wanting something is not the same as valuing it. Most obviously, people can desire something (for example, taking certain dangerous drugs) but not value it because they regard it as harmful, destructive, or otherwise troublesome. But such consequences aside, people may also desire something that they do not value because they regard it as in itself base and unworthy of our attention: for example, staring at a pile of corpses (Plato's example) or viewing violent and demeaning pornographic films. We often *want* what we value, though not everything we value is an object that we desire to acquire, possess, or control. (Consider past events, the welfare of future human and nonhuman animals, sunsets, mountains, etc.) Valuing, it seems, is typically a relatively stable attitude, capable of with-standing (some) critical reflection, reaffirmed over time despite significant alterations in mood, impulse, and momentary inclination. Some desires give those who have them little or no reason, even from the agent's perspective, to follow them—they disapprove of these desires or reasonably regard them as something alien to be resisted, altered, or suppressed. We typically filter out such unwanted *desires* as we form our *values*. So it seems that, with fewer exceptions, a person who values something has a reason, at least from his or her perspective, to do, say, and think various appropriate things with regard to it.

Valuing Instrumentally and Valuing for Its Own Sake

Some things we value only for other goods they may bring, not for themselves. We may value these persistently, insistently, and for very good reasons, while still valuing them only for their effects: for example, food, unpolluted water, and shelter for oneself and one's family. Other things we value and not just for their effects or accompaniments, and not unreasonably so. Contrary to some traditional assumptions, what we value for no further reason is not always an "end" to be pursued, nor need it be an object possessing a metaphysical property of "intrinsic value," natural or nonnatural. Despite Aristotle, arguably it need not be the natural *telos* for human beings or some constitutive aspect of this. Particular human beings are wonderfully diverse and complex, and the values they *all* happen to share, if any, have no preemptive weight per se, apart from context, over the things *individuals* care about for their own sake. It is unlikely that all human beings value aspects of the natural environment for their own sake, but surely the case for an appropriate environmentalist attitude does not assume otherwise.

Valuing and Being Valuable

Presumably we want to say not merely that many people do in fact value natural phenomena in themselves, but also that these phenomena *are valuable* in themselves. What more is implied in this last claim? This is a large and difficult question, but a few things seem clear enough. When we say that something is valuable, and not merely valued by some, we imply that its being valued is not (or need not be) simply the result of mistakes of various kinds—for example, failure to understand it, confusion, bad reasoning, judgment skewed by irrelevant biases, and so on.[6] Moreover, we seem to imply that what is valuable has in itself features that make it worthy of being valued even when it is not. We readily acknowledge this with respect to unappreciated items of potential utility or delight to human beings—for example, a scientific discovery before its time, an unfashionable poem or painting, or a secret act of kindness. But the point could be extended. We may think that the aspects of nature that we value in themselves have features worthy of being valued in this noninstrumental way even if ignorance, greed, and closed-mindedness prevent all remaining generations of human beings from appreciating them. That is, we do not merely value them noninstrumentally, but also regard them *as valuable in themselves*, at least if this is understood in an ordinary sense. In my view, this is not a judgment that presupposes an untenable metaphysical value realism, but it does at least imply that, if these aspects of nature were to continue to be valued noninstrumentally, the attitude need not rest on mistakes (factual misunderstanding, bias, faulty inferences, etc.).

---

[6] The possibility of such mistakes about what *is valuable* is important in order to distinguish the concept from the weaker ideas that the thing *seems valuable* and *is valued*. It must make sense to say, "It seems valuable, it is valued (e.g. by many others), and I did value it, but really it is not valuable." The distinction, however, need not be explained as the difference between false and true attributions of a metaphysical property of the thing in question independent of its relations to those who do or might observe, experience, or otherwise respond to the thing. The difference has to do both with other possible errors and misjudgments as well as endorsement of something as *worthy* of being valued, a normative judgment that needs more discussion but does not necessarily invoke the kind of metaphysics of which I am skeptical.

Moreover, as just noted, when we say that something is *valuable* in itself, not merely *valued* for its own sake, we imply that it is *worthy* of being valued for its own sake. We can perhaps imagine someone saying, "*I value X* for its own sake even though I admit X is not really worthy of this attitude," but could we understand someone who said, "X *is* intrinsically *valuable* but not worthy of being valued for its own sake"? Although we can only touch on the issue here, there are various ways that the further claim of worthiness could be interpreted without resorting to a metaphysics of intrinsic value as an independently existing property. For example, it seems, at least in part, to express the speaker's endorsement of valuing the object for its own sake, perhaps with an expectation that other reasonable, aware, and informed persons would tend to share this attitude if appropriately situated. Any analysis of the meaning of these expressions is likely to remain controversial, but consideration of how we actually make and revise our judgments can be helpful. When we confirm that something has market value, it is sufficient to observe that very many people value it enough to exchange other things for it. If we learned that many, even most people, familiar with something valued it for its own sake, however, this would not by itself prove to us that the thing is intrinsically valuable. Their attitude, and not merely their beliefs about the object, might have been shaped by political indoctrination, cultural pressures, irrelevant associations, and desires unrelated to the valued object. Discovery that the attitude was entirely due to such factors would undermine their claim that the object was intrinsically valuable. If, apart from such factors, the object itself has no stable disposition to lead anyone to value it for its own sake, then those who do value it for its own sake, we might say, do so not because it is worthy of such evaluation but for other reasons.

Is this Account Still too Human-Centered?

A persistent objection to accounts of the value of nature of the sort sketched here is that they still make the value too dependent on human nature. This is a kind of objection sometimes raised against any value theory that treats value judgments as involving a relation between facts, events, and objects in the world and those who actually or potentially observe, experience, or respond to them evaluatively. Such objections often rest on misunderstand-ings of the theories in question or groundless optimism about the possibility of developing a defensible metaphysically realist alternative. Here I can offer only a few brief comments on the issue—with apologies to both sides of a long-standing dispute.

First, it is mistaken, or at least misleading, to suppose that the only alternative to metaphysical value realism is that human beings "create" or "invent" the value of natural phenomena as opposed to their being valuable "because of what they are." In my view, we do "find value" in nature, *in a sense*, when we learn and experience "what it really is." We do not arbitrarily choose what to value but form our value judgments, over time, as we come to experience and better understand natural phenomena. Sometimes, to our surprise, we "discover" valuable aspects, and not just useful ones, that previously we had ignored or considered worthless. We often "correct" our superficial impressions and initial value judgments as we enlarge and correct our understanding of the natural phenomena. When asked for the reasons why such things, themselves, are valuable, we cite identifiable features of the things that have value. These facts about what we are judging, rather than facts about our human nature and individual tastes, are "what makes the things valuable" in the ordinary sense, even though in a meta-level philosophical discussion we might "explain" values by reference to a relation between features of what is judged and dispositional features of actual or potential judges. This meta-level philosophical discussion is not what is at issue in practical contexts when someone asks whether something in nature is valuable in itself. The question is usually whether all that matters about it is its effect on human rights and welfare. In the ordinary sense at work here, the *reasons* why some natural phenomena are valuable, even apart from such effects, are properties that they really have, but this is not to say that their value is a property, like physical mass and extension are often thought to be, that can be understood without any reference to the potential receptivity, experi-ence, and response of non-inert beings.

Second, the ordinary expressions "good in itself" and "valuable for its own sake," which (I believe) are quite appropriately applied to nonhuman natural phenomena, are often blown up (or stripped down) by philosophers into metaphysical categories that few ordinary users of these terms would even recognize if explained to them.[7] For example, expressions such as "good in itself" ("important in itself," etc.) typically make a contrast with another kind of evaluation (not always "good as a means") that becomes clear in context. At least we need to pause to consider whether the technical uses have anything to do with real environmental debates.

Third, the debate about what is valuable for its own sake should not be burdened with the familiar, but far from obvious, assumption that the right thing to do is always to produce the greatest possible amount of such (intrinsic) value. When we say that something is valuable, we almost always mean to convey some idea about the *reasons* someone has for doing, thinking, or feeling something, but what is implied varies with the expressions and context. The judgment that aspects of nature are valuable in themselves is not irrelevant to what we should do, but it is unnecessary and unhelpful to try to treat it as assigning points on a scale of commensurable values that always determine what we should do. The controversy on this point is old and familiar, of course, but it is worth keeping in mind when discussing intrinsic values in the context of environmental issues.

Finally, because "anthropocentrism" has become a term of abuse among some environmentalists, it may be helpful to raise again the question what this means and why it is a bad thing. "Anthropocentrism" can refer to significantly different ideas, and more and less radical ideas may be unfairly swept away with the same rhetorical brush.[8] The following, for example, are prima facie significantly distinct claims: (1) Everything in nature except human beings exists solely for the material benefit of human beings. (2) Everything in nature except human beings exists solely for the benefit of human beings; but this includes aesthetic and spiritual benefits as well as material benefits. (3) All valid concerns about the natural environment derive ultimately from human rights and duties to respect human interests. (4) It is good for us to value nonhuman animals, natural wildernesses, and ecosystems noninstrumentally; that is, it is a virtue of *human* beings, although not of other creatures, to do this. (5) All moral obligations and duties, virtues and vices, blameworthiness and praiseworthiness are, strictly and literally,

---

[7] Long ago, in the days of "ordinary language philosophy" at Oxford, I studied in some detail the common (nonphilosophical) use of these expressions, and this investigation (Hill (1961)) convinced me that G. E. Moore and other philosophers had changed the subject substantially when they wrote about "intrinsic value" in their technical sense.

[8] The following with minor revisions is from Hill (2001a).

attributed only to human beings (or other "rational" beings). (6) The ultimate justification for thinking that we should value nature noninstrumentally (and count it as "morally considerable") must appeal not only to the facts about the natural world and our place in it but also to the nature of moral justification—which is, in the end, a process dependent on human reason, sensibility, experience, dialogue, and reflection. (7) This process of moral justification, properly understood, is not a matter of either perceiving values that exist as facts in nature or of intuiting nonnatural "intrinsic values," and so, though we should *value* nonhuman nature and even *regard it as valuable* noninstrumentally, the ultimate justification cannot be "It simply exists with the nonrelational property of intrinsic value" which we "see" or "intuit."

If being anthropocentric is to be objectionable, we should be careful to indicate which claims it encompasses. My own view is that the first three claims are the primary ones that environmentalists should protest. The fourth is environmentally friendly, for it endorses valuing nature noninstrumentally without denying other environmentalist themes. Controversies about the fifth—that only human beings, strictly, have moral virtues—will, I suspect, largely turn on whether we use "moral" in a sense that is narrow or broad, perhaps literal or metaphorical. The last two points, concerning ultimate justification, are subject to philosophical disagreement, but I see no practical or theoretical advantage for environmentalists to treat these claims as the enemy. To do so would require them to draw up battle lines against the major developments in moral theory this century, and much before, and quite *unnecessarily* as far as I can see. I suspect that confusing these claims, i.e. (6) and (7), with some of the others has been largely responsible for the idea that serious environmentalists must deny them.

5

Kant on Weakness of Will

The topic of Kant and weakness of will is a large and complex one, made more difficult by the fact that Kant never gave us an explicit and thorough discussion of weakness of will.[1] Thus we must try to reconstruct his position from his many writings on ethics, taking into account that his views, or ways of expressing them, evolved to some extent over time even in his critical period. It may also be helpful to see his view in contrast with those of certain prominent predecessors against whom he reacted. In any case the plan for my discussion is this: (1) First, without regard to Kant, I review a common conception of weakness of will and some of the philosophical puzzles that it raises. (2) Next, I sketch briefly some views about weakness of will that Kant rejected, notably the views of Hobbes and Hume. (3) Then I discuss Kant's conception of the will in general, calling attention to distinctions that are important for understanding his view. This requires considering the relations between inclinations, reason, and will, and how these three are supposed to work in paradigm cases of morally good acts, morally indifferent acts, and immoral acts. (4) I turn to Kant's conception of virtue as a good will combined with developed strength of will to do what is right. (5) I take up the difficult issue of how to interpret strength and weakness of will. Kant held that our acts are not the causal product of natural forces but are based on freely chosen maxims; this view rules out familiar images of strength and weakness of will modeled on physical strength and weakness. So an alternative interpretation is needed. (6) Next I comment briefly on a puzzle raised by many commentators over the years: If the moral law is the fundamental principle of a will with negative freedom (i.e. absence of causal determination)

[1] Earlier versions of this chapter were presented at the Catholic University of America, the University of California at Riverside, and UCLA, and I am grateful to the participants at those sessions for their helpful questions and comments. I also thank Tobias Hoffmann for valuable suggestions and historical references.

and autonomy, how can anyone freely choose to gratify natural desires in an immoral way? Given the apparent identity between a free will and a moral will in the *Groundwork*, it may seem mysterious how anyone could *freely* will to do wrong through weakness, malice, or any other motive. So how can we be to blame when natural desires and impulses move us? (7) Finally, given Kant's assumption that we always have the capacity to do our moral duty despite our strongest inclinations, how can there be degrees of culpability and mitigation of responsibility for crimes of passion? For example, why are we less culpable, other things being equal, for weakly yielding to jealous rage than for carrying out a cold-blooded plan for revenge?

This is a large agenda, and I realize that I cannot do justice to all the questions that I raise; but at least, I trust, we will have something to discuss.

1. A Commonsense View and Some Problems

Weakness of will is a very familiar phenomenon and yet also very puzzling. All too often we seem to know what we ought to do, care about doing what we ought, and yet do not do it. When criticized, we deny that we acted maliciously, and yet we cannot pretend that we acted in ignorance. We knew what was right and we wanted to do it, we say, but we were weak. We might mention the pressures we were under, the strong feelings prompting us, and our understandable interest in acting as we did. But we realize that these are only a partial excuse because we still could have done the right thing if we had cared enough and tried our best. Recognizing that we have a long record of acting in this and similar ways, we will admit, if we are honest, that we are weak-willed persons. We may admit this without showing any shame just to demonstrate our modesty and to provide ourselves with a generic excuse for future failures, but in our hearts we realize that our weakness of will is both a moral defect and generally a detriment to our own interests. This at least seems a quite common and intuitively sound view.

Nevertheless, the view is puzzling in several respects. For example, often when people fail to do something they can and should do, especially when this is a pattern, we begin to doubt their sincerity when they say, "I *know* and *fully understand* that I should have done it." We may wonder: If they had *really* known and fully understood that they ought to, wouldn't they have done it? Further, considering the analogy with physical strength, we may ask, "Why are they to blame at all if the failure was due to their lack of strength?" As with physical weakness, we may sometimes blame someone for not previously developing the strength his or her responsibilities demand, but that seems a separate issue. If they lacked the strength to do what they ought at a given time, then it seems they should not be blamed for failing to do it then but at most for past neglect of proper self-development. Again, from a different perspective, we might wonder whether pleading weakness of will should excuse or mitigate guilt at all. To do wrong because one's *will* is weak seems very different from doing it because of a physical disability. It is our own fault, it seems, if in the face of temptations we only will weakly to do what is right. We should will firmly, strongly, with all our might to overcome our impulses to do what we know is wrong. One might even think that to fail to do so is to be guilty twice: guilty of an immoral act and guilty for willing so weakly to avoid it. In addition, we may wonder about the relation between weak-willed acts and a weak-willed character. Is a weak-willed act the primary notion and a weak-willed character just a disposition to do weak-willed acts? Or is it perhaps the other way around, that is, that weak-willed acts are simply those characteristic of the primary notion of weakness of will as a character trait? Also, is weakness of will a general phenomenon or is it always a matter of acting contrary to one's *moral* beliefs? Don't we sometimes do what is merely imprudent or detrimental to our personal projects through weakness of will? Finally, what is a "will" anyway? We commonly explain actions in terms of desires and reasons for acting. Do we need the idea of a will in addition?

2. Some Historical Views That Kant Found Unsatisfactory

Although Kant's idea of strength and weakness of will is quite distinctive, he did not develop it in ignorance of historical precedents. Some of these are especially worth noting. First, although he does not discuss them directly, Kant apparently knew and rejected several ancient views. For example, the Socratic position was that no one could know the good and not do it.[2]

---

[2] Plato, *Protagoras* 352b–58c.

Thus vice is due to ignorance, not a bad or a weak will. Plato gave us vivid metaphors for *appetites* and *passions* obeying or rebelling against *reason*,[3] but not of a *will* distinct from both that can choose between them. Aristotle tried to explain some of the phenomena that we attribute to weakness of will, but the explanations seem to turn more on distraction, short-sightedness, and lapses of focus than on willful refusal to act on the best reasons.[4] The Stoics emphasized the will and they inspired Kant in many ways, but, unlike Kant, they seemed to think that the way to virtue was to dispel or transform our troublesome desires and impulses, not to overcome them. Epictetus, for example, argues that we should will not to desire things beyond our control,[5] not that we should walk a straight path in spite of those desires.

An idea of the will closer to Kant's developed in Christian thought that no doubt influenced him, but it was sharply challenged by Thomas Hobbes. A traditional view was that as human beings we have *reason* to discern basic moral truths, *appetites and passions* that can lead us astray, and a *free will* that is responsible for our choice when appetites and passions conflict with reason. The will becomes especially important for those who, unlike Plato and Aristotle, affirmed that every adult person has the basic capacity and responsibility to discern and do what is right and to be (fully) virtuous.[6] Given that all responsible moral agents have reason, appetites, and passions, the difference between the virtuous and the vicious could not be attributed (entirely) to the presence or absence of these factors. Besides, apart from desires that follow upon our judgments, desires and passions also came to be understood as things given to us by nature or passively "happening" to us and in us. With this understanding of desires and the assumption that everyone has the basic rational capacity to *discern* the right, many thought that the shared responsibility to *do* what is right must lie in neither desires nor reason per se but in our free capacity to choose what to do when desire

---

[3] Cf. e.g. Plato, *Republic* 4. 435b–41c.

[4] Aristotle, *Nicomachean Ethics* 7. 3.

[5] Cf. e.g. *Arrian's Discourses of Epictetus* 1. 12 and 1. 15 (1925).

[6] Medieval authors developed this point in the context of their teaching on conscience and on natural law. For basic accounts of these problems, see Potts (1982), 687–704; and Luscombe (1982), 705–19. Many Christians, of course, added that this "basic capacity" needed to be supplemented by divine grace and the help of the Church, but this is quite different from Aristotle's denial that women, barbarians, and even Greeks without luck and good mentors could be virtuous. In *The Republic* Plato implies that the lower classes need to be told what is right by their betters; cf. 4. 433c–d, 434a–b.

and reason conflict.[7] Famously, however, Hobbes rejected this view and thereby set the agenda for much of the philosophical discussion of responsibility that followed. I want to sketch briefly Hobbes's view, and a variation by Hume, because they contrast sharply with Kant's view and posed a challenge that Kant needed to address.

According to Hobbes, all human behavior is causally determined in a mechanistic way by appetites, which are actually aspects of our bodies in motion.[8] These desires and aversions are often in conflict, and they can never be shaped by reason into an integrated coherent set. We are always moved by our strongest desires and aversions, and *the will* is nothing but the desire or aversion that finally causes us to act.[9] It follows that every act is a result of the agent's will: no act is involuntary, strictly speaking. It also follows that there is neither *free will* nor *weakness of will*, in the strict sense, for all our acts are caused by our will, which is itself caused by prior motions, and we can never fail to act when we will to do so (though we may fail to achieve our objective). Acts, but not the will, can be free but only in a sense.[10] For example, we freely leave the room, as opposed to being dragged forcibly out, in that we behaved as we willed and willed what we most desired. Reason can estimate consequences of our various acts and thus influence conduct indirectly, but it has no power directly to oppose, suppress, or overcome desires and aversions. What is ordinarily called "weakness of will," then, is really just a matter of being short-sighted or impulsive, that is, being moved by appetites and aversions (including one's "will") that were not influenced by due consideration of long-term consequences. The principles (or "natural laws") of right reason are really just precepts of prudence about how to preserve oneself and further one's interests.[11] In civil society one is responsible for not acting justly, but this is just a matter of public accountability and contractually based legal liability

---

[7] Free decision in cases of conflict between desire and reason was explained by some in terms of the will's capacity to restrain the impact of passions on reason; see e.g. Thomas Aquinas, *Summa theologiae* Ia IIa q. 10 a. 3. Acting against one's better judgment presupposes for Aquinas, as for Aristotle, that the judgment of what is best to do is not applied to the particular case at hand (*Summa theologiae* Ia IIa q. 77 a. 2 (cf. *EN* 7. 3)). By contrast, the view that the will can choose to follow sensuous desires even against a particular practical judgment of reason was prominent among voluntarist authors such as Henry of Ghent, *Quodlibet* 1. 16 (1979), 103–4; Duns Scotus, *Opus Oxoniense* 3. 36. 1 (1986), 400; and William of Ockham, *Quodlibet* 1. 16 (1980), 87. I am grateful to Tobias Hoffman for these references.

[8] Thomas Hobbes, *Leviathan* 1. 6 (1994).

[9] Ibid.   [10] Ibid. 2. 21.   [11] Ibid. 1. 14.

to punishment.[12] Injustice is never a matter of freely willing, when one could do otherwise, to act to satisfy one's desires *instead of* the moral demands of reason.

David Hume, whom Kant regarded as his immediate challenger, accepted many of Hobbes's basic ideas but made them gentler and subtler. He regarded human sentiments as more varied, more other-regarding, and more socially malleable than Hobbes did. But he still conceived of reason as a fact-finder and calculator rather than as a source of moral and rational imperatives.[13] In his view desires and passions are still passive "impressions" that we feel and dispositions that we infer from patterns of feeling and behavior.[14] They, and only they "move us" to act. Beliefs about matters of fact, which are discovered by reason and observation, only provide the context in which sentiments move us. Strictly speaking, there are no matters of fact or imperatives of reason about what we ought to do. The will is no longer an appetite or an aversion, as it was for Hobbes, but it still is just an event in a chain of causes.[15] I act freely, in a sense, when my behavior is caused by an occurrence of a will-event in me and this was caused by my desires. As we might say, "I *did it freely* because I had a *will* to do it and this was because I *wanted* to do it." Again, on Hume's view a free will would be an uncaused event, and this is contrary to nature and no help to morality anyway.[16] We are responsible for acts not because a random, uncaused natural event occurred but because the acts are caused by a will that is caused by our character. Given Hume's regularity theory of causation, a will to do something does not *necessarily* result in action.[17] For example, a person who has just lost a limb may for a time try or "will" to move the limb but without success. When a limb is detached, occurrences of a will-event have no immediate causal efficacy with respect to it. The will's power, we might say, is limited in scope this way, but the failure has nothing to do with weakness of will. What we call "weak-willed acts," instead, must be simply imprudent or foolish acts: that is, objectionable acts caused by ignorance, miscalculation, or strong short-term desires contrary to our own acknowledged best interests or acts caused by immediate impulses without thought of consequences. Choosing or willing is not, strictly speaking, an *activity* that we could do weakly or resolutely, and the will is not a weak or strong *power* that could choose between desire and reason.

[12] Leviathan 1. 15 and 2. 27.   [13] Hume (1978), 3. 1. 1.   [14] Ibid. 1. 1. 1.
[15] Ibid. 2. 3. 1.   [16] Ibid. 2. 3. 2.   [17] Ibid. 1. 3. 14.

Hume admittedly offers a more subtle account of moral virtue and responsibility than Hobbes does, but from Kant's perspective it is hampered from the outset by an untenable action theory.

Kant's theory, as we shall see, contrasts sharply with those of Hobbes and Hume. For example, according to Kant, the will is an active power of the mind, not something we passively experience. It is not a desire, strong or weak. Nor is it an inner event or "impression" that we come to recognize by introspection. We cannot understand the will as something in a series of natural causes, and so free or voluntary action cannot be reduced to behavior caused by will-events that are caused by our desires. And weak-willed acts cannot be reduced to behavior, against long-term or moral interests, caused by ignorance, miscalculation, or overpowering immediate impulses. But to see Kant's positive view, we need to review some basic elements of his action theory.

3. The Will in General, Negative Freedom, and Autonomy

A difficult but central aspect of Kant's moral theory is his idea of what human agents must be like in order to be capable of understanding and acting for moral reasons. Here the briefest summary will have to suffice. Moral agents have natural inclinations, reason, and the power to choose which to follow when inclination and reason conflict. Inclinations are natural dispositions to act, in themselves morally neutral but often temptations to act contrary to reason.[18] Reason regarding practical matters *enables us to discern* (within limits) what is prudent and what is moral. Its judgments about what we must do in a particular case depend on both rational principles and empirical facts.[19] Practical reason is also a *disposition to act* in

---

[18] Regarding this and subsequent points in this section, see Kant (2002). See esp. pp. 198–201 [4: 397–9], 215 n. (4: 414 n.). Useful commentaries include Paton (1958), esp. chs. 8–9, 20–1, pp. 78–102, 207–22; and Allison (1990), chs. 1–7, pp. 11–145.

[19] The rational principles that lie behind moral judgments, Kant held, are expressed (in imperative form) in his various formulations of the Categorical Imperative (see Kant (2002), 222–35 [4: 420–34]), and summarized at 236–7 [4: 436–7]. The rational principle behind hypothetical imperatives, Kant implies, is roughly, "One ought to take the necessary means within one's power to the ends that one wills (or abandon the ends)"; see ibid. 215–20 [4: 413–19]. Partly because he thought that previous philosophers often neglected the rational principles, Kant emphasized these rather than relevant empirical facts,

accord with the judgments of reason.[20] The dispositions stemming from our inclinations and reason often conflict, but not always. We also have the power (or free will) to choose whether to follow inclination or reason when these conflict. At least this is what we must presuppose from the practical standpoint of an agent deliberating about what to do.[21] Granted, empirical science must think of human behavior as causally determined; but this is not inconsistent with conceiving of ourselves for moral purposes as having negative freedom and autonomy.[22] Negatively free agents can act independently of their inclinations.[23] We must presuppose that such agents also have autonomy of the will, which is a capacity and disposition to guide themselves by rational principles that are not mere hypothetical imperatives prescribing the means to their desire-based ends.[24] The fundamental moral principles expressed in the Categorical Imperative, in its various forms, express the standards to which any rational will with autonomy is necessarily committed.[25] Unfortunately, not every moral agent with the capacity to live by the standard actually does so. But to violate it inevitably results in an inner conflict of will, reflected in the painful self-judgments of conscience and lowered self-esteem.[26] This is because in immoral action we use our free

encouraging some critics to suppose that he thought empirical facts have no place in ethics. Particular moral judgments, however, are applications of rational principles to the agent's circumstances and so require empirical understanding. Also Kant's own arguments, especially in his later ethical writings, often presuppose at least general empirical facts about the human condition.

[20] This is a theme throughout Kant's mature ethical writings. See e.g. ibid. 247–8 [4: 447–8], and (1998b), 50–2 [6: 26–8]. See also his (1996a), 13–14 [6: 213–14]: insofar as "practical reason" is regarded as power to discern what is rational to do and to be disposed to do it, it is "the will" (*Wille*) in one of the senses that he distinguishes in his later works. An ability to choose, even to follow inclination contrary to reason, is our "will" (*Willkür*) in another sense. Because we are responsible for our choices, this ability to choose must be "free" at least in the minimal sense that its exercise is not regarded as causally determined although what is chosen may be to satisfy an inclination. When we act immorally (and so "contrary to reason") for the sake of inclination, I think Kant's view allows that we can still be "acting for a reason" in an ordinary sense, guided by instrumental rationality and in the light of facts discerned by the theoretical use of reason. Some scholars suggest that such immoral acts must be either misguided attempts to follow the Categorical Imperative or else unfree in a sense that would undermine responsibility. For complex and subtly qualified versions of this suggestion, see Korsgaard (2009), esp. ch. 8, and Engstrom (2009), esp. 108–9. My comments on Engstrom, "Practical Reason, the Moral Law, and Choice," are forthcoming in *Analytic Philosophy* (Hill, 2012, forthcoming).

[21] Kant (2002), 247–8 [4: 446–7].

[22] Ibid. 247–57 [4: 447–58].

[23] Ibid. 246 [4: 446].

[24] Ibid. 240–7 [4: 440–7].

[25] Ibid. 236–41 [4: 436–41].

[26] Kant (1996a), 160–1 [6: 400–1] and 188–91 [6: 437–40]; (1998b), 27 [6: 267–8] and 178–80 [6: 184–7].

power of choice (our *Willkür* or "will" in one sense) in a way contrary to what is required by our practical legislating reason (our *Wille* or "will" in another sense).[27] By contrast, a person who willingly follows moral principles, even when contrary to natural inclinations, has a kind of integrity and self-respect that others lack. Immoral and morally weak persons do not in the same way express their nature as rational human beings with autonomy.

4. Virtue as a Good Will with the Developed Strength of Will to Do Right Despite Obstacles

Kant's *Groundwork* was meant to be preliminary to his more comprehensive work, *The Metaphysics of Morals*, published more than ten years later. The latter is divided into the Doctrine of Right (concerned with law and justice) and the Doctrine of Virtue (concerned with personal morality).[28] Duties of virtue, he tells us, are concerned with our maxims, motives, and ends. They result from the "inner legislation" of our own reason, not from governmental legislation. We cannot be coerced to follow them, but should do so out of respect for their moral grounds—for example, the dignity of humanity in each person. Unlike juridical duties, most duties of virtue are imperfect duties: they do not prescribe specific actions but rather tell us to make it our maxim to promote certain moral ends, especially our own perfection and the happiness of others. The widest duties, such as beneficence, leave a wide "playroom" for free choice as to when, how, and to what extent to promote the end.[29] Fulfilling these duties of virtue is meritorious but omitting them is not in itself demeritorious (or culpable).[30] Neglect of duties of virtue becomes culpable when it is due to a principled refusal to accept them or a failure to apply them in a particular emergency

---

[27] Kant (1996a), 13 [6: 212] and 18 [6: 226]. Gregor translates *Willkür* as *choice* and *Wille* as *will*; see Allison (1990), 129–36.

[28] For Kant's explanation of this division and the corresponding different types of duty, see (1996a), 20–2 [6: 218–21], 23–34 [6: 229–42], and 145–54 [6: 379–91].

[29] Ibid. 26 [6: 233], 153–4 [6: 390–1], 168 [6: 410–11], 195 [6: 445], 202–3 [6: 453–4]. Interpretations differ about the extent and kind of latitude allowed by Kant's duty of beneficence. See Gregor (1963), 95–112; Baron (1995), 88–107; Cummiskey (1996), 105–23; and Hill (2002), 201–43.

[30] Kant (1996a), 153 [6: 390].

situation in which the usually "imperfect" duty has become mandatory.[31] In these cases, predictably, our consciences will accuse us and cause us to suffer, but, generally speaking, it is not the business of others to judge and condemn us in this area.[32]

But what is it to be a virtuous person? First and foremost it requires having a *good will*—a sincere commitment and effort to do what is right.[33] This is the essential feature of a morally good person. Many other things are useful and valuable to those who have them but they are neither necessary nor sufficient for basic moral goodness. This is true, for example, of diligence, courage, intelligence, wealth, happiness, and useful accomplishments. A person with a good will is fundamentally good even if she is by nature scatter-brained, timid, stupid, unnoticed, miserable, and devoid of social achievements. A good will manifests itself when we act from duty, but we can *have* a good will even when acting at the moment from other innocent or good motives. The moral goodness of a *person* is not a function of number or kind of ("morally worthy") *acts* that the person does from duty. A commitment to morality can motivate us to do the right thing when we are tempted not to, but it can also serve as a *back-up motive* when we are doing things for other reasons. For example, we usually read novels for enjoyment but a person of good will is ready to stop reading if a friend suddenly needs help. Similarly, usually we take care of our children from love, not duty, but a parent with a good will is moved to continue even when stress overwhelms affection. A good will can also serve as *a filter* that rejects in advance certain immoral acts as not even options to consider. Unlike our desires, our feelings, and the *effects* of our actions, whether or not we have a good will, the commitment to act rightly is entirely up to us. At least, Kant argued, this is what we *must presuppose* as moral agents. But, as we shall see, being *virtuous* is more than having a good will.

---

[31] For the first point, see ibid. The second presumably follows from applications of the Categorical Imperative directly to emergency cases of dire distress, in which aid would not be automatically made mandatory by the wide imperfect duty of beneficence, when interpreted nonrigoristically.

[32] Ibid. 150–2 [6: 385–7]. Their general ethical duty, like ours, is to promote the happiness of others, not their virtue, and so apart from matters concerning the law, the moral education of children, and scandalous conduct, others should be focused more on our happiness (consistent with justice) rather than our moral virtue. This perhaps surprising theme is developed in my (1992a), 176–95.

[33] Kant (2002),195–203 [4: 393–402]. See Wood (1999), ch. 1, pp. 17–49.

Virtue and some other features of an ideally good person cannot be acquired at will.[34]

Virtue includes a good will, but virtue as a character trait is also a *developed strength of will* to do what is right.[35] Effort, practice, and time are needed to turn a basically good will into a strong and effective will that chooses the right thing even in the presence of contrary inclinations so intense that they might sway a weaker person.[36] With practice, a person of developed virtue would overcome such obstacles with regularity and relative ease. Those who have a good will have a general policy and aim that points them in the right direction, as it were, because the principle of any good will is "to do what is right." These general good intentions, however, may sometimes fail to result in right action because of the agent's weakness of will. In this case the will generally aims at the right, so to speak, but it is weak. In a person of developed virtue, the will is both strong and aimed at the right.

5. How Are Strength and Weakness of Will to Be Understood?

Kant's conception of strength and weakness is not easy to fathom, but a few points seem clear enough. For one thing, despite the metaphors, Kant did not think of a will as an empirical force that could do battle with felt impulses and inclinations.[37] So a strong will is not (as it was for Hobbes) a desire that, in a stream of conflicting desires, happens to overpower the others and cause the resulting behavior. Willing, in Kant's view, is something we *do*, not something we *experience passively*. Second, we will to act on *maxims*, which are personal policies or general intentions referring to a kind of act, its purpose, and sometimes its underlying reason.[38] From a practical perspective, we think of ourselves as acting on a rationale that could in

---

[34] Kant (1996a), 158–9 [6: 397]. Kant implies that being a person with cultivated "compassionate natural (aesthetic) feelings" is a goal that we have an (indirect) duty to pursue, but it is a trait that we cannot acquire at will but requires effort over time (e.g. by not avoiding sickrooms, debtor's prisons, and contact with the poor); see ibid. 205 [6: 457].

[35] Ibid. 146 [6: 380], 164–5 [6: 405–7], 166 [6: 408], 221 [6: 477]. See also Allison (1990), ch. 9, pp. 162–79; Guyer (2000), 303–23; and Wood (1999), 329–33.

[36] Kant (1996a),158–9 [6: 397], 221 [6: 477].

[37] Kant (2002), 250–7 [4: 450–8].

[38] Ibid. 202 n. [4: 402 n.], 222 n. [4: 421 n.]; (1996a), 17–18 [6: 225–6]; (1998b), 48–9 [23–4].

principle be articulated and is not reducible to a description of the empirical causes of our behavior. All acts for which we are morally responsible are supposed to be based on a maxim, whether we act dutifully or immorally, with a strong will or a weak will. Some maxims are quite specific, describing the actual intentions and aims with which we act on particular occasions. Other maxims, however, are very general, life-governing policies that guide, more or less effectively, our choice of more specific maxims. We adopt our maxims as human beings subject to the influence of both our sensuous inclinations and our morally legislative practical reason (*Wille*). All of our maxims, however, are presumed to result from the exercise of our power of free choice (*Willkür*).

Accordingly, weak-willed acts contrary to duty are not to be understood as the result of an agent's willing to act on a particular good maxim but lacking the power to do so.[39] Similarly, virtue or strength of a moral will is not just a matter of being committed to act on a good maxim and *being able* to do so despite obstacles. All moral agents are presumed to have *that* capacity insofar as they have freedom of will.[40] We often lack the power to ensure that our acts have the *effects* we intend, but it is presumed to be entirely up to us whether or not to choose to act on a maxim to try to achieve the end. *Depraved* persons act on bad maxims and without any general commitment to acting rightly.[41] Those who act rightly from *virtue* act on morally good maxims in line with their general commitment to do what is right. Those who do wrong from *moral weakness* act at the moment

---

[39] Kant says that failures to fulfill an imperfect duty, provided they are not based on a principle not to comply, display "weakness," or want of virtue ("strength of resolution"). Though they are not in themselves "culpable" (as are intentional wrongdoings), nevertheless they reveal a "deficiency in moral worth," not merely an excusable disability; see (1996a), 153 [6: 390]. Again, Kant says that "moral weakness" is "negative lack of virtue" where virtue is treated as "strength of soul," which is "strength of resolution in a human being endowed with freedom"; see ibid. 148 [6: 384]. Kant classifies "general weakness of the human heart" (or "frailty") with "impurity" and "depravity" as "three sources of moral evil," and in Kant's view lacking the ability to do what is right could not be a source of moral evil; see (1998b), 53–5 [6: 29–32].

[40] At least one passage might suggest that human freedom is merely a capacity *to acquire the ability to overcome opposing impulses*, but this would allow that, before we could successfully acquire the ability, our opposing impulses could completely excuse our wrongdoing, contrary to what Kant repeatedly implies. What must be acquired, I take it, is not the *basic ability* to do one's duty in the face of temptation but, as he says, *virtue*, a *strength of resolution* that we develop by "contemplating the dignity of the pure rational law and by *practicing* virtue"; see (1996a), 158–9 [6: 397].

[41] For the contrast between depravity, weakness, and impurity, see Kant (1998b), 52–5 [6: 29–32]. Here Kant explicitly discusses *propensities* to evil, but presumably the depraved and weak persons are those who choose to fulfill rather than to overcome the corresponding propensities.

on an immoral maxim but contrary to their practical reason (*Wille*) and their general commitment (of *Willkür*) to act rightly. They give in to inclinations contrary to duty, but this is not a matter of a stronger *force* (their inclinations) literally *overpowering* weaker ones (their rational predisposition to morality and their general intention to be guided by it). The comparison with physical strength and weakness is misleading here. What is needed, instead, is an interpretation of strength and weakness appropriate to Kant's action theory—with its complex conception of "will" and its understanding of acts as based on freely chosen maxims.[42]

The metaphor of strength of a will to be moral might be unpacked in at least two ways.[43] First, consider the content of our commitment to morality. Like laws of the state, resolutions and principles can be clear and definite or vague and somewhat inexplicit regarding specific implications. Some even have explicit "loopholes" permitting escape from their primary provisions. Many of us do wrong because our commitment to morality is vague or even qualified. For example, we have only a rather vague and indefinite resolve "to do good" or, anticipating potential sacrifices, we might adopt as an explicit policy the rule that "I will always to do right even against inclinations, unless the cost is really, really high." These imperfect commitments might account for a person's acting rightly in most circumstances, but occasionally failing when temptations are extraordinarily strong.

However, a qualification is needed here. Kant distinguishes *weakness, impurity*, and *depravity* as different grades of the natural propensity to evil.[44] The *weakness* or frailty, Kant describes thus:

---

[42] The best account of these matters, in my view, is Johnson (1998), 349–67. My reflections agree with his excellent discussion on most important matters, though I do not rely in the same way on a distinction between "motivation" and "values." Also at times Johnson seems to treat weakness of will as a kind of inability. For example, "The weak person we are interested in here is not simply a person who *drops* and *adopts* principles too easily, but is rather one who *cannot* live up to those she adopts and does not drop" (p. 360, my italics in the second clause).

[43] Here I offer an interpretation not explicitly mandated by Kant's remarks about strength and weakness of will but guided by a concern to reconstruct, compatibly with the texts, an account of weakness of will that fits the basic requirements of his moral theory: for example, the will is not a desire or inner force that we can introspect, weakness of will is not an incapacity that excuses wrongdoing, strength of moral will is developed virtue in a person with a basically good will, morally responsible acts (good or bad) are to be understood as acts on a maxim, and we have both specific maxims (as in the *Groundwork* examples) and more generic, life-defining maxims (such as "self-love" and "duty" in the second *Critique*). The interpretation is no doubt partly influenced by my earlier attempts to make sense of weakness of will in everyday life, as manifested by several patterns in the character of weak-willed persons over time. This is reprinted as "Weakness of Will and Character" in Hill (1991), 118–37.

[44] Kant (1998*b*), 52–5 [6: 29–32].

First, the frailty [*fragilitas*] of human nature is expressed even in the complaint of the Apostle: "What I would, that I do not" i.e. I incorporate the good (the law) into the maxim of my power of choice; but this good, which is an irresistible incentive objectively or ideally [*in thesi*], is subjectively [*in hypothesi*] the weaker (in comparison with inclination) whenever the maxim is to be followed.[45]

By contrast, *impurity* is the disposition to qualify our commitment to follow the moral law, saying, for example, "I will do what is right if it also serves my interests" or "I will do my duty if the cost is not too high." Even in their basic life-defining maxims, those who yield to this disposition are not committed to treating duty as a sufficient reason for them to act. Their general policy with regard to morality is, in effect, full of loopholes. Finally, Kant says, *depravity* is "the propensity of the power of choice to maxims that subordinate the incentives of the moral law to others (not moral ones)."[46] The paradigm of a depraved person is one who systematically chooses, on principle, to act from self-interest instead of duty, when these are in conflict.

Moral regret when one does wrong is a sign of a moral weakness insofar as the regret reflects a conflict between the weak agent's immediate choice of an immoral maxim and his or her general commitment to be moral. Regret for being morally weak does not indicate that, although the particular maxim on which the agent elected to act at the time was good, regrettably the agent was unable to act on it. Rather, the regret shows that, despite maintaining a long-standing commitment or "will" to be moral, on this occasion the agent chose to indulge other, competing concerns. This reveals an irrational "conflict of will," not an inability to do what is right. Those whose basic commitments are mixed or depraved do not necessarily have this sort of conflict of will with regard to morality. They may *wish* that they could satisfy both morality and self-love, because in Kant's view they are predisposed to both. But, strictly speaking, their particular immoral choices are not in conflict with their basic, life-governing maxims. In fact those maxims express their general intention (or "will") to favor inclination over duty in various circumstances.

My first suggestion is that weak-willed persons, by contrast, are committed unconditionally to doing right despite inclination, but they are typically not very clear, definite, and explicit about what specifically this

---

[45] Kant (1998*b*), 53 [6: 29].   [46] Ibid. 54 [6: 30].

implies for various particular choices. This vagueness, we might say, is a kind of "weakness" in their resolution to be moral, a weakness in the content of what they will analogous to the weakness of a vague law adopted by legislators who lack a clear understanding of its implications. A weak moral resolution of this sort enables us, especially when weak in other respects, to affirm a general, unqualified commitment to morality even though we sometimes act contrary to what that commitment, properly understood, requires. Vagueness opens a door for self-deception, inattention, and special pleading that enable us to live with a genuine conflict of will, of which we are aware enough to be responsible but not enough to prompt us to change.

A second way of thinking of moral strength requires us to distinguish *what we will* from *how seriously and resolutely we will* it.[47] Suppose two people have a *general intention* always to do what is right and the capacity to act accordingly if (as we say) they try hard enough. One person is wholeheartedly committed, treating the commitment as the highest priority, and is determined to be attentive, well focused, and clear-headed when inclinations conflict with moral responsibilities. The other person is sincere but habitually lets himself be easily distracted and indulges a tendency to make self-serving excuses. Both will to do what is right as their *life-governing policy* and have an adequate *capacity* to implement the policy in every case, but the second *wills it more weakly*.

Kant admitted that we cannot explain this commonsense idea empirically, as we might explain a person's failure to lift a certain weight as a matter of exerting too weakly a muscular capacity that one has. Nevertheless, Kant implies that a moral perspective needs a concept of this sort. Using the concept, he can suppose that both the virtuous and the morally weak person had the capacity to overcome inclinations contrary to what is right, but the virtuous or morally strong-willed person can do so—and typically does—more readily, easily, and confidently. Kant could even say, with Aristotle, that the virtuous person is not *tempted* to do wrong, insofar as the word *tempted* implies an initially wavering attitude characteristic of the morally weak person. This is not to say, however, that virtuous persons never

---

[47] This second point is meant to apply even to cases in which the agents' *policy* to do what is right is clear and definite. The moral weakness here is not due to vagueness, but is to be explained in a different way.

experience strong inclinations contrary to their moral responsibilities, for extreme enduring physical pain may be required and to be inclined to stop the pain is only natural.[48]

On the interpretations suggested here, the weakness of the morally weak person is either in the content of the person's moral resolution or in how resolutely, in a sense, the person willed it. In either case, however, those who are weak-willed often make particular choices contrary to their practical reason, the "will" (*Wille*) in them that "legislates" moral standards for them irrespective of their individual choices. Thus we could say that in the morally weak person "the will" (in this further sense) is weak in that it does not effectively govern all particular choices, as it does in the virtuous person. To say this, admittedly, is not to explain an inner mechanism at work, effective in some persons (the virtuous) but not in others (the morally weak). Rather, it is simply another way of noting that the morally weak person's particular choices, unlike the virtuous person's, do not regularly correspond with the moral commands of their practical reason. That moral weakness can be described in this way is worth noting, however, because in some passages Kant suggests that what is weak in the morally weak person is in fact the "will" in this sense (*Wille*).[49]

6. How Can We Be to Blame When Natural Desires and Impulses Move Us?

Philosophers have often wondered how we can be responsible for our behavior if it results from natural forces, such as desires, impulses, feelings, and sentiments. The problem can take several different forms. If we regard the fundamental human desires as good, we cannot explain wrongdoing and evil simply by reference to these good desires. The main problem, then, is to say why acts motivated by some desires are praiseworthy while acts motivated by other desires are blameworthy. We would also need an account of motivation that explains why agents should be *blamed* for their objectionable

---

[48] These points about temptation and inclination in the virtuous were first suggested to me by Karen Stohr of Georgetown University.

[49] Kant (1996a), 151 [6: 387] and 164–5 [6: 405–7].

behavior rather than *pitied* for the misfortune of having bad or perverse desires that overwhelm the "natural" good ones.

Kant's official position avoids these problems. Taking a broad view of "nature" as governed by causal laws, Kant rejects the idea that certain "natural" inclinations are in themselves good and others bad. He held that, although some inclinations and desires are more benign in their effects than others, all of them are in themselves morally neutral insofar as they belong to our sensible, empirical nature.[50] For this reason he does not rely on distinctions among such motives to explain the difference between morally culpable acts, morally indifferent acts, and acts of positive moral worth. In addition, Kant held that whether we have strong inclinations contrary to duty is often just a matter of luck (and so not our fault) and that such desires can merely *dispose*, not *compel*, us to do wrong.[51] Because we have the freedom of will to choose to satisfy desire or to follow reason, we are not to be pitied and pardoned, but held responsible, for our wrongdoing. The contrary inclinations do not literally "overpower" us but rather we choose to indulge or "give in" to them.

Nevertheless, Kant's account of desire-based wrongdoing seems to face a serious problem. At least critics have often thought so.[52] Here is the problem. In the *Groundwork* Kant argues that his supreme moral principle is the principle of a will that has the property of autonomy, which is "being a law unto itself (independently of any property of the objects of volition)."[53] Thus any rational person with autonomy wills the moral law as its principle. He also argues that autonomy is inseparable from negative freedom, which is a will's capacity to be active "independently of alien causes *determining* it."[54] This entails that anyone with a free will, in either sense, wills the supreme moral principle. Thus, it may seem, no one freely chooses to act contrary to the supreme moral principle. Those who act badly are really just caused to do so by the forces of nature, in fact by their own desires and inclinations. In other words, in "immoral" actions the will to do what is right is not just *weak*, but in fact utterly *powerless* against contrary inclinations. No one does wrong freely, and so no one is responsible for vicious

---

[50] This is Kant's mature position (see e.g. (1998*b*), 57 [6: 35]) but it seems in tension with (2002), 229 [4: 428].

[51] Kant (2002), 199–201 [4: 397–9].

[52] See e.g. Sidgwick (1981), app., 511–16; and Wolff (1973), 122–3, 210–11.

[53] Kant (2002), 240 [4: 440] and 246 [4: 446–7].   [54] Ibid. 246 [4: 446].

and harmful behavior. This, however, is an intuitively absurd result, and it contradicts the dominant theme explicit in all Kant's mature ethical writings. Clearly something has gone wrong.

This apparent problem rests on a serious misunderstanding. In saying that the supreme moral principle is the principle of a will that has the property of autonomy, Kant does not mean that a person who has such a will never acts immorally. To the contrary, Kant implies that autonomy and negative freedom are characteristics of all moral agents, good and bad.[55] In fact denying this point was the primary error of all previous moral theories, for in various different ways they assumed that heteronomy, not autonomy, was the basic feature of human wills. In Kant's view all moral agents have negative freedom, that is, the *capacity* to choose, rightly or wrongly, without being causally determined by their inclinations (*negative freedom*). This capacity is possible only because they also have *autonomy*, which is a rational *disposition* to govern oneself by rational principles not based on contingent inclinations. This moral disposition, however, does not guarantee morally correct choice on particular occasions. The key to the puzzle lies in a distinction between two aspects of the will that Kant distinguishes explicitly only in his later writings. As noted above, in Kant's view, we have a rational legislative will (*Wille*) and a free power of choice (*Willkür*).[56] To say we have a legislative will (*Wille*) is a metaphorical way of saying that, as moral agents, we inevitably recognize the moral law as imposing overriding rational demands on us. To say we have a free power of choice (*Willkür*) is just to say that whether or not we fulfill these demands is not causally determined but is a choice for which we are responsible. In more everyday terms, we all implicitly understand moral requirements as a *standard* that we should respect even when we violate it. Vicious people systematically refuse to let the standard constrain them. Morally weak people let themselves lapse from their general policy of doing right. For both, Kant thought, a troubled

---

[55] At least this is what we must presuppose from a practical standpoint. "Autonomy" here refers to a "property of the will" that is a capacity and disposition to use and follow the moral law as a rational standard that the agent with autonomy necessarily recognizes as not externally imposed. When contemporary writers write as if some people (the morally good) are "autonomous" and some (the morally bad) are "heteronomous," this would be less misleadingly expressed, if the point is Kantian, by saying that some (the good) express their rational autonomy in their choices, while others (the bad) do not, acting instead as if they were beings subject only to the laws governing beings with heteronomy of the will; see Allison (1990), 85–99, and Hill (1992a), 76–122.

[56] See e.g. Kant (1996a), 13 [6: 213–14] and 18 [6: 226–7].

conscience is inevitable because they realize that they willfully disregard a standard that they cannot help but recognize as inherent in their own practical reason.

7. How Can There Be Degrees of Culpability?

When Kant takes an empirical point of view, he often describes human beings as morally lax, self-deceiving, self-serving, hypocritical, and weak.[57] Usually, it seems, they do wrong while professing even to themselves that they aim to do right.[58] Principled wrongdoing and fiendish malice are rare, if not impossible, for human beings. Conscience can be dulled but not silenced. And yet Kant insists that, from a moral/practical point of view, we cannot excuse our misconduct by saying that we generally aim and want to do right and failed because of natural and universal temptations. We must take ourselves to be capable of doing our duty despite our strongest contrary inclinations. "I *really* wanted to do something else!" hardly excuses a serious neglect of responsibility. So, from a moral practical point of view, we are very often culpable regardless of our generally positive orientation toward morality.

Nevertheless, we ordinarily think that we are *less* to blame, other things equal, for the wrongs we do in moments of extreme passion or when acting rightly would require great sacrifice of our personal interests. These factors *mitigate* our culpability, we think, even though they do not completely excuse our behavior. Even Kant seems to accept this idea when, in *The Metaphysics of Morals*, he says:

Subjectively, the degree to *which an action can be imputed* [*inputabilitas*] has to be assessed by the magnitude of the obstacles that had to be overcome . . . The lesser the natural obstacles ["of sensibility"] and the greater the obstacle from the grounds of duty, so much the more is a transgression to be imputed (as culpable).—Hence the state of mind of the subject, whether he committed the deed in a state of agitation or with cool deliberation, makes a difference in imputation, which has results.[59]

---

[57] e.g. Kant (1998b), 60–1 [6: 38–9].   [58] See e.g. Kant (2002), 225 [4: 424].
[59] Kant (1996a), 19 [6: 228].

The point here is that, other things equal, when our moral offense is objectively worse, then we are more culpable; and if we could have avoided the offense without much sacrifice or struggle against our passions, then again we are more culpable. In effect, strong temptations to some extent mitigate our culpability for wrongdoing.

But now the question arises: If we are fully capable of doing what is right, why should we be any less to blame because we had strong temptations to do wrong? The temptations, in Kant's view, are not marks of diminished capacity. They do not literally overpower us. We freely choose whether to yield to them or not. We do not yield because the forces of reason were defeated in battle by the forces of inclination. We chose to act on the maxim to satisfy inclination when we could have done otherwise. We did wrong through weakness of will in Kant's special sense, but why is that any mitigation of our culpability?

Recall that weakness of will, as interpreted here, has at least two dimensions: first, our will to do right is somewhat vague and relatively inexplicit regarding its implications. Second, we will it weakly: that is, we resolve half-heartedly, waveringly, off and on, without willing specifically, in anticipation, the necessary and available means. Note that although these descriptions raise questions of their own, they are not ascriptions of power-lessness, diminished capacity, or lack of adequate troops for war against inclinations. Kant uses metaphors that can easily suggest these interpretations of weakness, but he cannot intend them literally when taking the practical/moral perspective. Arguably, such metaphors are unnecessary because the two dimensions of weakness of will just mentioned are sufficient to explain why strong passions and temptations tend to mitigate culpability to some degree.

Contrast two people who tell a lie when they should not.[60] For example, they flatly deny having made a serious culpable mistake of which they are aware, and they deny it in a context where others clearly have a right to hear the truth. The first person regularly tells such lies whenever they serve his advantage, however slight. Although he sometimes feels pangs of con-science, he has decided that these are worth the rewards of getting what he wants. He is amiable and well liked and does not do anything overtly monstrous, although he would if certain opportunities arose because his commitment to self-advancement would demand it. He has relatively little

---

[60] Any similarity to former political leaders may not be purely coincidental, even if exaggerated.

to lose by telling the truth on this occasion, and yet he tells the lie readily without any strong passion driving him to do so. The second person generally aims, wants, and does do what is right, but on this occasion his moral reputation, which he has worked hard to earn, is on the line. He feels deeply ashamed and guilty about his past mistake and the harm it caused but when asked point-blank about it, he suddenly feels a huge resistance to confessing it publicly. Besides, his career is at stake, and he wants *very, very much* not to lose his distinguished and important position. He inwardly wavers, feels torn, and tries to make excuses to himself, saying, "I just *cannot* let them know I did *that!*," but he dimly realizes that he could if he tried. He tells the lie, not merely because of the psychological obstacles he faced, but because his commitment (or will) to act rightly was always somewhat vague and he willed it weakly, that is, somewhat waveringly, off and on, without an explicit commitment to take the means necessary to sustain a moral will in the face of obstacles.

Neither person, of course, is a paragon of virtue. Both are culpable for telling the lie. But isn't the second person, for all his faults, less to blame than the first? The second fails because his will to do right was weak; the first fails because he did not actively will to do right at all. Neither was literally overpowered by temptations, but the second person's immediate passion and the threat to his personal interests help to explain his lapse despite his general commitment to morality. It is this commitment, his basic good will, that mitigates his culpability (as compared to the relatively shameless liar).

Conclusion

To summarize, my aim here has been to explore the place of moral weakness in Kant's moral theory. I first surveyed some questions raised by various popular ideas of weakness of will in general, and then briefly sketched the salient views of some of Kant's influential predecessors, especially Thomas Hobbes and David Hume. Then I reviewed the necessary background to Kant's alternative position, his special ideas of the will, negative freedom, and autonomy. These were crucial because Kant conceives of moral weakness by contrast to moral virtue, which he understands as strength of will to fulfill one's duty despite temptations. Kant, however, cannot consistently treat strength and weakness of will simply as a mental analogue of physical strength and weakness. This is because he takes all morally significant acts to be based on freely adopted maxims. These express the agents' rationale in acting—their policies, aims, and intentions—rather than causal forces that determine behavior.

The puzzle, then, was to explain, despite Kant's relatively sparse explicit discussion of moral weakness, how weakness of moral will can be interpreted consistently with the action theory implicit in his special ideas of reason, inclination, and will. One way to view moral weakness, I suggested, might be to see it as a kind of weakness (due to vagueness) in the *content* of one's resolution (or "will") to be moral. The problem here could also be expressed as a relative weakness in the agent's *rational legislative will* (or morally practical reason, *Wille*). Another possibility, I suggested, was to locate the moral weakness in *how* (weakly) one wills even clear and definite moral resolutions. These suggestions invite many further questions, but they are attempts to cash out the metaphors of strength and weakness of will consistently with Kant's ideas that we are responsible for our moral weakness and that significant moral acts are based on freely chosen maxims. The suggestions, even if further developed, would not "explain" how strong and weak wills work, but this fits with Kant's view that "the will" is ultimately beyond explanation, at least explanation of the kinds natural science or critical philosophy can reasonably hope for.

Next, I sketched a response to an old worry that Kant's texts at times imply that no one wills freely to do wrong and so no one is ever responsible for wrongdoing. Then, finally, I tried to illustrate how the conception of moral weakness suggested here might square with Kant's idea that culpability for doing wrong is mitigated, but not fully excused, by the fact that it was done under the influence of strong passions.

6

Kantian Virtue and "Virtue Ethics"

The reputations of various systematic ethical theories rise and fall over time, for good and bad reasons. Some rise like splendid towers only to be demolished by withering attacks from critics. Others, like castles on hilltops, were apparently too formidable to be destroyed by frontal assault, but their defenders abandoned them in search of newer, less cumbersome quarters, leaving only their impressive ruins behind as tourist attractions.[1] We can hope that, as in the history of medicine, there is progress in these changes guided by improved understanding and wise reflection; but we may fear that, as with fads and fashions, the changes are driven by enthusiasm for whatever is novel. Despite our hopes, progress is not guaranteed.

Similar remarks might be made of major *approaches* to ethics as well as particular ethical theories. For example, theological approaches were once dominant but lost ground to various forms of intuitionism and utilitarianism. Attempts to restrict ethics to the "metaethical" analysis of moral language have largely been abandoned in favor of more holistic approaches, as illustrated, for example, by the influence of Rawls's theory of justice. Today, it seems widely agreed, normative ethics is largely dominated by several competing approaches, including prominently utilitarianism, Kantianism, and virtue ethics. Utilitarianism has undergone many subtle transformations in response to criticisms and still survives with many adherents especially in Great Britain. Broadly Kantian approaches to ethics have been developed in a variety of ways that have earned new respect and attention for their source; but simultaneously a diverse movement commonly called "virtue ethics" has gained popularity especially in its opposition to other

[1] The imagery here comes from Isaiah Berlin's lectures at Oxford in the early 1960s.

approaches. In my discussion today I shall be concerned with the latter two of these trends, but mainly Kantianism. More specifically, I shall discuss first Kant's conception of moral virtue, its place in his overall ethical theory, and some questions that it raises. Then, in the final section, I shall consider briefly how Kant's ethics, or at least an expanded and supplemented Kantian ethics, might respond to certain criticisms and alternatives often associated with "virtue ethics."

My aim is to explore a wide range of related topics, to offer suggestions regarding the interpretation and development of Kant's ideas, and to raise questions about how these compare and contrast with some ideas in another tradition.[2] With apologies to scholars of both traditions, here I can only sketch various positions with broad strokes, passing over various complexities and controversies that may be important in another context. My suggestions often presuppose interpretations and arguments that I discuss more fully elsewhere, but even so they remain tentative as well as incomplete. Here my hope is just to call attention to some features of Kant's ethics that emerge mostly in his later writings, to address some problems, to warn against some misunderstandings, and to facilitate further discussion of the relative merits of different approaches.

I. The Apparent Conflict: Basic Points and Exaggerations

It may be useful, especially for those not already familiar with the controversy, to begin with a loose description of Kant's ethics and virtue ethics as they are often conceived—or caricatured. In an extreme (distorted) picture,

---

[2] Earlier versions of this chapter were discussed at the University of Tennessee and the University of Cincinnati. A lecture with some similar content to sections of this present chapter was given at The Catholic University of America and discussed at the University of California, Riverside, and the University of California, Los Angeles (Hill 2008a). I am grateful to participants in those discussions for their helpful comments. I cannot thank individually all the Kant scholars from whose work I have learned, but among the best accounts of these matters, in my view, is Johnson (1998), 349–67. My reflections agree with his excellent discussion on most important matters, though I do not rely in the same way on a distinction between "motivation" and "values." Also at times Johnson seems to treat weakness of will as a kind of inability. For example, "The weak person we are interested in here is not simply a person who *drops* and *adopts* principles too easily, but is rather one who *cannot* live up to those she adopts and does not drop" (p. 360, my italics in the second clause).

Kant's ethics is seen as exclusively focused on moral duty, the sole issue being how I must act and not what sort of person I should be. All duties are supposed to be derived from reason alone independently of any assumptions about human feelings or other empirical data about the human condition. Ethical standards are not scalar ideals of excellence, which we may "live up to" or "fall short of" to various degrees. Instead, moral principles are always definite and nonscalar, or all-or-nothing: either you obey the strict moral commands or you don't. Morality is completely rule-governed, like an all-encompassing legal code consisting of rigid, exceptionless laws that specify for all cases what is forbidden and what is required. The only good motive is devotion to duty: to do duty for duty's sake. Other motives are morally on a par: being moved by compassion, for example, is *no better* than being moved by malice. We should only do our duty from respect for moral law, not from habit, not to emulate virtuous persons, or even not to do what is noble and honorable. A moral life must be entirely governed by strict, inflexible moral rules that bind everyone, regardless of circumstance, without exception. Moral rules completely ignore special relationships between individuals and differences in historical and cultural contexts. Knowing what is right to do is obvious to even the most ignorant, unreflective, and corrupt persons: we never need to weigh expected consequences and virtue is not needed to discern the right thing to do. Acting rightly and having good traits of character are equally within the power of every minimally competent adult: *luck* has nothing to do with it. Justice requires judicial punishment and judgments of blame according to inflexible, exceptionless rules that serve the basic aim to make each person suffer according to their inner moral deserts.

By contrast, "virtue ethics" is sometimes conceived thus: its focus is *character* or what one should *be*, not how one should *act*. Virtues of character are derived entirely from the *study of human nature*, especially what enables us to flourish as human beings. This is determined entirely by our *natural end* (or *telos*) and our natural powers and vulnerabilities. All moral standards are scalar ideals of excellence, to which we may approximate more or less. Rules and principles are of little use outside a legal system. They have no authority independent of judgments on particular cases, and focusing on them inevitably leads to the neglect of morally relevant features of the case at hand. There are many virtuous motives, and the appropriate kind and degree depend on the context. Concern for the noble and honorable, for example, is a general mark of a virtuous person. Compassion and many other specific motives are good but only when their degree, time, place, and manner of moving us are fitting to the particular circumstance, as judged by a practically wise person. Acting from good habits should be encouraged; and to develop such habits, we should emulate those who are known paragons of virtue. Friendships and family relations are outside the scope of duty and moral rules. The standard of right action is to do whatever a thoroughly virtuous person would do—so the *right* is completely determined by prior judgments about what is *good* in particular cases. Virtue and knowledge make a person better able to judge what is right and good, and both depend heavily on how *lucky* one is in one's natural endowments, social circumstances, and friends and mentors. A good life requires sensitivity to the rich variety of personal relationships and historical contexts. Moralistic blame and punishment belong to an untenable legalistic model of ethics that values uniformity, abstract rules, and vengeance more than human flourishing and good character.

My sketch of Kant's ethics is a caricature combining mistakes and distortions that probably no one believes altogether. It reflects significant themes in Kant's writings but exaggerates and misrepresents them in unfortunate ways and omits important qualifications. It also fails to distinguish what is deep and basic in Kant's moral theory from ideas that are less so. My sketch of *virtue ethics* is perhaps less a caricature than an agglomeration of points from different versions of virtue ethics, or points offered from time to time by those inclined to favor a "virtue ethics" approach. A thorough treatment would need to clarify the apparent differences among these views, to sort out the deep contrasts from exaggerations and misunderstandings, and to identify precisely which moral theorists, if any, are committed to the views.[3] This chapter attempts to take a few preliminary steps in this direction, at least concerning Kant's ethics.

In contrast to most philosophers before and after him, Kant treats *virtue* as a kind of strength of the will to do what is right. Virtue is more than having good intentions, and we need to develop it over time. We have a duty to try to develop virtue, but we are also responsible if, lacking sufficient virtue, we

---

[3] Serious discussions of virtue representing contemporary versions of a broadly "virtue ethics" approach, as distinct from more popular and implausible representations, can be found in Crisp and Slote (1997); Darwall (2002); Foot (2003); Hursthouse (1999); Slote (1992); and Swanton (2005).

do wrong through weakness of will. We have particular virtues insofar as our will to fulfill various specific duties is strong, but it is not the implications of Kant's position for particular virtues (and vices) of character that is most interesting. Apart from that, Kant's ideas raise questions about moral responsibility and strength and weakness of will that present special problems of understanding, even though (arguably) in some respects Kant's ideas reflect familiar common sense views.

My discussion will be divided into three main parts. Part II reviews briefly basic ideas in Kant's *Groundwork for the Metaphysics of Morals* about methodology, a good will, morally worthy acts, categorical imperatives, and the supreme moral principle. Part III concerns ideas that Kant develops in his later ethical writing, notably two senses of "will," virtue as more than a good will, and a distinction between weakness, impurity, and depravity. Central questions here are: How can we understand moral weakness of will as a deficiency of virtue, not a disability, as culpable but better than impurity and depravity? And how does Kant's idea that we act on *maxims* fit with his metaphors of strength and weakness of will? In Part IV, I consider implications regarding four topics on which Kant's ethical theory might be contrasted with certain views associated with "virtue ethics": 1. the need for moral rules; 2. sensitivity to particular contexts; 3. morally good motivation; and 4. the standard for right action.

II. Some Basic Themes of the *Groundwork*

Let us review briefly ideas that Kant introduces in his *Groundwork for the Metaphysics of Morals*. These set the stage for his discussion of virtue in his later work, *The Metaphysics of Morals*.

II.1. *Methodology*

To begin, the method appropriate to *foundational* questions of ethical theory, Kant thought, was an a priori method that did not rely on empirical studies of human psychology. There were two main reasons: First, the way to "discover" and confirm a principle as the supreme moral principle, he thought, was to *analyze the common idea of duty*, and this is a matter of deep conceptual analysis, not empirical investigation. Second, foundational ethics needs to resolve the question *whether commitment to morality is rational*, and empirical studies cannot determine what constitutes practical rationality.[4] Although many philosophers today doubt Kant's conclusions, many still accept his main methodological point: that basic questions about the pre-suppositions of our concepts and the nature of rationality call for philosoph-ical reflection and cannot be resolved by empirical studies.

Unfortunately, this sensible point has been confused with another, utterly untenable idea: namely, that we can judge what is right to do in a particular situation without relying on any empirical facts at all. Although Kant's incautious remarks sometimes contribute to the confusion, the idea that empirical evidence is irrelevant to moral judgments about particular cases and specific (mid-level) principles is both absurd and contrary to Kant's own moral arguments. We must rely on empirical facts even to identify an act as a "lying promise," "a suicide," "an act of revolution," or an act of another kind. Moreover, as Kant acknowledged, his own substantive principles in *The Metaphysics of Morals* about political authority, punishment, internation-al relations, self-perfection, beneficence, gratitude, respect, and friendship presuppose general assumptions about the human condition. He argued that some acts are morally wrong, whatever the consequences, but he knew, as any sensible person does, that at some level *consequences matter.*[5] He held, for example, that we have duties to preserve our health, promote the happiness of others, and work toward world peace. One cannot even begin to do these things without estimating the probable consequences of our acts.

---

[4] These two tasks of fundamental moral philosophy in the *Groundwork* were to "seek out" and "establish" the supreme principle of morality: Kant (2002), 193 [4: 390].

[5] Consequentialists hold that *nothing but* consequences, and perhaps a few "side constraints," ulti-mately matter, and Kant is no consequentialist in this sense. Kantian moral reasoning to particular moral conclusions, however, is complex and consequences are potentially relevant at certain stages though constrained by certain principles and procedures. It should be noted that any substantive moral principle that constrains choice, even if justified by a procedure that takes consequences into account, will exclude in the particular case consideration of facts (including consequences) about anything but the criteria for judging the case as falling under the principle. As an absolute principle "Never lie," whatever its grounds, prohibits considering any facts beyond the criteria for determining what would be a lie in the case (among which, for example, is that my saying certain words now will likely cause the other person to believe what I think is false). Even a qualified principle, such as "Be truthful, except when deception is necessary to save lives and is directed to a person making an immoral threat (and other specified conditions)" says, in effect, "In the absence of these circumstances, you must not tell a lie regardless of *further* consequences." That substantive moral principles exclude (further) consequences in *this* way is not a radical Kantian thought but a thought that few, if any, who acknowledge genuine moral principles (in contrast with act-consequentialist "rules of thumb") would deny.

II.2. A Good Will: The Core Feature of a Morally Good Person

After describing his methodology, Kant begins his actual investigation with the famous assertion that *only a good will is good without qualification*. This thesis, he implies, is inherent in our ordinary rational cognition of morality. The basic point here is that what a rational and good person would seek and preserve, no matter what else must be sacrificed, is a *good will*—a basic commitment to do what is right, whatever the circumstances. Without this no one can be a morally good person. Other traits can be useful and admirable but are not essential or sufficient for basic moral goodness. Kant emphasizes that a good will expresses itself only in acts from duty, but insofar as a good will is a stable disposition over time one can *have* a good will even when acting from other motives. The moral goodness of a person, then, is not determined by *how many* "morally worthy" *acts* the person does from duty. That may depend in part on the moral challenges that the person faces. A person blessed with few temptations is not necessarily a worse person than others because she faced fewer occasions that called for explicit thoughts of duty.[6] A good will can serve as a *back-up* motivational commitment even when we are doing things for other reasons. We play games for fun, but a good person is ready to stop to help others in emergency situations. Often we help from love, not duty, but a person with a good will is ready to help, if necessary, even when wishing to do something else. Kant argues that the freedom presupposed in moral agency entails that whether or not we have a good will is up to us, not empirically determined. By contrast, our desires, our feelings, and the *effects* of our actions are often beyond our control.

II.3. Morally Worthy Acts and Acts Commendable in Other Respects

Kant turns next from evaluation of persons to evaluation of acts. His central point is well-known and often criticized: *assuming that an act accords with duty,*

---

[6] This interpretation may be controversial because Kant seems to imply (and *at times* it seems true) that to do what is right from nonmoral motives is a moral failing. Consider a teacher who never gives her favorite student (who happens to deserve high marks) a low grade *simply because she likes him*, with no thought of her duty as a teacher. At least in the case of various negative duties, however, there is no adequate reason to suppose that Kant was committed to the implausible idea that on each occasion on which one satisfies the requirement from a nonmoral motive one is morally deficient. For example, well-contented people who pass up many unwanted opportunities to commit suicide because they want to live need not be considered guilty of anything so long as, with a good will, they stand ready to avoid suicide when tempted and when it would be an escape from responsibilities.

it has moral worth if and only if it is done from duty.[7] To act from duty is to do something because it is right, not because it is profitable or immediately agreeable. The more difficult question is what is "moral worth"? The key is its connection with the essential feature of a good person: *morally worthy acts manifest a good will in action* whereas other acts do not. This is the feature that Kant was concerned about for purposes of his argument: his aim in *Groundwork* I was to "seek out" the supreme moral principle by asking, "On what principle is a good person acting when moved by the attitude or commitment essential to morally good persons?"[8] Kant's initial answer is: a person with a good will, when acting as such, does what is right, regardless of rewards and punishments. This account is later expanded: for human beings, acts motivated by a good will reflect the agents' *respect for the moral law* rather than their desire for a particular end. Finally, the principle of a good will in action is said to be *"Conform to universal law,"* which is all too quickly transformed into the famous first formulation of the Categorical Imperative: *"Act only on that maxim by which you can at the same time will that it should become a universal law."* The details of the argument are not necessary here. The point is that Kant's famous claim about morally worthy acts is not presented as a complete theory about how to assess the moral value of acts, still less a complete theory about how to assess character. To the contrary, it is a step, arguably even an unnecessary step, in an early argument to identify a fundamental criterion of right action.

The practical, forward-looking message of Kant's claim is that one should strive to be the sort of person who takes the fact that something is morally required as a sufficient reason for doing it. This does not mean that we should be always thinking of duty, especially not that we must always be focused on Kant's abstract principles. Kant suggests that traits of character other than a good will, such as moderation and self-control, can be (morally) commendable provided the agent also has a good will.[9] Later he adds that it is "an indirect duty to cultivate the compassionate natural (aesthetic) feelings

---

[7] Kant (2002), 199–201 [4: 397–9].

[8] At this point Kant's strategy of argument bears some resemblance to the idea in virtue ethics that we need to determine what is right to do by considering what a good or virtuous person would do. A significant difference is that Kant seeks a general *principle*, not particular judgments, by this strategy. Also his conception of a person with a good will is apparently different from the "thicker" ideas of a virtuous person typical of virtue ethics.

[9] Ibid., 195–6 [4: 393–4].

in us," and so such compassion has moral value at least as a trait that good persons must seek to cultivate.[10] Even if they are not done from duty, acts that manifest these traits may also be commendable as such, provided the agent has a good will (as a standing commitment and "back-up" motive). Kant does assert, however, that *only acts from duty* have the special kind of value he calls *moral worth*. To reconcile these ideas, we must distinguish between two perspectives from which we may evaluate the moral value of acts. One perspective focuses on the agents' commitment (or will) to act as they should; the other focuses on the agents' success in cultivating and exemplifying character traits that help us to live a moral life and achieve our moral ends. Because they manifest a good will, *acts from duty* are worthy of *esteem as instances of the agents' willingness* to live up to moral standards, even when otherwise inclined. Because they stem from character traits that, for moral reasons, everyone should *try* to cultivate, *acts that demonstrate moderation, self-control, and even sympathy* may be *commendable as exemplifying ideals that we should strive for*, even if success in cultivating these traits is not entirely up to us. Once we make the distinction, we see that, though Kant insisted that a good will and acts from duty have a special kind of moral value, he agreed with the common opinion that other character traits and acts can also have a kind of moral value that is undeniably important.

II.4. Moral and Nonmoral Reasons

Kant begins his argument in *Groundwork* II by considering the nature of *"ought" judgments in general* and then what is distinctive about the *idea of moral duty*. This chapter, like the previous one, aims to "seek out" the supreme principle of morality by an analytic mode of argument. It aims to discover the deep sources of morality presupposed in the common idea that we are subject to moral requirements that are distinct from the requirements of efficiency and prudence. The idea of duty serves as the second of two *starting points in Kant's initial investigation*, but it is the idea of *autonomy, not duty*, that he finds to be *the source of morality*. A good will and duty are *first for expository purposes*, but rational autonomy is *primary for purposes of deep explanation and justification*.

---

[10] Kant (1996a), 205 [6: 457].

"Ought" judgments in general, on Kant's analysis, purport to express "objective principles" that are "necessitating" for "imperfect wills."[11] In other words, they purport to say what we have good reason to do, and so "must" do, even though we might not. If justified, a judgment that one "ought" or "must" do something affirms an *imperative*—that is, a requirement of *reason* expressed in a form appropriate for those who do not automatically do what is rational.

Some "ought" judgments are nonmoral, for example, "You ought to practice shooting free throws" and "You ought to stop and smell the roses." Here the reasons for the prescriptions are dependent on the prescribed act serving as a means to an end the agent happens to want: for example, to improve as a basketball player and to be happy. Other "ought" judgments are moral: for example, "You ought to keep your solemn promises" and "You ought not to kill people for profit." Here, Kant argues, the predominant reason is not that the prescribed act or omission serves the ends you happen to have. And you cannot render the requirement inapplicable to you simply by altering your ends. In Kant's terms, the first "ought" judgments are *hypothetical imperatives*; the second (moral) "ought" judgments are *categorical imperatives*.[12] If they are genuinely rational requirements, they derive ultimately from a fundamental principle of rationality. In the first case, the principle seems to be "One ought to take the necessary means within one's power to the ends one wills, or else revise or abandon the ends." Commentators sometimes call this "the Hypothetical Imperative." In the second (moral) case, the fundamental principle is what Kant calls "the Categorical Imperative," and he argues that it can be expressed in several ways.

Three formulations should be mentioned, though they are not my main focus here. Famously, the first says: "Act only on that maxim by which you can at the same time will that it should become a universal law."[13] In other words, it is wrong to act on basic policies that you cannot reasonably choose as policies that others may (or should) follow. The second, equally influential, formulation says: "Act in such a way that you treat humanity, whether in your own person or in any other person, always at the same time as an end, never merely as a means."[14] On one reading, this says essentially that

---

[11] Kant (2002), 214–15 [4: 413–14].   [12] Ibid., 215–18 [4: 413–17].
[13] Ibid. 222 [4: 421].   [14] Ibid. 230 [4: 429].

we should treat all persons in ways consistent with their dignity as rational beings. Dignity is "an unconditional and incomparable worth," above all price, and without equivalent. A third formulation is "Act on the maxims of a universally law-giving member of a merely possible kingdom of ends."[15] Briefly, the point is that the general moral requirements on everyone are those that rational and autonomous persons would prescribe or "legislate" for all from an appropriate legislative perspective that is modeled on an analogy with an ideal commonwealth where everyone is both author and subject of the laws.

These topics—categorical and hypothetical imperatives and the formulations of the fundamental moral principle—are the most often discussed features of Kant's ethics, but for comparison with virtue ethics I want to highlight just two points, often neglected. First, although Kant notoriously endorsed certain strict prohibitions (for example, against lying) as unqualified, inflexible requirements, arguably the strictness of his personal convictions on these particular matters is neither inherent in the idea of a categorical imperative nor derivable from his fundamental moral principle. By definition, a categorical imperative is a principle of the form "Ought never..." or "Always ought..." and we cannot avoid its demands simply by revising our ends. But the concept of a categorical imperative allows that the principle itself may contain built-in qualifications, and Kant implicitly acknowledges this. For example, Kant apparently thought that it is a categorical imperative never to kill another human being except in self-defense, a just war, or legally authorized execution. Moreover, some categorical imperatives prescribe the adoption of general ends, such as the development of one's talents and the happiness of others. These requirements do not say definitely when, how much, or in what ways one should pursue the moral end, but rather leave details to judgment and choice in particular contexts.

Second, as Kant analyzes moral imperatives, they combine two distinct elements: (*a*) an affirmation that there are sufficient, overriding reasons to act in a certain way and (*b*) an implication that we are constrained to do the act, contrary to what we may want. The former is inherent in the idea that categorical imperatives express "objective principles." The latter is implicit in the rather demanding vocabulary: "must," "ought," "imperative," and

---

[15] Ibid. 239 [4: 439]; see also 233–5 [4: 433–4].

"necessitating." Now, for various reasons, Kant concentrates on cases where both elements are apt: there is a rational requirement and we are disinclined to fulfill it. But the elements can come apart in other cases. For example, those who simply acquire their moral beliefs from authorities may accept that *they are constrained* to do or avoid certain acts though *they have no awareness of the reasons* for doing or avoiding them. Alternatively, we may be well *aware of the reasons* but *lack any sense of constraint*—because we are not in the slightest tempted to do otherwise on the occasion. These distinctions are important because they open up the possibility that we might often act from our recognition of the good moral reasons behind a categorical prescription without the sort of reluctant, unhappy, self-sacrificing attitude commonly associated with the idea of "acting out of duty." Arguably, even by Kant's criteria, such acts should be counted as "morally worthy" because they manifest a good will insofar as they are motivated by good moral reasons. Kant himself did not address the possibility of such unconstrained moral acts, perhaps because he was so pessimistic about human inclinations and so keen to emphasize that a moral life can be hard and demanding. But the possibility is not ruled out by the basic elements of his theory.

III. Kantian Virtue

A good will is the essential feature of a morally good person, but virtue is more than a good will. In *The Metaphysics of Morals* Kant gives an account of virtue as strength of moral will, something that requires time and practice to develop.[16] A good will is a fundamental commitment to doing what is right, despite obstacles, but a good will may be weak. A virtuous person has a will that is both good and strong. It is not only able but fully ready to overcome inclinations to act contrary to duty, and it does so effectively and without wavering before temptation. One has particular virtues insofar as one has a strong will to fulfill the various moral requirements of justice, truthfulness, self-improvement, beneficence, gratitude, respect, and so on. The common core of virtue, however, is a good and strong will to do what is right.

---

[16] Kant (1996a) 145–6 [6: 380], 148–9 [6: 383–4], 151 [6: 387], 153 [6: 390], 156–7 [6: 394–5], 163–8 [6: 404–10], 223 [6: 479–80]; Kant (1997b) 72 [5: 84–5] and 107 [5: 128].

The basic idea here may seem familiar, but to understand it in the context of Kant's philosophy requires some background. Once the idea is placed in this larger context we can see what is special about it. In particular, Kant's idea of strength of will contrasts sharply with empiricist conceptions, and it raises special problems.

The background includes prominently Kant's ideas of inclination, practical reason, and will (in two senses). Briefly, we have *inclinations* by nature and social influence. These are feelings and dispositions of which we are aware empirically—impulses, desires, aversions, and steady interests.[17] They are not all self-directed even though Kant classifies maxims based on them under "self-love."[18] We can try to cultivate or rid ourselves of particular inclinations, but our ability to do so is limited. Inclinations and feelings are often obstacles to clear thinking and right acting, but in themselves they are neither good nor bad.[19] They provide impetus to action, but they are not to be seen as sufficiently determining causes.

As human beings we also have *reason*, theoretical and practical.[20] *Theoretical reason* enables us to discern facts about what there is (the world as it appears) through logic, fundamental concepts of understanding, science, and everyday learning processes. *Practical reason* enables us to discern the fundamental principles of what we ought to do. It can guide deliberation, judgment, and choice, not merely telling us what is right but disposing us to act accordingly.[21] In his later work Kant distinguishes two senses of *will*—a power of choice (*Willkür*) and a rational legislative will (*Wille*).[22] Neither is an empirically observable "thing," but we need ideas of both to make sense of moral deliberation and judgment. Rational legislative will (*Wille*) is an aspect of practical reason, metaphorically represented as the will of an authority (reason), which is necessarily a part of each rational agent, and this authority "legislates" to the agent universal principles of conduct. As rational human agents we cannot help but feel respect for this authority, and yet its prescriptions often conflict with our inclinations. The result is not a mere battle of opposing forces, for we also have a power of (free) choice

---

[17] See e.g. Kant (2002), 215 n. [4: 414 n.].

[18] Kant (1997b), 19–20 [5: 22–3].

[19] Kant (1998b), 46–7 [6: 20–2] and 57–8 [6: 34–5]. But see also (2002), 229 [4: 428].

[20] Kant (1997b) 2–5 [5: 4–6].

[21] Ibid. 29 [5: 32].

[22] Kant (1996a), 13 [6: 213] and 18 [6: 226]. Gregor translates *Willkür* as *choice* and *Wille* as *will*.

(*Willkür*). When inclinations and rational dispositions conflict, we must presume that we are able to choose and are responsible for our choices.[23]

Our actions are interpreted as based on *maxims* reflecting our intentions, ends, and (sometimes) underlying reasons.[24] At least for morally significant cases, we must view ourselves as acting on freely chosen rationales, not merely exhibiting behavior that is the product of causal forces. When we act from inclination, we are not causally determined by forces within us but instead we "incorporate" the inclination into a maxim on which we freely choose to act.[25] Or so, for moral purposes, we must suppose. For example, we must see ourselves as freely adopting the policy or intention to satisfy our lust rather than supposing that the lust causally determines our behavior. What is presupposed here is *freedom in a negative sense*—an ability to act without being causally determined or unavoidably motivated by empirical factors beyond our control ("alien causes").[26] This, Kant argues, is inseparable from *autonomy of the will*, or freedom in a positive sense.[27] The core of this idea is that as rational agents we are able and disposed to guide our conduct by rational principles of conduct that are not desire-based, do not merely prescribe taking means to our ends, and yet are products of our own reason. As human beings that have both inclinations that often oppose reason and a (negatively free) power of choice, unfortunately we do not always express our autonomy by following those rational principles. Nevertheless only mistaken moral theories deny that moral agents have it.[28]

Particular maxims or rationales may be good, bad, or indifferent, and Kant acknowledges maxims of different levels of generality. The *Groundwork* provides examples of relatively specific maxims regarding suicide, lying promises, neglect of talents, and helping others.[29] Later Kant refers to fundamental, life-governing maxims reflecting one's deep and persistent priorities when morality and self-interest conflict.[30] Here our choices are more limited: the only good choice is that of a good will, which has a basic commitment to prioritize morality over self-interest. Any other choice is

---

[23] Kant (2002), 247–8 [4: 447–8]; (1997b), 37–44 [5: 42–50]; Kant (1996a), 18–19 [6: 226–7].
[24] Kant (2002), 202 n. [4: 402 n.] and 222 n. [4: 421 n.]; Kant (1996a), 17–18 [6: 225–6].
[25] Kant (1998b), 48–9 [6: 23–4].
[26] Kant (2002), 246 [4: 446].
[27] Ibid. 246 [4: 446], 231–5 [4: 431–4], and 240–1 [4: 440–1].
[28] Ibid. 241–5 [4: 441–4].
[29] Ibid. 222–4 [4: 421–3].
[30] Kant (1998b), 45–60 [6: 19–39]. See also Kant (1997b), 17–24 [5: 19–26].

evil. This is the background for Kant's distinction between human tenden-cies to weakness, impurity, and depravity.[31] Human beings, in Kant's view, are never fiendishly evil in the sense of willing to do evil for evil's sake.[32] Moral *depravity* is the systematic subordination of morality to self-love in one's fundamental, life-governing maxim.

Impurity consists in having an unstable, ultimately incoherent mixture of conflicting elements in one's basic maxim, manifesting a failure to make an unqualified commitment to either morality or self-love. A person with an impure moral will may, for example, adopt as a basic maxim "I will do what is morally required, unless the cost is too high."[33] Neither a morally *depraved* person nor a morally *impure* person is committed to the unconditional moral law as a life-governing maxim, and therefore neither has a *good will* in the primary sense of the *Groundwork*.[34]

A morally *weak* person, by contrast, has a fundamentally good will but lacks virtue. That is, such persons incorporate the moral law into their life-governing maxim, giving it in principle priority over self-love, but they deviate from the moral law on particular occasions because they have not developed a sufficiently *strong* will to do what is right. As Kant says, the

---

[31] Kant (1998b), 52–4 [6: 29–31]. Kant introduces the terms to describe "propensities" to evil in human nature in contrast to several "predispositions" to what is basically good (ibid. 50–2 [6: 26–8]). I extend the terms to characterize those who have voluntarily incorporated these propensities into their basic, life-governing maxims.

[32] Ibid. 58 [6: 35]; Kant (1996a), 160 [6: 399–400] and 208 [6: 461].

[33] The incoherence of this position stems from the fact that Kant understands a "moral requirement" (or duty), when fully stated, as an unconditional imperative, expressible as "Do (or avoid) X, regardless of how it affects your contingent interests." Thus the mixed maxim would be, in effect, "I will do what is morally required, *regardless of how it affects my interests* but *only if it does not too much damage my interests*." Note, however, that this point is compatible with thinking that sometimes effects on one's own contingent interests are relevant in deciding the specific content of a moral requirement, for example whether one must give absolutely all one's goods to the poor.

[34] In the *Groundwork* Kant does not explicitly distinguish a *good will* and *virtue*, but it is clear that a "will" (or resolve or firm intention) to act as moral law requires is at least the core of both. At (2002), 196 [4: 394] Kant describes a good will as not "merely a wish but a summoning of every means in our power." This implies that a person with a good will exerts (or at least intends to exert) every effort to follow moral requirements. This is characteristic of virtue, but it is unclear at this point whether it necessarily includes the virtuous person's *strength or fortitude of will*, a developed moral resolve that is persistent and effective over time. At ibid. 253–4 [4: 454–5] Kant writes of a "malicious villain" as "conscious of possessing a good will which, on his own admission, constitutes the law for his evil will as a member of the world of sense—a law of whose authority he is conscious even while transgressing it." At this point "a good will" seems to refer to what Kant later identifies as a rational legislative will (*Wille*) rather than an adoption through a free power of choice (*Willkür*) of a basic, life-governing maxim to follow the moral law. A malicious villain might have a "good will" in that sense (*Wille*) even though morally depraved (as opposed to morally weak or virtuous).

weakness or "frailty (*fragilitas*) of human nature is expressed even in the complaint of the Apostle: 'What I would, that I do not!' i.e. I incorporate the good (the law) into the maxim of my power of choice, but this good, which is an irresistible incentive objectively or ideally (*in thesi*), is subjectively (*in hypothesi*) the weaker (in comparison with inclination) whenever the maxim is to be followed."[35]

It is moral weakness that is especially important for understanding how *virtue* is more than a *good will*. Those who in their basic life-governing maxims yield to the propensities to impurity or depravity lack a good will: they have no commitment to moral standards as unconditional requirements. As moral agents, both inevitably have a rational legislative will (*Wille*) and so feel respect for morality, and therefore they are liable to suffer for their wrongdoing the self-disapproval that Kant pictures metaphorically as a sentence in the inner court of conscience.[36] Unlike the impure and the depraved, morally weak persons have a good will—the basic life-governing maxim that expresses their most fundamental choice regarding morality and self-interest places morality above self-interest, unconditionally, in case of conflict. They have a good will, then, but lack virtue because their will to live by this basic commitment is weak. Virtue requires a good and strong will. But how are we to understand this?

Because we are responsible for our basic, life-governing maxims, these must be represented as due to our free power of choice (*Willkür*). Those who are *depraved* have elected (by *Willkür*) to subordinate the prescriptions of their rational legislative will (*Wille*) to self-love and those who are *impure* have chosen to accept only *qualified* conditional versions of those prescriptions. Thus neither has a good will. The *morally weak* have a basic commitment (through *Willkür*) to follow the full, unqualified prescriptions of their rational legislative will (*Wille*), but they fail to live up to this commitment on some particular occasions. (If they failed readily and regularly, however, we would naturally doubt that they had the basic commitment.) They have a good will, but, as we say, it is weak. By contrast, the fully *virtuous* have the same basic commitment (through *Willkür*) but, unlike the weak, they do not deviate from it on particular occasions. This is because they have a developed strength of moral will to overcome the obstacles of inclination. Their will is both good and strong.

---

[35] Kant (1998*b*), 53 [6: 29].   [36] Kant (1996*a*), 188–91 [6: 437–40].

The question remains: How are we to understand strength and weakness here? In Kant's view, those who do wrong through moral weakness, though better than the impure and the depraved, are nevertheless directly responsible for their wrongdoing.[37] Their weakness, then, is not a disability, like underdeveloped or atrophied muscles. Thus the special strength of moral will that virtuous persons have (and the morally weak lack) cannot then be literally the capacity or ability to do right despite contrary inclinations because, having a free power of choice, even the morally weak have that capacity. We cannot free ourselves from responsibility for serious wrongdoing by citing the weakness of our will to do right, as if this is a disability such as a physical weakness that causes us to fail in an attempt to rescue someone drowning. Kant suggests that we should take a charitable view toward others' weakness, but, strictly speaking, his theory implies that we must suppose that they too have the capacity and freedom to do whatever morality requires.

Kant also rejects the position (for example, of Thomas Hobbes and David Hume) that choices between good and bad are ultimately to be explained by whether the agents' broader-based desires and sentiments were causally more efficacious than their more immediate, impulsive ones. Moral weakness, then, is not simply a matter of having dispositions to act rightly that have *greater force* than our dispositions to act wrongly. By his own admission, indeed insistence, the exercise of agency (or "will") cannot be explained or comprehended theoretically, either in empirical or metaphysical terms.[38] So strength and weakness of will, as conceived in moral discourse, must be treated as metaphorical (or "noumenal") ideas needed and valid only for practical purposes. Thus we cannot expect references to strength and weakness of moral will to provide a "nuts and bolts" type of causal explanation. These are not terms that fit into any empirical science, though Kant grants that any "phenomena" associated with morally significant acts, indeed any acts, can also be viewed from an empirical perspective that presupposes causal determinants.

---

[37] This is entailed by Kant's repeated insistence that we can do what we ought. Even the innate human "propensity" to moral weakness, Kant held, must be seen as chosen, despite any apparent empirical evidence to the contrary: (1998b), 52–5 [6: 29–32]. Insofar as moral weakness is merely "want of virtue," as evidenced by neglect (rather than principled rejection) of imperfect duties (beneficence, etc.), it is not "vice" but "lack of moral strength" (of "resolution") and assessed as "a deficiency in moral worth," (1996a), 153 [6: 390].

[38] Kant (2002), 254–62 [4: 455–63].

Drawing from the previous chapter, here is one way we might interpret or reconstruct Kant's position. The morally weak, unlike the virtuous, act contrary to their own basic commitment (good will) to place morality above self-love in their lives, but they fail to live up to this commitment, too often, on particular occasions. When they fail, doing wrong through weakness, they are morally responsible. Therefore, by Kant's theory, they choose (through *Willkür*) to act on the particular occasion contrary to their basic, life-governing maxim regarding self-love and morality (to which they are also committed through *Willkür*). This cannot be simply a momentary change of mind or heart—as if one could choose on every day but Saturdays to treat morality as unconditionally and always prior to self-interest but then on Saturdays suddenly choose to make an exception of Saturdays, and then on Sundays again revert to the unconditional commitment, week after week. This is not a coherent picture, especially if the basic, life-governing maxim is viewed (as Kant presents it in *Religion*) as somehow representing a person's most fundamental choice over time.[39] The supposed "flip-flopper" or Saturdays-only immoralist is more plausibly seen as having a morally impure will, which for Kant remains a form of "evil."[40] The morally weak, then, must be viewed as having two conflicting maxims at the time of weak-willed wrongdoing: a basic maxim to conform to morality's unconditional requirements and a shorter-term maxim reflecting an intention to indulge self-love on the particular occasion despite its conflict with morality and their own fundamental commitments. To preserve responsibility, in Kant's theory both must be choices through our power of choice (*Willkür*). There is, so to speak, a double conflict of will here: one freely chooses on a particular occasion (through *Willkür*) to act contrary to one's basic choice to prioritize morality (an act of *Willkür*) and in violation of the inevitable demands of one's own rational legislative will (*Wille*). The virtuous person has neither kind of inner conflict.

This reconstruction raises a number of potentially troubling questions, which I can address only briefly here. First, we may ask, when someone does wrong through moral weakness, *what* is weak? We commonly say that the person's *will* was weak, but how does this play out in Kant's terms? The person's power of choice (*Willkür*) is presumed to have the freedom, or ability, to act independently of the causal force of inclinations. So it cannot

---

[39] (1998b), 61–73 [6: 39–53].   [40] Ibid. 53 [6: 30].

be utterly weak in the sense "incapable of choosing" to do right. To conjecture that it is a "diminished capacity" to choose is to invoke empirical analogies that do not fit well with Kant's theory of agency. Nor is it necessary to invoke a "weak muscle" imagery to explain why pleading moral weakness tends to reduce blame but does not excuse wrongdoing. Those who lie or steal through moral weakness still have a basic commitment to morality and so at least have a conflict of will about the lying or stealing. They may be blamed less than those who behave similarly from an immoral policy that they wholeheartedly endorse, whether they follow the policy passionately or from cold, calculated self-interest.[41] The difference is not in what they *can* do, or can easily do, but in whether their bad act is a deviation, albeit a voluntary deviation, from their persisting, overall commitment to act well or rather a reflection of their bad fundamental commitments.

An alternative reconstruction would attribute the weakness to the agents' rational legislative will (*Wille*). At least one passage supports this interpretation, but it is apt to be more misleading than helpful.[42] The interpretation suggests that the explanation for wrongdoing through moral weakness is a deficiency in the agents' basic moral *capacities*: a crucial aspect of their practical reason (*Wille*) is substandard, unable to function effectively as it does in the virtuous. This invites us, when morally weak, to blame our equipment rather than our choices, which is hardly a Kantian idea. Moreover, attributing the weakness to the agents' rational legislative (*Wille*) still seems to reflect and reinforce the idea of moral conflict as a tug-of-war between two opposing forces, reason and inclination, leaving responsibility for choice out of the picture. We might say, speaking loosely, that practical

---

[41] Kant implies that, other things equal, the degree of culpability for a wrongdoing is greater when the agent acts deliberately on a fixed bad policy than when giving in to strong inclinations (presumably against a moral disposition). He writes: "*Subjectively*, the degree to *which an action can be imputed (imputabilitas)* has to be assessed by the magnitude of the obstacles that had to be overcome.... [T]he less the natural obstacles ['of sensibility'] and the greater the obstacle from grounds of duty, so much the more is a transgression to be imputed (as culpable).—Hence the state of mind of the subject, whether he committed the deed in a state of agitation or with cool deliberation, makes a difference in imputation, which has results," (1996a), 19–20 [6: 228]. Note that what mitigates culpability is not that the agent acts in an emotional state, which would not lessen the blame of those passionately committed to their immoral policies. It is the "state of agitation" that reveals a moral commitment in conflict with temptation that shows the weak wrongdoer's deed not as bad as the whole-hearted wrongdoer's otherwise similar deed.

[42] Ibid. 165 [6: 407].

reason (or *Wille*) was not as strong in the morally weak wrongdoers as in the virtuous, but, to avoid misunderstanding, we should avoid thinking of this as an explanation of failure due to defective *capacities*. Instead, we can view the expression as a loose, metaphorical way of describing someone who tends to yield to strong inclinations that are contrary to both their practical reason (*Wille*) and their fundamentally good will. Moral practical reason both *directs* and *predisposes* everyone to do what is right despite contrary inclinations, and in addition the morally weak (like the virtuous) have a *basic commitment* to do what is right. We might say that sometimes *all* of this "on the side" of moral practical reason (*Wille*) may not be "strong enough," as it were, to defeat the "other side"—strong contrary inclinations.[43] We would do better, however, to attribute moral weakness simply to the *agents* them-selves, or their particular choices, rather than to their moral capacities—*Wille* and *Willkür*. In a manner of speaking, they *will weakly* to do what is right, though they have adequate capacities to do otherwise.

How could this be so? Kant does not explain, and attempts to make sense of the idea must respect central points in Kant's action theory, especially that we act on maxims and that reason and inclination are not literally two opposing forces (phenomenal or noumenal). A first step might be to think of an individual's willing basic maxims on analogy with a governing body's exercising its power to adopt binding policies and regulations for its own members as well as others. Imagine it functions under a constitution that defines and limits its legitimate aims and activities, just as the fundamental moral laws of practical reason (*Wille*) impose limits on what basic maxims individuals can legitimately, or rightfully, adopt as their life-governing policies. The governing body may adopt rules and policies that are, in a sense, weak or strong, depending on their content. They are relatively weak insofar as they are vague and indeterminate about what is prohibited (or required) and relatively unspecific about the means of implementation. Weak policies are especially open to disagreements in interpretation, to self-deceptive special pleading, and to irregular and ineffective efforts at implementation. Similarly, in many cases moral weakness might be partially

---

[43] It is noteworthy that in the troublesome passage where Kant seems to treat virtue as an aptitude "not as a property of choice (*Willkür*) but of will (*Wille*)," he characterizes the latter as "a faculty of desire that, *in adopting a rule*, also gives itself a universal law (my italics)." Here "will" (*Wille*) seems to refer to more than merely the aspect of practical reason that rationally *legislates* moral laws and *predisposes* even the worst moral agents to follow them.

understood as a matter of individuals' incorporating the moral law into their basic life-governing maxim but in a somewhat vague and indeterminate form and without any specification about how to carry it out in the face of obstacles. This allows us to think that they still have the same fundamental moral commitment even though sometimes they willfully deviate from it. Their will of the moment is in conflict with their fundamental will to be moral, partly because the content of that will was weak, in a sense. But, assuming they were at least dimly aware of the conflict, this sort of weakness is not an excusing incapacity. Their basic maxim that gave precedence to morality over self-love was, in a sense, a weak maxim. It was not, however, the immoral basic maxim of a person who yields to the propensity to "impurity," for that would include acknowledged exceptions, as in "I will behave as morality prescribes except when this calls for significant sacrifices."

This sort of explanation would not, of course, account for morally weak deviations from explicit and definite basic maxims that even anticipate and specify how to guard against and manage contrary inclinations. Here we seem to need the idea that a person can will a fully explicit and definite moral maxim, specific about means of implementation, but will it so weakly that deviations still make sense even though they are not excusable. The appropriate analogy might be a school board that, by full vote and repeated decisions of principle, adopts, reaffirms, and usually follows a "zero-tolerance" policy for expelling illegal drug users. When the mayor's son is caught with drugs, let us imagine, they give in to political pressure and make an unjustified exception. To make sense of the idea that they still, in a sense, hold the policy and yet knowingly deviate from it, we perhaps need to attribute to them imperfectly rational mental states and dispositions, regret, a guilty conscience, and a "will" to change. If so, we might say that they willed the zero-toleration policy, it remained their basic governing policy, but they failed to implement it in this particular case, without excuse. They willed the policy more weakly, we might say, than a different governing board that resisted all pressures to deviate from it. Some cases of moral weakness, perhaps, give evidence of a moral commitment, or will, that is weak in an analogous way. That is, our basic commitment over time was to an explicit and specific basic maxim to do what is right but, as imperfectly rational beings, we were capable of conflicts of will, choosing sometimes on particular occasions to deviate from deeper commitments that we never abandoned.

As Kant leads us to expect, such descriptions do not satisfy the criteria of empirical, scientific explanations, but I suspect that nevertheless they echo common moral thinking on these matters. And, from Kant's point of view, an advantage is that these ways of thinking do not treat reason, will, and inclinations as opposing forces of the same sort and they allow us to interpret morally significant acts as based on maxims. There remains, however, much that is puzzling and incomplete about this account. For example, some explanation is needed about why Kant allows (with Aristotle) that time and practice are required to develop virtue.[44] As strength of moral will, virtue does not consist in good habits and trained dispositions, but, like those, it cannot be acquired at will. What morally weak persons need is not, strictly, more power, ability, or habits of choice and feeling, but a better use of capacities they are presumed to have to adopt and implement a commitment to morality.

To conclude this section, I want to emphasize that my aim has been to sketch broadly Kantian ways of understanding some puzzling ideas in Kant's ethics and to suggest connections with familiar moral thoughts, but not to defend these ideas as correct or even strictly Kant's views. I turn now to some equally broad, and perhaps provocative, comparisons of Kantian ethics with "virtue ethics."

IV. A Brief Comparison: Kant's Ethics and "Virtue Ethics"

Finally, and all too briefly, let us take a look at some main themes commonly associated with virtue ethics to see how Kant's ethics compares. Here I will comment on four main points: (1) the need for moral rules, (2) sensitivity to particular contexts, (3) morally good motivation, and (4) the standard for right action.

IV.1. Are Moral Rules Necessary?
Advocates of virtue ethics tend to deny or downplay any need for moral rules, and they especially object to strict, inflexible moral rules such as Kant's

---

[44] e.g. Kant (1996a), 158–9 [6: 397].

absolute prohibition on telling lies. First consider: Do we need rules of conduct at all? Where does Kant stand? In *law*, of course, he thinks we need public, authoritatively legislated, and judicially enforced rules.[45] These should state explicitly what is prohibited and what is required, without incorporating *arbitrary* exceptions; but there is nothing in principle wrong, in Kant's view, with built-in complexities, including *well-grounded* qualifications. The laws, he held, should normally be enforced and obeyed rigorously, but there is one notable exception with implications far beyond what Kant himself envisioned, namely, we should not obey or (presumably) enforce a government's laws or orders if they require us to do anything "intrinsically immoral."[46] Regarding *social rules*, the shared moral codes taught and informally enforced by communities, Kant is remarkably unsupportive. Unlike Mill, who gave such rules a central role in his *Utilitarianism*, Kant relies almost entirely on general principles for law and for individual decision-making instead of informally enforced social codes. Contrary to his reputation, Kant was deeply opposed to moralistic meddling in others' lives: our duty is to promote others' happiness, not to make them good.[47] Even judicial punishment, in his legal theory, is authorized only to prevent interferences with legitimate freedom, not to make wrongdoers suffer because they intrinsically deserve it.[48]

Laws and social codes, then, are not really the issue. Advocates of virtue ethics do not argue that *criminal and civil laws* are unnecessary, and Kant does not argue that *informally enforced social rules* are necessary. What remains controversial is whether *general principles for morally guiding individual moral decisions* are unnecessary. Critics charge that in Kant's theory these constitute a hierarchical system of ethical principles analogous to a legal system, and this legalistic ethics, they argue, serves no good purpose. A better alternative, they sometimes say, is to promote character development through the emulation of virtuous exemplars and the formation of good habits. Kant's position, recall, is that moral principles are sharply distinct from legal rules and, unlike legal rules, their purpose is not to serve as the basis for the mechanisms of public enforcement. The moral principles that he presents in

---

[45] Ibid. 23–34 [6: 229–42], 89–120 [6: 311–51].

[46] Ibid. 136–7 [6: 371] and (1998*b*) 153 n. [6: 154 n.].

[47] Evidence for this is assembled in Hill (1992*a*), 176–95.

[48] Some evidence for this controversial thesis is presented in Byrd (1989), 151–200; Scheid (1989), 262–82; and Hill (2002), 310–39.

his Doctrine of Virtue are a philosopher's attempt to articulate reasonable answers to recurrent moral questions that human beings face despite many differences in their circumstances. The principles are offered, with supporting arguments, in order to convince a reflective, critical audience that *doing what these principles prescribe* is necessary for a morally good life. Moreover, he proposes the principles as considerations that anyone would need to *respect as grounds for their decisions* in order to be fully virtuous. Behind this is Kant's thought that emulation, cultivated sentiments, and good habits are at best aids to virtuous living, not by themselves sufficient. Kant insisted, as in fact Aristotle did also, that judgments of practical reason are also essential; but Kant goes further than Aristotle apparently did in claiming that the grounds on which practical judgment relies can be reliably and usefully articulated (at least by philosophers).

IV.2. Are Kant's Moral Principles Insensitive to Relevant Differences in Contexts?

Advocates of virtue ethics sometimes suggest *any moral rule* is liable to oversimplify the complexities of particular situations, causing rule-followers to neglect morally relevant factors needed for correct judgment. This problem, if it is one, seems to be compounded by Kant because he endorsed rules, such as "Never tell a lie," that are simple, substantive, unqualified, and absolutely inflexible. What can we say on Kant's behalf? First, I think we must agree both that Kant endorsed such principles and that doing so was a mistake. We may question, however, how deep this problem goes in Kant's theory. Arguably, further reflection on the implications of Kant's basic moral framework does not actually support many of his extreme opinions about particular issues, such as lying, "unnatural" sex, and revolution.[49] We should also recall that Kant's main principles, beyond justice, for dealing with other people are "imperfect duties" concerned with moral attitudes and ends, for example, principles of gratitude, beneficence, respect, and friendship.[50] These, as Kant says, prescribe rather indefinite "maxims" rather than specific actions.[51] Whether even these are objectionably insensitive to context, as many of his "perfect duties" are, readers must judge for themselves.

---

[49] Kant (1996*a*), 182–4 [6: 429–31], 178–80 [6: 424–6], and 95–100 [6: 318–25].
[50] Ibid. 198–218 [6: 448–74].   [51] Ibid. 150–6 [6: 385–94].

Underlying the objection, however, may be a deeper issue. Are the grounds for moral judgment so relative to historical, cultural, and particular contexts that they can never be encapsulated in general principles? Particularists of various kinds answer "yes" and so reject moral principles, except as rough and potentially misleading heuristic devices. Most traditional moral philosophers, who were usually far more flexible about rules than Kant was, argue to the contrary that moral judgment presupposes that, at some level, there must be some common grounds for the legitimate variations in particular moral judgments. Bathing in lots of water may be fine in the monsoon season in India but wrong in the drought season in a desert community. There must be some reason, it seems, why the practice is wrong in one context and not the other, and the ultimate reason cannot be just that "that's what people say." Like utilitarians, perfectionists, intuitionists, and others, Kant tries to articulate and defend an account of ultimate and penultimate moral reasons. He expresses these in his fundamental principle (the Categorical Imperative) and some very general choice-guiding derivative principles, many of which are far from the specific "dos" and "don'ts" that critics of rules are most concerned to avoid. A number of Kant's specific principles, for example about sex and lying, are rightly rejected, but we do not need to embrace particularism of various sorts to avoid these.

IV.3. Does Kant Ignore Relevant Features of Good Character and Motivation?

Here again Kant's position is controversial and may be unsatisfactory, but misunderstanding and exaggeration often confuse the issue. Consider first Kant's views about good character. As we have seen, having a *good will* is the essential feature and to be fully virtuous we must have developed, in addition, *strength of will* to do what is right. We have the *particular virtues* of beneficence, gratitude, truthfulness, and so on, when we have a good and strong will to do what is right with respect to helping others, acknowledging our benefactors, communicating with others, and so on.[52] Besides these essential features, Kant acknowledges that there are other morally desirable traits of character (or perhaps personality) that we should try to cultivate, such as sympathetic feelings for others.[53]

---

[52] Ibid. 157 [6: 395].   [53] Ibid. 205 [6: 457].

Kant did not emphasize the need to develop affective sympathy, compassion, and other feelings, perhaps for two reasons. First, he saw British sentimentalism, his main competitor in moral theory, as false and dangerously seductive in its two respects: its explanation of the apparent authority of moral judgments and its idea of what makes acts morally commendable. Thus a major part of Kant's agenda was to emphasize the limitations of the role of feeling and emotion in moral judgment and motivation worthy of moral esteem. Second, he believed that wrongdoing and misguided moral judgment are to a great extent due to the way that passion, affects, and inclinations distort our moral judgment and provide self-deceptive excuses for making ourselves an exception to moral principles that we apply to others. His extreme and perhaps false empirical beliefs on these matters, arguably, bear considerable responsibility for his emphasis on the aspects of the moral life conceptually independent of affect and feeling. Arguably, however, Kant's basic moral theory offers a more expansive role for feeling than Kant himself acknowledged. There are several points to note.

First, Kant did acknowledge some role for feelings in the moral life. Respect for the moral law, and through that for persons, has an affective aspect. In beings like us, he argues, recognition of moral requirements inevitably causes feelings of respect, akin in some ways to fear and awe.[54] Other moral feelings include a kind of satisfaction or "pleasure" at having done what is right, and guilt and diminished self-esteem from having knowingly done wrong.[55] His thesis is not that we lack such feelings but, first, that they are a product of our moral awareness rather than its source and, second, that morally esteem-worthy motivation is not the same as doing what our feelings at the time prompt.[56]

Another point Kant conceded, but did not emphasize, is that we should cultivate positive other-regarding feelings to counteract the negative feelings that tempt us to do wrong, thereby making it easier for us to do our duty. For someone committed always to do what is right, cultivating such positive feelings is among the means, or facilitating conditions, that should be taken. Kant grants that this is true even of the merely "aesthetic" or

[54] Kant (1997b), 62–75 [6: 71–89].
[55] Kant (1996a), 15 [6: 221], 151 [6: 387], and 160 [6: 399–400].
[56] Ibid. 141–2 [6: 375–7].

affective feelings for others, as distinct from the "practical" love and benefi-cence that consists of a commitment to promote others' well-being.[57]

But Kant's basic moral theory has the resources to say much more than this. Two further points in particular he *could* have added. First, from experience it seems that sympathy and compassion are important, and often necessary, to awaken our awareness of the needs of others and the way our choices may affect them. As feminist theorists rightly remind us, sensitivity to others and caring for them is needed to open our eyes to their needs and their suffering. Without these, callous, unfeeling moral agents, no matter how conscientiously determined to do what is right, will blunder repeatedly with potentially disastrous results. In short, affective sensibility provides essential information about the context that no one seriously committed to a moral life can allow him/herself to neglect.

A further point is this. Among the moral principles that Kant (and any reasonable moralist) endorses is a prescription to promote the happiness of others. In fact, the two primary ends Kant proposes in his Doctrine of Virtue are the moral and natural perfection of oneself and the happiness of others.[58] Kant was no expert about what specifically promotes happiness and what hinders it, but Kant's critics (among feminists and virtue theorists, for example) point to empirical facts that (arguably) Kant's basic moral theory requires us to take seriously into account. For example, whether you have genuine affection for your friend while visiting her in the hospital usually matters greatly to the quality of your relationship, to the happiness of your friend, and so to what feelings and attitudes you should cultivate and even to what you should do about visiting now, given how you feel. Cultivating our kindly feelings toward others and trying to transform our tendencies to indifference and feelings of hostility are required for virtually anyone who takes seriously the moral requirement, or desirability, of promoting others' happiness. Similar remarks could be made regarding other moral require-ments that Kant acknowledges, for example, gratitude, friendship, and respect.

There is another point to consider. As Aristotelians remind us, failure to have the feelings morally appropriate to a given context is evidence that the agent is less than fully virtuous. This means, at least in part, that the agent does not have the sort of affective dispositions that we should all aim to

---

[57] Ibid. 198–203 [6: 448–53].   [58] Ibid. 154–6 [6: 391–4].

acquire and that virtuous persons, through long practice by emulating exemplars, have succeeded in making habitual. In other words, according to the Aristotelian, everyone should aim to cultivate dispositions to feel in certain ways in various contexts even though success is not guaranteed because it depends on social setting, the availability of good mentors, and good luck. Having such dispositions to appropriate feelings, on this view, is a mark of a good and "virtuous" person in the sense that it amounts to success in achieving what everyone should strive for but not all can achieve, even with the best of efforts. Let us consider how this view compares with Kant's.

According to Kant, whether we have, or can develop, such traits depends as much on nature as on our good efforts. The mere possession of such traits, such as compassion, does not in itself make us *worthy of moral esteem*, but we can call them *good traits of character* to indicate that they are among the traits that, for moral reasons, we should strive to acquire. Even though Kant himself was inclined to minimize this point, arguably this follows from his basic moral theory together with a realistic understanding of human psychology. If we find someone lacking in the moral feelings we come to expect of everyone, this does not *necessarily* mean that the person is morally bad or blameworthy but it may well be *symptomatic* of real moral failures. This is because, given human nature, if someone is *genuinely committed* to moral principles and *strives to become well suited* for a moral community, then typically that person will develop moral feelings as a natural consequence. Human beings are inescapably sensuous as well as rational. If our commitments, aims, and efforts are sincere, we are inevitably prone to feelings of disappointment when we fail, satisfaction when we succeed, and longings and worries when we are still striving. Similarly, if we genuinely respect others and "make their ends our own," as Kant directs, we are liable to indignation when oppressors abuse them, guilt when we ourselves mistreat them, delight when we see them succeed, and sadness when tragedy strikes them. Because of this, persistent emotional indifference to another's plight virtually always reflects a deeper failure of moral commitment. In Kant's view, moral feelings are the typical products and signs of moral commitment, though not its cause or what makes it worthy of esteem.

Now consider moral motivation. As we have seen, Kant thought that only acts from duty have "moral worth" in his special sense but, if one *has* a good will, acting from other motives in various situations can be appropriate and even commendable as exemplifying good character traits. A virtuous person, for example, may be commendable for caring for her children out of love, rather than duty, assuming that duty would move her if love should fade.

Another point also deserves mention. Critics sometimes ridicule the idea that virtuous people act justly and charitably "merely for the sake of duty" because they assume this means that they are focused on nothing but a lifeless, abstract principle. Understandably, they say, we should be concerned about the real people with whom we are interacting, not conformity to a philosopher's abstract idea. The problem here rests mostly on a misunderstanding, albeit one that Kant's own incautious remarks encourage. Expressions such as "respect for the moral law" and "acting for the sake of duty" call up images of submission to the commands of external authorities, divine and secular, but these images are inappropriate because utterly incompatible with Kant's thesis that the ultimate source of morality is the practical reason and autonomy of all moral agents. Your moral obligations stem from your own reason insofar as you reflect on human problems in a way that appropriately acknowledges the claims of others. In addition, we cannot "respect the moral law" if we disregard its core message. In the formulation most directly concerned with the "matter" or content of the supreme moral principle, Kant says that we must treat all persons as ends in themselves, a status and unconditional value that demand that we treat them with justice, respect, and concern for their (permissible) personal ends as individuals. In acting from a commitment to morality, then, we are rightly focused on the dignity, needs, and aspirations of actual persons rather than merely an empty formula.

IV.4. What Is the Standard of Right Action?

Those associated with virtue ethics hold different views about the standard of right action, but some conceive of the right act as the act that a virtuous person would do in the situation.[59] Now most people, including Kant, would agree with this on one interpretation; but, as stated, the claim is ambiguous. We need to ask: Is the act right because a virtuous person would do it, or would a virtuous person do it because it is right? One cannot have it

---

[59] e.g. Hursthouse (1999), esp. 17, 18, 28–31, 49–52.

both ways. Kant held that, factual errors aside, a virtuous person does what is right because it is right. Then Kant offered criteria of rightness, attempting to draw relatively formal features from the concept of duty as a categorical imperative. Some virtue ethicists, apparently, hold that acts are right because they are what a virtuous person would do. Then they offer various suggestions about how to specify what a virtuous person would do. This position is coherent and understandably motivated by reaction to excessively legalistic moral theories, but nevertheless the position raises questions. For example, in cases where most clearly there is a right thing to do, are the standards of virtuous character by themselves determinate enough to identify the right act? They would be, of course, if virtuous character were defined in part as understanding and respecting the principles of justice, honesty, beneficence, gratitude, friendship, and so on. The difference between virtue ethics and Kantianism might be minimal if virtue ethics were to spell out these independent standards in certain ways. An extreme virtue ethics, however, would deny that there are such independent standards of right action. Arguably, without them, the idea of virtue becomes very thin, too insubstantial to guide our decisions or adequately explain morality.

Kant raises a related objection twice: when criticizing the divine command theory and when arguing that the supreme moral principle cannot be found by studying examples.[60] His point about the divine command theory is this: we could not derive our standards of rightness and goodness from the commands of a powerful deity because in order to *recognize the deity as worthy of obedience* we would *need to rely on our prior understanding* of rightness and goodness. Regarding empirical study of examples, he first notes that, for all we know, there may not be any actual examples of perfect virtue. His deeper point, however, is that trying to find the standards of right and virtue in examples is a fundamentally flawed procedure because *we must already have and apply such standards* in order to *identify* anyone *as an example*. Despite its far-reaching implications, Kant's basic idea in both cases is not radical but rather an idea implicit in ordinary moral thinking: that is, *to be virtuous*—and properly beneficent, grateful, honest, just, and so forth—*just is* in part to know and respect the *prior* reasons for acting rightly. And to respect these independent reasons is ultimately just to acknowledge fully the value of

---

[60] Kant (2002), 243 [4: 443], 208–10 [4: 406–9].

humanity in each person. To be sure, we should *do the things* that a fully virtuous person would and from the *same motives*, but *in moral theory* we should not try to derive our standards of rightness and goodness from alleged instances of perfect virtue, human or divine. And the morally best motive is respect for moral reasons, not a desire to emulate admired exemplars.

7

Kant's Tugendlehre *as Normative Ethics*

1 Introduction

In *The Metaphysics of Morals*, especially the *Tugendlehre* or Doctrine of Virtue, Kant clarifies, develops, and extends ideas that he presented in the *Groundwork for the Metaphysics of Morals* and the *Critique of Practical Reason*.[1] These earlier works attempt to articulate and defend the fundamental moral law, and they argue that all previous moral theories fail to appreciate the autonomy of will that we must attribute to ourselves as rational moral agents. They provide only a few brief examples of how this supreme principle can guide moral deliberation, a task that the *Groundwork* explicitly postpones for a later "metaphysics of morals" (Kant (2002) [4: 391]). Kant published a two-part work of this title late in his life (1797–8), and it is here that we find his fullest official presentation of his normative ethical theory (or here "normative ethics").

My plan is to review and highlight certain features of Kant's normative ethics as I understand it. My focus will be primarily on general features, especially its aim and structure, rather than on specific first-order duties. The discussion will be wide-ranging, though not comprehensive. The interpretations that I propose may be controversial at points, but I shall not defend them here.[2] My hope is that together they present the *Tugendlehre* as a normative ethics that is coherent and contrasts with other normative ethical theories in interesting ways.

---

[1] All references to Kant's works are to the Cambridge Edition, with the exception of those to the *Groundwork*, which are to Kant (2002).

[2] For other perspectives, see Allen Wood, "The Final Form of Kant's Practical Philosophy," and other essays in Timmons (2002).

More specifically, the plan is this: First, I review some features of normative ethics that distinguish it from science, metaphysics, metaethics, and theories of law. Second, I discuss the role of the basic moral principles in Kant's theory and how they relate to more specific principles. Third, I consider Kant's idea of duties to oneself and their relevance to certain contemporary discussions. Fourth, I discuss second-order duties to oneself that anticipate our liability to errors in moral judgment, ulterior motives, and weakness of will. Fifth, I comment briefly on Kant's idea of what should motivate us to fulfill our ethical duties. Finally, I note some ways in which the *Tugendlehre* is incomplete.

2 Normative Ethics

Normative ethics may be distinguished from science, metaphysics, meta-ethics, and theories of law. Kant has much to say about all of these, but they are not the same. The boundaries are sometimes unclear, but rough distinctions should serve well enough here. Normative ethics traditionally proposes general answers to such questions as "What ought I to do?," "What may I do?," "What ends are ultimately worth pursuing?," and "What are features of a morally good person?" These contrast with questions of sociology and psychology, such as "What do people in various groups *believe* about moral requirements, permissions, worthy ends, good character?" and "What are the causal influences on their moral beliefs and behavior?" In the *Tugendlehre* Kant addresses normative ethical questions as distinct from scientific ones. Scientific inquiry uses "theoretical reason" focused on the world as it is—the objects that exist, events that occur, and their causes. In Kant's view, ethics must use "practical reason," which is focused on the ends, conduct, and character that we *ought* to strive for.[3] Insofar as history and anthropology (in Kant's sense) attempt to describe and explain behavior, they too contrast with normative ethics.[4] Even if history

---

[3] Although he never gave a full explanation of "the unity of reason," Kant held that "theoretical reason" and "practical reason" refer to reason used in two different ways, a theoretical use and a practical use ((1997*b*), 100–2 [5: 119–22]; (1965), 617–18 [A776–7/B804–5], 635–6 [A804–6/B832–4]).

[4] When history and anthropology are strictly empirical, they are uses of theoretical reason; but for certain purposes Kant allows moral concerns to shape the interpretation of historical events and to draw practical lessons from descriptive anthropology.

and anthropology never rise to the level of science, they primarily use theoretical reason to investigate what is and has been, rather than what ought to be.

In contemporary philosophy *normative ethics* is also distinct from *metaphysics*. Kant works with a similar distinction, but his term "metaphysic of morals" may mislead readers accustomed to current usage. "Metaphysics" now commonly refers to philosophical inquiry into the most general nature of things that exist ("Being"), including space, time, substance, causation, particularity and generality, and mind and body. Metaphysics is also distinguished from epistemology and empirical science, though the boundaries are sometimes unclear. For Kant "metaphysics" can mean different things, including *unwarranted speculation* about entities beyond our comprehension and an *appropriately modest attempt* to lay out systematically the most general features of things as we can know or justifiably view them. Kant divided the more modest aspirations into *metaphysics of nature* and *metaphysics of morals*. The *Tugendlehre* is Kant's presentation of the part of his metaphysics of morals that is concerned with character and moral ends, as distinct from law and justice. This metaphysics of morals is not speculative metaphysics that tries to use theoretical reason beyond its limits, even though its use of practical reason borrows some "ideas" from speculative metaphysics for its choice-guiding (practical) purposes. A metaphysics of morals is also distinct from a *metaphysics of nature*, which attempts to use theoretical reason, appropriately limited, to develop a system of general principles about the natural world.[5]

By contrast with both speculative metaphysics and a metaphysics of nature, Kant's metaphysics of morals relies primarily on practical reason, not theoretical reason. That is, it uses reason to develop a system of principles to explain not the natural world as it *is*, but what we *ought* to do, treat with respect, and set as ends. The system outlines what we can justifiably regard as moral ends and virtuous character but which we can legitimately claim only to be adequate for purposes of rational deliberation and choice.

[5] A metaphysics of nature would be a system of rational principles distinct from particular empirical sciences and beyond the principles of causation, substance, etc., discussed in the first *Critique*. It is not surprising that Kant found this aspiration hard to achieve. See Kant, (1965), 13–15, 653–5 [Axix–xxii, A832/B860–A851/B879]; and (2002), 189–904 [4: 387–9].

A metaphysics of morals is also not *metaethics* in the current sense. Metaethics is conceived as investigation of the *meaning* of terms used in ethical judgments (e.g. "good" and "ought") and the ontological *status* of alleged moral facts and properties (e.g. whether "real" or "unreal"). Sometimes it encompasses moral epistemology, which asks how we can know or justify our moral claims. Although it uses some definitions, metaphysical ideas, and justifying arguments, Kant's metaphysics of morals is not primarily a work of conceptual analysis, ontology, or epistemology.

Finally, Kant's normative *ethics*, as presented in the *Tugendlehre*, is distinct in various ways from his theory of Right.[6] The distinction has been variously interpreted, but some points are evident.[7] Both are included in *The Metaphysics of Morals*, but only the *Tugendlehre* concerns duties and ends that are *ethical*, in a sense evidently narrower than "morals" in the work's title ((1996a) 20–2, 145–8 [6: 218–21, 379–84]). The basic ethical duties are to adopt the maxims to respect humanity as an end in itself and, more specifically, to pursue self-perfection and the happiness of others. Unlike juridical duties, ethical duties cannot be externally legislated or coercively enforced. Their source is inner legislation, and full compliance with them requires being motivated by the moral law. They include wide *imperfect* duties that leave some room for choice about how and when to pursue moral ends. By contrast, juridical duties, as *perfect* duties without latitude, prescribe particular actions, and insofar as these are legal requirements they do not require moral motivation.

These differences are important, but we should not overlook the fact that principles of Right limit and supplement duties of virtue. The *Rechtslehre* not only comes before virtue in the order of exposition, but there is a structural priority as well. Principles of law and justice limit what we may do to promote morally good ends. Duties of virtue are to be understood as qualified, "Promote these ends, but *only* by means compatible with Right." In addition, the *Rechtslehre* adds content to the *Tugendlehre* because, Kant says, it is an indirectly ethical duty to conform to juridical duties ((1996a), 20–2 [6: 219–21]). This implies that fully virtuous persons, for moral reasons, will not only avoid taking unjust and illegal means to their ends

---

[6] Kant's *Rechtslehre* is about "rightful" relations in private, public, and international relations. The term "Right" is broader in English whereas *Recht* only concerns rights, justice, and enforceable laws.

[7] Among the less evident and still controversial questions is how the first principles of the *Rechtslehre* and the *Tugendlehre* are related to the Categorical Imperative.

but will also obey the positive requirements of their legal system, within certain limits.[8] But the structural point remains that Right constrains and adds to the requirements of virtue.

3 The Role of the First Principles

The principles in the *Metaphysics of Morals* have a hierarchical structure in which more basic comprehensive principles articulate reasons for more specific ones. Kant states the supreme moral principle as follows: "[A]ct on a maxim which can also hold as a universal law.—Any maxim that does not so qualify is contrary to morals" ((1996a), 18 [6: 226]). Each Part, however, starts from a general principle more specific to its subject matter. In Part I, the *Rechtslehre*, this is "The Universal Principle of Right: Any action is *right* if it can coexist with everyone's freedom in accordance with a universal law, or on its maxim the freedom of choice of each can coexist with everyone's freedom in accordance with a universal law" (ibid. 24 [6: 230]). In Part II, the *Tugendlehre*, the first principle is: "act in accordance with a maxim of *ends* that it can be a universal law for everyone to have" (ibid. 157 [6: 395]).[9] Here my concern is just with how these relate to more particular principles and judgments, and my main aim is to relate Kant's theory to contemporary discussions.

3.1 Details depend on interpretations of the first principles, but several general points regarding their use seem evident. For example, although Kant's metaphysics of morals is supposed to start from a priori first principles, its development and application must take into account at least general

---

[8] Kant acknowledges that official orders to do something contrary to "inner morality" should not be obeyed ((1996a), 136 [6: 371]). Examples, presumably, would include orders to bear false witness or to commit rape. (See also (1998b), 153 n. [6: 154 n.].) As Lara Denis (2010) notes in ch. 9, perfect duties to oneself grounded in "the right of humanity" account for some limits to what law and justice can legitimately require. Also, there are arguably some limits to how unjust and contrary to the rule of law an alleged government can be before losing all claim to being a legitimate government as opposed to being a mere rogue regime without any legal or moral authority.

[9] Kant adds: "In accordance with this principle a human being is an end for himself as well as for others, and it is not enough that he is not authorized to use either himself or others merely as means (since he could then still be indifferent to them); it is in itself his duty to make man as such his end" ((1996a), 157 [6: 395]). Whether intended as a paraphrase, an explanation, or application, this articulates the standard that Kant most often appeals to throughout the *Tugendlehre*.

empirical facts about the human condition. Also, arguments for more specific ethical conclusions cannot always be strictly deductive. Kant acknowledges that experience, judgment, and wisdom are required.[10] This is especially true when trying to fulfill the imperfect duties regarding the ends of self-perfection and the happiness of others. Even perfect ethical duties raise "casuistical questions" that have no simple deductive answers.[11] Moreover, arguments to and from its substantive principles may require *interpretation* of normative ideas. Applying basic ethical principles may be sometimes more a matter of finding a reasonable instantiation than of finding a unique solution. This fits with Kant's understanding of ethics as employing ideas of reason that are neither reducible to empirical concepts nor as precisely determinate as mathematical concepts are.

3.2 In what sense are the first principles prior to more specific ethical principles? This is an especially pressing question if the first principles are not viewed as the axioms of a purely deductive system or as referring to metaphysical (ontological) bedrock.[12] An alternative that can be neutral regarding the ontological status of values and duties is to think of the first principles as epistemologically prior to more specific duties. That is, the first principles may be known independently of more specific duties and they are the only basis for inferring more specific duties. Unlike contemporary theories that rely on the method of reflective equilibrium, this interpretation would give no weight to common "intuitions" about what we ought to do in various situations.

Alan Donagan interprets Kant's moral epistemology differently.[13] That is, although Kant presents the results of his rational reflections on morals in the form of a hierarchy of principles, this does not necessarily mean that the force of evidence flows from top to bottom. As in mathematics, Donagan suggests, we may sometimes reasonably have more confidence in some mid-level principles than in the abstract first principles that we later accept as expressions of the normative concerns that they have in common. The order of

---

[10] See Kant (2002), 191 [4: 389–90]; Kant (1996a), 10–11 [6: 217–18, 411–12, 478].

[11] See Kant (1996a), 117–18, 179–80, 184, 186, 188 [6: 423–4, 426, 428, 431, 433–4, 437].

[12] Some commentators suggest that Kant held, as a metaphysical/ontological thesis, that "humanity" is an ultimate "value" that exists and is the ground of our various ethical duties.

[13] See Alan Donagan, "Moral Dilemmas, Genuine and Spurious: A Comparative Anatomy" and "The Relation of Moral Theory to Moral Judgment: A Kantian Review," in Malpas (1994), 153–68 and 194–216. Donagan (1977) presents a modified Kantian "metaphysics of morals."

discovery and grounds for belief may not be all top-down even though the principles are finally presented in an ordered structure analogous to a system of mathematics. Even the neat structured arguments in that discipline, e.g. proofs in geometry, do not necessarily reflect the mathematicians' order of thought or even grounds for belief. This opens the possibility for a more holistic or reflective equilibrium epistemology in ethics. This would fit with Kant's brief remark in the Preface to the *Groundwork* that, although "apparent adequacy" is not "secure proof of correctness," his first principles would be "clarified" by working out the whole system and "strongly confirmed by the adequacy the system would manifest throughout" ((2002), 194 [4: 392]). It would fit too Kant's use of examples to invoke awareness of "the fact of reason" in the *Critique of Practical Reason* ((1997*b*), 27–8, 40–4 [5: 31, 46–50]).

Whatever we conclude about logical and epistemological priority, it is clear that Kant attributed a normative *moral* priority to the moral law. A persistent theme is that we have specific duties *because* the moral law requires them, and we should strive to fulfill them because we respect the moral law. This contrasts with one form of contemporary intuitionism, represented prominently by Jonathan Dancy, which holds that what we ought to do is determined by the complex cluster of particular facts that constitute "reasons" of various kinds in each particular case.[14] General moral principles, in Dancy's view, are at best only approximate heuristic generalizations and often useless or harmful. Kant's view of the prior moral authority of the law also contrasts with any holistic theory that counts particular moral intuitions as among the factors that determine the truth or constitute the authority of the moral law. Kant's view, I think, is not that the ordinary person's immediate grasp of the wrongness of false witness, and the like, is what makes the moral law true or authoritative.[15] Rather, the strength and immediacy of such judgments make one aware of the fundamental difference between mere self-interest and morality that is expressed by the moral law. If so, Kant's theory treats the moral law as the fundamental moral authority even if it is not first in our moral awareness and not a decision procedure that entails determinate answers to all moral questions. A better analogy would be an ideal constitution for a moral commonwealth that authoritatively fixes basic values and procedures for legislating principles that represent the general will (or practical reason) of each citizen.

---

[14] Dancy (2004).   [15] See Kant's example (1997*b*), 27–8 [5: 30].

3.3 Kant's first principles and most general principles regarding ends are categorical imperatives. This means that they are strict duties with which everyone must comply, even though they allow considerable latitude of choice in application. To respect and value the end of humanity is fundamental and not optional. To adopt and pursue the ends of self-perfection and others' happiness is also rationally and morally required. These are obligatory ends, not merely ends prescribed by *prima facie duties*.[16] We must also make these our ends for the right (moral) reason—respect for the moral law. When, how, and to what extent we should further these ends, however, is somewhat indeterminate. The imperfect duties to develop our natural powers and to promote the happiness of others permit some "playroom" for free choice (Kant (1996a), 153 [6: 390]). For example, each profession calls for different skills, but choice among responsible professions is normally optional; and, barring emergencies and special obligations, we have some choice about where to spend our charitable effort, time, and money. The end of moral perfection is "narrow and perfect in quality" but "wide and imperfect in degree" (ibid. 196 [6: 446]): we must strive to fulfill *all* our duties from a moral incentive, but *how* exactly to do this and the *extent* to which we can at any given moment is somewhat indeterminate.

Despite their latitude and indeterminacy in practice, Kant's duties to promote the obligatory ends still differ from Ross's prima facie duties of self-improvement and beneficence.[17] Most obviously Kant's duties imply that it is morally necessary *to adopt these ends* as one's own—merely promoting ends by chance or in ways that are incidental to another purpose does not suffice. Also, as noted, Kant's duties cannot be completely fulfilled without adopting and pursuing the end from a moral motive. Perhaps surprisingly, Ross's famous list of prima facie duties allows *less latitude* for choice than Kant's imperfect duties. This is because Ross's system implies that, unless there is another conflicting prima facie duty (e.g. fidelity, justice, reparation, gratitude, non-injury, or self-improvement), one must promote a small pleasure for someone else even at the sacrifice of one's own much greater pleasure.[18] Both Ross and Kant accept that it is not in general a *duty* to promote one's own pleasure or happiness, but (arguably) the latitude in

---

[16] Ross (2001), 16–64. [17] Ibid. 21–2.

[18] Ross attempts to rectify this bizarre result by asserting, implausibly, that it is a prima facie duty to promote one's own pleasure if one sees it just as someone's pleasure rather than one's own. Ibid. 24–6.

Kant's imperfect duties allows *permission* to forgo doing minor favors for others, at least sometimes, so that we can pursue our own ends.[19]

3.4 Because the idea of natural teleology dominated much of ancient and medieval ethics, we should consider briefly its role in Kant's *Tugendlehre*. Is it a basic assumption expressed or presupposed by the first principles of his ethical theory? Modern philosophers such as Hobbes, Hume, and Spinoza rejected the traditional natural teleology, and so Kant's repeated appeals to "nature's purposes" in the *Tugendlehre* may seem an unfortunate regression. Nevertheless, the claim that an end is "natural" in Kant's theory cannot be a foundational moral claim. All Kant's major ethical writings make clear that the first principles are necessary principles of practical reason that require (and admit) no empirical justification. Kant does argue that there are moral and epistemological reasons for the "regulative" principle that we should try to conceive of natural events as ordered toward an ultimate end, and in the *Tugendlehre* he writes as if specific human capacities (e.g. for speech and reproduction) have natural ends. Underlying his familiar teleological language in presenting his specific duties, however, is the conviction that practical reason endorses the aims and dispositions that are said to be natural ends. Often this is only implicit, but there is ample precedent for this understanding. Even Thomas Aquinas identifies the basic natural ends relevant to the first precept of natural law as natural inclinations *approved by reason*.

In his gloss on the first principle of the *Tugendlehre* (as well as in the *Groundwork*), Kant presents the fundamental moral imperative in teleological language ("the duty to make man as such his end" ((1996a), 157 [6: 395]) but it has moral force because it is a necessary requirement of reason, not because of morally neutral empirical facts about human nature. In the *Groundwork*, drawing from "common *rational* knowledge of morality," Kant famously says that nature's purpose for human reason is to produce a good will, not happiness ((2002), 198 [4: 396]). It soon becomes evident, however, that the special value of a good will lies in the fact that its basic principle is always to follow the unconditional requirements of reason (ibid. 202–3 [4: 402]). Practical reason unconditionally requires us to strive for a

---

[19] There has been some controversy about the kinds and extent of latitude that Kant's principles allow. See e.g. Marcia Baron and Melissa Seymour Fahmy, "Beneficence and Other Duties of Love in *The Metaphysics of Morals*," in Hill (2009), 211–28; and "Meeting Needs and Doing Favors," in Hill (2002), 201–44.

perfectly good will, and ultimately this is why we should think of it as "nature's purpose" for giving us reason. In Kant's teleological framework, the reason we *ought* to seek a certain end is not that it is *nature's purpose* for us, in an independent, morally neutral sense. To the contrary, the deep rationale for thinking of an end as nature's purpose for us is in large part the prior underlying belief that that there are compelling reasons for us as human beings to pursue it.

4 Duties to Oneself

A striking difference between Kant's theory and most contemporary ethical theories is that Kant not only includes but gives special priority to duties to oneself. Many people today see morality as only concerned with how we treat others. Harming yourself, for example, is said to be foolish but not morally wrong unless it indirectly harms others. Advocates of "virtue ethics" tend to treat harming or degrading yourself as reflecting defects of character rather than violations of duty. Classical utilitarians, such as Bentham and Sidgwick, hold that one's ultimate duty is to consider one's own good as only a tiny part of the aggregate good that determines right and wrong. Special attention to oneself and one's inner circle may be justified in practice but only from a moral point of view in which one's own welfare is ultimately no more important than the comparable welfare of each other sentient creature. On this view, self-harm and self-benefit have some weight on the grand scale that determines moral right and wrong, but not much. In addition, many philosophers hold that, independently of such substantive issues, it is conceptually confused to suppose that one could have a duty *to* oneself in the strict sense in which we have duties *to* others. They argue, for example, that one cannot literally *violate one's own rights* or create a binding obligation by making a promise to oneself.

In Kant's theory, by contrast, ethical duties to oneself are prominent.[20] Suicide, gluttony, drunkenness, lying, servility, and sexual "self-defilement," Kant argues, are contrary to perfect duties to oneself. Self-perfection is an end that one has an imperfect duty to oneself to adopt and pursue. Leaving the

---

[20] For an excellent detailed examination, see Denis (2001).

details aside, let us compare and contrast Kant's position with the contemporary views just mentioned.

First, like many today Kant distinguishes morality from mere prudence. A foolish use of one's money, for example, becomes (indirectly) a moral issue for Kant only when it threatens to throw one into poverty that leads to vice or makes one unable to fulfill one's responsibilities ((1996a), 152–3 [6: 388]). Kant condemns certain ways of harming and debasing oneself, however, as contrary to perfect duties to oneself. For example, severely damaging one's rational capacities by abuse of food, or drink and (presumably) other drugs, is wrong, regardless of its harm to others; and the same holds for degrading sexual practices and servility (for example, "making oneself a worm" before others) (ibid. 176–81, 186–8 [6: 422–28, 434–7]). Also, Kant held that deliberate failure to develop one's natural and moral powers is culpable and to neglect them shows "lack of virtue" (ibid. 153 [6: 390]).

Second, unlike the position associated above with "virtue ethics," Kant's theory does not relegate all acts that merely harm oneself to a realm of vice and virtue that is *distinct from duty*. In fact, for Kant virtue *is* the strength of moral will to fulfill all one's duties despite opposing inclinations.[21] Acts contrary to perfect duties to oneself or based on rejection of the obligatory end of self-improvement are morally wrong, not merely signs of imperfect virtue.

Third, Kant is obviously no utilitarian. More specifically, for him the question whether abusing and degrading oneself through drugs, sexual practices, servility, and lying is wrong is not determined by weighing the consequences for oneself and all others. Along with law and justice, these duties are firm constraints on what one may otherwise reasonably do to promote the happiness of anyone.

Finally, Kant insists that we have duties *to* ourselves even though he was aware of a distinction between duties *to* persons and duties merely *toward* persons or things. He affirms duties *to* oneself and *to* other human beings, but he denies that we have duties *to* God, nature, and nonhuman animals (ibid. 32–3 [6: 240–1]). Instead, he holds that we have duties *towards* (or regarding) nature, animals, and at least the idea of God (ibid. 192–3 [6: 442–4]). It is difficult to be sure that we understand the relevant terms in exactly the same way, but it seems clear that Kant meant to say that we have

---

[21] See Kant (1996a), 145–6, 148, 153, 156–7, 163–7 [6: 380, 383–4, 390, 394, 404–10].

duties *to* ourselves and *to* others in the same sense. A duty to oneself in this sense, Kant implies, means that one is both the person under obligation and the person who imposes the obligation (or to whom it is owed). He anticipates the current objection that a duty to oneself is conceptually impossible because as the obligating person (to whom it is owed) one could always release oneself (as the obligated person) from the duty (ibid. 173–4 [6: 417–18]). If true, Kant says, this objection would undermine all duties, but he finds a "solution" in the different perspectives one takes when conceiving oneself as the one who is obligated and as the one who imposes the obligation.

In several ways Kant's position is less radical and unappealing than it may seem.

First, note that many common arguments against duties to oneself do not apply to Kant's conception of them. For example, assuming that all "duties *to*" are correlative with "rights *against*," some argue that a duty to oneself would entail the absurdity of having a right against oneself. One cannot literally violate one's own rights or, as the traditional slogan says, no one can do an injustice to himself. Kant himself accepts the point, reserving duties to oneself for ethics (*Tugendlehre*) rather than the domain of rights and justice (*Rechtslehre*) (ibid. 147–8 [6: 383]). Also wide of the mark is the familiar disdainful association of owing something to oneself with doing oneself favors, for example as a reward that one deserves or promised oneself. Kant's duties to oneself are concerned instead with not damaging or degrading oneself and with working to improve one's natural and moral powers. Some also object to Kant's position because it implies that the last person on earth would still have duties to himself, and they find this counterintuitive. Intuitions about such remote examples are hardly decisive, but in any case Kant's duties to oneself are primarily about the sort of person one should try to be as a person living in relations with others. Consider, for example, the duties to oneself not to lie or be servile and, more positively, to "make oneself a useful member of the world" and develop the strength of will to fulfill *all* one's duties (ibid. 182–4, 186–8, 194–7 [6: 429–31, 434–7, 446]). To be sure, these are not derived from duties to others but they are duties to oneself concerned with how to be a rational agent living among others.

Consider next the familiar argument that a duty to oneself would entail the absurdity that one is bound by a duty from which one could release oneself at will. This seems to assume that the model for all duties *to* a person, in a strict sense, is a promise, contract, or other voluntary commitment (ibid. 173–4 [6: 417–18]). The idea of a morally binding "promise to oneself" is indeed suspect, even though morally significant resolutions are sometimes described as such. Kant, however, does not invoke this idea. He seems to appeal instead to an older idea of an involuntary and irrevocable duty to someone by virtue of that person's inherent authority or awesome superiority. The idea apparently is that the ideal human being (with pure practical reason) in us imposes the obligations that bind us as the obligated moral agents. To make sense of this, as Kant suggests, we must conceive of ourselves in both these roles but from different perspectives (ibid. 173–4 [6: 418]).[22] The obligation is not voluntarily imposed or undertaken, as with promises, but is permanent and essential to being a moral agent. It is, in part, a metaphorical way of representing the thesis that to be under moral obligation *is* to be an imperfect rational agent who cannot but acknowledge the authority of the principles of rational autonomy that, in Kant's view, are expressed by the Categorical Imperative.

What some contemporary readers may find troubling is that Kant calls the relevant concerns *duties* at all, not that he classifies them as *to oneself*. If so, disagreement may run deep, but a few words of caution are in order. First, Kant's duties are not narrow requirements that are attached to social roles or meant to be enforced by busy-body neighbors. One's own reason, conscience, and self-respect are the ultimate motivators for compliance with ethical (as opposed to juridical) duties. Duties are constraints, but they are not imposed arbitrarily by tradition, culture, or any person, human or divine. They are in a sense self-imposed by our own rational recognition of the principles to which we, as rational agents with autonomy of will, necessarily accept as authoritative. All duties potentially limit what we may do to satisfy our inclinations and pursue happiness, but common sense and virtually all ethical theories recognize some such limits.

A final note regarding the relevance of Kant's duties to oneself to contemporary ethics should at least be mentioned, though it is too large a theme to develop here. Social contract theories from Hobbes to Rawls attempt to derive social and political obligations by asking what principles and institutions rational self-regarding agents would accept from a common

---

[22] See also ibid. 149 n., 150–2, 154, 157, 194–6 [6: 379 n., 386–7, 392, 395, 445–7].

deliberative perspective. Even T. M. Scanlon's theory, more focused on ethics, tries to determine what we owe to others by contractualist thinking based on intuitive "reasons" from different agents' perspectives.[23] In each case what matters is not just the kind of impartiality or reciprocity the contractualist deliberations involve but also the nature of rational self-regard.

Kant acknowledges that morally constrained prudence is rational and that, more generally, rational agents will take the necessary and available means to their subjective ends unless they deliberately abandon or suspend those ends (for example, for moral reasons).[24] Equally important, however, is the rational self-regard that, in Kant's view, underlies the ethical duties to oneself. To extrapolate, Kant thought that, apart from duties to others, finite rational agents will place a high priority on continuing to exercise and preserve rational capacities, on living among other rational agents as equals, and on communicating with others in a straightforward rational manner. They will also be rationally self-concerned to develop useful physical and mental powers, and to live under conditions favorable for maintaining their self-respect and following their consciences. These are not concerns they have primarily for the sake of others even though, as moral agents, they must respect the same rational interests of every other person.

These claims may be challenged in various ways, but their relevance to contemporary contractualist thinking should be obvious. The rational interests that each individual can bring to the table, as it were, for deciding on (further) principles are not merely self-preservation and desire satisfaction (Hobbes), or natural rights and property (Locke), or primary social goods (Rawls), but (arguably) those rational interests that lie behind Kant's duties to oneself. If so, this would partially explain how duties to oneself are fundamental in Kant's ethics.

5 Negligence and Second-Order Duties

Kant's system of ethical principles includes first-order principles regarding actions, such as suicide, lying, and disobedience to law, as well as commitment

---

[23] Scanlon (1998).
[24] Kant (2002), 215–20 [4: 414–20], and Editor's Introduction, ibid. 51–7.

to moral ends and attitudes. The principles primarily address the first-person questions "What ought I to do?" and "What should I especially value and strive for?" These are the questions we raise when we are morally alert, reflective, and ready to make our acts and attitudes conform to our best judgments. It seems, however, that the most pervasive, if not the worst, wrongs and vices are due to moral negligence, self-deception, and weakness. In these cases we do not raise the moral question, see the moral problem, or anticipate how hard it is to live up to our best intentions. In these contexts principles that merely tell us how to assess our intentions seem to offer little help. At a later time we may become aware of our negligence, self-deception, and weakness, and then we may blame and hold ourselves responsible—as perhaps others will. Such retrospective and third-person assessments of blameworthiness and responsibility, however, are at best a secondary concern in Kant's theory. The first moral concern is not "Who is to blame?" but "What should I do and strive for now?"

On reflection, however, we can and should face the problems of moral negligence, self-deception, and weakness in our thinking about what we should do and strive for *now*. These are common human tendencies that underlie much wrongdoing, and we can know in general that we are liable to them. We may be unaware, or only half-aware, that we are being negligent, self-deceiving, or weak at the moment of decision, but our ever-present liability to these faults is well known. We should expect, then, that a complete system of principles for guiding first-person deliberation will include principles about preparing ourselves to reduce the influence of these propensities insofar as we can.

Kant's system includes very general principles of this sort. The first stems from "a human being's duty to himself as his own innate judge" ((1996a), 188–91 [6: 437–40]). This concerns conscience, which Kant imagines as an inner forum analogous to a criminal court. In it one must think of oneself as different persons, by turns the accuser, the defender, and the judge. As judge one hears evidence and then condemns or acquits oneself as the accused, with the best outcome (a clear conscience) being relief, not reward. The conscience is also seen as observing, warning, and even threatening us unbidden. We can "distract" or "stun" ourselves to avoid its message temporarily, but it is an innate predisposition that is inescapably bound up with our moral agency. One's specific duty regarding conscience is to cultivate it and "sharpen one's attentiveness to the voice of the inner judge" (ibid. 161 [6: 401]). The metaphor of courtroom activity, however, also suggests that the duty is to take on seriously the active role of the judge, scrupulously weighing evidence before exonerating the defendant or rightfully imputing the act as a violation of moral law (ibid. 188–91 [6: 437–40]).[25] Importantly, this self-judging can only compare *our own understanding* of our acts (past, ongoing, or proposed) with *our own best judgments* about what ought to be done in the context ((1998*b*), 179 [6: 186]; (1996*a*), 161 [6: 401]).[26] A clear conscience at best signals that we are blameless, not that the acts are objectively right.

Kant's metaphors of conscience may be questioned, but the main forward-looking message is hard to deny. That is, we should be careful to see that what we intend to do can survive our own critical moral scrutiny. This means that, at least for serious matters, we may need to investigate our facts further, examine our assumptions, rethink our moral reasoning, and consult others to challenge our understandings. This presumably is the *duty of due care* that, Kant suggests, the well-intentioned Spanish Inquisitors failed to heed when they burned heretics at the stake ((1998*b*), 179 [6: 186]).

A further second-order principle is "the first command of all duties to oneself," namely, "*know* (scrutinize, fathom) *yourself* . . . in terms of your moral perfection in relation to your duty" ((1996*a*), 191 [6: 441]). Kant's concern here is with our deepest predispositions and commitments as well as more specific motives. Self-scrutiny can make us more aware of our respect-worthy predisposition to the good ("the moral law within"), but it can also reveal a deep, actual will that is impure, contemptible, and evil ((1998*b*), 52–61 [6: 29–39]; (1996*a*), 191 [6: 441]). Although it is "difficult to fathom" the depths of our hearts, self-scrutiny may also expose particular ways in which we deceive ourselves, for example by taking "wishes empty of deeds" as proof of our good will. Deceiving ourselves about our true motives can also distort our moral deliberations and allow us to persist in

---

[25] In judging oneself, however, one must think of the judge as another person, even if "merely an ideal person that reason creates for itself" (Kant (1996*a*), 189 [6: 439]). Earlier Kant implies that this ideal judge ("conscience") is our practical reason (ibid. (1996*a*) 160 [6: 400]). We do not have a duty to *acquire* a conscience because it is something moral agents inevitably have, and we must not follow the initial promptings of conscience blindly. We should, however, listen to conscience and follow its verdicts insofar as they express our best judgment about what practical reason requires.

[26] For a fuller discussion see Hill (1998), 13–52.

wrongdoing. We need to expose self-deception not just to achieve purity of motive but to avoid wrongdoing and neglect of positive duties.

Finally, the duty to oneself to increase one's moral perfection includes not only striving for purity in one's dispositions and motives but striving to "fulfill all one's duties" and "attain completely one's moral end with regard to oneself" ((1996a), 196 [6: 446]). These duties correspond to the biblical commands "be holy" and "be perfect" (ibid.).[27] The latter requires us to develop *virtue*, which Kant conceives of as an inner fortitude or strength of moral will with which we can overcome obstacles to duty more easily and in a good spirit. Because persons of good will can be weak, virtue is not merely a good will basically committed to duty above self-interest. Virtue is the opposite of weakness of moral will, which we must strive to overcome. This weakness—or lack of virtue—does not excuse wrongdoing, because, in Kant's view, we must presume we can do what we ought to do even if it is hard and unpleasant. We exercise our will by adopting and acting on maxims, so "weakness" and "strength" here cannot be understood literally as forces, physical or metaphysical. The good-willed person who does wrong from weakness of will, then, should apparently be seen as (voluntarily) acting at the moment on a bad maxim that is inconsistent with his or her own higher-order good maxim to avoid wrongdoing. If so, the person would be responsible for the act and reveal an imperfect character (though not as bad a one as if the person had acted with a thoroughly bad will).

Kant may have thought instead that as a result of human frailty a person who has not yet developed virtue will sometimes find it impossible (not just difficult) to do her (normally binding) duty on a particular occasion. The important point here, however, is that he clearly thought that it is a duty to strive to develop virtue and that over time we can improve in that regard. This is an important second-order duty—the duty to increase our moral strength of will to fulfill our other duties despite obstacles.

In sum, Kant's system of ethical principles includes at least three second-order duties in recognition that failure to fulfill first-order duties is often due to moral negligence, self-deception, and weakness. These second-order duties require us, first, to be alert to the warnings of conscience and respond appropriately; second, to scrutinize our motives to expose our tendency to make excuses; and, third, to strive to develop virtue conceived as strength of

---

[27] See 1 Peter 1: 16; Matthew 5: 48; Philippians 4: 8.

will to do the right thing despite temptations. These are not criteria for assessing blameworthiness but principles for guiding first-person moral decisions about what to do now. Their ability to guide us, however, presupposes that, despite our failings, we are to some extent aware of their message, do not completely refuse to see their implications, and are not always too weak to follow them.

6   Moral Motivation

An important feature of Kant's system of ethical principles is its requirement of a moral incentive for avoiding wrongdoing and adopting the obligatory ends. This feature is one of several that distinguish principles of Right from ethics as conceived in the *Tugendlehre*, and it also distinguishes Kant's ethics from most ethical theories prominent today. Kant's requirement of a moral incentive, however, raises questions of interpretation as well as objections.

Principles of Right, according to Kant, forbid or demand particular actions, not maxims or motives. Ethical duties, by contrast, require us to adopt maxims regarding ends to respect and promote.[28] This means that ethical duties essentially concern our attitudes, goals, and intentions, contrary to contemporary theories that relegate such concerns to theories of character. These theories reserve *duty* and *obligation*, *right* and *wrong*, for "the acts themselves" as described apart from such variable ("subjective") factors. In addition, Kant held that ethical duty, the product of "inner legislation," prescribes a moral incentive—respect for the moral law. Duty requires not only that we respect and pursue obligatory ends but that we do so for moral reasons. This demand contrasts sharply with mainstream contemporary theories. It is off-putting to many readers and, perhaps for this reason, is often de-emphasized by those who try to present Kant's theory in a favorable light.

How should we understand the *requirement of a moral incentive*? Is it that we must strive to make the thought of duty present and salient every time we do something to promote an obligatory end? Must I, for example, try to

---

[28] All duties, including perfect duties to oneself and respect for others, are based on "the end of humanity"—that is, the imperative to treat humanity in each person as an end in itself (Kant (1996a), 157 [6: 395]).

live so that each time, or even usually, when I help others, the immediate honest explanation for my doing so would be that duty requires me to promote the happiness of others? Must I strive to make the thought of duty my dominant and explicit reason for visiting a friend in the hospital, taking care of an aging parent, or not committing suicide today? To suppose so strikes many of us as implausible and even repugnant.

Perhaps, then, we need to think of duty explicitly only when we are disinclined to act as we should. Even if so, Kant still says that we must strive to develop *virtue*, the perfection of which requires "actions being done not only in conformity with duty but also *from duty*" (ibid. 196 [6: 446]). Does it show a defect in virtue if any motive but duty keeps us on the right path when we are otherwise inclined? Is it, for example, a moral failing or defect for someone to overcome a temporary suicidal impulse from love of his family rather than from duty, assuming that duty would have been by itself a sufficient motive? Similarly, suppose someone who cannot altogether expunge urges to eat or drink excessively would be moderate from duty alone if need be, but her desire to avoid the social consequences of gluttony and drunkenness is her immediate and sufficient motive. In this case again the thought of duty may be unnecessary, and to insist on it as required for virtue may be to insist on one thought too many. Assuming that we accept duty as a sufficient reason in general for avoiding suicide, drunkenness, and gluttony, it is at least counterintuitive to suppose that striving for virtue means trying to ensure that duty is always our immediate conscious motive.

An alternative way to understand the ethical duty to have a moral incentive might be this: we should strive always to count the moral law as a sufficient, overriding constraint and guide as we shape our plans, policies, and characters, and then we should try to strive to live our everyday lives accordingly.[29] On this understanding the thought of duty need not be our immediate and conscious motive whenever we act as we should. It would suffice, for example, if the moral law serves as an incentive to adopt, and reaffirm as need be, the obligatory ends as a permanent part of our life-plan. The ends may be internalized, not as blind habits, but as deep-rooted commitments that play a role in a full explanation of our choices even though they are not always the salient factors we call "the reason" for each act of kindness, self-improvement, etc. When other permissible aims and

---

[29] See Herman (2007), 1–28, and Baron (1995), pt. 11, 117–94.

affections converge with our deep moral commitment, then there may be no meaningful choice about "making" one or the other our immediate reason. We would then have *both* an overriding commitment to morality and more specific maxims to promote our permissible ends. When sufficient motives "cooperate" happily in this way, it could be misleading to say that either is "the reason" for which one is acting.

In *Groundwork* I Kant asserts that only acting from duty, as opposed to inclination and mixed motives, has "moral worth" ((2002), 198–201 [4: 397–9]). This may seem incompatible with the broader interpretation, but arguably is not. Kant's aim is to reveal the principle of a good will, and so he focuses on actions from duty, which most directly express a good will. Such acts have special "moral worth" as manifesting the agent's commitment to duty above self-love. Acts from inclination and mixed motives, by contrast, may reflect the ultimate commitments of a depraved, impure, or weak will, none of which consistently subordinates self-love to duty. In these cases (in contrast to cases of cooperating motives discussed above), acts from inclination and mixed motives would be morally defective, not merely expressive of a good person's morally constrained personal values. It is immoral to subordinate duty to self-love (and "evil" to do so systematically), but it is not necessarily wrong or less than virtuous to do the right thing from other immediate motives.

On the broader understanding of the moral incentive requirement, I have suggested, sometimes conforming to duty without the explicit thought of duty is not a moral failing or defect. This reflects common understanding about the examples reviewed earlier. In other cases, however, the immediate thought of duty does seem appropriate and a sign of virtue. Consider, for example, a teacher trying to grade a favorite (or disliked) student, jurors trying to reach a verdict on a notorious (or popular) defendant, or a lifeguard rescuing a distressed millionaire known for her generous rewards. If the moral incentive guides as well as constrains our plans, policy, and character development, it should lead us to be more alert to duty in these cases than in the cases considered previously.

The broader understanding may also to help deflect some common objections. Consider, for example, the objection that we could not have a duty always to act as we should *from duty* because we cannot control our motives at will. Kant seems to recognize this problem when he says that the duty to increase one's moral perfection, though "narrow and perfect in terms of quality," is "wide and imperfect in terms of its degree, because of the frailty (*fragilitas*) of human nature" ((1996*a*), 196 [6: 446]). We cannot expect ourselves to be perfect but only to strive sincerely to make progress toward the ideal. Given the conditions of human life, however, is it really ideal to have duty always at the forefront of one's mind, even when overcoming inclinations to act badly? Would this be an essential feature of moral perfection for us even if we could achieve it? The broader understanding of the moral incentive opens the way for a more attractive ideal, which is to have all our plans, attachments, and character traits so shaped by our fundamental commitment to morality that we always conform to duty but think explicitly of duty only as most appropriate to the circumstances. This is still an ideal beyond the reach of most of us, an ideal of human perfection and not a mere second-best that falls short of virtue, and it does not demand that we can call up at will a sufficiently moving thought of duty each time we act as we should.

Another familiar objection is that Kant's motive of duty represents a joyless recognition of burdensome constraint. By contrast Aristotle's ideally virtuous person seems fully engaged, ready, and pleased to do the right thing in each situation. The broader understanding of Kant's moral incentive may help with this objection too. Undeniably Kant did think that recognition of the moral law constrains us, humbles us, and strikes down our natural self-conceit. He did not believe that nonrational human nature is as well-disposed or malleable as Aristotle did, and so he could hardly imagine that we could dispense with the constraining thought of duty. How often and how prominently the explicit thought of duty should appear in our daily lives, however, is not clear from these general features of Kant's view. If we have a good will, we are committed to doing what is right whether or not we feel so inclined, but this commitment may not need to be explicitly invoked when we have no temptations to the contrary. Similarly, assuming a good will, perhaps we need not experience duty as a constraint if such temptations are easily rejected from other (permissible) concerns that are part of our life-plans and good character. Moral law, in Kant's theory, represents both what we have good reason to do and (in imperative form) what duty constrains us to do. The more we acknowledge and come to care about the moral reasons, the less work there may be for explicit thought of duty *as a constraint*.

Finally, consider the objection that the idea of a duty to act *from duty* is incoherent because it leads to an infinite regress. For example, if I have a duty to tell the truth from duty, then it seems I must have a duty to fulfill *that* duty from duty, and then a *further* duty to fulfill that second duty from duty, and so on and on. The regress could be blocked by stipulating that the second-order (motivational) duty is only to fulfill all first-order duties (e.g. regarding specific actions or ends) from a motive of duty. The mistake, one might argue, is to assume that literally every duty must be fulfilled "from duty." This reply, however, may at first seem arbitrary. What is so special, one might ask, about the duty to act rightly from a moral incentive? Why is a moral incentive not required for this as well?

The answer, I suspect, is that if we properly understand the requirement of a general moral incentive, the request for a further moral motive makes little sense. The issues here are complex but roughly the idea is this: to have duties for Kant is basically to have sufficient, overriding, rational considerations for certain choices, often experienced as constraints because they can conflict with inclinations. For a *rational* person to recognize such considerations *is* to be rationally predisposed to be moved by them, at least to some extent. As imperfectly rational agents, however, we also have conflicting inclinations and a propensity to subordinate duty to self-love. Our most fundamental choice—for Kant the choice between good and evil—is which dispositions to incorporate into our basic life-governing maxim ((1997*b*), 29–35 [5: 32–9]; (1996*a*), 191 [6: 441]). A fully rational person would choose a fundamental maxim always to give priority to the moral predisposition, and as imperfectly rational agents it is our duty to choose as we would if fully rational. If so, it is a fundamental duty, in this sense, to choose the principle of a good will, to respect and follow the unconditionally rational moral law. In other words, it is a duty to incorporate the moral disposition (or incentive) into one's life-governing maxim. To do this is to maintain the attitude that, for the sufficient reason that the moral law requires various specific choices, one is ready and willing to make them.

This understanding of the requirement of a moral motive does not treat it as an extra duty added on to each particular duty, for example a duty always to remember to think of the moral law whenever one conforms to it. To the contrary, the requirement is to take up a fundamental and comprehensive attitude that should shape and permeate all one's plans, policies, and choices. Although Kant presents the duty to strive for a pure moral motive ("be holy") as one among many in his catalogue of duties of virtue, it has a special status as part of a prior higher-order duty. On this view, choosing and maintaining the attitude of a good will makes one ready and willing to fulfill specific duties, even though the thought of duty need not be ever-present. If one could fulfill the higher-order duty completely, conformity to specific duties would follow; but mere conformity to specific duties does not fulfill them *as ethical duties* if one lacks that comprehensive commitment to the priority of the moral law (a good will). Although it sounds paradoxical, this understanding gives a sense to "a (comprehensive) duty to do one's (specific) duties from (one's ultimate commitment to) duty." To make that ultimate commitment for duty over self-interest (good over evil) is what a fully rational person would do and so by definition it is what we should do, but it makes no sense to suppose it is a still further duty to make *this* ultimate choice for duty over self-love *from a prior commitment to duty*.

7 Concluding Note

The *Tugendlehre* is obviously ambitious and far-reaching in its scope, but in several ways it is also incomplete. It is incomplete partly because Kant's aim was only to present the first principles of "the doctrine of virtue," and perhaps too because he never managed to explain and illustrate even that system of first principles as fully as he may have wished. That aside, the system is also meant to be incomplete in another way because Kant wisely realized that there are limits to what even the best ethical theory can do. Some ethical principles leave a wide latitude for choice, and applying any principle requires judgment and understanding of the particular context. There are many matters on which moral principles do not speak, and regarding these our consciences—and Kantian moral theories—should also remain silent.

III
Moral Rules and Principles

8

The Dignity of Persons: Kant, Problems, and a Proposal

The idea that all persons have a special worth, or dignity, is widely shared, quite apart from any particular philosophical theory. The idea is invoked in many different contexts, and sometimes on different sides of debates on the same issue. For example, in discussions of abortion and end of life decisions, the need to respect the dignity of persons is cited as a reason both for preserving and for terminating a life. But what is the meaning and underlying basis of these appeals to dignity?

In the following section, I comment on some common replies that, in my view, prove to be philosophically unsatisfying. Next, I sketch briefly some main features of Kant's idea of human dignity and note some of its implications. Then I review different ways in which the Kantian idea has been interpreted and call attention to problems raised by common interpretations. Next, in response to these problems, I describe briefly a proposal for incorporating the idea of human dignity into a two-level, Kantian normative theory. Finally, I note that several different values implicit in common appeals to human dignity are affirmed in the two-level Kantian normative theory, which also provides a framework for assessing priorities when these common values conflict.

An Unsatisfying Response: Just Treat Persons as Persons

Flagrant violations of human dignity are often described by comparison with the way we treat nonhuman animals and things of inferior value. For

This chapter was initially presented at the 25th Conference of the International Wittgenstein Society, on the topic "Persons—An Interdisciplinary Approach," in Kirschberg, Austria, August 2002. I thank the participants, and especially Ralf Stoecker, for their comments.

example, we complain that persons are treated as mere instruments, play-things, commodities, or (worse) as dogs, vermin, or garbage. This suggests that to treat people with dignity is simply to treat them, instead, *as persons*. In particular contexts often it seems plain enough what this requires. The suggestion also *seems* to provide its own justification: we should treat persons as persons *because*, in fact, they are persons. Despite its rhetorical force in particular moral debates, however, the idea that respecting dignity is just treating persons as persons raises many problems.

First, what is the underlying premise in the supposed justification "We should treat persons as persons *because* they are persons"? If it is that we should always treat everything as what it is and not as something different, the premise is not at all plausible. There is nothing wrong, for example, about treating a stone or clock as a paperweight, if it serves the purpose. A person may be a duke, or a king, but it does not follow that we should treat him *as a duke* or *as a king*, as that would be commonly understood. The concepts of *duke, king, judge, professor, film star*, and so forth, attribute to a person a social role and status that, by conventional norms, call for respectful treatment. The fact that a person has such a conventional status, however, does not by itself determine the person's *moral* standing: that is, how, morally speaking, the person should be treated.

Now it might be thought that the concept of a *person* is not merely functional (like "paperweight") or conventionally normative (like "duke" and "king"), but moral. For example, some say that in moral discussions an essential part of the conception of a person is that it is "a being with moral rights." This is analogous to the idea that for legal purposes a "person" is a possessor of legal rights. The suggestion, then, is that to treat a person as a person is to respect the person's inherent moral rights. The term *person* may be used in this way, but, in this sense, to say, "They are persons" *by itself* tells us nothing specific about *how* the persons should be treated or *why* certain treatment is called for. As philosophers, we must still ask the further questions, what rights do persons as such have, and on what are they based? Sometimes, in actual situations, the rights in question may be taken for granted, and then the imperative "Treat them as persons" can serve as a reminder of what is assumed to be common knowledge. A man who treats a woman as merely an object for his own pleasure might well be reminded: "She is a person: so you must not treat her like that." This is apt in some practical contexts, but it does not take us far toward understanding what she is entitled to by virtue of being a person, and why.

If we drop the normative connotations of the term *person* and treat it as a purely descriptive term, then, whatever the descriptive criteria are for being a person, from the mere fact that someone is a person we cannot infer anything about how the person should be treated. Clearly, the moral injunction to treat persons as persons means more than "Treat them as beings with X, Y, and Z descriptive properties." At times a reminder that those who are being oppressed, exploited, or ignored have these properties may awaken moral sensibilities in those who already have them, but to say "They are persons" in a descriptive sense would not by itself indicate how those referred to should be treated, or why such treatment is necessary.

Another interpretation is suggested by some remarks of Wittgenstein.[1] The idea is that *seeing persons as persons* is not a matter of believing certain descriptive or normative propositions about them, but rather a matter of responding to them in certain ways. Somewhat over-simply, we could say that, on this interpretation, the difference between those who see someone as a person and those who do not would be a difference in their attitudes, rather than their beliefs. For example, surgeons, soldiers at war, and bureaucrats may temporarily see certain persons as mere objects while sympathetic observers see them as persons. The difference, it may be argued, lies not in their understanding of the facts but in their affective reactions and attitudes. In most contexts, perhaps, we can expect that those who see persons as persons will treat them more decently than those who do not, but this is not invariably the case. A surgeon, for example, may be better able to benefit the patient by temporarily objectifying the person on whom she operates. So it is not necessarily a good thing always to see a person as a person. Also, arguably, the most sadistic torturers see their victims as persons. Their pleasure depends on their vivid awareness that they are torturing a person rather than a nonhuman animal. Seeing persons as persons, then, seems neither necessary nor sufficient for treating them decently.

---

[1] Wittgenstein (1958), pt. II. xi, pp. 193 ff.

Basic Elements of Kant's View

The idea of the dignity of persons is pivotal in Kant's *Groundwork for the Metaphysics of Morals*. Persons are conceived of as free and rational beings. Their freedom of will, autonomy, and practical reason are Ideas presupposed in all moral thinking. Kant argued that we cannot act at all without presupposing these Ideas, despite the fact that they cannot be explained empirically. As he puts it in *The Metaphysics of Morals*, a person is a being to whom we can *impute* actions as their "free cause."[2] With freedom goes responsibility for our acts and for the consequences of wrongdoing. Above all, persons are responsible to themselves. The Idea that, as rational agents, we can act without being determined by prior natural causes is coherent only if we also assume that we have "*autonomy* of the will." This means that, as persons, we are unavoidably committed to rational principles not based on our inclinations.[3] The constraints that derive from these principles are seen as self-imposed and overriding. Accordingly, if we intentionally choose instead to act from some inclination, we are inevitably acting contrary to our own implicit rational standard. Among the implications are that we expect that all persons, if subject to inclinations, will have *respect* for the moral law, at least as a standard, and will feel pangs of *conscience* if they violate it. Because the moral law is presumed to be the will of all rational agents, for themselves and others, we show respect for others by doing what is right and we show disrespect to all persons when we do wrong. Empirical science takes a different perspective when it considers human beings as a part of nature, but, Kant argues, it cannot disprove our normative moral framework with the Ideas of freedom and practical rationality that it attributes to moral agents.

---

[2] Kant (1996*a*), 16 [6: 223].

[3] "Commitments" in the sense intended here are not voluntary undertakings, like making a promise, swearing an oath of allegiance, or even choosing over time to be a person with a "good will" who tries to give morality priority over self-love in their lives when these conflict. What I have in mind is the sense in which our evaluations, judgments of others, and use of practical reason generally have implications to which one is "committed," whether one likes it or not, in that one cannot disown them unless one is self-deceived, confused, or incoherent. Kant held that all moral agents, even those who make the "evil" choice to subordinate morality to self-love, are committed to the moral law as a rationally authoritative standard that they cannot violate without a conflict of will and liability to self-disapproval in the court of conscience. There is a partial analogy with the way in which our beliefs about the world and use of theoretical reason "commit" us to propositions and standards that we did not voluntarily choose but cannot coherently disown even when we defy them in practice.

This is the background of Kant's normative ideas about the dignity of persons, but here I focus primarily on those normative ideas rather than their background in Kant's systematic philosophy.[4] How much of that theoretical background is necessary to support the moral ideal of human dignity remains a controversial question.

The fundamental principle that expresses Kant's idea of dignity is the famous humanity formula of the Categorical Imperative: "Act in such a way that you always treat humanity, whether in your own person or in the person of any other, never simply as a means but always at the same time as an end."[5] Kant says both that *persons* are ends in themselves and that *humanity* (or *rational nature*) in persons is an end in itself.[6] Apparently these terms were intended to express the same basic idea, namely that persons are ends in themselves *because of their rational nature* and this requires us to respect them *in special ways appropriate to rational beings*. Ends in themselves are "objective ends," valid for all rational beings, in contrast to the "subjective," personal ends that we adopt because of our various desires and inclinations.[7] Strictly, ends in themselves are not ends in the sense of an end to be produced or a goal to be achieved. They are ends "against which we should never act."[8] But the idea is not entirely negative, for Kant argues that if we fully appreciate the idea that persons are ends in themselves we will try to further the ends of others.[9] That we should not treat persons merely as means follows from the idea that we must always treat them as ends in themselves, but the latter idea is more comprehensive than the former. For example, we do not treat people as mere means when we utterly ignore them, but indifference and neglect fail to respect persons as ends in themselves.[10]

Kant explicitly connects the idea of ends in themselves and dignity after his discussion of the "kingdom" (*Reich*) of ends. This is an ideal model of "a systematic union of rational beings under common objective laws."[11] Using political metaphors, Kant describes the members as both legislators of the law and (except for the "head" (*Oberhaupt*)) subject to the law.[12] It is an

---

[4] I review some of the broader context in "Kantian Perspectives on the Rational Basis of Human Dignity," (Hill, forthcoming).

[5] Kant (2002), 230 [4: 229].   [6] Ibid. 428–30.

[7] Ibid. 427–8.   [8] Ibid. 236 [4: 437].

[9] Ibid. 231 [4: 430].   [10] Kant (1996a), 157 [6: 395].

[11] Kant (2002), 233–4 [4: 433].   [12] Ibid. 234 [4: 433].

ideal condition that would become actual only if everyone followed the moral law (and God ensured that the personal ends of the virtuous were not systematically frustrated).[13] Nonetheless, it is a moral imperative to obey the "laws" that we and other rational legislators would make as members of a kingdom of ends. The members are conceived not only as rational but also as having a set of personal ends, though we must "abstract" from the content of those ends and from personal differences in thinking of the kingdom of ends.[14] The idea of a kingdom of ends is constructed from elements in the previous formulations of the Categorical Imperative (universal law-giving, humanity as an end in itself, and autonomy), and these are supposed to be rational values not dependent on individual preferences or even universal contingent human sentiments. This, presumably, is why we must abstract from the content of the ends of the members of the kingdom. Only the values of rational persons as such are constitutive values of the legislators; but to apply the ideal to human circumstances, we must try to work out the implications of those basic values for the human condition, and for various local conditions, in the light of facts about our circumstances and more specific concerns.

Everything in the kingdom of ends, Kant says, has *dignity* or mere *price*. The rational members, as ends in themselves, have dignity, which is an "unconditional and incomparable worth" that "admits of no equivalent."[15] Persons with dignity, then, have a kind of worth that does not depend on class, culture, race, popularity, or social utility. It is a worth "above all *price*" in the sense that it has priority over all values dependent on their utility or relation to our sentiments. Moreover, as "without equivalent," dignity is not a commensurable value on a scale that permits trade-offs for things of greater value.

Old and New Applications

In the *Grundlegung* Kant's familiar examples of using his principle obviously rely on certain background assumptions. The conclusions are that it is wrong to commit suicide because life promises more pain than pleasure,

---

[13] Kant (2002), 239 [4: 438].   [14] Ibid. 234 [4: 433].   [15] Ibid. 235 [4: 434–5].

wrong to borrow money that one cannot repay in order to escape financial problems, wrong not to develop one's useful capabilities, and wrong to refuse to aid the needy on a policy that respecting their rights is enough. In the ethical part of *The Metaphysics of Morals* (*Tugendlehre*) the idea of the special value of humanity is the main normative idea to which most of Kant's arguments appeal, and it plays a role in the first part (*Rechtslehre*), concerned with law and justice, as well. For example, Kant implies that it opposes certain unequal sexual relations, punishment for purely pragmatic reasons, lying, servility, drunkenness, and various forms of disrespect for others.

More recent writers have extended the application of Kant's idea to issues of racial discrimination, sexual objectification, respect for cultural diversity, respectful social dialogue, informed consent in medical practice, and other matters. On a more theoretical level, the idea of the dignity of persons as rational agents opposes the utilitarian doctrine of "negative responsibility," that is, the idea that we are *just* as responsible for all the bad things that we do not prevent as we are for our own wrongdoing and its bad consequences.[16] The Kantian idea of the dignity of persons poses a strong constraint on the consequentialist thinking on which this doctrine of negative responsibility rests, for the Kantian position denies that all values are commensurable. Dignity is a value that cannot be quantified, and it limits what we may do in pursuit of quantifiable goods.

The idea of dignity is also a part of contemporary Kantian responses to the alleged problem of "agent-centered restrictions."[17] This is posed by the question: How could it be that it is *wrong* for us to do something that would promote the greatest good by preventing others from doing something even worse? If two murders are worse than one, for example, how could it be wrong to commit a murder in order to prevent two murders? The Kantian response is that, for every moral agent, the most fundamental value is, in all actions, to respect humanity in each person, not to promote an outcome that is maximally desirable by some other standard. The alleged "problem"

---

[16] See Bernard Williams, "A Critique of Utilitarianism" in Williams and Smart (1973).

[17] The terms "agent-centered restrictions" and "agent-centered privileges" were apparently introduced by Scheffler (1982). The former prohibit each agent from doing certain acts (e.g. murder) even if the result will be that more acts of that kind are committed by others. The latter are moral permissions for each agent to do certain things or not, as they please, even though they would thereby be doing less than possible to produce the most good for all.

posed by agent-centered restrictions stems from assumptions that belong to the consequentialist tradition, not to the Kantian tradition. It assumes, for example, that acts and their consequences have a value that is commensurable and quantifiable (in theory, if not practically). It assumes, further, that there is a strong presumption that we ought always to maximize this value. These assumptions are directly contrary to central Kantian ideas: (*a*) that dignity is another kind of value, "incomparable," "without equivalent," and not a something "to be produced", and (*b*) all genuine value is grounded in reason, which arguably imposes constraints on the means that we can permissibly use to promote good ends. What is good is whatever is rational and reasonable to choose, not an independent natural or metaphysical property that can be measured and aggregated.

Similarly, consequentialist (not Kantian) assumptions underlie the so-called problem of agent-centered privileges. This is posed by the question: How can it be morally permissible for us to do anything if we could promote the greatest good by doing something else? From a Kantian point of view, acts are morally permissible unless there is compelling reason to adopt principles forbidding them, and there is no measurable "greatest good" independent of rational and reasonable principles of moral conduct. The "problems," in short, are internal to consequentialist approaches to ethics that Kantians oppose.

Each of these issues deserves further discussion, but I turn now to different interpretations of the Kantian position and some of the problems that they raise.

Interpretations of Kant's Principle and Some Problems

Not surprisingly, there are disagreements about how Kant's ideas should be interpreted and developed. I shall review three of these in order to call attention to problems that, in my view, a tenable Kantian ethics should try to avoid.

First, the prescription to treat rational nature (or humanity in us) as an end in itself has been interpreted as nothing more than the prescription to act only on maxims that we can will as universal law.[18] Although there are

---

[18] e.g. Singer (1961), 235.

considerations that suggest this, most scholars seem to agree that the humanity formula (and the related idea of the dignity of persons) goes beyond the formula of universal law in making explicit a further essential aspect of a moral perspective. Kant's formulas of the Categorical Imperative are supposed to be expressions of fundamentally the same principle, but neither the humanity formula nor the formula of universal law, by itself, articulates all aspects of that supreme moral principle. In any case, this first interpretation would impose on the humanity formula all the notorious difficulties of using the universal law formula as a decision guide, for example the problems posed by alternative maxim descriptions.[19]

Another interpretation treats dignity as a high-priority value, above all "price," but nonetheless a value that permits trade-offs within the category of dignity.[20] On this interpretation, our humanity, or rational nature, is a set of rational capacities to be preserved, developed, and promoted. Unlike things with mere "price," these capacities always have value, regardless of their utility and independent of our sentiments. However, although the dignity of humanity in one person always gives us reason to try to preserve and promote that individual's life as a rational, autonomous person, the dignity of other persons may give us reasons that override this and even justify sacrificing the individual for the good of others. The result is a sophisticated kind of consequentialism with a two-tiered value system.

This interpretation is worth mention because it makes explicit a way of understanding dignity that, I suspect, will strike many as natural and tempting. This is because thinking of all values as commensurable is a pervasive feature of our commercial and even philosophical culture. To think this way, however, is to miss what is especially distinctive and (in my view) attractive about Kant's idea of the dignity of persons. That is, dignity is not a value to be produced but a status always to be honored and respected, never violated. It is not a value that can be sacrificed in a few persons for the sake of many more persons. How specifically this value should guide our thinking about cases of conflict is a difficult question, to which I shall return. It seems clear, however, that from a Kantian perspective choices in dilemma-like situations cannot be justified by thinking every person has equal

---

[19] These problems have been often discussed. A good recent review is in Wood (1999), 76–110.
[20] See Cummiskey (1996).

dignity, so two persons must be worth twice as much as one, ten worth ten times more than one, and so on.[21]

Another quite common line of interpretation is well presented by Alan Donagan.[22] Donagan believed that Kant's formula of humanity as an end in itself best captured the heart of a long tradition of Judeo-Christian ethics. (Thomas Aquinas came close, he thought.) Donagan interprets the formula as a universal prescription to respect every person as a rational creature. Rationality is the feature of persons that ultimately grounds moral principles, and the expression "respect a person as rational . . . " also indicates what morality requires. Appealing to commonsense understandings of this phrase, he argues for many specific moral principles regarding suicide, self-development, coercion, injury, beneficence, truth-telling, property, law, family, and military service. His list is, in effect, a modified version of Kant's *The Metaphysics of Morals*. Donagan's principles are sometimes more qualified than Kant's, but nevertheless quite strict. He would allow, for example, lying to a would-be murderer to save a friend, but only because the person threatening murder has forfeited his right to the truth, not because good consequences outweigh the obligation to respect every person.

Donagan was vehemently opposed to W. D. Ross's influential idea that moral principles express only "prima facie" duties because that idea, like consequentialism, can be used to justify promise-breaking, coercion, and even murder if necessary to promote enough happiness.[23] To be sure, Ross's doctrine is typically seen by Anglo-American philosophers as strikingly opposed to consequentialism, for it can also be used to justify keeping a promise and telling the truth in cases in which breaking the promise and lying would produce more good. The problem, of course, is that Ross leaves it to intuition, or hunches, to determine what we actually ought to do when different prima facie duties conflict. A merit of Kant's humanity formula, in Donagan's view, was that it draws clear and definite lines between what is permissible and what is forbidden. Moreover, he thought

---

[21] As I argue elsewhere, there are times when "the numbers matter" and moral deliberation that fully respects the dignity of every person must take into account e.g. how many lives will be saved and how many lost. The justification, however, cannot be that two are *worth* more than one. See Hill (1992*a*), ch. 10.

[22] Donagan (1977).

[23] See Ross (1930). Prima facie duties are, in effect, considerations that count in favor of regarding an act to be one's actual duty.

that the lines it draws are in accord with the Judeo-Christian tradition and Donagan's own moral convictions.

Problems: Inflexible Prohibitions and Moral Dilemmas

Unfortunately, Donagan and many others treat decisions about what is required to treat persons with due respect as determined simply by focusing on particular interactions between persons in isolation from broader questions about justifiable policies for recurrent problems. When we try to rely on our intuitive sense of what is "respectful" to settle directly which interactions are forbidden and which are permitted, we are likely to generate indefensible prohibitions. This procedure leads us to think of morality as consisting of absolutely strict principles that admit no exceptions even for cases in which adhering to the principles will have disastrous consequences. Kant himself held some particular principles (e.g. regarding lying) in this inflexible way, but now this extreme rigorism is widely rejected, even by contemporary Kantians. It is also doubtful that it actually follows from Kant's basic principles, properly interpreted.

To illustrate the problem, consider a hypothetical situation in which telling a lie to an innocent company employee is the only nonharmful way that security investigators can persuade the employee to reveal information crucial to preventing a disastrous act of terrorism. If we focus entirely on the false communication between two persons, we may be tempted to see it as "disrespectful" and so, by Donagan's account, immoral. But looking at the larger context of the two persons' relations to everyone else affected, the lie may well seem justified. In principle, it could be justified to the employee herself, even though secrecy was required at the time. Arguably, from the larger perspective, the lie was the best way to give proper regard to the dignity of every person.

Again, we can imagine an "undercover" agent secretly opposing a totally oppressive tyranny, possessed of vital information needed to prevent massive destruction. Suppose she could keep from exposing herself as a resistance worker ("blowing her cover," as we say) only by standing idly by, or even cheering, as the tyrant's henchmen mock and humiliate an innocent citizen. Respect for the citizen seems to demand protest, but from a larger perspective respect for the dignity of other oppressed victims seems to demand cooperation. It is a tragic case, no doubt, but locally focused, rigoristic interpretations of Kant's humanity formula would apparently condemn the most reasonable course of action.

The narrowly focused interpretation of the humanity formula also seems to generate irresolvable moral dilemmas. Donagan argued forcefully that rational systems of moral principles, such as his and Kant's, cannot admit that there are any genuine moral dilemmas, except when it is the agent's own fault. His narrowly focused interpretation of respect for persons, however, apparently generates more dilemmas than he could reasonably blame on the agents faced with the problem. If we think of the prohibition on violating human dignity as demanding absolute refusal to engage in any interpersonal exchanges that seem intuitively disrespectful, then, unfortunately, we may be often caught in situations where we are, so to speak, damned if we do and damned if we do not. Suppose, for example, one has made a solemn promise to a brother to preserve an innocent secret but circumstances arise in which one can keep the secret only by means of telling a lie to a friend. Considered narrowly, both the lie to a friend and the breaking of a promise to a brother seem "disrespectful" and so wrong; but from a wider perspective there may be a solution that could be justified to all, at least as permissible.

A broadly Kantian ethics that determines specific principles from a wider perspective is unlikely to endorse absolutely exceptionless prohibitions of lying, promise-breaking, or whatever two-party interchanges are *intuitively* disrespectful. It cannot, however, settle moral problems simply by counting the number of people favorably and unfavorably affected by an action or by adding up amounts of benefit and harm. Whatever else they may be, Kantian responses to cases of conflict must regard respect for human dignity as a constant constraint on consequentialist thinking. What is respectful of dignity in one context, however, may be significantly different from what is respectful of dignity in another context, especially in tragically abnormal situations.

A Proposal: Dignity as a Value in Deliberation about Principles

Too often the debate between Kantians and consequentialists is presented as a stark choice between a utility maximizing theory that would sacrifice innocent people for slight increases in the general welfare and a rigoristic Kantian theory that insists on adhering to simple, narrowly conceived rules no matter what disaster will ensue. The former says, "Always go for the best balance of costs and benefits," and the latter endorses a particularly narrow reading of "Let justice be done, though the heavens should fall." Many philosophers in the consequentialist tradition now acknowledge constraints on their utility calculations. Examples include rule-utilitarians (such as Peter Railton) and consequentialists with nonhedonistic value theories (Shelly Kagan, David Cummiskey, and Donald Regan). Neo-Kantians too attempt to modify and supplement Kant's insights in a way that both respects the dignity of persons and takes seriously the need for principles responsive to the complex problems that we confront in our very imperfect world. This has, in fact, been my project now for many years.[24]

The basic idea is that Kant's formulas of the Categorical Imperative, including his formula of humanity as an end in itself, should not be treated as decision-procedures to be used case by case in the absence of serious reflection on general principles. Just as rule-utilitarianism distinguishes two levels of thinking about moral problems, theories that are Kantian in a broad sense should do likewise. In everyday, ordinary moral deliberation, we need to focus on the facts of the particular situation, keeping in mind the moral principles and ideals that we affirm. The principles and ideals help us to pick out the facts that are relevant, and they provide the basis for judgment about what we should do in the particular case. Questions may arise, however, that call for reflection and deliberation at a more general level. For example, we need at times to ask why we endorse the principles and ideals that we do, and we should look critically at our reasons. Even when convinced that a given principle is reasonable, we often need to think further about how to interpret it, define its range of application, and qualify it to allow for extraordinary cases. Keeping in mind the social and personal roles that

---

[24] This project is the underlying theme in many of the essays in Hill (1991), (1992*a*), (2000), (2002). These essays develop more and fully the proposal that I only sketch briefly here. My Kantian perspective is in the spirit of John Rawls's theory of justice, to which I owe much, but focuses more often on the real problems we face when we try to adjust theory for ideal conditions to address conditions that are far from ideal. Perhaps the most pertinent essays are "Making Exceptions without Abandoning the Principle: or How a Kantian Might Think about Terrorism" (Hill 1992*a*), ch. 10, and "A Kantian Perspective on Rules," "Basic Respect and Cultural Diversity," "Must Respect be Earned?," and "A Kantian Perspective on Moral Violence" (Hill, 2000), chs. 2, 3, 4, and 8, and "Moral Dilemmas, Gaps, and Residues" (Hill, 2002), vol. 4.

principles and ideals play in our lives, Kantian reflection at this more general level seeks to identify, interpret, and, if necessary, revise working principles and ideals that we can reflectively endorse.

This two-level structure is familiar in rule-utilitarianism, but what is distinctive about a Kantian two-level theory? The general idea, suggested by Kant's "kingdom of ends," is that the more specific working principles and ideals that we seek for guiding everyday moral decisions are those that would be affirmed, after due reflection, by Kantian ideal "legislators." Kantian legislators would deliberate about principles as rational and autonomous persons. They aim for agreement on "universal principles," which can be seen as reasonable from the perspective of any member. At least at first, their concern is with ethical principles, not principles for an enforceable legal order. As legislators with autonomy of the will, they are appropriately detached from special interests. In picturing the kingdom of ends, Kant says, we "abstract" from all differences among the members, but at later stages of deliberation certain differences will prove to be relevant.[25] More specific principles can be derived from a general principle of beneficence, for example, only by considering specific facts about the range of cases for which those principles are intended.

Unlike rule-utilitarian legislators, Kantian legislators are not motivated by an all-encompassing aim to maximize utility. They aim instead to identify a set of specific principles and ideals that, assuming facts about the human condition, best express the most fundamental values in Kantian ethics. The most prominent of these, and the most pertinent here, is human dignity or treating persons as ends in themselves.

In Kantian ethics value concepts are inseparable from ideas about what it is rational and reasonable to do. The former do not ground the latter, as they do in consequentialist theories. Rather, an assertion that something has value (e.g. dignity) is more like an abbreviation for a cluster of related judgments about the policies and attitudes that it is rational and reasonable to adopt.

---

[25] The two-level Kantian theory suggested here has affinities with Rawls (1999c), and this is no accident. There are also, however, important dissimilarities. For example, Rawls focuses only on the justice of basic social institutions, his "original position" members (who determine the principles of justice) lack moral commitments (e.g. to human dignity), and they are "mutually disinterested" (and so care nothing for the personal ends of others). Rawls wisely distinguishes several stages of deliberation, from the most abstract and universal to the more concrete and historically focused, and, though I cannot develop the idea here, I think that two-level Kantian theory needs to work with something like his distinctions.

Although I cannot argue the point here, I suggest that the cluster of judgments encapsulated in Kant's idea of human dignity includes most of the different values we find in appeals to dignity in everyday moral discussions. Not all of these are absolute values in the sense that they are decisive whenever they are relevant. In Kantian ethics what is absolute is the imperative always to treat persons as ends in themselves and so never to violate the human dignity of anyone. According to the two-level Kantian theory described here, this imperative is violated, strictly speaking, only by acts contrary to the principles and ideals reflectively endorsed from the Kantian legislative point of view. Unfortunately, in hard cases the principles that, all things considered, best express respect for human dignity may not allow us always to express it directly, fully, concretely to every person, but following those principles in such regrettable circumstances still respects the fundamental imperative.

In brief, the cluster of practical judgments associated with the Kantian idea of human dignity, in my view, includes the following.

First, and most formally, we must treat persons only in ways that we could in principle justify to them as well as to all other rational persons who take an appropriately impartial perspective. That is, we respect the dignity of persons by constraining ourselves by the principles we think all would endorse from the Kantian legislative perspective, assuming that this can be adequately defined.

Second, because dignity is not a commensurable value, our deliberations about specific principles must not proceed as if the dignity of persons can be compared and weighed against the dignity of others. We can speak of their "equal dignity" as persons, but, like "equality before the law," this refers to their common standing with rights and duties under moral principles, not "the same amount" of exchangeable value.

Third, we must treat persons as beings with moral rights that restrict how we may treat them even to achieve good ends. This idea acquires full practical import only insofar as moral rights can be specified from the legislative perspective. Even apart from these details, however, the general attribution of rights calls for recognition that morality attributes to each person a status honored and protected by some significant restraints on how he or she may be treated.[26] Kantian legislators, then, will try to find

---

[26] I use the term "moral rights" here more broadly than what Kant includes under *Recht*, for they do not imply legitimate enforceability by the state.

reasonable principles that define the individual rights, understanding that ignoring or trivializing rights is not an option.

Fourth, and more specifically, the existence of each rational person is an objective end and so something to be valued by all rational persons. This implies a strong presumption against killing persons and for helping them to maintain the conditions necessary for living as a rational autonomous person. Objective ends take precedence over subjective ends, and so we honor human dignity by placing a higher priority on preserving human life than on goods and services whose value depends on nonrational inclinations. To make the preservation of life an absolute value, however, would generate many paralyzing moral dilemmas.

Fifth, very important to Kant and to most people is the implication that dignity calls for *expressions* of respect and honor for persons, not for their social position, education, or achievements, but just as persons worthy of some deference and concern. How this can be expressed depends on the context. Often conventional gestures suffice, but at times what is needed is consulting, listening, respecting privacy, and trusting in ways appropriate to the context.

Finally, as Kant implies, we fully respect human dignity only if we count the personal ends of others as worthy of our attention and aid, even if the ends are based on morally indifferent preferences rather than basic needs. Arguably this is a lower priority than preserving life and avoiding expressions of disrespect, leaving considerable flexibility in practice. What clearly fails to respect dignity, however, are attitudes and policies of indifference to others' personal ends.

A Kantian legislative perspective, then, would be a framework constituted by basic Kantian values that is intended to be appropriate for thinking about the more specific moral principles that guide everyday judgments. The perspective obviously needs further explanation and development, but enough has been said to distinguish it from rule-utilitarianism and also from John Rawls's theory of justice (to which it has some resemblance). Arguably it also helps to avoid the problems raised by alternative interpretations of Kant's humanity formula: for example, multiple maxim descriptions, consequentialist justifications of intuitively immoral practices, and unreasonably rigid principles and moral dilemmas. Many questions regarding justification and application remain, and I conclude in the next section by mentioning a few potential problems and possible Kantian responses.

Problems with the Proposal and Suggestions for Response

Every type of moral theory raises characteristic problems, and developing a moral theory is to a large extent a matter of identifying and addressing these problems. Here I can only mention briefly some characteristic problems raised by the neo-Kantian perspective sketched here. First, like any theory that gives a prominent place to moral principles (or "rules"), the perspective sketched here raises questions about the place of principles in a moral life. Contemporary particularists, virtue theorists, and often feminists charge that modern moral philosophy has over-emphasized the importance of principles and rules, neglecting moral virtue, perception, habit, and the value of particular relationships. A reasonable theory, in my view, must not neglect these matters, and so neo-Kantian theorists need to think seriously about the reasons for having principles and rules and the limits of the role of principles and rules in a moral life.

Second, all theories face, in one way or another, the fact that reasonable people often disagree about moral matters. Disagreements, however, may seem a special problem for any theory that seeks general principles justifiable to all in reasonable deliberation. Such theories may address the problem in different ways, but one possibility is to think of a moral perspective not as generating universal moral principles that can win the actual agreement of all, but rather as guiding our reflections about what principles we can conscientiously endorse. The perspective calls for more than deliberation by ourselves in isolation from others, for we must consult, listen to, and reason with others in an honest effort to find principles that, in our best judgment, are based on reasons adequate to justify the principles to others. Nevertheless, realizing that disagreements may persist, we can only act conscientiously by those principles that, in our best judgment after due consultation with others, are supported by such reasons.

Third, two-tiered moral theories have been charged with promoting "moral schizophrenia," or "alienating" moral agents from the values by which they live in daily life.[27] The idea is if a theory distinguishes two levels of moral deliberation, one for deciding on principles and one for applying

---

[27] See Stocker (1976), 453–66.

them, then the theory must rely on two distinct sets of values, one for the first level and another for the second level. Rule-utilitarianism, for example, tells us to value only maximum possible utility when deliberating about moral rules, but then tells us to treat as valuable in daily life whatever those rules prescribe (such as honesty, acting from personal affection, etc.) Theories that are Kantian, in a broad sense, are supposed to decide principles from an "impartial" viewpoint that sets aside personal attachments and the more concrete values expressed in moral practice. Granted, Kantian impartiality is very different from, say, hedonistic utilitarians' equal consideration for equal pleasures, no matter whose, but critics tend to tar both "impartialist" theories with the same brush.

Many of the values in Kant's ethical theory are, as Kant thought, implicit in the thoughts and practice of ordinary conscientious people. Arguably, Kant's theory expresses at a higher level of abstraction the fundamental moral commitments commonly found in daily life. At least that was one of Kant's basic aims. Neo-Kantian theories, likewise, should confront the charge of alienation by developing, as far as possible, the constraints of moral deliberation about principles in a way that enables them to say, honestly, that the constraints reflect the basic values implicit in common thought and practice. There are, of course, limits to what can be done, given other aims of moral theory. But a theory, like rule-utilitarianism, that proposes deliberating about principles from a perspective alien to common thought and practice invites rejection. When offered principles derived from the alien perspective, we may well object, "Why should *we* count as authoritative the principles that would be adopted from the perspective of utility maximizers who are quite unlike us?" Ideally, neo-Kantian theorists should be able to say, among other things, that our theoretical guidelines for reasonable deliberation about moral principles express at a higher level of abstraction basic commitments implicit in your own moral judgments.

9

Assessing Moral Rules: Utilitarian and Kantian Perspectives

There has always been some disagreement about the importance of principles and rules in morality, but in recent years the disagreement has sharpened radically among philosophers. Traditional thinkers of many kinds, natural law theorists, intuitionists, Kantians, and even utilitarians, emphasized the need for moral principles and rules that are publicly acknowledged, deliberately taught, and socially enforced. Despite significant differences, there seems to be broad agreement on the main content of many of these principles. Respected philosophers associated with virtue ethics and particularism, however, have challenged these common assumptions, arguing on various grounds that the role of principles and rules in a moral life has been grossly exaggerated. Some of the objections stem from abstract metaphysical and epistemological considerations. Others express the more practical moral concern that traditional ethical theories have neglected the significance of judgment, character, and particular context in determining what is best to do. Wittgenstein's followers emphasize the limits of guidance by explicit rules as opposed to values inherent in ongoing social practices. Elizabeth Anscombe led many to suspect that modern ethical theories employed legalistic ideas of "obligation" that make no sense apart from theological beliefs of an earlier age. These are all important challenges, but not my concern in this chapter. Here I take up another major source of doubt about moral rules and principles: the common perception that rule-utilitarianism, the most prominent contemporary type of rule-oriented ethics, is subject to devastating objections.

My plan is to revisit some of these objections, for I suspect that the objections to rule-utilitarianism are also seen as reasons to doubt any normative ethical theory that is similar in giving a prominent role to publicly affirmed, deliberately taught, and socially enforced rules and principles.

My main point is that certain common objections to rule-utilitarianism do not undermine all theories that affirm the importance of such rules and principles. More specifically, I suggest that an alternative "Kantian" way of identifying and justifying the morally significant rules and principles is not open to the objections in question. The alternative does not merely add another epicycle to the latest version of rule-utilitarianism, but proposes a different understanding of the relevant values and how they enter into deliberation about rules and principles. The alternative is to some extent drawn from Kant's ethics, but I am not concerned here with tracing its roots. I call it "Kantian" in a broad sense, but do not insist on the label.

My plan is as follows. First, I describe what I take to be a familiar view of the role of rules and principles in everyday life independently of any particular theory. I think of this as the commonsense view, but for now I present it merely as a starting point. Rule-utilitarianism offers a systematic normative explanation of this commonsense view, but arguably not the best explanation. Second, I review briefly how rule-utilitarianism treats moral rules and principles, and why it is supposed to be more satisfactory than act-utilitarianism. Third, I set aside two persistent controversies about rule-utilitarianism that are not relevant for my purposes, the first because it is a dispute internal to utilitarianism and the second because it is irresolvable. Fourth, I review some further objections to rule-utilitarianism (and more broadly, to some other forms of rule-consequentialism).[1] Fifth, I sketch a Kantian alternative that, like rule-utilitarianism, ascribes an important role to rules and principles but differs significantly in its structure and value theory. Finally, I point out ways in which the alternative addresses the concerns behind the objections to rule-utilitarianism. This comparative study is not intended as a refutation of rule-utilitarianism, but it suggests

---

[1] My discussion will focus on rule-utilitarianism, but for the most part it will be applicable to familiar versions of rule-consequentialism, such as Brad Hooker's. There are many versions of rule-utilitarianism and rule-consequentialism. Here I follow Brad Hooker's ((2000), 1–2) account. Rule-consequentialist theories "make moral permissibility turn on considerations about ideal codes." They hold "that the code whose collective internalization has the best consequences is the ideal code." Rule-utilitarian theories are rule-consequentialist theories that have a specific idea of "best consequences": they evaluate "rules solely in terms of aggregate well-being" (ibid. 33). Other rule-consequentialist theories often take into account how well-being is distributed. Hooker's favored version, for example, says (in part): "An act is wrong if it is forbidden by the code of rules whose internalization by the overwhelming majority of everyone everywhere in each generation has maximum expected value in terms of well-being (*with some priority for the worst off*)." The italics are mine. Hooker gives references to other versions at p. 33; see also 43 n. 13.

that there may be a better way to understand and defend moral rules and principles. More specifically, a broadly Kantian theory may give a more plausible account of the grounds on which moral rules should be evaluated, the reasons why they are needed, and the limits on their role in a moral life.

A Familiar Pre-theoretical View of the Role of Rules and Principles

A common view, which I find plausible, is as follows. First, there are some general moral principles that are valid for everyone, at least for everyone in the more or less familiar circumstances within which we interact with others. These, in contrast with specific rules, are quite basic, and reasonably treated as grounds for more specific rules and judgments. The general principles, unlike the standards that moral theorists aspire to articulate, are usually treated as platitudes but are obviously open to different interpretations. A list of familiar examples, loosely expressed, might include: "You ought not to inflict needless pain," "You should honor your commitments," "You should do your fair share of what needs to be done," "Don't be mean," "You should not exploit people," "Life is precious, not to be wasted." These commonsense principles serve various roles. We offer them to children in moral education. We appeal to them in arguing and exhorting others to behave well. We cite them in blaming others, and ourselves. And they serve as implicit background assumptions in our deliberations about what to do.

In addition to these vague general principles, we appeal to more specific precepts that I shall call "rules" (even though they may more commonly be called "principles"). Some are quite specific and context-dependent whereas others are broader and less limited in scope of application. There are often disagreements about their interpretation, stringency, and context of application, but some core requirements are commonly seen as socially enforced standards appropriately invoked in moral education, deliberation, argument, exhortation, and blame. They sometimes conflict in tragic cases, and even in relatively trivial everyday cases. When they conflict, we can often (though not always) reasonably judge which rule is most important to follow in the circumstances. Many moral rules overlap with legal requirements, but, typically, moral rules are enforced more informally and are regarded as "immune from deliberate change."[2] Like legal rules, moral rules often have at least a penumbra of indeterminacy; but this does not prevent their serving an important role in our moral lives. There are no official moral judges to render precedent-setting decisions about how to remove indeterminacies, but we manage well enough in practice by exercising individual and group judgment and sometimes by just "plumping" for one interpretation or another.[3] Having such rules widely accepted and internalized helps to coordinate our activities and assure us that others will reciprocate. The rules give shape to our social practices and their social enforcement counteracts our fear that moral restraint will make us "suckers" easily exploited by others.

Although nonphilosophers rarely discuss the matter explicitly, most seem to treat moral rules, like legal and religious rules, as standards for particular judgments rather than as "rules of thumb" that approximately generalize what was initially perceived as correct in particular cases. It is commonly understood that the rules actually accepted in a community as moral requirements may be imperfect and subject to gradual change under critical scrutiny but also that even imperfect rules often create legitimate expectations that deserve consideration. People may differ widely in their assumptions about the ultimate source of the authority of moral principles and rules even when they share a common understanding of their content and importance. Few, if any, imagine that all aspects of moral life are rule-governed. It is generally understood that developed moral attitudes, good character, and judgment are needed for wise application of rules and for situations for which rules do not apply.

Rule-Utilitarianism

The commonsense idea of moral principles and rules is largely accepted by rule-utilitarians (and, more broadly, by rule-consequentialists), but in

---

[2] See Hart (1961), 171–3. Professional codes of ethics may be altered by official acts of the governing bodies of professional associations, and in this respect their rules are more like legal regulations than moral rules and principles. However, insofar as they are regarded as morally binding on members of the profession, they are generally thought to be supported by moral reasons beyond the governing body's power to change. Hart also says that moral requirements are taken to be serious requirements, whereas at least some legal requirements may be seen as quite trivial.

[3] This is Simon Blackburn's term for what we often must do in a moral dilemma situation.

addition they offer a normative ethical theory that is supposed to systematize, clarify, and explain the role that particular moral rules serve and the
reasonable basis for accepting them.[4] As theories of "normative ethics" as
opposed to "metaethics," these theories do not claim to answer all the
linguistic, epistemological, and metaphysical questions that philosophers
have raised about moral judgments. The normative theories themselves do
not tell us how their basic normative principle and value theory can
ultimately be justified (though their advocates often have views about
this). Questions about ultimate justification of normative theories and the
meaning of evaluative terms are left for metaethics or moral epistemology.
Rule-utilitarian theories, however, have been subject to a number of
apparently compelling objections that leave them suspect even as normative
theories.[5] These objections (to be considered shortly) are of broad interest
because they may seem to cast doubt on all theories that try to systematize,
clarify, and explain the common view of moral principles and rules
described above. Before turning to objections, however, we should review
some basic points about rule-utilitarianism.

Rule-utilitarianism (RU) developed in response to objections to act-
utilitarianism (AU). There are various versions of both types of theory but
subtle differences need not detain us here. AU, as commonly conceived,
holds that acts are right if they promote at least as much expected utility as
any alternative open to the agent and they are wrong otherwise.[6] Classic
utilitarians, such as Bentham, Sidgwick, and perhaps Mill, are hedonists,
counting pleasure (under various names) as the only thing intrinsically good

---

[4] From now on I will simplify discussion by reserving "principles" for the most basic standards in a
theory and (somewhat artificially) calling all other, more specific norms "rules."

[5] Most of the objections I shall consider, unlike some other familiar objections to rule-utilitarianism,
can be raised as well to forms of rule-consequentialism such as Hooker's, but it does not matter for my
purposes here whether or not some versions of rule-consequentialism (perhaps radically modified) could
meet the objections. The point is to identify the objections and to see how a broadly Kantian alternative
theory might handle them.

[6] John Stuart Mill, whom many (but not all) regard as an act-utilitarian, had a more subtle view. He
said that right acts tend to promote happiness and wrong acts tend to promote the reverse, but he later
explained that the concept of a "wrong" act implies that we may be compelled by law, social opinion, or
conscience to refrain from the act. Some acts recommended by utilitarianism as utility-maximizing, then,
are not wrong not to do, strictly speaking, in Mill's ((1976), 60) sense. Note also that, although I describe
AU as assessing acts by their expected utility (as Bentham and others do), some (e.g. G. E. Moore) hold
that for utilitarianism the right act is what maximizes actual utility (for him " 'intrinsic value' "). Nothing
in my discussion hangs on the distinction, but I shall generally assume that expected utility is what most
utilitarians are concerned to maximize.

and pain (under various names) as the only thing intrinsically bad. G. E. Moore and his followers deny the accompanying hedonistic value theory, but typically they and other consequentialists regard intrinsic values and disvalues to be commensurable in principle. Most consequentialists believe that we can reasonably think in terms of aggregating intrinsic values and of increasing and diminishing the total amount, even if strict quantitative measurements are not possible.

Among the many objections raised against AU in its various forms, the most persistent has been that it leads to counterintuitive moral judgments. If we use AU as a decision guide, it is argued, our ignorance and wishful thinking will often cause us to misestimate the expected utility of what we propose to do. More seriously, even if our estimates are correct, we will sometimes judge it permissible to do things that are dishonest, unjust, ungrateful, and disloyal because in many empirical circumstances, the honest, just, grateful, and loyal options are not utility-maximizing. Defenders of AU generally argue that this does not in fact happen very *often,* but critics reply that it happens *all too often* for AU to be a satisfactory theory.

Some act-utilitarians deny that the AU principle should be used as a working guide to moral decision-making. Instead, they treat it as stating what would make agents' acts *objectively* right even if the agents could not know what is objectively right, should not even try to discern it by estimating utility in the particular case, and are often utterly blameless in failing to do it. Such utilitarians can consistently recommend following rules the general acceptance of which would apparently maximize expected utility, but they can only recommend this as a useful heuristic guide likely to result in right action more often than trying to estimate utilities in particular cases. Sometimes, AU must concede, following such rules may lead to wrong acts because what maximizes utility (and so by AU is objectively right) in the particular case is not always what is prescribed by rules the general acceptance of which would maximize utility.

RU, in its more subtle versions designed to avoid "collapse" into AU, construes right acts as acts permitted by a set of "ideal" rules the general acceptance of which by most, but not all, people in the relevant community would produce at least as much utility as comparable acceptance of other moral codes. The rules are taken to be public, teachable, socially reinforced rules that should be internalized by all. Such rules may include "built-in" standard exceptions, but they would not be useful if they were too complex.

The rules in the "ideal" set or code may sometimes conflict, but allowing too many conflicts among the rules would diminish their usefulness as rules. RU can offer various procedures for resolving these conflicts, but to stipulate that we should resolve conflicts simply by attempting to maximize utility in each particular instance of conflict would threaten to undermine what is distinctive about RU even if it would not, strictly, reduce it to AU.

Having a set of rules might promote utility for several reasons. For example, when we guide ourselves by appropriate rules, conscientiously or from habit, we are not open to the objection to AU that we are prone to misestimate the expected utilities in particular cases because of ignorance, wishful thinking, and self-deception.[7] Having a common set of generally acknowledged public rules also helps to solve problems of coordination. When most of us internalize the rules and rule-breakers are at least informally sanctioned, we have needed assurance that others will generally act in mutually beneficial ways. The rules can serve as the basis for interpersonal moral persuasion, argument, and criticism, which help to reinforce moral motivation, channel disagreements constructively, and form bonds of trust and community. As Mill noted, developing common moral precepts through experience over time enables us to act quickly when it might be disastrous for us to take the long time necessary for utility calculations in a particular case.[8]

Act-utilitarians can consistently acknowledge that having common rules can be useful and adhering to these regularly may be the best strategy for maximizing utility in most cases. However, as Rawls noted, under AU rules remain rough generalizations or "rules of thumb."[9] The crucial point distinctive of RU is that it implies that particular acts in accord with a useful rule can be right even though an alternative act would actually produce more utility—and particular acts contrary to useful rules can be wrong even though they would actually produce more utility than any alternative would. This feature, and the structure of RU, enables rule-utilitarians to

---

[7] There is, of course, always some danger that these distorting influences might affect the interpretation and application of rules, but arguably this is a lesser danger than we would face in trying to estimate utilities case by case. Also, the objection in question does not apply to the version of AU that says that maximizing utility is the criterion of objective rightness but not an appropriate guide for actual decision-making.

[8] Mill (1976), 30–2.

[9] Rawls (1955).

argue that the ideal moral code includes many intuitively important moral rules regarding honesty, justice, gratitude, loyalty, etc. that demand or forbid acts independently of the utility they produce on the particular occasion. RU says it is right, not just a generally useful rule of thumb, to conform to rules provided general acceptance of those rules by most people in the relevant community produces at least as much utility as such general acceptance of any alternative moral code.

Sophisticated versions of RU take into account that blindly following rules ideal for a non-actual world might be disastrous (and morally wrong) to follow in our imperfect, real world. Various strategies help to address the problem: for example, in assessing the utility of general conformity to a given set of rules we must take into account the feasibility and costs of maintaining it as a moral code as well as legitimate expectations generated under the actual moral code to be reformed.

Rule-consequentialism (RC) is, in effect, RU expanded in its value theory to allow the relevance of consequences other those traditionally associated with utilitarianism (pleasure, pain, happiness, unhappiness, etc.). Also some versions may not insist that all values are commensurable and quantifiable; and partial or qualified versions of RC can allow some side-constraints on the ideal of maximizing good consequences. These modifications may make the theory more plausible, but they also move it away from its initial structure and inspiration. For simplicity of comparison I will focus on RU, but much of my discussion would apply equally well to recent forms of RC such as Brad Hooker's.[10]

Two Controversies about Rule-Utilitarianism Set Aside

Two kinds of dispute have dominated much of the contemporary discussion of utilitarianism of all kinds, but they are not the points most relevant to my purpose here. First, utilitarians disagree among themselves, as well as with others, about what is intrinsically valuable. Familiar forms of utilitarianism combine a theory of right (asserting that acts or rules are to be assessed by the

---

[10] Hooker (2000).

amount of intrinsic value they produce) with a theory of value (identifying what has intrinsic value). Hedonistic versions, such as Bentham's, hold that pleasure and only pleasure is good in itself and pain and only pain is bad in itself. Many have argued that this view is too narrow, ignoring the intrinsic value of human experiences and relationships that cannot be measured in terms of pleasure and pain. Mill famously tried to expand hedonism by acknowledging different "qualities" of pleasure, but for various reasons many have found this move inadequate.[11] G. E. Moore, and followers, said that intrinsic value was an irreducible property—simple, nonnatural, known by intuition, and distinct from pleasure.[12] Objections to the metaphysical and epistemological implications of this view, as well as other problems, convinced most subsequent moral philosophers that the view was untenable. Many question the very idea of agent-neutral intrinsic values that can be compared, weighed, and aggregated. Recent versions of utilitarianism avoid the older ideas of intrinsic value and focus instead on comparative amounts of satisfaction, well-being, fulfillment of agent's informed desires, etc., but how to understand *utility* remains controversial.

The second dispute that I shall bypass here concerns the objection that has dominated critical discussions of utilitarianism from Mill's time to ours. This is the charge that utilitarianism, even rule-utilitarianism, entails judgments of right and wrong that conflict with judgments that are widely and deeply held by most competent, reflective people. Just as AU is said to recommend acts that are unjust, ungrateful, breaches of promise, and insensitive to moral deserts, it is charged that RU recommends moral codes, or sets of rules, that are not adequately sensitive to claims of justice, gratitude, fidelity, and desert.[13] The reason is that, although rules requiring justice, fidelity, gratitude, and desert obviously promote well-being in many ways, the moral code that *maximizes* (expected) utility (e.g. aggregate well-being) does not necessarily or obviously accord with our convictions about these matters. Given the complexities of the relevant empirical facts, the utility-maximizing code would apparently allow many more exceptions than our reflective moral convictions would.

The problem with this line of objection for present purposes is that we are not in a position to know exactly what a utility-maximizing code would prescribe regarding matters involving justice, fidelity, gratitude, and desert.

---

[11] Mill (1976), 11–15.   [12] Moore (1959), ch. 1.   [13] See e.g. Frankena (1973), 39–43.

We cannot argue that its recommendations are inferior to those of an alternative normative theory without knowing what the specific recommendations of each theory would turn out to be. Fictional counterexamples that simply stipulate what maximizes utility do not show that RU yields unacceptable results in the real world for which, presumably, normative ethical theories are intended. Actual or realistic counterexamples, however, are always controversial because it is uncertain what the long-term consequences of various complex sets of rules would be. Thus it is best to turn to different kinds of objection.

Further Sources of Doubt about RU

A general question lies behind several more specific doubts. *Does RU adequately reflect our understanding of the relevant grounds for assessing moral rules?* RU implies that moral codes are rightly assessed solely in terms of their expected contribution (compared to other codes) to maximum utility (aggregate well-being, satisfaction, or intuited intrinsic value).[14] Insofar as it guides debates about what is the best code, it implies that we are to consider nothing else as ultimately important. Even if the theory is not meant to be a guide to actual deliberation about rules, it still implies that the *correct* moral rules are those that *would* be selected by rule-makers who were *perfectly informed* and *exclusively concerned* to advance utility. But, we may wonder, is producing maximum utility the only relevant consideration? Is it always a decisive consideration? Even if a moral theory does not, in the end, make specific recommendations contrary to our considered moral judgments, it may offer an intuitively inadequate account of the grounds by which we should assess sets of moral rules. The following, more specific questions reflect this general concern.

---

[14] For simplicity I will hereafter drop the qualification regarding different things that rule-utilitarians can count as utility. My discussion will proceed as if utility is simply well-being, but similar questions arise about other interpretations of utility. Special problems arise if utility is treated as an intuited "intrinsic value" in the manner of G. E. Moore. This allows the theoretical possibility that there is *intrinsic* value, and so utility, in the mere fact that a promise was kept, justice done, gratitude shown, etc. This move in effect loads the utilitarian theory with deontological considerations in a confusing way in order to meet standard objections. I will not discuss this "ideal utilitarianism" further here because the problems with it have been well recognized.

1. *Does the permissibility of pursuing one's own personal projects depend upon whether or not the moral code that maximizes utility allows these pursuits?* Some have argued that utility-maximizing moral codes would be too demanding, ruling out personal pursuits that are intuitively permissible. This objection, like the charge that RU prescribes acts that are intuitively unjust, cannot be fairly assessed unless we can determine with confidence how various moral codes would actually affect aggregate well-being. This depends on complex empirical facts that we are in no position to judge with any assurance. There is a limit to what can be settled by reference to alleged counterexamples. Even though we cannot judge with confidence exactly which moral codes would be utility-maximizing, however, we can and should question whether the permissibility of personal pursuits is entirely dependent on the empirical question whether moral codes allowing them in fact would maximize utility.[15] This is a question not about the particular judgments prescribed by RU but rather about its account of the *grounds* for assessing moral rules. RU holds that maximizing utility, and only this, is the ground for assessing sets of rules, and so we may pursue our personal projects only if the utility-maximizing moral code would allow it.[16] We have no moral freedom to do what we want, even if it harms no one, except insofar as the rules allowing particular freedoms turn out to maximize utility.[17] Whether or not utility-maximizing rules would in fact allow an intuitively acceptable range of permissible pursuits, we may well doubt whether our moral

---

[15] Any plausible ethical theory implies that the pursuit of some personal projects is morally optional but also that there are some stringent moral restrictions on what kinds of personal projects we may pursue. The issue now is not where to draw the line, but whether the only consideration relevant to drawing a line is what utility-maximizing codes require and permit. Note that on versions of RU with an intuitionist theory of value, what will maximize utility is not entirely an empirical question.

[16] Here (and elsewhere) I pass over the complication that, for all we know, two different codes might both bring about the same maximum possible utility. Brad Hooker's ((2000), 32) rule-consequentialism contains this proviso: "If in terms of expected value two or more codes are better than the rest but equal to one another, the one closest to conventional morality determines what acts are wrong."

[17] Similar concerns are sometimes expressed in terms of "agent-centered privileges." The concerns typically arise for those who already accept that all relevant values are commensurable, and that there is at least a strong presumption that our acts or rules ought always to be chosen so that they maximize utility. Given this framework, it appears puzzling how one could justify the "privilege" of particular agents to pursue their own projects if they were less than utility-maximizing. RU justifies this by stipulating that rules, not particular acts, must be utility-maximizing and then arguing that utility-maximizing codes in fact include ample permissive rules (or its mandatory rules are sufficiently limited to allow ample moral liberty by default). But then the further question arises, whether the stipulation that rules, not particular acts, are to be assessed by utility is arbitrary given the background assumptions. For utilitarians, this is the worry that RU may reflect an irrational "rule-worship."

freedom to do these things rests entirely on this (hard to discern) empirical fact.

2. *Do the traditional restrictions on the legitimate means that we may use to prevent the wrong and harmful acts of others depend entirely on their maximizing (expected) utility?* Again the issue here is not whether, given empirical facts, RU supports such restrictions, but whether its support is needed. It is commonly believed that no one should use murder, torture, perjury, or rigged elections as a means even toward the commendable end of reducing the total number of comparable acts by others. Even those who would allow exceptions for certain extraordinary catastrophic circumstances rarely argue (at least publicly) that in general we may murder, torture, lie under oath, and fix elections whenever we expect that this would result in more expected utility by hindering others from murdering, torturing, etc., in the future. Rule-utilitarians can argue that, for various empirical reasons, utility-maximizing moral codes would include something like these traditional restrictions; but we may well doubt whether our convictions in this area rest on that empirical claim. If, contrary to fact, we knew that the code that would maximize expected utility lacks the traditional restrictions on the means we may permissibly use, would that settle the issue whether or not they should be abandoned?[18] The question prompts a suspicion that RU assessment of rules omits relevant considerations.

3. *Even if there were good grounds to believe that a certain moral code would maximize expected utility, would an unconditional commitment to follow its rules* for that reason *be a reasonable and morally worthy attitude?*[19] Again, we are not questioning for now the claim that RU supports morally acceptable rules that have built-in exceptions that are intuitively plausible. Nor are we

---

[18] For those who begin with the framework of thought described in n. 17, this is the problem of "agent-centered restrictions." That is, given those assumptions, how can one justify restrictions such as "One must not murder even to prevent another from murder." If the initial guiding idea is that harm, deprivation, and suffering are bad (e.g. as diminishing aggregate well-being), then it seems one ought to do what diminishes the number of murders, severity of harms, etc., without regard to *who* does these things. Most agree that this conclusion is counterintuitive, but the background framework calls for justification. Advocates of RU can argue that moral codes with the traditional restrictions would maximize utility, and so prohibit murder to prevent future murders, etc. My question is whether that sort of argument is what should settle the matter.

[19] By "reasonable" here I do not mean "rational from a self-interested point of view" or even "rational to choose as a way of maximizing satisfaction of one's desires." My question concerns the evaluation of RU as a normative ethical theory, and so thinking about whether the commitment is "reasonable and morally worthy" calls for evaluating it by our considered moral judgments.

raising linguistic, metaphysical, and epistemological questions that traditionally belong to metaethics. The issue, rather, is how RU squares with our normative views about respectful commitment to systems of rules. RU, as usually conceived, is a normative ethical theory about the features of acts that make them permissible or wrong. Specifically it holds that what makes acts right or wrong is whether they are allowed or forbidden by a set of rules that maximizes expected utility.[20] It is almost a truism, and not just among Kantians, that it is reasonable and morally worthy to do acts that are right because of features that ultimately make them right, i.e. the reasons why they are right.[21] So we naturally wonder whether RU identifies the ultimate right-making feature in such a way that it is a reasonable and morally worthy resolve to do whatever acts have that feature just because they have it.

   To illustrate, consider a fanciful example. Suppose I could articulate the ideal moral code that my maternal grandmother taught me. Imagine that its content fits as well as any code our considered judgments about justice, gratitude, permissible personal projects, murder, and so on. In other words, the advice "Follow the rules of the code that Hill's maternal grandmother taught" serves as a reliable way to identify right and wrong that matches (as well as any theory) the core of common moral opinion. By strictly adhering to Grandmother's Code, let us suppose I would act correctly, meeting my responsibilities and avoiding wrongdoing. But if the reason I did so was *just* that Grandmother's Code required it, I would not be acting in a reasonable and morally worthy way. A commitment to whatever the code demands just because it is the set of rules that a certain person taught is not a worthy attitude.[22] Now the supposition that a code is utility-maximizing is

---

[20]   An advocate of RU could deny that RU explains what ultimately makes acts right (the reasons why the acts are right), saying merely that it reliably picks out right acts. This strikes me as an unpromising move, however, because it is so hard to show that it actually does reliably identify right acts and because what initially inspired utilitarianism was the relatively uncontroversial thought that it is at least in general a good reason for doing something that it prevents harm or promotes well-being.

[21]   Note that I set aside here the controversial question whether *only* such motivation is morally worthy.

[22]   We can perhaps imagine that I was committed to acting morally because I recognized the good moral reasons that lie behind moral requirements, but then I came to see that, oddly enough, following Grandmother's Code would reliably lead me to act in a morally correct way. Suppose further that I followed Grandmother's Code strictly because I was resolved to act morally and had seen good moral reason to do all the particular things prescribed in the content of Grandmother's Code (independently of the fact that grandmother taught it). My ultimate commitment, then, is not to "Do whatever Grandmother's Code says" but to "Do what I judge, from moral reasons independent of grandmother, to be morally required." Although it is no doubt just a fiction that anyone's grandmother devised such a

obviously of more moral significance than its being favored by my grand-mother, but a similar doubt arises. Even if RU would lead to morally correct action, does it adequately explain what makes acts right and what makes commitment to rules morally worthy?[23]

4. *Are only forward-looking considerations relevant to the assessment of moral codes?* RU is like AU in that both hold that the primary objects of evaluation, whether they are particular acts or sets of rules, must be evaluated entirely by their expected consequences.[24] For AU what matters ultimately is whether a proposed particular act brings about a better future (or one at least as good) as does any alternative. A common objection was that some moral considerations, such as fidelity, gratitude, and reparations, are "backward-looking." That is, they appeal to *past* facts as reasons why we should *now* act in certain ways, such as keeping a promise, returning a favor, and compensating those whom we have wrongfully injured. RU was designed in part to acknowledge the validity of such principles, and in other respects too RU

---

perfect moral code, if we imagine that I correctly and reasonably judged that my grandmother's code was a perfectly reliable indicator of moral requirements, then my *basic* commitment and resolve (to morality, not grandmother) would be morally worthy. Something similar might be said of RU. Suppose we knew exactly what code RU picks out and also knew that code reliably identifies acts as right or wrong even though not by their most basic right-making features. Then the code would have a derivative value as a handy device that enables us to make particular moral judgments without further reflection on basic values. But the background hypotheses here seem quite unrealistic.

[23] This general worry is related to the more specific objection to RU that arises within the utilitarian family: to follow RU is to be guilty of "rule-worship." The charge, made by act-utilitarians, expresses the thought that following a set of rules, even rules the general acceptance of which maximizes expected utility, is arbitrary, i.e. without good reason, if one is confident that in the particular case one can bring about more good, all things considered, by breaking the rules. The particular objection gets its bite from background assumptions that utilitarians typically (but not necessarily) accept—the framework of thought described in n. 17. Given this background, it seems that, although utilitarians usually have good reasons to follow the moral codes general acceptance of which maximizes expected utility, and to encourage others to do so, it would be arbitrary, unreasonable, and unworthy "rule-worship" to follow the rules in particular cases in which breaking them clearly brings about more (intrinsic) value. This is a special conundrum for utilitarians, and some have offered solutions. For example, Brad Hooker avoids defending his version of rule-consequentialism from initial claims about "intrinsic value" as the source of all reasons (and so morality), and defends them instead by appeal to more general methodological criteria (fit with initially "attractive" general beliefs about morality, coherence, consistency, capacity to system-atize and impartially justify our considered judgments, and helpfulness regarding contested cases).

[24] This is a slight exaggeration. A hedonistic utilitarian, for example, can count the enjoyment of an activity as part of aggregate utility even if it is not conceived as a separable "consequence" of the activity. So, strictly speaking, the better "future" that right acts are supposed to promote can include pleasures and satisfactions simultaneous with the utility-maximizing act. Also, as mentioned earlier, "ideal utilitarians," such as G. E. Moore, allow the theoretical possibility that facts such as "a promise was kept" and "justice was done" have intrinsic value, and these are not normally considered "consequences" of the acts that fulfill promises and do justice.

requires us to pay attention to the past. Most obviously, RU allows that the past may be relevant to the assessment of rules insofar as it offers valuable lessons enabling us to predict future consequences. (Even AU requires us to try to learn from the past.) In addition, insofar as we actually care about how our past and future are related, our future happiness depends to some extent on whether the future that results from our present choices coheres with our past in the ways we want. Arguably a code that maximizes expected utility would contain transitional rules telling the individuals committed to them to adjust their conduct in various ways that respect legitimate expectations in the previously accepted code. For all these reasons in following RU we could not reasonably assess moral codes with the attitude, "Forget the past and just look to look to the future."

The fact remains, however, that *what finally* determines RU assessment of moral codes is the sort of future it is expected to bring about—specifically whether, compared to alternatives, it would maximize expected utility (aggregate well-being, satisfaction, or intuited intrinsic value). We may well ask, however, is this *all* that is relevant? Is it always relevant? More specifically, we may doubt whether our respect for the backward-looking and cross-time values of mutual respect,[25] justice, and fidelity to commitments are entirely dependent on whether or not the general acceptance of a code that requires them is expected, all things considered, to bring about more aggregate well-being than any other.

A Kantian Perspective on Moral Rules

In several previous essays, I have sketched an alternative way of thinking about moral rules drawn from Kant's idea of ideal moral legislation in a "kingdom of ends."[26] The main idea is that everyday decision-making should be guided and constrained by rules (mid-level principles) that would be endorsed by rational moral "legislators" who deliberate under specified conditions, including autonomy and respect for humanity as an

---

[25] Particular relationships of mutual trust and respect as examples of cross-time values, where a valued relationship over time requires certain responses even if they are not calculated to bring about the best future state of affairs, are discussed in Hill (1991), 189–211.

[26] Hill (2000), chs. 2, 4, and 8; (2002), ch. 3; and chs. 8, 10, 11, and 13 of this volume.

end in itself. As in RU, deliberation about moral rules must take into account reasons for and against having rules with respect to various areas of life, but in the Kantian alternative these reasons are not fixed by an overarching concern to maximize utility. Consequences matter, but only in ways prescribed and limited by the Kantian values stipulated in the legislative framework. These values are supposed to reflect the most fundamental Kantian standards expressed in formulations of the Categorical Imperative, including interpretations of *autonomy, universal law-giving,* and *humanity as an end in itself.* At a minimum the framework presupposes (as an *autonomy* constraint) that ideally in deliberating about moral rules we maintain an appropriate detachment from our personal projects and preferences, though the kind of detachment appropriate for various stages of deliberation varies. Respect for *universal laws* is reflected in two ways: moral legislators rely on basic values regarded as valid for all human beings, and they seek to find or construct rules (mid-level principles) that are justifiable for everyone within the scope of the problems under consideration.

The most fundamental values that are to guide and constrain deliberation about rules are drawn from the idea of human dignity, or *humanity as an end in itself.* In Kantian normative ethical theory, as I understand it, attributions of value are to be understood, for practical purposes, as claims about reasons for taking certain attitudes and actions. Saying that something is valuable, then, can be understood as equivalent to saying how we ought to regard and treat the thing that is said to have value. Accordingly, we should understand the idea of human dignity, or humanity as an end in itself, as a cluster of prescriptions about how to regard and treat human beings. For now, let us take the main prescriptions as follows.

In sum, they are, *negatively,* not to regard persons as having a merely commensurable value and not to violate principles that rational autonomous persons would endorse, all things considered; and, *positively,* to exercise, preserve, develop, and honor rational nature in all persons, to prioritize the needs for rational autonomous living over more trivial concerns, and to count the happiness of others (or, strictly, their permissible ends) as significant in our deliberations. The proposed Kantian perspective regards the second negative prescription as an inflexible constraint on action: *never* violate the principles that, in one's best judgment, rational autonomous deliberators would endorse, if guided and constrained by the idea of human dignity and mindful of the complexities of the real world for which the principles are intended. The first negative prescription (*"never* regard persons as having a merely commensurable value") and the remaining positive prescriptions are also non-optional demands, but they directly concern our *attitudes* when we deliberate and act.[27]

Further details must be left aside here, but a few further remarks may be helpful. First, the Kantian legislative framework, as I conceive it, is not a decision procedure but at best an aid to thinking about moral rules, pulling together various morally relevant considerations and excluding irrelevant ones. Even when deliberating with the stipulated Kantian values, we cannot expect that reasonable people will always agree about the relative importance of various rules and the exceptions they allow. For this reason the deliberative procedure might be best viewed as an aid to conscientious judgment and debate rather than a criterion of moral truth.

Second, the Kantian perspective asks what rules we would endorse if deliberating with certain stipulated values whereas RU asks what rules, if generally accepted, would maximize utility. In effect, however, the RU question is the same as asking what rules would be endorsed by ideal legislators who were *exclusively concerned* and *perfectly informed* about the utility of the consequences of the general acceptance of the rules. If we could assume there is always an objective fact about which codes would maximize utility, then we could infer that all who deliberate from the RU perspective *correctly* would agree about the rules to be followed. It seems doubtful, however, that *utility,* on any plausible interpretation, is a sufficiently determinate concept to permit the assumption that there is always a fact of the matter about what rules maximize utility. More important for present purposes, such theoretical determinacy, even if possible, would be no practical advantage of RU when this is treated as a normative guide, because those who use RU as a guide in the real world, not being omniscient, can be expected to disagree often about what maximizes utility. As normative standards, neither RU nor the Kantian perspective can guarantee that reasonable, conscientious followers will always agree. The real issue

---

[27] Of course, they will rule out certain acts as immoral and show that others are morally required, but they do so by demanding that our deliberations, choices, and intentions are compatible with the prescribed attitudes. It is not as though one could muster up a motivationally inert and non-reason-giving "inner state of mind," a mere wish or "pure thought," and then anything one does will be permitted.

between them is about what counts as relevant in the process of assessing moral rules.

A Kantian Response to the Objections

In this final section let us consider briefly whether the alternative, Kantian perspective is liable to the same doubts as RU. The general worry concerned the grounds by which moral rules are to be assessed. The apparent problem for RU was that it eliminated all but one relevant consideration—maximum utility. The Kantian perspective is both more pluralistic and more restrictive in its value theory. The value of humanity is understood as providing a cluster of relevant considerations, with various priorities. To preserve human life, promote mutual respect, and maintain conditions favorable for rational autonomous living are high-priority ends. Promoting the happiness, or personal ends of individuals, is also a moral end, provided it is compatible with higher-priority ends and other constraints. To assess moral rules, however, we cannot focus exclusively on a set of ends to be promoted. Persons have a status of *dignity* that does not allow us to assign an initial value to the lives or interests of each and then select rules that maximize aggregate value. In fact the Kantian perspective does not acknowledge any strictly commensurable values relevant to morality. Persons, as ends in themselves, have dignity, "an incomparable worth," "without equivalent."[28] Respecting their dignity requires us to adopt a general maxim to regard the permissible ends of others as our ends, but the requirement is indefinite, in part because there is no interpersonal measure of the value of personal ends. What we may do as a means to promote even morally desirable ends is limited by the requirement to respect each person as a rational agent now. To do so we must give due regard to our relationships with others over time, our past commitments and mutual interactions, and not just as a way of promoting an independently desirable future. We must not treat persons merely as means, and the formal test is whether they too could accept our proposed treatment of them when deliberating from the Kantian perspective.

---

[28] Kant (2002), 228–31 [4: 427–30], 235–6 [4: 434–6].

This sketch of the Kantian alternative leaves open many questions, but it points toward the complex plurality of Kantian values that contrast markedly with typical RU conceptions of utility. Let us consider briefly the implications of the alternative with respect to the four critical questions posed to RU.

1. *Does the permissibility of pursuing one's own personal projects depend upon whether or not the moral code that maximizes utility allows these pursuits?* RU affirms this dependency, but the Kantian alternative denies it. The obvious point is that Kantians do not assess rules by a standard of maximum utility. In fact they acknowledge no commensurable intrinsic values that can be aggregated across persons and maximized. The Kantian perspective on rules, like RU, does call for a kind of impartial assessment, a reflection that sets aside special regard to one's own projects and personal attachments. The Kantian task, however, is not to aggregate utilities impartially assigned to each person's interests, satisfactions, well-being, etc., but rather to identify rules most favored by a complex set of considerations, the most basic of which are associated with the idea of humanity as an end in itself. Arguably, these favor mutual aid and strong prohibitions on various acts destructive of the conditions needed for living with others as rational, mutually respecting, autonomous agents. Within the limits of these requirements, as rational agents we also value setting and pursuing our own ends and arguably, given this, mutual respect provides a strong presumption against rules that stifle individuality and demand constant attention and effort to bestow relatively minor benefits on others. Following RU we might also oppose such excessive demands because they lead to more unhappiness; but from the Kantian perspective, while acknowledging that as a relevant consideration, we would primarily make the case in terms of respect for persons as rational agents.

2. *Do the traditional restrictions on the legitimate means that we may use to prevent the wrong and harmful acts of others depend entirely on their maximizing (expected) utility?* The general Kantian response remains the same, that is, the proper standard for assessing rules is not utility maximization. Some further comments, however, might help to highlight the contrast between the RU and Kantian perspectives. As Bernard Williams points out, act-utilitarians are committed to the doctrine of *negative responsibility:* "that, if I am ever responsible for anything, then I must be just as much responsible for things

that I allow or fail to prevent, as I am for things that I myself, in the more everyday restricted sense, bring about."[29] Williams argues that this has strikingly counterintuitive results, for example that it is obvious that, other things equal, we should kill one innocent person if necessary to save two or more others. Now RU suggests a reply to this sort of objection, which is simply to argue that, because of the abuses and insecurity that would result, a set of rules that permits murders to prevent murders, etc., would not actually maximize utility. That may be a good guess at what RU would favor, but the problem remains that RU gives us no reason, when assessing sets of rules, to care about anything but the bottom line of costs and benefits of their general acceptance.

For the Kantian, the reason to forbid a person to commit murders to prevent others' murders is not just that there would be a net increase in general welfare—or even a net decrease in the number of murders. At least in part the reason is that the prohibition belongs in a set of restrictions that together affirm and give shape to the basic requirement to respect the dignity of each person as having a value that cannot be calculated. Even if the best RU code would contain adequate restrictions, the attitude that causes RU legislators to endorse it seems morally deficient. Although, by hypothesis, they prescribe restrictive rules for everyday living, their reasoning about rules reflects an attitude of indifference toward everything but consequences. The RU legislators must think, "As long as the ultimate outcome would be the same, it does not matter whether the rules require or forbid a conscientious person to deceive, abuse, or kill an innocent person if doing so would prevent a vicious person from doing these things to someone else." The question now is not which set of rules would actually be utility-maximizing, but whether RU legislators are thinking about them in the right way.

In assessing rules, the Kantian legislators will also consider as relevant, in itself, whether the rules affirm and express rational autonomous persons' concern to relate to each other with mutual respect and dignity. They aim to endorse rules with the understanding that these will guide and constrain most people to whom the rules apply, but also knowing that even the best rules will sometimes be ignored and flagrantly violated. They have reason to endorse both first-order rules that prohibit everyone from fraud, abuse, and

---

[29] Smart and Williams (1973), 95.

murder, and second-order rules (for example, of censure and punishment) intended to discourage even the least conscientious persons from violating the first-order rules. The aim is not simply to preserve life and promote aggregate well-being but, in large part, to identify and prescribe rules that express and honor the ideal of mutually respectful relations among rational autonomous persons. From this perspective there is a strong intrinsic presumption against rules that would require conscientious persons, who respect and strive to live by the ideal, to deceive, degrade, and kill other innocent people even if it would prevent malevolent people from similar acts. Here, again, the objection is not that RU favors the wrong rules, but rather that it tries to assess them from a morally inadequate perspective.

3. *Even if there were good grounds to believe that a certain moral code would maximize expected utility, would an unconditional commitment to follow its rules* for that reason *be a reasonable and morally worthy attitude?* Let us suppose, for the sake of argument, that utility-maximizing rules happen to coincide with the best dignity-respecting rules that Kantian legislators can propose. Then RU and Kantian legislators would have no disagreement about the content of the best moral code. But consider the attitude of those who abide by the rules. No doubt they will often conform to the rules without much thought, acting from habit, social conformity, and various nonmoral motivations, but presumably it is not morally desirable that they follow the rules without any understanding or concern about why it is right to follow these rules. Ideally they should have at least a general understanding of the reasons for the rules and a willingness to abide by them for these reasons. Moreover, it seems reasonable and morally admirable for them not to make this commitment conditional, for example on whether following the rules is profitable, convenient, likely to be praised by others.

As noted above, it seems doubtful that RU gives us a satisfactory answer to our question (3). The comparable question for the Kantian perspective is whether it is reasonable and morally admirable to make an unconditional commitment to rules that, in one's judgment, best respect the complex set of values inherent in the Kantian idea of the dignity of all persons. Readers must judge for themselves, but the Kantian set of values for evaluating rules and following them seems to me more promising. Neither the Kantian perspective nor RU yields clear and certain answers in particular hard cases, but arguably it frames the questions more appropriately.

4. *Are only forward-looking considerations relevant to the assessment of moral codes?* Many have argued that backward-looking and cross-time values are intrinsically relevant to moral judgments in particular cases. RU can accommodate this thought by arguing that the utility-maximizing set of rules would include such backward-looking considerations as promises, reparations, and desert. The question now, however, arises at another level of concern. Is it appropriate for the "legislators," who determine which rules are best, to consider only the ultimate future consequences of different sets of rules? In effect the legislators are none other than we who try to evaluate rules and whether we have adequate grounds to follow them. Arguably the broader, yet also more constraining, values of Kantian legislators turn our attention appropriately to past and cross-time considerations in evaluating the whole set of rules. Justice, desert, respect, and fidelity to commitments are not merely relevant in daily practice because respecting these rules makes for a better future. They stem from basic values that should shape and constrain deliberation about what rules to endorse.

A Final Note

In his admirably clear and thoughtful book *Ideal Code, Real World*, Brad Hooker ((2000), 4) argues for rule-consequentialism on the basis of reflective equilibrium or its coherence with "moral convictions we have after careful reflection." He acknowledges that these include familiar convictions about how justice, promises, desert, etc., must constrain our daily pursuit of individual and general welfare. His methodology allows, even requires, these convictions to influence the development and defense of rule-consequentialism. In effect, then, he takes up a perspective with Kantian elements when defending rule-consequentialism, arguing that the rules it prescribes will not be offensive from a more Kantian perspective. This requires, as a crucial step, arguing that Kantian elements are so utility-promoting that they will be incorporated into the best moral code from the rule-consequentialist perspective. My suggestion has been that this is unknown, perhaps unknowable, and in any case it is an unnecessary and problematic step.

10

The Importance of Moral Rules and Principles

In everyday life we take for granted that some rules, such as prohibitions of torture and rape, are important to respect and maintain, and not just because they are incorporated into our legal system. We also show an implicit awareness that rules have a *limited* role in our lives: morality is not all about following rules. Also but less obvious, in our moral deliberations and debates we presuppose that there are more general principles that stand behind our particular moral judgments and arguments. We may rarely articulate our most general principles, but we implicitly appeal to principles when we try to justify our particular decisions and our reliance on certain rules. For centuries moral philosophers have worked to state, refine, and defend their conceptions of the most fundamental and comprehensive moral principles. They and their followers have used these basic principles as guides and constraints in their deliberations about the importance and limits of more specific principles (or "rules").[1]

Many of the disputes within moral philosophy today reflect "in-house" disagreements about whether or not the most fundamental moral standards are expressible in one principle, whether or not they are concerned exclusively with consequences, and whether or not their use together with relevant facts leads to particular moral conclusions that match our ordinary considered judgments. These debates typically take place within a broad area of agreement on the need for moral principles and rules. For example,

This chapter was initially presented as the annual Lindlay Lecture at the University of Kansas in October 2006. I thank participants in discussion there for their comments.

[1] The sort of more specific principles or "rules" I have in mind are e.g. prohibitions of rape, torture, murder, assault, promise-breaking, deception, and theft. The general importance of these principles may be rarely questioned, but disagreements often arise about how to articulate and interpret them and about when, if ever, they admit of exceptions.

rule-consequentialists, Kantians, and various social contract theorists all accept the general structure that I ascribed to ordinary moral thinking. That is, all justified particular moral judgments are ultimately based on more fundamental moral principles; sometimes the particular judgments rightly rely on less comprehensive rules (for example, about physical violence, promise-breaking, and fraud); but then those rules must be justifiable by the fundamental principles in light of relevant facts.

There have always been skeptics about the common assumptions of these "in-house" disputes in moral philosophy, but in recent times the skeptical voices have become louder and more articulate. The voices express a variety of different objections, some more convincing than others. Aristotelians and other theorists associated with "virtue ethics" tend to deny any special significance to moral *rules*, and they do not appeal to fundamental *principles* to explain or justify their claims about how a virtuous person would feel and act.[2] Act-consequentialists endorse one basic principle (or goal), but they often deny that this basic principle should serve as our day-to day decision guide and they insist that more specific rules are at best fallible heuristic guides.[3] Most radically, moral particularists (such as Jonathan Dancy) hold that rules and principles are not needed in moral theory and they tend to distort and corrupt moral practice.[4]

As my title suggests, I accept the standard assumptions about the importance of moral rules and principles, but with qualifications that acknowledge some good points raised by skeptics. Much of my previous work has been an attempt to understand Kant's ethical and political thought and to develop a broadly Kantian moral theory. Today I will not comment specifically on Kant's texts but instead sketch a broadly Kantian perspective on moral rules and principles that also draws from David Hume, John Stuart Mill, and John Rawls. I shall distinguish and comment on two quite different issues in the larger debate about *whether* moral rules and principles are important. Then, all too briefly, I shall describe elements of the broadly Kantian conception of

---

[2] "Virtue ethics" is a term often used for a cluster of related moral views. See e.g. Crisp and Slote (1997) and Hursthouse (1999). Hursthouse rejects many contemporary ideas about the importance of moral rules, but she allows there is a place for rules learned "at mother's knee" and "v-rules," such as "Be honest" and "Do not do what is mean." See ibid., esp. 36–9.

[3] Regarding act-consequentialism see Hooker (2000), 5–6. Roughly, it is the view that the rightness of acts depends entirely on their consequences.

[4] Dancy (2004).

why certain rules are important and review some common objections. The occasion of a Lindlay lecture, I trust, gives me license to offer a wide-ranging rather than narrowly focused discussion.

To preview, the issues to be considered are these:

(I) Is it morally important to have shared moral *rules* about specific types of problems, rules that are distinct from laws of the state and yet not merely heuristic guides?

(II) If there are such morally important rules, does their moral authority or the justifiability of particular moral judgments depend on more fundamental moral standards that can be expressed in the form of *principles*?

(III) If there are such fundamental moral principles, what sort of framework do they provide for deliberation about the content of moral rules, their limits, and the priorities among them?

(IV) If principles and rules are important, how can we respond to common objections to their use and abuse in philosophy and in ordinary decision-making?

My answers, not surprisingly, will be (I) we need specific moral rules; (II) justification presupposes more general principles, as illustrated in a Kantian account of practical reason; (III) one sort of deliberative framework can be drawn from Kant's basic moral principles; (IV) common objections show the limits but not the unimportance of moral rules. All these issues are controversial. My aim here is not to settle the disputes but to sketch a view of moral rules and principles worth taking seriously.

I. Moral Rules Are Needed

For convenience, I use the word "principles" for general comprehensive moral standards and the word "rules" for norms regarding specific types of act. The distinction is somewhat artificial and imprecise, but it is not uncommon in philosophy (for example, among rule-utilitarians).[5] It simplifies exposition, and nothing important depends on the labels. Apart

---

[5] For a good example of rule-utilitarianism see Brandt (1979), 286–300. See also Hooker (2000). For another sort of theory that makes central use of moral rules see Gert (2005).

from its convenience in marking a certain distinction, the word "principles" in some respects would be preferable to the word "rules" when speaking of fairly specific, substantive, derivative, and often implicitly qualified moral norms such as "One ought not to lie." The word "rules" may remind us too much of strict, narrowly focused regulations imposed by institutions—tax codes, dress standards, graduation requirements, and the rules of poker, baseball, and so on. Such associations naturally make us resist talk of *moral rules* because we take morality to be less formally structured and context-relative than these other practical rules. Nevertheless, for present purposes, the term "moral rules" may serve as a handy label once we understand more fully what is intended and try not to rely on misleading analogies with other sorts of rules.

In saying that we need moral rules, what I have in mind, more specifically, is that there are strong moral reasons for endorsing, following, and supporting the general acceptance of norms or standards requiring or forbidding certain rather specific kinds of conduct. Examples would be "rules" against lying, promise-breaking, incest, rape, assault, torture, and murder. Moral rules, as understood here, refer to rather specific types of conduct but are wide-ranging in application. That is, they are not regulations that make sense only within a classroom, only within the jurisdiction of a particular city or country, only for doctors or social workers, and so on. Some would say that to be a *moral* norm of any kind, the norm must be universal in that it applies to everyone at all times and places; but my terminology is not meant to be restrictive in this way. Moral rules, for present purposes, are quite wide-ranging, if not universal, do not depend for their authority on particular institutions and legal jurisdictions, and are ultimately justifiable by basic moral principles that also explain the limits of their application. Moral rules, as understood here, are not merely the "maxims" that Kant says conscientious individuals can test and adopt in proper moral reflection.[6] They are norms that should be socially taught, supported, and enforced beyond their place in the law, and they should serve as constraints on public as well as private deliberations.[7]

---

[6] For "maxims" see Kant (2002), 202 n. [4: 402 n.] and 222 n. [4: 421 n.]. Bracketed numbers refer to volume and pages in the standard Prussian Academy edition.

[7] It is important to keep in mind several distinctions here. What I have been calling "moral rules" are not the same as either *laws* of the state or *mere* social conventions. They are similar to social conventions, for example of etiquette, in being shared norms of conduct, socially taught and reinforced, used to guide deliberation and assessments, public and private. Moral rules are not *mere* social conventions, however, if

In *Utilitarianism*, John Stuart Mill presents a strong case for respecting and socially supporting certain rules or "precepts" of justice, such as showing fidelity to promises, honoring moral and legal rights, and judging impartially.[8] Long experience, he argues, has shown that such precepts not only tend to promote the general happiness but are virtually essential to a minimally decent level of well-being in any society. They are normally "wrong" to violate because compliance "can be exacted like a debt." This means that the basic moral principle, for him the principle of utility, not only recommends following the rule but calls for its enforcement by law, public opinion, or at least (socially developed) conscience. The precepts are rules of justice, according to Mill, because (unlike, say, precepts of charity) they also assign *rights* to individuals. Rights are important to respect and enforce, but they are not free-standing moral norms. Rather, rights are derived from the basic moral principle: they are legitimate claims as defined by rules without which societies could not achieve even a minimal level of happiness.

In my view, Mill's utility principle is not an adequate standard for assessing moral rules, but otherwise there is much wisdom in his account of the social role of moral rules and the need to justify them by more basic principles. From David Hume we can draw further lessons, especially about how to think about exceptions to moral rules. Mill allowed that even the precepts of justice admit of exceptions, but he left scholars much room to debate how we should conceive of the exceptions. Are the precepts, as act-utilitarians say, merely rough summaries telling us what the utility principle usually prescribes when applied directly to particular cases? Or are the

---

their role is justified, as especially important, by basic moral principles. Moral rules differ typically from laws in the informality of their origin and enforcement, and in other ways as well. Philosophers and moralists, however, often propose rules or "mid-level principles" conceived in a still different way. For example, in Part II of *The Metaphysics of Morals,* Kant outlines a system of intermediate principles to guide "ethical" deliberation of individuals. These are quite distinct from both laws and Kant's principles regarding law and public justice. The ethical principles are intermediate between Categorical Imperative and particular judgments but are not presented as rules to be socially maintained and enforced. To the contrary, Kant insisted (mistakenly, I think) that, apart from law and justice, we must each take charge of our own ethical decisions, leaving it to others entirely to handle theirs. Intermediate moral principles can inform our consciences and guide individual choices, but regarding others, our duties are to respect them and promote their happiness, not to socially promulgate and enforce norms for them to follow. Kant (1996a), esp. 150–1 [6: 385–8].

[8] Mill (1998), ch. 5.

precepts, as rule-utilitarians say, useful but strict limits on what individuals may do in pursuit of the general good?

Hume was not, properly speaking, a utilitarian of either kind, but he gave reasons why within certain limits we should obey and enforce certain systems of rules, such as rules of justice and promise-keeping, without regard to whether or not conformity is beneficial in each particular case.[9] These systems of rules tend to be mutually advantageous, he argued, generally better for each of us than abandoning them or revising them to allow exceptions whenever someone thinks (even rightly) that she could do more good by deviating from the rule. Such rules may have implicit "built-in" exception clauses, for example one should keep promises *unless* the person to whom one promised releases one from obligation and *unless* unforeseen circumstances undermine the point of the promise. Most rules leave an area of indeterminacy about what counts as an exception, but they could not serve their function *as rules* (as opposed to mere heuristic guides) if they allowed an *all-purpose exception* for every time deviating from the rule was judged, rightly or wrongly, to do more good in the particular case.

Kantians do not assess moral rules by either the utilitarian standard of aggregate welfare ("the greatest happiness") or Hume's standard of utility (what tends to be mutually advantageous), and so they are not engaged in the special debates between act-utilitarians and rule-utilitarians. Nevertheless, the broader lesson from Hume should be acknowledged in any moral theory—that is, there are good reasons, stemming from our basic moral concerns and our human condition, to develop, respect, teach, and socially enforce certain rules, apart from the law, even if following the rule in each particular case is not always most beneficial. These reasons include, for example, the fact that maintaining such rules, as more than optional heuristic guides, can help to *coordinate* our individual acts and encourage morally desirable behavior by giving needed *assurance* of others' compliance. Beyond this, shared moral rules become incorporated into our practices and help to shape morally valuable forms of life. Also, criminal law is often an ineffective, costly, clumsy device for deterring and preventing undesirable behavior. Legal systems sometimes fail to address egregious moral offenses when they should, and yet they become oppressive when they try to criminalize every serious moral offense. There is a need, then, not only to reinforce

---

[9] Hume (1981), bk. III pt. II sect. II, "Of the Origin of Justice and Property."

good laws, but to go beyond law by teaching, internalizing, and socially supporting more informal moral rules against violence, abuse, betrayal, and other offenses. The reasons need not be only forward-looking considerations of future benefits and harms. Kantian values of human dignity, mutual respect, moral integrity, solidarity, and even hope may underwrite certain moral rules as guides and constraints that are to some extent independent of legitimate concern for future consequences.

A full and direct defense of the claim that we need moral rules (as understood here) would be long, complex, and no doubt controversial. It would require specifying the particular moral rules to be defended, then articulating and defending the basic moral principles or values from which the argument proceeds, and also citing evidence for whatever empirical claims the argument requires. That is obviously not a short-term project. In the next sections I propose a few preliminary steps—first, in section II, I explain how, at least in Kantian theory, particular facts become reasons to act insofar as they are aspects of a more fully expressible rationale that appeals to basic rational principles, and then, in section III, I sketch some elements of a framework for thinking about moral rules drawing from basic Kantian principles. This illustrates how in a Kantian theory we might try to identify which moral rules are important and why. Finally, in the concluding section IV, I review a few familiar objections to reliance on moral rules. These are good objections to some extreme views—and apt warnings to all of us—but they do not, I think, undermine the qualified defense of moral rules sketched here.

II. Moral Rules and Particular Moral Judgments Presuppose General Standards

Radical moral particularists, such as Jonathan Dancy, are not simply concerned to warn against the reliance on substantive and specific moral rules of the sort we have been considering. They have a deeper point, sometimes presented as metaphysical: that is, particular moral judgments do not depend for their validity on any general moral principles. The "reasons" that determine what we ought to do are particular facts, in a cluster of other particular facts, that ground the "ought"-judgment without the help of general standards. A particular reason in a given context, for example, might be "Robin needs help now," though a person's needing help is not a reason to help in all contexts. Moreover, there may be no correct generalization about when we ought to help. What is a positive reason in one context may be a consideration that is indifferent or of the opposite valence in another, rather similar context. A particular fact is a reason only if certain other facts ("enablers") are present and still other facts ("defeaters") are absent. But again, in Dancy's view, there are no true or useful "principles" to indicate reliably when a cluster of facts ("reasons," "enablers," and absence of "defeaters") constitutes, all considered, a case that we ought to give (or deny) help. The claim is not just that principles tend to be unreliable heuristic guides, but that they offer no "ground" or "justification" for either mid-level rules or particular judgments. Ultimate principles are not needed and they serve no purpose.

Other moral theorists who are less radical (or less clear and explicit) hold similar views. Those identified with "virtue ethics" may concede a limited role for principles learned at "mother's knee" in the process of a child's moral development, but deny that these, or any principles, play an important role in the deliberation and judgment of virtuous adults. They also tend to deny that *principles of conduct*, as opposed to ideals of character, have a significant role in moral theory as explanations *why* a virtuous agent would make a decision, say, to help a friend, in particular circumstances. If we have the moral virtues, we will "see" or somehow wisely judge what to do, but the judgment is not a "conclusion" from grounding "principles."

Much of this sounds right as description or phenomenology of ordinary moral judgment, and it reflects reasonable doubts about a purely "legalistic" morality that would treat all moral problems as if they can be resolved by reference to a determinate system of primary rules, and further rules for interpreting those rules, and so on. Relevant moral considerations, as they say, cannot be determinately "codified" to tell us what to do in every conceivable circumstance. Beyond these undeniably good points, particularists and virtue theorists tend not only to avoid but also to deny the value of theoretical investigations of the general grounds for particular moral judgments. Why, for example, does Robin's suffering in a particular case constitute a reason for the moral judgment that I should help her? For practical purposes, of course, there may be no need for further comment; but the philosophical issue is whether we may reasonably ask for further explanation of *why certain facts are reasons* in a given context—an explanation that is not just a more specific description of the context but a general explanation of what facts constitute reasons and why.

Radical moral particularists and virtue theorists are not the only philosophers who rest content with their unexplained intuitions about what is a good reason to act in a particular context. In fact it is an increasingly common trend to assume that "a reason to do X" just means "a consideration in favor of doing X" and that this is a primitive notion that cannot be further explained. Further, it is assumed that whether a particular fact is a good reason, or stronger reason than some other, must be left to intuition case by case.[10] Particular reasons are regarded as basic and in need of no further explanation. Rationality, then, is simply a matter of responding appropriately to the best particular reasons in each case. It is important to note the order of explanation that is implicit in this view. That is, the quality and strength of reasons is to be determined intuitively case by case,[11] and then being practically rational or reasonable is defined, in effect, as acting on the best reasons. The issue is not, of course, whether to be rational we must respond appropriately to particular facts, for no one would deny that. It is whether particular reasons can be identified and weighed independently of principles of practical reason or whether, instead, such principles partially explain why certain facts are reasons in a particular case.

All these philosophers reject an ambitious *project* that was at the core of Kant's philosophy. Whatever we may think of Kant's conclusions, his work remains of interest because he set himself the task of finding and defending

---

[10] These ideas seem to be common assumptions in many discussions of practical issues. A source of encouragement may have been Scanlon (1998). Scanlon treats a "reason for" or "consideration in favor of" an attitude as a primitive notion for purposes of his normative theory, but he sets aside further metaphysical and metaethical questions about this. He describes an interpersonal intuitive process for identifying and determining the relative strength of practical reasons, but he does not commit himself to traditional intuitionism as an epistemological and metaphysical theory. Unlike particularists, Scanlon relies on the idea of "generic" reasons that apply to *types* of cases, and his account of the relation between rationality and reasons is more complex than the simple view I sketch here.

[11] Particularists, such as Dancy, insist on intuition in each *particular* case because, in his view, even the smallest difference between that case and a quite similar case *could* warrant a radically different judgment. Others, such as Scanlon, rely on intuition (or consensus of pre-theoretical judgments) to identify and weigh reasons pertinent to *generic* situations, described in *general* terms, in order to judge whether there is any applicable permissive *principle* (i.e. one that cannot reasonably be rejected from a specified perspective). Nevertheless, Scanlon shares the particularists' view that practical reasons are not derived from general principles. To the contrary, Scanlon holds that moral principles presuppose prior identification of reasons: Scanlon (1998), chs. 4 and 5.

basic principles of rational choice, principles that explain why some particular facts are good reasons to act and others are not. His primary ambition was to find and defend rational principles of moral choice, but in the process he offers an interesting account of instrumental rationality. Rather than argue directly that particular reasons presuppose general principles, I want to use Kant's theory to illustrate one nonparticularist way of explaining this relation. What is most dissatisfying about the particularists' position is that, having shared their intuitions about what particular facts are good reasons, they deny that further philosophical questions are in order. But, we wonder: What explains why these particular facts, not others, are good reasons to act? What do the good reasons have in common? What explains the normative force or authority of the facts alleged to be reasons?

Here I can only sketch some structural features of the Kantian account.[12] What matters for present purposes is not so much the content of Kant's proposals but the challenging idea that what makes certain particular facts reasons is determined by their role in a rationale that is grounded in principles of rational choice.

1. Reconstruction of Kant on Reasons and Rational Principles: General Remarks

An initial problem is that Kant does not express his ideas in terms of "reasons" in the way that is common in everyday discourse and current philosophical fashion. We hear much from Kant about rational principles and objective and subjective "grounds of the self-determination of the will," but these do not translate readily into familiar talk of "reasons for action." So here is my suggestion.

Propositions about what we ought to do, both general and specific, are essentially statements about what it is rational to do (and contrary to reason not to do). "Ought" expresses *objective principles*, that is, principles a fully rational person would follow, but in the special vocabulary of *imperatives*, which includes "must," "bound," "obligated," "constrained," and so on. So long as we are dealing with what Kant calls *imperfect wills* that can follow rational requirements but might not, the transition from a valid statement about what is rationally required to "oughts" and "imperatives" is more or

---

[12] Here I draw from Kant, especially (2002), 214–22 [4: 412–22]. See also the introductory notes, pp. 49–64.

less automatic. So, leaving aside this special vocabulary of constraint, let us look at the structure of arguments to a conclusion that reason requires a particular act or otherwise limits our options for choice. There are at least two patterns, one characteristic of hypothetical (nonmoral) imperatives and the other of categorical (moral) imperatives.

2. The Pattern for Hypothetical Imperatives

The basic presupposition is a general principle of rationality: (HI) *Fully rational persons, acting in a fully rational way, will take the necessary and available means to the ends they will or else revise or abandon their ends.*[13] In other words, we ought, if we persist in holding to an end, to take the required means when opportunity arises. A controversial assumption here is that we can give up or suspend any contingent end when we have reason to, even if our desire for the end persists. (Kant says that we have our happiness as an end by natural necessity,[14] but his theory implies that we can suspend the pursuit of happiness on any occasion when it conflicts with moral requirements.) Note that the "ought" here does not "detach" to yield any unequivocal prescription. It always leaves an option: one ought, when one has an end for which available means are necessary, either take the means or abandon the end. That is, these are the only rational options even though confused, self-deceiving, and weak-willed persons may try to avoid both. Although there is a kind of irrationality in balking at taking the necessary means to a persisting immoral end, this does not imply that it is rational to take the means. The only rational option is to abandon the immoral end. The means-end principle here may be regarded as an implicit standard of rational decision-making.[15]

---

[13] Here I offer a reconstruction of Kant's ideas rather than an exact description or strict interpretation. Many philosophers prefer to treat what I call principles of reason as rules of inference rather than premises in arguments, but I see no compelling reason for this preference, at least regarding the principles HI and CI. The usual principles of logic serve as the rules of inference and presenting HI and CI as basic principles just highlights them as presuppositions of instrumental and moral reasoning. There is no implication that in ordinary practical reasoning we do or should consciously structure our thought in the patterns I sketch.

[14] Kant (2002), 217 [4: 415].

[15] In first-person deliberation, which was Kant's primary concern, the principle indicates how we should proceed with the fallible information that we have; but obviously our (rational) aim is to do what the principle would direct if our choice of means and ends were not skewed by ignorance of the facts. If we needed a conception of the "objectively" rational, not essentially tied to the agent's beliefs, we could perhaps say that one does what is *objectively rational* in the circumstances only if, having an end, the person

To argue explicitly from the basic principle to a particular conclusion, we would need at least two further premises. (i) *Person P wills end E.* (For example, I will to finish writing these remarks in time to present them.) And (ii) *Means M is necessary and available for P to achieve E.* (For example, I must and can work enough hours to finish in time.) The conclusion is the conditional particular judgment: (iii) *If fully rational and acting in a fully rational way, P will take means M or abandon the end E.* (For example, if sufficiently rational, I will put in the work hours or give up the plan to present the paper.)

Setting aside for now problems and refinements, let us turn instead to the supposed structure of moral judgment.

3. The Pattern for Moral (Categorical) Imperatives

Again, an explicit reconstruction would begin with a general principle about what is supposed to be universally rational: (CI) *Any fully rational person, acting in a fully rational way, will act in such a way that it satisfies the supreme moral principle, the content of which is expressed in the various formulations of the Categorical Imperative, all of which say in effect: "Always do or avoid A (an act of a specified type), independently of whether it promotes your happiness or serves your other contingent ends."* Here my concern is with structure, not content, but, expressed cryptically, for Kant himself the acts prohibited would be (*a*) acts on maxims that cannot be willed as universal law, (*b*) acts that fail to treat humanity as an end in itself, and (*c*) acts contrary to the principles of legislators in the kingdom of ends.[16] The general principle might be applied in stages, involving derivative moral principles and "rules," but the most direct applications would proceed thus. After the general principle, we would cite the complex particular facts of the case that (we judge) make the case fall under the principle: (i) *Person P is in a context to which the general principle applies and P can do A.* (For example, the guard's torturing the prisoner for amusement is not treating him as an end, and he could refrain.) From these and the general principle (CI), an explicit rationale would draw the particular conclusion: *If P is fully rational and acting in a fully rational way,*

---

either takes what are *actually* the necessary and available means (whether known or not) or else abandons (or revises) the end. Note that this would be a necessary, not sufficient condition for objective rationality.

[16] Kant (2002), 221–37 [4: 420–37].

P will do A. (For example, it is rationally necessary for the guard to refrain from torturing the prisoner.)

I call adequately specified bits of reasoning along these two patterns *rationales*, but I do not suppose that what we ordinarily count as a reason, even a sufficient reason, for an act needs to make explicit reference to all the background assumptions in the fullest statement of a reconstructed rationale.

A reconstructed rationale might take into account intermediate principles, for example principles of the sort Kant presents in *The Metaphysics of Morals*, principles that are supposed to apply broadly in recurrent human conditions.[17] Politics and law aside, these are mostly expressed in terms of "thick concepts"—self-improvement, beneficence, gratitude, respect, and friendship. The idea is that such principles are supported by ideas inherent in the supreme moral principle, but their application calls for experience, knowledge of local conditions, and judgment that cannot be governed by further rules. Also these intermediate principles typically prescribe ends to adopt, leaving much room for individual choice.[18]

4. Where in These Patterns Are the "Reasons" for Action?

Kant does not write of particular "reasons" in the way that is common now, but here is a suggestion. What counts as "the reason" for doing something in ordinary conversation is partially relative to context in a way analogous to ordinary causal explanations. What might be called "the fullest explanation" of the outbreak of a fire might include the careless dropping of a match, its falling on combustible material, certain wind conditions, the absence of rain, many other background facts, and certain causal laws or relevant generalizations. Observers talking about "the cause" of the fire might mention any of several factors, depending on what they assumed their audience knew and what they considered most relevant to their concern— for example, responsibility for the fire, prevention of similar outbreaks, or surprise that it could have occurred. So "the cause" might be that the normally careful park ranger absent-mindedly dropped a match, or that contrary to the hearer's assumptions it hadn't rained in a year in that area, or that the stuff on which the match fell was surprisingly flammable. Perhaps in most cases, the salient factor will be of the same kind, but there seems to be

---

[17] Kant (1996a), 10–11 [6: 216–18].   [18] Ibid.

no guarantee that this is so. Philosophers might come along and try to force a division of these factors into Dancy's categories of "contributory reasons," "enablers," "intensifiers," and absence of "defeaters," but the analogy suggests that we are still talking about pieces of a fuller explanation that has causal laws or relevant generalizations at least in the background.

The suggested analogy is that what we count as "the reason" in explaining why an action was instrumentally rational presupposes general principles and can vary with the context in a similar way. If you are wondering why I drove to town and were unaware of my plans, I might explain as my reason, "I intend to make dinner for many guests tonight." Or, if you assumed I had all the necessary ingredients already, I might say, "The reason was that I had no milk or flour." If you were wondering why I did not walk to town as usual, I might say, "The reason I drove to town was that I have injured my leg." If you imagined I was going to town out of duty, I might just say, "I needed some things for what I planned to do tonight—and, despite the extra trouble, I decided not to change the plans." All of these are particular facts, but they are reasons because they are especially salient features of a possible fuller rationale that we might give—one that includes HI or other principles of rational choice. For practical purposes, of course, we usually do not need to articulate the basic principles, and in moral theory we do not need to treat them as explicit premises of arguments rather than implicit rules of inference.

In a similar way, perhaps, "the reason" as ordinarily understood for what one morally ought to do might vary with context but presupposes the possibility of a fuller justification that (perhaps boringly) identifies all the relevant factors that we can think of, including the basic principle to which we are appealing. So the reason might be "she needs help," or "the doctor was out of town," or "she saved my life last year," or "it would be an even more callous and dangerous world if no one would lend a hand to others in distress," or "she is a terrorist suspect, but also a human being." On this picture, in theory a moral judgment regarding a particular case depends on a complex set of background assumptions, immediately salient facts, perhaps some derivative and qualified moral principles, and ultimately presupposed general ideas about what moral justification is or ought to be. The latter perhaps rarely figure in ordinary moral arguments, but Kant set it as a task to articulate those background assumptions. In fact Kant's ambition went beyond finding the general principles that explain why particular facts are moral reasons. He also thought he had the elements of a unified theory of rational choice, one which would support his belief that compelling moral reasons always trump merely prudential ones.[19] Skeptics may doubt that either project can succeed, but, especially regarding the first and more modest ambition, final judgment seems premature.

III. A Broadly Kantian Perspective on Moral Rules[20]

Let us suppose for now that specific moral rules are needed and that they are based on more fundamental moral standards expressible as principles. Moral theories offer competing conceptions of what these basic standards are. In Kantian, rule-consequentialist, and contractarian theories these conceptions can be understood as different frameworks for thinking about what moral rules are needed, how they should be interpreted, and what (if any) exceptions they allow. A broadly Kantian framework may be drawn from Kant's idea of moral legislation in "kingdom of ends" and, to some extent, from his later ideas of "original contract" and ideal political legislation. To the dismay of some of my Kantian friends, this makes the framework for assessment of moral principles similar in structure to John Rawls's theory of justice. Strict fidelity to Kant's texts would not underwrite this reconstruction, but arguably it reflects the spirit, and some of the letter, of Kant's moral philosophy. In any case, my project is to draw from and extend some of Kant's ideas, not to reflect them with full historical accuracy.

The basic idea is that particular moral reasons depend on general moral principles, and moral principles are conceived as determined by what rational autonomous persons, in an appropriate deliberative situation, would accept or "legislate" for themselves and others. Without the Kantian

---

[19] In Kant's theory "perfect duties" should always take precedence over morally optional personal projects, but the "imperfect duty" to make others' happiness our end allows some freedom of choice as to when and how to do this. Although interpretation here is controversial, I understand this to mean that we may sometimes pursue merely personal projects even when we could instead do a favor for someone else. In the misleading but common way of speaking, in such a case one would have a "moral reason" to do the favor but would not be wrong to act on a "nonmoral" or "merely prudential" reason. We should note, however, that much of what we ordinarily consider prudential concerns—e.g. preserving one's life and health—Kant classifies as moral "duties to oneself."

[20] Here I review again some main features of the Kantian perspective discussed in previous essays, such as Hill (2000), chs. 2 and 8, and chs. 8 and 9 of this volume, but I acknowledge that it remains underdeveloped and controversial.

terminology, the core idea is that justified moral constraints and guidelines are those that reasonable, relevantly informed, and mutually respectful people would agree to as standards for their practices and personal interactions. One might try to develop this idea into a metaethical alternative to various forms of intuitionism, naturalism, and expressivism, but for practical purposes it is best seen as just a way of thinking about principles that brings together various factors relevant to their moral assessment.

This approach invites many specific questions, but here I will only mention a few points. First, the deliberative framework requires that in assessing principles the "legislators" appropriately set aside their particular personal preferences,[21] but they rely on certain values that we (at least Kantians) might argue are rational for any *human being* (at least when considered apart from particular context and attachments).[22] These presumably would include a rational interest in continuing to live, in having

---

[21] The kind and degree of detachment from particular personal preferences that is appropriate depends, of course, on the level of deliberation. The level suggested by Kant's "kingdom of ends" is very abstract and concerned with whatever substantive principles are applicable universally. Deliberation at the level of Kant's *The Metaphysics of Morals* concerns principles appropriate to pervasive human conditions. We can expect that any principles that would be acceptable to all "legislators" at these abstract levels would be quite general, somewhat indeterminate, and often open to exceptions, more so than Kant himself suggested. Assessing principles for more limited contexts, relying on specific information about the contexts, could be guided and constrained by the more general principles (if any) adopted in the prior deliberations. Thinking of working from the most abstract principles to principles specified for more local conditions is analogous to Rawls's applications of his principles of justice in various stages (constitutional, legislative, and judicial), but there would need to be significant differences noted: Rawls (1999c), 177–80.

[22] Many issues would need to be addressed here. For example, in a Kantian account the sense of "rational" will not be merely instrumental rationality, or this combined with rational ends understood as those chosen with full information, but it cannot serve the purpose without circularity if it means "reasonable" in the most loaded sense of responsiveness to all good reasons, especially moral ones. I postpone further discussion, except to note that Kant seemed to rely at times on a traditional notion of a rational person as, among other things, one who thinks for himself, controls impulses and emotions by informed and consistent reflection, cares about acting for reasons that make sense to others as well, cares about being acknowledged as such and about treating others, when possible, the same way. It seemed obvious to Kant e.g. that no rational person as such wants to be treated as a mere means, or to be manipulated by lies, to be mocked as worthless, to be regarded and dealt with as an animal, etc. Moreover, I suspect that he thought that, aside from moral arguments, rational persons—reason-governed persons—are rationally disposed not to treat other rational persons in these ways and would not but for their conflicting sensuous desires. In the Kantian deliberative framework I have suggested, these rational values (or presumed "reasons") would not enter as moral convictions or altruistic concerns, but preferences that the rational legislators are presumed to have apart from their particular ends and projects (which they set aside). Assuming such values is far from settling practical questions, however, because in the real world not all values can be fully realized. A community of perfectly rational agents, perhaps, might never lie to each other, but lies (and even killing) are necessary sometimes to preserve other values.

freedom and opportunity to choose and pursue personal ends, in avoiding the severe pain and suffering to which all human beings are averse, and, more controversially, in relating to rational persons in ways that respect our mutual rational capacities and dispositions. Second, while any broadly Kantian ethics would be primarily concerned with how we regard and treat the people that we directly encounter and affect, it cannot reasonably be indifferent to how we may influence future conditions. Our moral decisions are not determined by any idea of aggregate welfare over time, but arguably Kantian values include proper respect for past generations and hope for future ones. Third, although the most abstract moral thinking (in the "kingdom of ends") may articulate ideals for a perfect world in which everyone conforms to moral principles, obviously practical deliberation must address the real problems generated by noncompliance due to ignorance, weakness, and malice. Rational people may prefer to live by the ideal principles of a more perfect world, but reasonable adjustments must be made when that world is impossible. Finally, disagreements in applying the Kantian framework, like disagreements in application of any theory, are to be expected, but that need not negate its value as perspective for thinking about what we can conscientiously do and recommend to others.

Now, moving beyond abstract theory building, let me summarize briefly a cluster of Kantian values that may have independent appeal. These include the idea that a practice is morally permissible only if it is, in principle, justifiable to all those affected by it. This is a familiar theme in contractualist theories, such as Scanlon's, but, as noted, in a Kantian version it is the requirement that the practice be compatible with the principles that could and would be endorsed by rational, autonomous moral legislators who properly value their own humanity and humanity in each person. The proper valuing of humanity includes, in part, accepting that persons have a basic worth that is not subject to trade-offs, like commodities with market value. Although hard choices often must be made, the justification cannot be that the value of persons is commensurable so that, for example, fundamentally two are worth twice as much as one, one hundred worth ten times more than ten, and so on. To be a human being is to have a status that must always be respected, in oneself and in others. The status imposes limits on how each person *may be treated,* even in the pursuit of good ends; and it constrains what each *may do,* even to ameliorate the treatment of others. In the Kantian version, this status of human dignity is not earned and cannot be forfeited, though our acts may be worthy or unworthy of it. The *particular* rights and responsibilities inherent in that status, and their *more specific* implications and limits, need to be identified, or constructed, through practical reasoning that takes into account in an appropriate way the interests and perspective of each person.

In the Kantian view, as also for many others, certain strong presumptive values are presupposed in a morally appropriate assessment of principles. All too briefly, these include the importance of allowing each person to live as a rational, autonomous person in conditions of mutual respect. This corresponds to traditional values of respecting life and liberty, and avoiding practices that are deceptive, manipulative, and degrading. Apart from these primary constraints on how one may treat persons, arguably a proper deliberative perspective also values positively the ability of every person to pursue and achieve his or her (morally permissible) personal ends. Thus, not only must we refrain from mistreating others (for example, by murdering, deceiving, or humiliating them), we also have some reason to promote others' happiness, both by preventing others from mistreating them and by supporting them in their (permissible) projects. Note that we have here two quite different sorts of moral concern, and these can apparently be in tension: first, each person has strong moral reason *not to do* anything to persons that is incompatible with a basic respect for their humanity, and second, each person has moral reasons, of varying strengths, to promote others' happiness by preventing mistreatment of them by others as well as by offering other sorts of aid. Kant often gave absolute priority to the first concern over the second—for example, refusing to allow lying to a person in order to prevent another from being murdered.[23] We may doubt, however, both whether Kant had adequate grounds for this absolute priority in his basic theory and whether his position about lying is actually required by the priority.

---

[23] Kant presents a division of duties into "perfect" and "imperfect," implying that the former always take priority over the latter in that one could not use means forbidden by perfect duties to fulfill the ends prescribed by imperfect duties—e.g. lying or murdering to aid someone in distress. To avoid strict moral dilemmas—cases in which all one's options are absolutely forbidden—he grants that apparent dilemmas arise when "the grounds of duty" conflict and call for judgment as to which determines what one ought to do, all things considered (Kant (1996a), 16–17 [6: 224]). Clearly it was an absolute ground of duty for him to *regard* everyone as having a basic worth as a person, but it is not clear that the derivative duty not to mock anyone as worthless would stand as absolute.

Setting aside details of Kant interpretation, the important point is that moral perspectives even remotely similar to Kant's hold that, in the idiom of the day, morality is *not all about* producing desirable results, not even about promoting outcomes that Kantians should seek and hope for. Often the end is good, but the means are unacceptable. Our acts do not simply affect the future; they treat people, well or badly, *now*. Moreover, the moral quality of what we do often lies in the values that we **express** by our choices, where expressing a value is *putting it into practice*, not merely trying to communicate or make a gesture. Expression in this sense, is especially important to the moral virtues of integrity, respect, solidarity, and hope.

What I have suggested here is just a bare sketch of a possible Kantian perspective for thinking about moral rules, but it is perhaps enough to show, for those familiar with rule-consequentialism and other theories, that there are some distinctive features of the Kantian perspective. Most strikingly, rules are not evaluated solely by reference to good outcomes to be produced. The Kantian perspective incorporates values (aspects of human dignity) that arguably constrain the pursuit of the general welfare and other goals that, in themselves, would be worthy.[24] For purposes of thinking from the Kantian perspective these values associated with human dignity are stipulated, but of course in another context they may be challenged and defended. Contrasts with various forms of contractualism and contractarianism may also be evident, but cannot be so easily summarized.

IV. Some Common Objections

Finally, let us review some common objections, theoretical and practical, to the use or abuse of moral rules.

1. *Rules are no substitute for good judgment.* Sometimes those skeptical about using moral rules make a general procedural point that no one should deny. That is, even the best rules need to be interpreted and applied with good judgment, and we cannot keep giving rules for interpreting rules, and further rules for interpreting those rules, endlessly. As Aristotle warned,

---

[24] The contrast between rule-consequentialism and the Kantian perspective I have sketched is discussed more explicitly in ch. 9 of this volume.

we should not expect more exactness than the subject matter affords. The warnings are easy to forget, perhaps especially because many of us were initially attracted to philosophy because, like mathematics, it gave hope of precision in areas where confusion and indeterminacy are common. But "all or nothing" thinking is unwise in philosophy, as elsewhere, and even seemingly determinate rules need to be applied judiciously. In my view, the role of moral rules is important, but limited. We need good rules *and* good judgment. Both require practical wisdom and other virtues of character.

2. *Rule-worship is irrational.* Act-utilitarians raise the objection, usually against rule-utilitarians, that it is irrational *rule-worship* to follow a rule in a particular case if no one actually benefits. Is this a valid objection to the broadly Kantian conception of moral rules suggested here? To charge someone with *rule-worship,* I take it, is to charge the person with a kind of idolatry—worship of something unworthy of that attitude. No one, surely, is guilty of literally worshipping rules, but the charge is fitting sarcasm for someone who, when challenged to defend his rigid adherence to a dubious code, has nothing to say but *"Rules are Rules."* Sarcasm and exaggeration aside, the underlying point of the charge is that one need not follow rules, even generally useful ones, *unless one has a sufficiently good reason* to do so. According to standard act-utilitarian theory, the only sufficient reason to act as a rule prescribes is that doing so in the particular case maximizes utility or expected utility, for example it promotes or is reasonably expected to promote "the greatest happiness." *Given their assumption,* no rule is worthy of being followed when it would (predictably) do more good, all considered, to break it. Their major objection to rule-utilitarians was that the rule-utilitarians seemed to share the assumption that the ultimate goal of morality is to maximize utility but still insisted that we should stick to generally useful rules even in particular circumstances when doing so does not actually benefit anyone.

This is an old debate the details of which need not detain us further. What is important here is to see that the disputes about *rule-worship* are really about whether there are sufficiently good *reasons* for having moral rules and adhering to them in various particular circumstances. Kantians, like everyone else, should agree that we should not stick to rules without good reason. The real issue is the deeper one—from what perspective do we determine whether there is good reason for having a given rule and, if so, whether there is good reason to allow for certain exceptions? Kantians reject the utilitarian assumption that these matters are to be determined from a perspective exclusively focused on maximizing (expected) utility. Any reasonable moral theory, in my view, should grant that moral rules often admit of exceptions and do not govern all aspects of life. A broadly Kantian perspective is a way of reflecting on the reasons we have for both rules and exceptions, not a perspective that endorses "rule-worship" understood as blindly following rules without good reason.

3. *Morality is not all about social rules*. Socially taught and sanctioned moral rules, the kind of primary concern here, limit our options in some specific ways but are not relevant to all choices. Few of us, I trust, are tempted to rape, incest, fraud, theft, murder, and assault, but we know many others are. Moral rules against such things are important, but there is no reason to suppose the whole of life should or can be governed by socially sanctioned rules. Some moralists may talk as if everyone should be made to conform to a comprehensive list of such rules conceived as fitting and sufficient for all situations, and some philosophers, perhaps inadvertently, encourage this unfortunate idea. My suggestion, to the contrary, has been just that there is a limited, but important, role for *some* socially supported moral rules, namely those that can be justified from the broadly Kantian perspective briefly described in the last section.

4. *Moral thinking is not all about systems of possible rules*. This is an objection to the idea that moral thinking should *always* be a two-stage process—using basic principles or values to identify an ideal code of conduct and then applying the rules of that code to particular situations. The objection now is not that life is over-burdened with socially enforced prohibitions. The concern, rather, is that philosophers construe moral deliberation as if it must always be about justifying and applying an ideal system of rules that may exist only in our thoughts. Richard Brandt and Brad Hooker, for example, hold that right and wrong are determined by what an "ideal moral code" would prescribe, the ideal code being that possible code the general acceptance of which *would* maximize aggregate welfare. Also, in Part II of *The Metaphysics of Morals*, Kant outlines a system of intermediate principles that express "ethical" requirements regarding individual conduct. These are more specific than the basic moral standard expressed in several

formulations of the Categorical Imperative, and they are apparently meant to be somehow derivative from that basic standard. The derivative principles are not presented as rules to be socially maintained and enforced, but as thoughts to guide and constrain individual decision-making. (In fact, contrary to his reputation, Kant strongly opposed moralistic social pressures to make people good, arguing instead that the sanctions for wrongdoing should be primarily legal punishment and individual conscience rather than public opinion.) Like Brandt and Hooker, then, Kant proposes to justify an "ideal" set of intermediate ethical principles to guide individual deliberation regardless of whether the principles are in fact socially taught and enforced. Thus, although their theories differ in other respects, Kant might be suspected along with Brandt and Hooker of picturing all moral deliberation as a matter of consulting an ideal system of rules. If so, the worry is that "moral thinking is not all about rules, not even about ideal systems of possible rules."

Again, the critic's concern is a legitimate one, but its force and scope are limited. For one thing, the moral theories in question make use of the idea of ideal rules (or intermediate principles) in a philosophical explication of what morality requires, but this does not imply that we need to be always thinking about the rules and principles when deciding what to do in particular situations. Furthermore, although Hooker and Brandt write as if full and explicit moral justification of actions must always appeal to rules of conduct, this is not my broadly Kantian view and (arguably) not Kant's. Kant's main ethical prescriptions in *The Metaphysics of Morals* are broad and indeterminate ends—one's own perfection and the happiness of others. His principle of beneficence states a rather minimal requirement for everyone regardless of circumstances, not a determinate rule that dictates precisely when, how, and to what extent to help others. Again I would add, as Aristotelians have wisely insisted, there are aspects of a moral life not helpfully explained by reference to rules, actual or ideal. Kantians, focused on duty and moral necessity, have not always sufficiently acknowledged this.

5. *Moral rules are unnecessary.* Undeniably people have been needlessly constrained, bullied, and bludgeoned in the name of rules alleged to be morally justified or self-evident. Naturally, then, we may wonder whether there is any *need* for moral rules to guide or motivate moral conduct. Arguments about this issue are often at cross-purposes. Some focus on

whether a *fully virtuous person* needs moral rules. Others are more concerned with whether moral rules are needed in our real world, which includes many who are imperfect, some who are vicious, and rather few who are saintly.

It is often suggested that a truly virtuous person would not need to think about any socially promulgated and enforced moral rules. The virtuous may have internalized the rules, or they may be guided by the ultimate values that the rules, perhaps clumsily, express and promote. Alternatively, some say the virtuous can perceive the good and be moved by a practical wisdom, or intuition, that works apart from any standards that can be articulated. Whatever the explanation, there is a good but familiar point here: moral rules, principles, and values need not enter explicitly into practical deliberation as premises in a logical argument to a practical conclusion. Granting this, we may still question whether moral rules should play no role for the fully virtuous. By hypothesis, we are talking here about "rules" that are socially promulgated and enforced and for good reasons. Such rules sometimes form a crucial part of the fabric of social life and discourse. A good person may never have to think, "For good reasons we have prohibitions of murder, rape, and torture, and so I must be sure to avoid these." But understanding the rule, its social role, and its justification can nevertheless serve to filter out, as unavailable options for choice, certain immoral means to otherwise good ends. It is potentially relevant that other well-meaning people have relied on the rule, committed to it in the face of uncertainty, and lived and died by it in hopes of a better future. A virtuous person may not consider such considerations as decisive in all contexts, but, if the issue arises, they should not automatically dismiss or ignore them.

The project of describing a fully virtuous agent's life and thought has been attractive to philosophers, but questions about the *need* for moral rules can have a broader focus. We must consider also the role of moral rules in the lives of those who are imperfectly virtuous, even those initially inclined to vicious behavior. Hume and Mill apparently took this more seriously than Aristotle and Kant did. Even if perfectly virtuous agents need not guide themselves by moral rules, it matters whether or not they stand behind such rules as a social practice. If the practice is warranted by more basic principles or values, then this is relevant to how the perfectly virtuous agent should relate to others.

If such rules form the framework for valuable and stable forms of life in communities where many are imperfect, then as community members the virtuous cannot reasonably dismiss the importance of these rules. And if, for good reason the virtuous endorse moral rules for the imperfectly virtuous, they may reasonably ask themselves, "Can we justify systematically treating ourselves as exceptions because of our superior virtue?"

11

Moral Construction as a Task: Sources and Limits

I. Preliminary Remarks, Aims, and Preview

Many different questions have been debated under the rubrics of "objectivity" and "relativity" of morals. My plan is to begin by distinguishing several of these questions as background discussion. Then, after a few remarks about the earlier questions, I sketch a broadly Kantian position on the last two of these questions: First, how, if at all, can we derive, justify, or support specific moral principles and judgments from more fundamental moral standards and values? Second, how, if at all, can (alleged) fundamental standards be defended? Famously, Kant attempted to provide nonskeptical answers to both questions. His explicit answers and arguments have often been criticized, and there are probably few today who accept them all without qualification. Many contemporary philosophers, however, have been influenced by his ideas about the nature and structure of moral thinking, his attempt to articulate a supreme moral standard, and his strategy for defending moral principles. My sketch here of a broadly Kantian perspective represents my attempt to develop and extend some of these ideas beyond Kant's texts.[1] The influence of John Rawls's theory of justice may also be evident.

This chapter was first presented at a conference on "Objectivism, Subjectivism, and Relativism in Ethics," sponsored by the Social Philosophy and Policy Center at Bowling Green University, November 2006. I am grateful to the participants for their comments.
[1] By calling a perspective "broadly Kantian" I mean to acknowledge that it draws heavily from Kant's ethical writings but does not follow Kant's texts in all respects. The broadly Kantian perspective that I sketch here and elsewhere modifies and supplements Kant's theory in various ways, one of which is its attempt to disassociate normative aspects of the theory from Kant's theory of noumenal freedom (as this is usually understood). I give a fuller (though still incomplete) description of the broadly Kantian perspective I have in mind in other essays, esp. Hill (2000), chs. 2, 4, and 8; (2002), ch. 3. See also chs. 8–11 and 13 of this volume.

To preview, the main features of my broadly Kantian position on our two main questions are these. First, Kant's later formulations of the Categorical Imperative provide important elements of a deliberative procedure that can be used to guide and constrain our thinking about more specific moral principles in a way that helps to correct for mere personal preference and parochial bias.[2] The procedure is far less than a determinate decision procedure or strict "derivation" of particular moral conclusions, but it promises a way of supporting judgments that initially may have appeared more doubtful. Second, Kant has two strategies for defending the ideas in his various formulations of the Categorical Imperative. The first has merit, at least when modified and presented more modestly as akin in some respects to Rawls's method of reflective equilibrium. The background of this strategy, too frequently ignored, is Kant's principled rejection of previous errors in foundational moral theory. Also, though not a major focus here, Kant's second line of defense, at least in its final modified form, may still serve its purpose in practical, rather than metaphysical, reflection and dialogue. If what is questioned is the rational authority of the basic standards identified by the previous method, the best we can do, and often all that is needed, may be to appeal to deep pervasive commitments and consistency in the practice and serious thinking of each rational moral agent.

Words such as "construction," "objectivity," and "relativity" are at best blunt instruments for discussion, and by now they have been used in so many ways they may have outlived their usefulness. Nevertheless, to connect my discussion with some recent literature, I propose that the broadly Kantian perspective sketched here leaves us with two ways in which moral *construction* is an ongoing *task*. First, and most obviously, *defining the broadly Kantian deliberative perspective* is an incomplete work in progress—an attempt to articulate for practical purposes an appropriate framework for deliberating about the interpretation and limits of specific moral principles (or "rules"). This construction project starts from the assumption that Kant's own efforts to articulate a comprehensive supreme moral principle were inadequate for the purpose but contain important, promising elements. The aim would be to put these Kantian elements together, modifying and supplementing them as needed in light of arguments, to build an account of an appropriate deliberative perspective or stance for addressing more

---

[2] Kant (2002), 222–37 [4: 421–37].

specific moral issues. The challenge would be to identify and defend certain more basic values as constituting the framework for deliberation about further, often more controversial issues, for example the interpretation and limits of rules about lying, preemptive killing, and torture. To continue the metaphor of construction, this *substantive deliberation about more specific principles* can be seen as a second, more practical construction project. In any broadly Kantian view, controversies about the interpretation of (and exceptions to) specific moral rules cannot be resolved by science, metaphysics, theology, or appeal to any authority based merely on power, tradition, or convention. Instead, such principles and their limits must, in a sense, be "constructed" in reflection from an appropriate moral point of view by the moral agents who must be subject to them.[3]

My remaining discussion will be divided into the following three main sections: In Section II, as background, I distinguish several different questions that arise in debates about moral relativism and objectivity. Then, in Section III, I sketch my broadly Kantian perspective for assessing specific moral principles. Finally, in Section IV, I describe briefly Kant's grounds for rejecting previous moral theories and his two strategies for defending a proposed deliberative perspective.

---

[3] The idea that moral principles can be *constructed* is a metaphor that can be illuminating in some respects but is also liable to be misleading. For example, the metaphor is intended to suggest that in order to reach reasonable conclusions about what moral principles require and what exceptions they allow, what is needed for practical purposes is not acute "perception" of natural or nonnatural metaphysical facts but rather reflection and discussion about what standards we have most reason to endorse in light of certain basic moral values, norms of rationality, and relevant facts about the human condition and the more local conditions in which the principles are to be applied. The metaphor of construction would be misleading if it suggested that we may construct whatever principles we please as if we were children given a pile of miscellaneous materials with which to build something but without any given blueprint, purpose, or standard for construction. When I suggest that we may think of *substantive principles* (for example, about lying, stealing, and killing) as *constructed* (or to be constructed) from a broadly Kantian deliberative perspective, I do not mean to imply that they are (or are to be) constructed from morally neutral or value-free assumptions or from values that are themselves constructed in the same sense. In saying, in addition, that we may think of *articulating the broadly Kantian deliberative perspective* as a *task for construction*, I mean to suggest only that it remains an unfinished task in moral theory to work out and express as clearly as possible a description of the most basic constraints and guiding values that are reasonable, and appropriately called (broadly) "Kantian," as a framework for assessing more substantive and derivative moral principles. When understood this way, construction of substantive principles need not be redundant or viciously circular, and construction of the deliberative basic perspective does not necessarily presuppose any particular metaethical theory. A more radical and controversial claim would be that *all* moral values and principles, including those treated as basic in a broadly Kantian deliberative perspective, are *constructed* in some further sense.

II. Different Questions Regarding Relativism and Objectivity

Some worry and others happily accept that moral principles and judgments may be "relative" and "subjective," as opposed to "absolute" and "objective." These terms, unfortunately, have been understood in so many different ways that they are now more often confusing than helpful toward understanding deep philosophical concerns.[4] At least their use in each context needs to be explained and supplemented with discussion in other terms. So I shall try to distinguish several questions without *relying* on the terms "relative," "absolute," "subjective," and "objective," even though I will use some of these terms as temporary *labels* for ideas that I explain.

A. Linguistic Relativity and Related Deeper Disputes

Some words are incomplete without explicit or implicit reference to something further. An obvious example is "relevant." Back in the 1960s, students often clamored for new courses that were "relevant" but without specifying what they were supposed to be relevant *to*. Some no doubt had the general idea that new courses should be relevant to their interests in stopping the war in Vietnam, reforming or destroying the existing government, living untraditional lifestyles, etc., but others seemed to think that the word "relevant" by itself expressed a complete idea. More commonly, people often talk about various things being *important* without saying *to whom* or *for what* they are significant. No doubt many could pause, if asked, and fill in the assumed or neglected qualification, but too often conversations proceed as if no further comment is required, some things just being important period, not *for* any specifiable purpose and not *to* you, or to me, or even to all human beings, to all rational beings, to all living things, etc. In these cases, we naturally wonder what the standards for evaluating such claims are and whether, after all, the claims make sense.

Thomas Hobbes says that "good" is always "relative to the person," usually relative to the person that uses the word but relative to the sovereign authority in a state when the sovereign makes a ruling about what is to be

---

[4] Philosophers have often noted important distinctions among the questions relevant to discussions of relativism and objectivity. An excellent example is Brandt (1959), ch. 11.

regarded as good.[5] At least part of the point seems to be that the word "good," like "relative" and "important," is incomplete by itself, and to make sense needs to be supplemented, for example by specifying to or for whom or from whose perspective something is alleged to be good. We might add a variety of other possible supplements, such as "good for . . . (a purpose)," "a good . . . (kind of thing)," or "good from the point of view of . . . (a group, project, or institution with shared aims, etc.)." Similar things might be said of "valuable," "desirable," "ideal," and other value terms (including negative terms such as "bad," "undesirable," "repugnant," etc.). If we want a label, we might use *linguistic relativity* for this idea that familiar value terms, such as "good," are incomplete without further specification.

Underlying any dispute about the linguistic point, however, is likely to be a deeper disagreement in moral theory or metaphysics. Plato held that there is a Form of Goodness that exists independently of existing earthly beings, their purposes, and their natural kinds. Hobbes made his linguistic point in a way that also expressed his antipathy to a Platonic conception of goodness. Unlike Plato, he thought that we call things *good* because we desire them, not that we desire them because (independently) they are good. Like Plato, G. E. Moore also implied that various things are good in themselves, or good *period*, as opposed to good *for* something, good *to* someone, good *of a kind*, etc. His underlying point was not merely linguistic but a controversial metaphysical thesis about the existence of goodness as a real nonrelational, nonnatural property.[6] Disputes about this go beyond linguistics and more properly fall under later questions about basic standards and justification.

B. Causal Dependence on Culture and History

When discussing whether morality is "relative," one often hears the claim that moral beliefs are determined by cultural and historical factors that vary widely. This is an empirical thesis about the causes of moral beliefs. Its relevance to disputes about the truth or validity of universal moral principles

---

[5] Hobbes (1994), pt. I, ch. 6, pp. 28–9. This famous passage in Hobbes is open to several different interpretations. My concern here is with the idea I draw from Hobbes, which may or may not be exactly what Hobbes meant.

[6] Moore (1959).

is less clear than is often supposed. There are two main points to consider. First, if true, the thesis would suggest (but does not entail) that there are no moral principles that are universally *believed*. Although it is not necessary, it is perhaps natural to expect that variable causes will produce variable effects. So the causal dependence claim is significant partly because it can be taken to support a "relativist" position on the next issue on my list, that is, whether or not all moral *beliefs* vary with cultural and historical conditions. The second and more important point to consider, however, is that the causal dependence of moral beliefs on variable cultural and historical factors is thought to undermine moral theories committed to other sources of moral belief—intuition, conscience, innate reason, divine commands, or universally shared sentiments. It is a fallacy to argue that a belief must be false because it was caused by something other than evidence for its truth. Hence, tracing the causes of moral beliefs to variable cultural conditions unrelated to moral theorists' alleged sources does not prove that the normative principles of these theorists are false, but it tends to undermine moral theories that depend on alternative causal stories to explain how they know their principles are true or valid.

C. Diversity of Many or All Moral Beliefs

As I just noted, sometimes the "relativist" position is an empirical thesis that what is *accepted* as morally right or good varies widely over times and places. A radical version would hold that there are *no* universally shared moral beliefs or values, and for every moral belief and value accepted in one culture there are *incompatible* beliefs and values in some other culture. That many particular moral beliefs diverge (for example, beliefs regarding sex, property, or the conduct of war) is undeniable, but it remains controversial whether there are some general moral values underlying the diversity of particular moral beliefs accepted in different cultures. This is an empirical question that cannot be easily settled. (A complication is that to assess evidence one must first take a position about what beliefs and norms count as *moral*.) When there is cultural variance in beliefs about facts such as the shape of the earth, there are ways to resolve the issue, showing that certain beliefs are true (the earth is round) and others mistaken (the earth is flat). Mere diversity of belief does not entail that there is no fact of the matter. The claim that all moral beliefs vary with cultural and historical conditions, then, does not entail that there are no true or valid universal moral beliefs. It does, however, raise doubts about moral theories committed to certain explanations of moral beliefs that would lead us to expect almost universal agreement about moral issues. If, for example, the theorists tell us that learning moral truths is like perception of colors or "seeing" simple mathematical propositions to be "self-evident," then they will be hard-pressed to explain pervasive and persistent diversity of moral beliefs.

D. *Normative Dependence of Specific Moral Rules and Particular Judgments on Context*

Some believe that there are fairly specific, substantive moral rules that are true or valid in all human conditions. Many understand the Ten Commandments this way. In a notorious late essay, Immanuel Kant argues that telling lies is always wrong, and even some who espouse "virtue ethics" hold that acts of certain kinds (such as torture or intentionally killing innocent persons) are always wrong.[7] By contrast, act-utilitarians maintain that specific conclusions about right and wrong depend on whatever will have (or is expected to have) the best consequences in the context. They typically affirm this act-utilitarian standard as true or valid but grant that the rightness or wrongness of specific acts can vary with the circumstances. For example, according to the act-utilitarian standard, malicious self-serving lies tend to be wrong because they cause more harm than good, though it would not have been wrong to tell a lie to a Nazi at the door to save the Jewish family hiding in one's attic. Even deontologists such as W. D. Ross hold that, although there are true universal principles of prima facie duty, particular judgments about one's "actual duty" in a situation depend also on the variable facts of the case at hand.[8] Contemporary moral "particularists" (for example, Jonathan Dancy) go even further, maintaining that

---

[7] For Kant's extreme position on lying, see "On a Supposed Right to Lie from Philanthropy," in Kant (1996b), 605–15 [8: 423–30]. Elizabeth Anscombe's view is expressed in her classic essay "Modern Moral Philosophy," Anscombe (1958), 1–19. Some other philosophers associated with virtue ethics (e.g. Philippa Foot) have reportedly endorsed this view in discussions.

[8] Ross (1930), ch. 2. Ross held that it is the principles of prima facie duty together with the facts of the particular case at hand that determine one's actual duty, but because none of those principles is absolute and they cannot be ranked with respect to one another, one's actual duty can vary with even slight changes in circumstance. To say that one has a *prima facie duty* to keep one's promise in a particular case is, in effect, to say that the fact that one promised is a *pro tanto* or defeasible moral reason to keep the promise or, in other words, a reason for doing what was promised that is sufficient in the absence of weightier countervailing moral reasons but not necessarily decisive in all contexts.

correct moral judgments are determined by the particular facts of each case independently of moral principles.[9] Dancy does not deny that *particular* moral judgments are true, "objective," and supported by reasons, but only that there are valid and useful moral *generalizations*. All these theorists hold that there are true or valid particular moral judgments, as determined either by universal moral principles or by good reasons in a context. Their primary disagreement is about the *scope* of intermediate-level moral rules or principles—for example, those forbidding lying, promise-breaking, torturing prisoners, and engaging in extramarital sex.[10] Are these valid rules or true generalizations for everyone, or only within certain cultures, or only for certain groups or individuals, or not at all?

E. Questions about the Scope and Authority of Basic Standards and Deliberative Procedures

Those who hold that specific moral rules and judgments are true or false, or valid or invalid, depending on their context, typically believe that there are more basic, general standards or procedures that explain this variability of specific rules and judgments. Both act-utilitarians and rule-utilitarians affirm such basic standards, and so do deontologists such as Ross and Kant.[11] The standards or procedures are commonly regarded as true or valid for all competent adults. They are conceived as the ultimate test of what is moral, and for many they are also (or thereby) an ultimate rational authority.

---

[9] Dancy (2004), ch. 1.

[10] Principles can be more or less general and comprehensive. In Kant's moral theory, the various formulations of the Categorical Imperative are supposed to express the supreme moral principle, which is the most general principle relevant to all questions about what we morally ought to do. What I call "intermediate-level principles" (or sometimes just "specific principles") are not as general and comprehensive, applying only to certain kinds of often-recurring cases, for example cases involving lies, theft, various sexual practices, developing one's talents, giving aid to the needy, etc. These are intermediate in generality between the Categorical Imperative and extremely specific rules and judgments concerned with a narrowly restricted range of cases (e.g. the special responsibilities of doctors and social workers regarding patients with Alzheimer's disease). Kant (1996a) outlines a system of intermediate-level principles for law and individual ethics in *The Metaphysics of Morals*.

[11] The act-utilitarian standard (roughly) is that one ought to do whatever brings about, or is expected to bring about, the most good (e.g. pleasure or well-being) in the long run. The standards of rule-utilitarianism are more complex to state because of various necessary qualifications, but the main idea is that one ought to conform to a set of rules (a code) the internalization of which by most people would bring about the most good. See Hooker (2000), 1–2 and 33. Ross's basic standards are his principles of prima facie duty concerning fidelity, gratitude, reparation, justice, self-improvement, non-injury, and beneficence. See n. 8. Kant's basic standards or deliberative procedures are expressed in the several formulations of the Categorical Imperative. See n. 2.

Opposing theorists (and some who are opposed to all theory) deny that there are universally valid basic moral standards or deliberative procedures that can guide and constrain our assessment of more particular moral rules and judgments (or make some true and others false).[12] There are different ideas, of course, about what it means for basic standards to be true, valid, and rational.

F. The Possibility of Proof, Justification, or Defense of Basic Standards

Many who accept that there are true or valid basic moral standards offer arguments of various kinds in support of their position, but some simply pronounce their standards to be self-evident. Kant and John Stuart Mill are two prominent moral philosophers who took seriously the tasks of explaining a sort of "proof" or defense that they believed possible and of offering arguments to serve the purpose. There are different views, of course, about what would constitute a proof, justification, or defense, and many theorists are skeptical about whether these are possible in any form. What constitutes a proof, justification, or defense depends heavily on how a given moral theory construes moral judgments—as stating natural facts, expressing the speaker's attitudes, ascribing real nonnatural properties to things, applying necessary rational principles, and so on.

There are, no doubt, other questions and further distinctions in disputes about moral relativity and objectivity, but my aim here has been only to set the stage for discussion. The primary focus of the rest of this chapter will be on the last two issues—more specifically, on a broadly Kantian position on *whether there are general and basic moral standards* that determine which more specific moral principles and judgments are justifiable and *how, if at all, the more basic standards can be defended.* These are difficult questions because they require not only interpreting and extending Kant's ideas but also discussing them in the terms of our contemporary debates in moral theory.

Before turning to the main two questions, however, here are a few brief comments on my broadly Kantian perspective on the other questions—

---

[12] The opposing theorists include not only nihilists (who dismiss morality entirely) but also subtle expressivists (who deny literal *truth* and validity to moral principles but do not deny their importance) and particularists (who affirm particular moral truths, possibly even similar ones in different cultures, but deny that there are basic *general* standards). Another possible view would be that there are general standards that are basic and true or valid within different historical or cultural contexts but no basic moral standards that are true or valid for all contexts.

comments which may explain why those are not my focus of concern. The questions in subsections B and C above are entirely matters for empirical investigation. Kant had opinions about them but no relevant expertise, and the main features of his moral theory, arguably, do not depend on his opinions on such empirical questions.[13] The main question in subsection A presumably belongs to traditional metaethics because it concerns the meaning, or proper use, of the word "good" and related terms. Kant's position on this matter could easily be misunderstood. He repeatedly writes of moral acts as "good in themselves" and thus does not buy into Hobbes's thesis that "good" is always "relative to the person" (more specifically, to the desires of the speaker or the command of the sovereign). In Kant's view, however, there is nothing, not even what he calls "good in itself," that is "good" in a practical sense independent of its relation to actual or possible rational agents and their reasons for intending, willing, and acting. Kant

[13] The relevance of various empirical facts to Kant's basic normative claims is not obvious. Kant evidently believed that virtually every mature and competent moral agent, at least every one in relatively "advanced" or "enlightened" parts of the world (and history), has practical reason and a conscience that acknowledges "the moral law," no matter how badly he or she may behave. He also thought that reason can be latent and conscience dulled, and that "evil" people intentionally elect to subordinate their moral predispositions. See Kant (1996a), 160–1 [6: 400–1] and 189–91 [6: 438–40], and (1998b), 179–80 [6: 184–7] and 45–65 [6: 19–44]. Kant's deplorable anthropological remarks about peoples of other "races" at least suggest that, in his opinion, even the capacity for morality may be more limited than his inspiring words about human dignity would seem to imply. See Boxill and Hill (2001), 448–71. It remains a difficult question to what extent Kant's main theses and arguments depend on his empirical beliefs and prejudices. *Groundwork* I starts with assertions about common rational knowledge of morality and proceeds to analyze their presuppositions. If Kant was mistaken about how wide the community that shared the "common" beliefs is, this would limit the interest in his main argument, making it applicable only to those who share the common beliefs. This, however, would not necessarily refute or render useless the sort of conditional ("analytical" style) argument that he admitted the argument in *Groundwork* I to be. Similarly, *Groundwork* II argues that our common conception of duty has certain striking presuppositions, but Kant concedes rather dramatically that this does not entail even that "we" who have that conception are really under moral obligations—and, all the more, the argument clearly does not entail that human beings who lack the conception are under moral obligations. In *Groundwork* III, and the *Critique of Practical Reason,* Kant tries to convince readers of the stronger claim that all agents with practical reason are subject to the moral requirements prescribed by the Categorical Imperative, but he is committed to the idea that these arguments cannot rest on empirical claims (e.g. the claim that, as a matter of fact, all cognitively competent human beings acknowledge these moral requirements or would do so after being given rational arguments). See sections I and II of Kant's *Groundwork* and, for an interpretation of the main arguments of those sections, see my "Analysis of Arguments," in Kant (2002), 195–245 [4: 393–445] and 109–14. See also Kant (1997b), 28–64 [5: 30–50]. If Kant's conception of duty and a good will were limited to eighteenth-century Prussians, the interest in his arguments would be severely limited in scope, but there is apparently a wider audience that shares Kant's conception of duty, or at least the belief that a moral duty is what one has sufficient reason to do and not just because it serves one's interests. Whether, despite objections, Kant's arguments have any merit remains a controversial question, not easily settled by reference to anthropological facts and still subject to doubts of other kinds.

does not believe in intrinsic values in the metaphysical sense that, for example, is central in G. E. Moore's intuitionist ethics.

Regarding the issue discussed in subsection D, Kant famously held that there are some specific moral principles that hold for all people at all times. His notorious example was an absolute prohibition on (serious) lying, but it is noteworthy that even famous advocates of "virtue ethics" (for example, Elizabeth Anscombe) apparently accept some completely inflexible universal principles about other matters, such as the intentional killing of innocent people.[14] On my broadly Kantian view, when (if ever) principles regarding lying and killing innocents are subject to exceptions must be determined by reflection from a more basic deliberative perspective. What this is and whether it is defensible—the questions in subsections E and F—are the topics for my remaining discussion.

III. A Broadly Kantian Perspective for Assessing Specific Moral Principles

Here I can give only a brief summary of relevant points in the Kantian perspective that I have in mind. Kantian moral theory belongs to a rationalistic tradition that maintains that the most fundamental moral values and standards are accessible through the use of practical reason, applicable to all rational human beings, and contrary to reason to dismiss or violate.[15] These fundamental values and standards are supposed to be expressed in Kant's several formulations of the Categorical Imperative and accompanying explanations.[16] Kant regarded these basic standards as presupposed by, and even implicit in, ordinary moral deliberation and judgment. He illustrates

---

[14] See n. 7 above.

[15] In Kantian theory, as I understand it, "values" are not entities or facts independent of what rational agents would care about (or "value") in various conditions. To say that humanity is a basic Kantian value, then, is not to claim that it has a perceptible quality that explains and justifies the idea that we have a rational requirement or good reasons to respect it. Saying that humanity is a basic value implies that it should be respected; i.e. we have a rational requirement or good reasons to respect it, because these are just different ways of saying the same thing. The Kantian view, so construed, is an instance of what T. M. Scanlon calls the "buck-passing" view of value—that is, value-claims do not state the *justifying basis* of reason-claims but rather *express* the idea *that there are* good reasons for taking certain (not yet specified) attitudes and actions toward the thing: Scanlon (1998), 95–100.

[16] Kant (2002), 222–37 [4: 421–38].

the guiding function of two versions of the Categorical Imperative by applying them directly to four examples that he sketches. In his later, more thorough treatment of practical problems, however, he appeals to basic standards together with general facts about the human condition to identify and (sometimes) argue for a system of general principles about property, marriage, legal authority, punishment, lying, self-neglect, helping others, gratitude, respect, and friendship.[17]

This is a system of principles of mid-level generality, standing between the most comprehensive supreme moral principle (expressed in the Categorical Imperative) and moral judgments in particular contexts. Some principles state *juridical duties,* which can and ought to be enforced by state authorities. Other principles state directly *ethical duties,* which require us to adopt maxims of various sorts to promote the ends of self-perfection and the happiness of others. The strict *perfect duties* have the form "Never . . . " or "Always . . . ," but the *imperfect duty* to help others leaves room for judgment and choice regarding when, how, and to what extent to help. According to Kantian theory, then, there is a structure that can guide us to correct moral judgments in particular cases. The ultimate standard, a principle or procedure expressed as the Categorical Imperative, is taken to be a comprehensive, fundamental, and even necessary requirement of practical reason—and so the standard for our reasoning about what we ought to do. Applying this standard to pervasive human conditions, Kant attempts to identify (and justify relative to the standard) a system of mid-level principles of several kinds intended to be applicable independently of variations in local conditions. The principles of perfect duty must never entail contradictory prescriptions, but the "grounds of duty" from which they are drawn may be in tension.[18] All the more, imperfect duties may be in tension, for promoting one moral end may limit the ways that one can pursue another. The system is supposed to be structured and consistent, but its imperfect duties allow considerable room for choice, and all duties require interpretation and judgment appropriate to the context.[19]

When explaining the basic Kantian standard for identifying more specific moral principles, most contemporary reconstructions and developments of Kant's moral theory concentrate on interpretations of either Kant's formula

---

[17] Kant (1996a), pts. I and II, 1–170 [6: 203–413].
[18] Ibid. 16–17 [6: 224–5].   [19] Ibid. 153 [6: 390].

of universal law or his formula of humanity as an end in itself.[20] Skeptical of these (or any formulas) as case-by-case moral decision procedures, I have suggested that a Kantian framework for assessing moral rules (or mid-level principles) might be constructed from Kant's idea of the perspective of a lawmaking member of a community of rational, autonomous, and mutually respectful persons (what Kant calls a *Reich der Zwecke* or "kingdom of ends").[21]

In section II of the *Groundwork for the Metaphysics of Morals*, Kant's attempt to articulate a basic moral standard unfolds in a progressive argument through the earlier formulas (of universal law and humanity as an end) to the idea of rational persons with autonomy legislating universal laws without basing them on contingent personal desires. Loosely paraphrased, the argument proceeds from "Conform to universal law" to "Respect and place the highest value on humanity in each person," followed by an explanation that this requires, among other things, respecting each person as a rational autonomous legislator of universal laws. This idea, in turn, is further developed in a formula of the Categorical Imperative that Kant suggests is his most complete characterization of moral requirements, the principle that says that we should conform to the laws of a possible *Reich der Zwecke*, or ideal commonwealth in which all rational autonomous persons, "abstracting from personal differences," legislate the moral laws that unite and bind them.[22] Although Kant still preferred his famous formula of universal law as the best guide for judgment in particular cases, he obviously regarded this

---

[20] The formula of universal law states: "Act only on that maxim by which you can at the same time will that it should become a universal law," Kant (2002), 222 [4: 421]. A variation that Kant uses in discussing his examples is: "Act as though the maxim of your action were to become by your will a universal law of nature," ibid. The formula of humanity states: "Act in such a way that you treat humanity, whether in your own person or in any other person, always at the same time as an end, never as a means," ibid. 230 [4: 429]. Distinguished scholars have interpreted these formulas in different ways, many of which I review in ch. 2 of this volume.

[21] See n. 1 for references to my fuller discussions of this Kantian perspective. A *Reich* (literally) is a state or commonwealth, a governing legal system that may or may not involve a king or monarch. There is a possible analogy with biblical talk of a "kingdom of God" that may have influenced Kant but is not essential to his idea. When Kant describes the "kingdom of ends" (*Reich der Zwecke*) in the *Groundwork*, it has a "head" with features only possible for a divine being, but the head has no function apparently but to endorse the same rational principles as every other member. The primary difference is that the "head," who is not conceived as a political sovereign with independent legislative authority, lacks sensuous temptations to act contrary to reason and so is not "subject to" or "bound by" the rational principles. That is, they are not moral "imperatives" for the divine being.

[22] Kant (2002), 231–7 [4: 431–7].

later principle as an inspiring conception of the moral point of view, "closer to intuition" and "feeling."[23]

The main elements of Kant's idea of moral legislation are the following. The legislators are rational, seeking to legislate a consistent and coherent set of "laws" (moral principles), making no law without sufficient reason or in ignorance of relevant facts. They are committed to finding and respecting laws that apply to all and respect human dignity in all, and so, in legislating, they must rely on reasons that any moral agent can acknowledge and take into account apart from special interests. Their "autonomy" also implies freedom from various distorting and morally irrelevant influences and a genuine acknowledgment that the rational standard behind particular moral reasons is not merely rational prudence or efficiency in the pursuit of one's own personal ends. Obviously, and for good reason, certain moral values, assumed to be fundamental, are built into this conception of moral legislation. The aim is not to give a bootstrapping argument for basic moral values but rather to construct from these an intuitively appealing and inspiring conception of the moral point of view that should frame our thinking about more specific moral requirements.

A more modest application of Kant's idea, akin to Rawls's initial theory of justice, would make use of the model of "legislation" from an ideal perspective adapted for a more specific range of practical problems. For example, we might use this approach in addressing the question whether the prohibition of torture is open to exception. Given certain basic moral values, the presumption against torture (as well as against murder, rape, fraud, and manipulation) is rather obvious. The difficult questions are about cases in which moral values conflict. Granting that some particular hard cases may have no resolution, we can still ask whether it is morally important to maintain shared public principles about such matters, independently of law, and what exceptions, if any, these principles should allow. The broadly Kantian idea is that it may be helpful to treat such questions in two stages—articulating the relevant standpoint for joint deliberation (in effect, the rules of debate) and then reviewing arguments for proposed principles.

From the Kantian perspective, the most fundamental values that are to guide and constrain deliberation about rules are drawn from the idea of human dignity, or *humanity as an end in itself*. In Kantian theory, as

---

[23] Kant (2002), 237 [4: 436–7].

I understand it, saying that something is valuable is equivalent to saying how we ought to regard and treat the thing that is said to have value. We can interpret the idea of human dignity, then, as a cluster of prescriptions about how to regard and treat human beings. Previously, I summarized these prescriptions thus:[24]

In sum, they are, *negatively*, not to regard persons as having a merely commensurable value and not to violate principles that rational autonomous persons would endorse, all things considered; and, *positively*, to exercise, preserve, develop, and honor rational nature in all persons, to prioritize the needs for rational autonomous living over more trivial concerns, and to count the happiness of others (or, strictly, their permissible ends) as significant in our deliberations. The proposed Kantian perspective regards the second negative prescription as an inflexible constraint on action: *never* violate the principles that, in one's best judgment, rational autonomous deliberators would endorse, if guided and constrained by the idea of human dignity and mindful of the complexities of the real world for which the principles are intended. The first negative prescription ("*never* regard persons as having a merely commensurable value") and the remaining positive prescriptions are also non-optional demands, but they directly concern our *attitudes* when we deliberate and act.[25]

Obviously much more needs to be said, but it may be helpful to conclude my sketch with a few general remarks about a significant difference between the Kantian perspective and some theories that are in other respects similar. For example, the Kantian framework is meant to reflect what deliberation from a moral point of view about the issue at hand would be like, not necessarily what rational self-interested agents would choose in a state of nature or what "mutually disinterested" rational agents would choose under a "veil of ignorance."[26] Because those who deliberate from the broadly

[24] Ch. 9 of this volume.

[25] Of course, they will rule out certain *acts* as immoral and show that others are morally required, but they do so by demanding that our deliberations, choices, and intentions are compatible with the prescribed attitudes. It is not as though one could muster up a motivationally inert and non-reason-giving "inner state of mind," such as a mere wish or "pure thought," and then anything one does will be permitted.

[26] As Fred Miller has noted in discussion, theories that aim to derive specific principles from a "self-interested" or any other deliberative point of view will not be able to reach any substantive conclusions unless they explain the interests or values that motivate the parties taking the deliberative (or contractual) perspective. "Self-interest" can be conceived in different ways, for example: as having the most pleasure possible, as realizing one's most important personal ends, or as Aristotelian *eudaimonia*. In Hobbes's state of nature, those who make the social contract are conceived as moved by their various desires, especially

Kantian perspective are directly moved and constrained by basic moral considerations, the Kantian perspective, as construed here, resembles Locke's social contract theory more than Hobbes's.[27] In this respect, the Kantian perspective also appears to differ from T. M. Scanlon's contractualism, for Scanlon stipulates that in determining what principles can reasonably be rejected we must restrict ourselves to comparing the weight of reasons that different agents have *from their perspective*.[28] The reasons for endorsing or rejecting a principle that must be weighed are not *moral* reasons, even though the outcome of Scanlon's contractualist reasoning is supposed to be judgments about what is (or is not) morally wrong. My broadly Kantian approach, then, is just one of several ways of thinking about morality that attempt, first, to define an appropriate point of view for deliberation and debate and then, second, to use this perspective to derive specific principles about how to deal with various recurring practical problems. My approach differs from various contract-oriented theories,

the predominant desire to survive, and their desires are always for some "good" for themselves. In Rawls's "original position," the parties are exclusively motivated to secure, within the constraints of the choice situation, the most favorable mix of "primary goods" (e.g. wealth, income, opportunities, powers, and self-respect) for themselves. Both Rawls and Hobbes conceive of the parties in the relevant deliberative position (Rawls's original position and Hobbes's state of nature) as *not* motivated by explicitly moral concerns. The choice situations are deliberately defined to ensure that *we* can draw moral conclusions from arguments that the parties in those choice situations would endorse certain principles, but *the parties themselves* are not engaged in moral reflection. There are some theoretical advantages in conceiving of the parties' motivations as nonmoral, but, following Kant, my broadly Kantian deliberative perspective nevertheless conceives of the "legislators" of specific moral principles as motivated in part by stipulated basic moral values (for example, humanity as an end in itself). This approach, of course, invites questions about how the stipulated values can be defended and whether, given that moral values are stipulated, arguments for specific principles are circular or redundant. My brief discussion here suggests Kantian responses, but these questions obviously require more attention.

[27] John Locke's political philosophy employs the idea of reasonable agreements or contracts that were, or would be, made by persons who take for granted certain fundamental moral norms (the "laws of nature") as requirements of reason. Locke then tries to justify various specific principles regarding government, revolution, etc., by arguing that these principles would be endorsed by contracting parties who have personal interests but are also committed to these laws of nature (as moral guides and constraints). Thomas Hobbes, by contrast, tries to justify principles regarding government, law, etc., by arguing that rational persons in a state of nature would have sufficient prudential grounds, apart from any *independent* moral commitments, to accept those principles to be enforced by a sovereign power. Interpretations differ, but, on my reading, Locke, like Kant, is explicitly arguing from basic general moral values to more specific moral principles. See John Locke, *Second Treatise of Government*, in Morgan (2005), esp. chs. 1–9; and Thomas Hobbes, *Leviathan*, pt. I, esp. chs. XIV and XV. We should note, however, that I have been comparing a Kantian *moral* perspective with the *political* theories of Locke and Hobbes. A comparison of the latter with Kant's political and legal theory is complicated because the relation between the Categorical Imperative and Kant's principles regarding law is unclear and controversial.

[28] Scanlon (1998), esp. chs. 2, 4, and 5.

however, in explicitly calling for reliance on basic moral values in deliberating about specific principles.

IV. Strategies for the Defense of the Deliberative Perspective

To sketch Kant's strategies, we must review three main points: a background of critical arguments and then two different lines of defense for
Kant's own perspective. The background (sketched in subsection A below)
consists of objections to previous moral theories. Then the first positive
strategy (subsection B) is an attempt to show "analytically" that the basic
values in Kant's deliberative perspective are presupposed in concepts essential to our ordinary understanding of morality. The second positive strategy
(subsection C) is simply to appeal to each reader's moral consciousness,
which Kant thought was a virtually inescapable recognition of being under
moral obligation (as Kant conceived this).[29] Apart from the details of Kant's
own exposition, arguably these general background arguments and strategies are potentially relevant in assessing contemporary moral theories,
including the broadly Kantian perspective sketched here.

A. The Background: Critique of Previous Moral Theories

The background consists of negative arguments to reject other (non-
Kantian) views about the nature and source of morality. These arguments
are most explicit in Kant's *Groundwork for the Metaphysics of Morals* and *Critique
of Practical Reason*.[30] Kant categorizes all previous moral theories into four
types, which we may label "ethical egoism," "moral sense theories," "divine
command theories," and "perfectionism." Having argued that moral concepts

---

[29] Those who were looking for a logical demonstration or empirical confirmation of Kant's basic
value claims are likely to find this appeal to their moral consciousness initially disappointing and perhaps
not even worth calling a "defense." It also falls short of Kant's ambitious project in *Groundwork* III to
"establish" that anyone who acts for reasons does so "under the idea of freedom" and is therefore
committed to the Categorical Imperative as a supreme standard. However, given a background of
arguments against other moral theories, the attempt to get us to see, in our own reflections, that we
deeply and persistently acknowledge certain basic moral values as rational might suffice, for practical
purposes, in response to certain kinds of theory-driven doubts about whether acting morally makes
sense.

[30] See Kant (2002), 242–5 [4: 441–4], and Kant (1997b), 32–6 [5: 35–41].

presuppose that "autonomy of the will" is the fundamental source of morality, Kant charges that all the previous moral theories are mistaken because they fail to acknowledge this fact. Here, I take it, Kant is engaging in what is now considered "metaethics," for he maintains that his "analytical" argument in *Groundwork* II shows that the theories in question fail to understand common moral concepts and, further, that they leave us without any resources to argue (as Kant attempts in *Groundwork* III) for the rational authority of basic moral standards. Kant alleges that each type of moral theory is open to special objections, but the common error of each theory is to suppose that morality is something other than following principles that moral agents with practical reason and autonomy would give (or "legislate") to themselves as constraining their social relations and personal choices. We do not need to accept the full Kantian idea of autonomy to appreciate his critique of other moral theories.

Roughly, the main negative points, reworked and modified for contemporary discussions, are these: (1) Some moral theories attempt to derive the content and rational authority of moral principles from the idea that, fundamentally, each person should (or has sufficient reason to) do whatever most effectively promotes his or her interests. This approach is inadequate, Kant argues, because it is a constitutive conception of *moral* requirements that they prescribe what we must do independently of whether they advance our own interests. Thus, even if only the pursuit of self-interest is rational, the requirements that would be prescribed by this method would not be *moral* requirements. Kant classifies egoistic theories as "empirical," apparently because their advocates typically base them on psychological egoism[31] and because they make specific moral requirements vary widely with each person's empirical circumstances. Kant's main critical point, however, is that moral requirements cannot be derived from egoistic principles of any kind, rational or otherwise.

Further, (2) Kant also rejects moral sense theories, presumably in part for reasons that comparable theories tend to be rejected now. Such theories attempt to derive moral conclusions from patterns of moral feelings that human beings typically have in recurrent situations—for example, impartial

---

[31] Psychological egoism, as I understand it, is the view that, as a matter of fact, every person is always ultimately motivated by the desire to advance his or her own interests. It can take different forms, depending on how "one's own interests" is interpreted and how deep or near the surface self-interested desires are taken to be.

spectators' feelings of disapproval of cruelty. The core objection is that judgments about what we ought to do are *normative judgments* about what we have *good reasons* to do, and these do not follow (without further premises) from facts about human sentiments, no matter how universal these may be. The point for contemporary discussions would be that empirical psychology alone cannot establish moral claims about what we ought to do, even though it can undermine ill-informed particular moral judgments and cast doubt on our capacity to live by certain alleged moral standards. Assuming (with Kant and others) that moral claims purport to give us good reasons to act, empirical studies by themselves cannot determine which moral claims, if any, are true or valid.

Turning to theories that Kant classifies as nonempirical or rational theories, (3) he rejects theories that attempt to derive moral requirements from theology on the ground that either their derivations are circular or the derivative commands are not moral. In other words, either the divine source is *defined* as giving only rational moral commands or else its commands are nonmoral because the authority comes from divine power, not reason. This objection also poses a challenge for any contemporary moral theory that rests the ultimate reasons for being moral on actual commands, secular or ecclesiastical. Similar considerations might apply to the assumption that the "force" of tradition, custom, or common opinion (alone) is the basis of moral requirements.

Finally, (4) Kant rejects forms of perfectionism that base the rational authority of moral requirements on their alleged promotion of the metaphysical value of "perfection," an idea prominent in the work of Leibniz and Christian Wolff. This idea, Kant suggests, is too indeterminate to be action-guiding unless we interpret "perfection" in a morally loaded way that would make derivations of moral requirements from it circular or question-begging. Again, details aside, we can draw a message relevant in moral theory today. Metaphysical properties, whether labeled "perfection" or "intrinsic value" or whatever, are supposed to be features of *the world as it is*, not necessarily *as it ought to be*. What we have reason to do cannot be determined by such facts alone. Although we are not concerned with the sort of perfectionism that Kant explicitly rejected, his objection may be relevant to current theories that rest too easy with "intuitions" about which facts are practical "reasons" (or "considerations that favor" choices), in the absence of any general account of what constitutes reasons of various kinds.

Returning now to my review of Kantian strategies for defending alleged basic moral standards, the first main point (which provides background for more positive arguments) has been that certain other strategies are *inadequate for the defense* of Kantian basic standards and, equally important, that those strategies *cannot by themselves refute* Kantian proposals about what the rational moral standards are. This is a strong negative metaethical claim that, perhaps for good reasons, most contemporary Kantians do not wish to debate at length, but it is a background idea that, if correct, makes it easier to move on to positive considerations.

B. *Argument that the Perspective is Presupposed in Common Moral Judgments*

Kant's main attempts to defend his conception of the basic moral standard are presented in the first two chapters of the *Groundwork,* where he argues that concepts deeply embedded in common morality presuppose the supreme principle expressed in his versions of the Categorical Imperative. His aim in these chapters is not to "establish" his basic principle or standard as rational but only to identify formulations of that standard that express its essential features and can serve to guide moral deliberation. If successful, these arguments taken by themselves would provide an important but limited "defense" of Kant's basic deliberative perspective as reflecting the indispensable core of our common morality, rather than mere custom or personal preference.

Kant's arguments do not start from a survey of moral opinions about particular matters, such as lying and suicide, but from relatively formal ideas about duty and a good will. An essential feature of these ideas, supposedly pervasive in ordinary moral thinking, is that being good and doing what one ought is, among other things, a matter of respecting constraints that we have sufficient reason to follow and not just because doing so advances our interests. This could be so, Kant argues, only if there is a basic rational standard, distinct from instrumental and prudential rationality, which can support more particular moral judgments. Moreover, Kant argues that the content of the basic standard(s) is expressible in different ways, which are supposed to be fundamentally the same. Most abstractly expressed, the standard is that we must (rationally) choose in a way that respects "universal laws." As eventually interpreted, the standard is to respect the more specific principles of conduct that would be "legislated" by rational agents who have "autonomy of the will" and respect humanity in each person. The form of Kant's argument is conditional, and so is his conclusion. That is, essential concepts of common morality *presuppose* his basic deliberative perspective as the standard from which genuine moral obligations derive. This defense is distinct from his later attempt, in *Groundwork* III, to show that common morality is not mistaken in taking its requirements to be *rational* to follow.

Let us set aside details and doubts about Kant's actual argument (and my brief summary) and focus instead on the kind of positive strategy Kant uses to defend his attempt to articulate a basic moral standard. Kant's strategy is similar in some respects to Rawls's method of reflective equilibrium, but there are also important differences.[32] Some differences in their methods stem from differences in their ambitions and hopes for moral theory, but others reflect Rawls's greater respect for the empirical realities which influence and provide the context for moral reasoning. These differences understandably make Rawls's method more acceptable to contemporary philosophers, but the ways in which Rawls's method remains similar to Kant's are also instructive.

To set the background very briefly, Rawls draws from widely accepted, relatively uncontroversial assumptions about basic moral and political values to develop (or "construct"?) an appropriate idealized point of view ("the original position") for assessing competing conceptions of justice.[33]

He proposes two general principles of justice and then argues that these would be preferred to certain alternatives from the perspective of the original position. Then Rawls argues that applications of the principles, in several stages, more or less match the "considered judgments of competent judges" in due reflection. When arguments from the appropriate deliberative standpoint ("the original position") *as this was initially defined* lead to conflicts with our "considered judgments," we need to reflect further on the definition and arguments for the original position, its application, and our own pre-theoretical considered judgments. The task of seeking *reflective equilibrium* is to revise the arguments, refine the original position, or abandon our initial moral judgments, until we can find no more acceptable way to bring our various convictions into a coherent whole. Like Kant, Rawls argues from what he takes to be deep and pervasive ordinary moral ideas to support an account of an appropriate deliberative perspective for assessing

---

[32] Rawls (1999c), 18–19, 42–5, and 507–8.   [33] Ibid., esp. pt. I, 10–19.

more specific principles, and then he illustrates the application of the deliberative perspective by applying it to several practical problems.[34]

Significant differences, of course, should be noted. Most obviously, Kant's ambition was to present a comprehensive moral standard, whereas Rawls aims to construct a deliberative perspective for a more limited project. That is, even in *A Theory of Justice*, Rawls constructs his "original position" primarily to assess competing, historically prominent conceptions of justice as they apply to the basic structure of well-ordered, cooperative, closed societies—in particular, with regard to how the basic structure affects the distribution of primary social goods. Later, in *Political Liberalism*, he restricts his project further to "political conceptions" of justice that reflect background assumptions common in Western liberal democracies.[35] A significant feature of Rawls's arguments for his deliberative procedure for assessing principles is that, unlike Kant, Rawls does not try to make his case by drawing out the implications of a few, relatively formal and allegedly essential features of common morality (such as the idea of duty and the value of a good will). Rawls rightly acknowledges more places where empirical facts are relevant to his arguments, and he is obviously more aware of the possibility that revisions may be necessary.

Important similarities remain, however—and for good reasons. Both Kant and Rawls see moral theory as a project with a structure that distinguishes basic deliberative procedures from derivative principles, and both distinguish arguments *for* the deliberative procedure from arguments *from* the procedure to derivative principles. Although both rely on assumptions about common moral opinions, neither treats these opinions as self-evident or infallible. Despite his repeated warnings about not basing moral theory on examples, Kant (like Rawls) draws out the (supposed) implications of his principles as some sort of confirmation of them.[36] Neither Kant nor Rawls

---

[34] Rawls (1999c) takes up various practical problems in pt. II of *A Theory of Justice*, e.g. toleration of the intolerant (190–4), governmental institutions to promote just distribution of wealth and income (242–51), justice between generations (251–8), and civil disobedience (319–31).

[35] Rawls (1996).

[36] Kant says: "[M]y claims about this central question [the nature and justification of the supreme principle of morality] would be greatly clarified by seeing the application of that supreme principle to the whole system, and they would be *strongly confirmed* by the adequacy the principle would manifest throughout." Kant (2002), 193–4 [4: 392]; emphasis added. He nevertheless strongly condemns any attempt to *derive* fundamental moral principles from examples. See e.g. ibid. 208–14 [4: 406–12]. *The Metaphysics of Morals* contains his most systematic attempt to present and support a system of intermediate-level principles.

addresses his theory to radical moral skeptics or pretends to have arguments sufficient to show that living a moral life is necessarily in one's interest. Finally, both Kant and Rawls seem to realize that, in the end, defense of their projects and results depends on a different sort of appeal to each reader—the subject to which I turn next.

C. Appeal to Each Rational Agent's Awareness or Acceptance of the Basic Standards

A final strategy for defending an account of basic moral deliberative standards is suggested by Kant's attempts to address the question that he so dramatically poses at the end of *Groundwork* II. That is, even if an account is demonstratively reflective of common moral ideas, is it really *rationally necessary* to accept it? Might it not be that morality's claim to be rational is just an illusion? Kant tried in *Groundwork* III to meet the challenge by arguing that whenever we act for reasons, we cannot help but see ourselves as free in a sense that ultimately commits us to the Categorical Imperative.[37] To meet the objection that he may have argued in a circle, he adds that in the theoretical use of reason (for example, in scientific investigations) we must take ourselves to be following reason independently of causal determination, and this again commits us to the Categorical Imperative.[38]

Later, in his *Critique of Practical Reason*, Kant reverses his argument, apparently conceding the inadequacy of the early arguments. He then proposes that consciousness of the moral law is "a fact of reason," adequate for practical purposes.[39] Scholars debate what he meant, but apparently at least part of the idea is that for us—human beings who take ourselves to be rational moral agents—no further argument is needed because, try as we will to deny and escape moral requirements, we cannot. That is, although self-deception, special pleading, and moral disagreements are all too common, in serious honest reflection we cannot consistently regard ourselves as rationally entitled systematically to ignore the claims of others as not (rationally) binding on us. The rational authority that supports such claims, Kant suggests, is inevitably recognized as the authority of our own reason, however much we may wish to deny it. This is not presented as a

---

[37] Kant (1996*a*), 245–8 [4: 444–8].
[38] Ibid. 248–57 [4: 448–58].
[39] Kant (1997*b*), 28–64 [5: 30–50].

demonstration, or a claim to perceive self-evident rational truths, or an appeal to moral feelings. As I understand Kant's point, it is an appeal to individuals, in their own first-person reflections, to acknowledge that they are under moral obligations or at least cannot help but conceive of themselves in this way. Arguably, despite Kant's own views, such reflections should not be used to justify assuming that others are as committed to morality as we are—assuming this, for example, when we are inclined to justify harsh moralistic treatment of criminals without regard to their actual background and attitudes. Nevertheless, Kant apparently thought his appeal to each person's moral consciousness a relevant kind of response to certain kinds of doubts about morality, given the fact (argued earlier) that contrary claims about rational choice could not be proved by science, theology, metaphysics, or social practice.

Kant's expectations for the practical success of this appeal to each person's moral consciousness were higher, I suspect, than the expectations most of us share. This is especially so if the person's moral consciousness is supposed to acknowledge Kant's particular statements of the moral law and associated ideas about freedom of will. But at least when our aim and context is practical, rather than an attempt to establish a universal truth of metaphysics or abstract moral theory, we may find that the best we can do, and all that is needed, is to appeal to the commitments of each rational moral agent. If agents profess to deliberate and debate in terms of shared reasons, reasons about which others outside their circle should care, then they may be able to see, on due reflection, that their moral and reason-based commitments exceed their wishes to escape moral obligation. And perhaps a more modest, reasonable contemporary account of moral obligations (compared to some ideas in Kant's actual texts) can facilitate this process, and arguably it can be a (practically) rational process. Rawls's appeals to each reader to consider, revise, and endorse his theory of justice is similar and, in my view, remains worthy of serious consideration.

V. Conclusion

In this wide-ranging chapter, I began by distinguishing different questions that are often confused in discussions of moral relativism and objectivity, and then I attempted to sketch the responses that a broadly Kantian theory might give to two of these questions. The first of these questions was: How (if at all) can we derive, justify, or support specific moral principles and judgments from more fundamental moral standards and values? In response, I briefly sketched a broadly Kantian deliberative perspective designed for this purpose, drawing from Kant's later formulations of the Categorical Imperative. The second question was: How (if at all) can fundamental standards such as those found in the Kantian perspective be defended? In response, I briefly described two of Kant's strategies for defending his fundamental standards and the important background of arguments against previous moral theories.

The Kantian deliberative perspective, like rule-utilitarianism, sets us the task of finding or constructing a set of specific moral principles (or "rules") that satisfy basic values and constraints but also take into account relevant facts about the human condition and the circumstances in which the principles are to apply. Unlike rule-utilitarianism, however, the Kantian perspective essentially includes values associated with human dignity that shape Kantian deliberations about the set of specific principles to be adopted. Kant's strategies for defending the basic values inherent in the deliberative perspective are, first, to try to show that these values are presupposed in common moral thought and practice and, second, to appeal directly to the moral consciousness of the would-be skeptic. In neither strategy does Kant argue for his standards from (allegedly) more self-evident premises or appeal to intuitive "perception" of an independent moral order. Instead, he analyzes the presuppositions of common moral concepts and appeals to each person to acknowledge his or her own deep and persistent practical commitment to the basic standards as rationally authoritative. How far such arguments can succeed in the world today is an open question. Kant's own confidence in them was a kind of morally based faith not refutable by empirical studies, but it is hard to share that confidence in today's world.

IV
Practical Questions

12

Questions about Kant's Opposition to Revolution

Kant is well known for taking a hard, inflexible line on certain particular moral issues, such as lying and revolution. Despite this, there has been a revival of interest in Kant's basic moral theory in recent years. The explanation is not that contemporary moral philosophers have been converted to Kant's rigorism about particular matters, but rather that they assume that his untenable rigoristic judgments on substantive issues do not strictly follow from his basic moral theory, at least if this is properly understood and perhaps modified in some respects. This assumption is well justified regarding Kant's stand on revolution. Kant held that revolution, even against a tyrant, is always impermissible, but he did not make a compelling case for this extremely conservative position. In fact, for several reasons, Kant's attitude about revolution was puzzling. Arguably, however, although Kant was mistaken, he had a more consistent and coherent view than at first it might seem and, moreover, he had the resources for developing a more moderate position.

Several related questions need to be considered. How could Kant consistently and coherently express enthusiasm for the French Revolution while endorsing an absolute prohibition against taking part in revolutions? How can Kant reconcile this Hobbesian absolute prohibition against revolution with his acknowledgment, contrary to Hobbes, that rulers can be tyrants who violate the requirements of justice? Does Kant argue convincingly that there can be no legal right to revolution? If so, are there, within his systematic moral theory, adequate grounds for inferring that participating in a revolution is always morally impermissible? In particular, does his appeal to the publicity requirement for maxims provide more than illusory support for his position? Do not the reasons implicit in the Categorical

Imperative, which must be the ground for allowing passive resistance to legal authority, also justify active participation in revolution in some cases?

In brief, the best response is arguably the following. Although Kant was mistaken to hold that participation in revolution is always wrong, his position is compatible with his insistence that rulers are bound by justice and his hopeful attitude toward the French Revolution. Kant does make a convincing case that there cannot be a legal right to revolution, provided we do not confuse genuine revolution and the constitutionally sanctioned removal of officials with delegated authority. It does not follow, however, from either this or his publicity argument that revolution is always immoral, and there are reasons to think that his basic theory would support the contrary conclusion.

Does it Make Sense to Hail the Revolution While Condemning the Participants?

Kant's position on revolution strikes many readers as bizarre. At the same time, Kant is adamant in his stand against instigating and participating in revolution against the de facto rulers of our state.[1] Regardless of how tyrannical the head of state may be, Kant says, no person has the right to attempt to overthrow him. Revolutionaries must be punished by death, he insists, even if their motives were honorable.[2] Attempting to punish a deposed head of state is always wrong and unlawful.[3] Few themes in Kant's political philosophy seem as forcefully and repeatedly asserted as these. Even so, Kant was optimistic about revolutions as forces for moral progress that we might otherwise never achieve. He was known as a supporter of the French Revolution, reportedly referred to as "the old

---

[1] See Kant (1996a), 95–8, 106–7, and 111–13, and Kant (1902–), vi. 319–22, 333–4, and 339–42. See also Kant, "The Contest of Faculties," "Perpetual Peace," and Reiss, "Postscript," in Reiss (1991), 81–4, 126, 182 n., 188 n., and 261–8. Note that what is at issue is revolution against the "rulers" or the "head of state," with the understanding that there is a government that meets Kant's minimal standards for legal authority. Arthur Ripstein, for example, argues that rogue regimes such as that of the Nazis are mere "barbarisms" and not legitimate governments even by Kant's minimal standards. See Ripstein (2009), 336–43. See also ch. 14 n. 5 below.

[2] Kant (1996a), 106–7 [6: 333–4].

[3] Ibid. 104–5 [6: 331].

Jacobin."[4] The way the French Revolution inspired spectators throughout Europe, Kant says, was among the most significant events in history, for it reflected a moral disposition that gives hope for continuing moral progress.[5] To many philosophers, this is a puzzling, even inconsistent, combination of views, suggesting that Kant was ambivalent or vacillated in his position.

The combination of views just described is no doubt unusual, but, properly understood, it is a consistent and coherent position.[6] In the end it is not defensible both because it implies that participating in revolution is always wrong and because it rests on an untenable faith in historical progress. Nevertheless it is worth showing why it is a coherent view because this highlights vividly the nonconsequentialist and agent-centered structure of Kant's moral thinking. Kant may sometimes have been ambivalent about revolution, but it is not necessary to suppose this in order to understand his official position in published work.

The key to understanding Kant's position is to realize that "What is morally permissible to do?" and "What will have the most morally desirable effects?" are distinct questions. Answers to the question of morally desirable effects are often relevant to the answers to the question of moral permissibility, but not in any simple and direct way. Let us by "morally desirable effects" understand effects that morally good people, as such, should hope for and seek to promote through permissible means. There are grounds for assessing the means to desirable results as morally permissible or not independently, or partly independently, of whether the predicted effects are such that morally good people would wish for them and seek them, when they can, through permissible means. Unlike consequentialists, Kant can consistently maintain that at times, unfortunately, it is not morally permissible to do what would be necessary to achieve the results that are morally most desirable. For example, the outcome of an election might be a morally more desirable state of affairs if Goodfellow wins, but the only means to defeat his rival Badfellow may involve bribery and spreading false rumors. Kant presupposes the key distinction when he defends his extreme stand against revolution, for he implies that no matter how greatly desirable and certain the morally desirable results of revolution might be, revolution

---

[4] See Korsgaard (1997), 300 and n. 6.

[5] Kant, "The Contest of Faculties," in Reiss (1991), 182.

[6] Peter P. Nicholson, "Kant, Revolution, and History," in Williams (1992), 249–68. See also Beck (1971).

is an impermissible means. We cannot infer the moral permissibility of means to an end from the moral desirability of the end because these must be assessed, to some degree, independently.

Thus Kant, unlike consequentialists, can consistently maintain that participating in a revolution is among the means to morally desirable ends that it is morally impermissible to employ, no matter how great and certain the good results might be. For Kant's position to be fully coherent, he needs an account of why, despite this, good people should applaud the spirit of the revolution and regard its outcome as moral progress. How does it make sense for Kant to adopt such a favorable attitude toward the French Revolution despite his belief that active participation in it would be wrong?

Considering an analogy may be helpful. Suppose a citizen in a town oppressed by corrupt bosses had always insisted vehemently that murder is absolutely wrong, but then he cheerfully joins others in rejoicing at the murder of a particularly vicious boss, expressing delight at the good that resulted from the murder, say, more peace and security for law-abiding citizens. Initially, there seems a tension in the citizen's attitudes. Some explanation or qualification is called for. He could preserve consistency by pointing out that he did not condone the murder, which he still says was absolutely wrong, but only welcomes the outcome that, luckily, a deplorable deed had in this case. This would disassociate the immoral act sharply from its fortuitous good consequences but it also severely dampens the enthusiasm expressed for the beneficial murder. It is at least a consistent position, as is the analogous position regarding revolution.

It is not clear, however, that Kant's enthusiasm for the French Revolution was so carefully and explicitly restricted to its outcome. He also hailed the spirit of the revolution, which was exemplified in the motivating ideals of the revolutionaries and spectators throughout the world who cheered for them. To make this coherent with his absolute prohibition of revolution requires expanding the analogy with murder.

To improve the analogy, we might try to imagine an idealistic and inspiring murder. In Kant's view, apparently, at least some French revolutionaries, though wrong, acted for the sake of the moral ideals of freedom, equality, and human solidarity, thereby inspiring the public reaction of enlightened people all over the world in favor of their ideals, even if not all their deeds. The closest parallel might be a homicide committed in a moment of passion by someone inspired by high ideals and responding to grossly unjust treatment, where not only the outcome but also the motivating ideals became a public inspiration even for those who deplored the act itself. Herman Melville's story of Billy Budd might be seen as a case of this sort, for when unjustly accused, Billy, a saintly fellow deeply troubled by the oppressive treatment of his fellows, finally strikes out in moral outrage against the evil first mate, killing him, not as a deliberate means to a good end but as a spontaneous expression of commitment to certain ideals. Spectators and readers are supposed to be inspired with the strength of his ideals, despite the Captain's cogent arguments that he did what he had no right to do and so was justly punished. We can coherently agree with the Captain while still admiring Billy's deep commitment to moral ideals.

Similarly, it seems, Kant's denial that French revolutionaries had a right to overthrow the governing authority does not render incoherent his enthusiasm for the moral ideals expressed by the French revolutionaries and echoed by spectators. He could not approve of their belief that revolution was a means justified by their idealistic end, but from Kant's perspective that belief was only a part of their larger, morally admirable ideology.

Another factor that helps to make sense of Kant's position is his philosophy of history, according to which it is reasonable to believe that revolutions and even wars are steps in a historical process leading to a morally better world.[7] The end toward which history is progressing is a world in which republican governments will have replaced other, less just forms of government, and nations will live in perpetual peace. This, we are to believe, is the direction of all wars and revolutions, regardless of the intentions of the participants. The good results of the French Revolution, then, are in Kant's view unlike the unexpected fortuitous benefits of a murder because moral progress is to be expected from revolutions and their benefits can be welcomed as a part of a historical progressive pattern. Kant admits that his claims about historical progress are not derived from empirical evidence, though they are supposed to be compatible with such evidence. The claims get their force, instead, from a moral imperative to avoid debilitating cynicism and despair. This, Kant thought, requires us to try to see history, despite all its particular tragedies, as progressing in a way that

---

[7] Kant, "Idea for a Universal History with a Cosmopolitan Purpose," "Perpetual Peace," "The Contest of Faculties," and "Conjectures on the Beginning of Human History," in Reiss (1991), 41–53, 108–14, 177–200, and 229–34.

ultimately affirms the worth of humanity. Even if we cannot share Kant's belief in the enlightened motives of the French revolutionaries or his faith in historical progress, we can see how with this belief and faith Kant could coherently applaud the spirit and expected outcome of the revolution without thereby retracting his belief that it is wrong to rebel against the state authority in power.

Another factor that also helps to make Kant's position on revolution less puzzling, though not necessarily defensible, is this. What was called "the Revolution" was a complex movement that extended long after the initial destruction of the monarchy. Although Kant, like Hobbes, held that acting to overthrow the effective power in the state was wrong, he maintained that citizens have no obligation to the former ruling powers once anarchy breaks out or a new effective political power emerges. In fact, much of the activity of so-called revolutionaries after the fall of the old regime can be seen as escaping from an anarchical condition by creating a new state authority or as carrying out the orders of a new authority. The activities, Kant thought, were not wrong even though they required the use of coercive force against unwilling people. The focus of Kant's condemnation was on acts aimed to overthrow the de facto ruling powers, but there was much in the French revolutionary movement apart from such acts. No doubt many revolutionaries joined only in interim stages of anarchy or after a new revolutionary authority had emerged. Noting this makes it easier to see how Kant could coherently condemn an aspect of all revolutions, their attempts to overthrow a legitimate state authority, but nonetheless express enthusiasm for other aspects of the French Revolution as a movement, such as its ideals of justice and liberty, the movement from anarchy toward a republic, and the willingness of citizens to obey the lawful orders of the new regime.

Can Justice Demand Unqualified Obedience to Unjust Rulers?

Like Hobbes, Kant insisted that it is always contrary to justice to rebel against the sovereign authority of the state, but Kant could not accept

Hobbes's account of why this is so.[8] Hobbes argued that all requirements of justice stem from a basic natural law to keep valid contracts, that sovereign authority could only arise from a virtually unqualified social contract binding subjects but not the sovereign, that it is conceptually impossible for the sovereign to do injustice to its subjects, and that therefore subjects, who are contractually and so justly bound not to rebel, can never justify or excuse rebellion by charging the sovereign with injustice. Kant refused to equate justice with obedience to contracts, denied that sovereign authority stems from an actual social contract, and emphatically rejected Hobbes's claim that requirements of justice do not restrict a sovereign's treatment of its subjects.[9] To the contrary, Kant held that rulers as well as subjects are bound by universal principles of justice, grounded in pure practical reason. Everyone has natural rights to freedom and equality that ought to be respected in every legal system, and even in anarchy or a state of nature we would have a duty to create a legal system, by force if necessary, as a step toward a fully just social order in which the rights of all are respected. The prima facie problem, then, is how Kant can reconcile his Hobbesian claim that revolution is always contrary to justice with his anti-Hobbesian conviction that there are universal standards of justice that apply to sovereign authorities. When a sovereign exercises authority in a grossly unjust way, even to the point of tyranny, how can justice demand obedience to it?

Again, we see Kant holding a combination of views that seem at first to be in tension with, if not contradictory to, one another; but again the combination is coherent, given further features of Kant's beliefs. Kant's claim is that trying to overturn lawful authority is always wrong, not that we should never disobey lawful authorities. Passive refusal to obey state laws when they would require us to do something "intrinsically immoral" is justified, even obligatory.[10] What needs to be reconciled with his other beliefs is not the extreme thesis that we must always obey the law, no matter how unjust.

Kant does hold that the fact that a law is unjust does not, by itself, mean that it is just for us to disobey it; but this is no paradox either. It is in fact a coherent, modest, and widely held view, consistent with many different

---

[8] See Hobbes (1962), esp. pt. I, chs. 13–16, and pt. II, chs. 17–21.

[9] See Kant, "On the Common Saying: 'This May be True in Theory, but it does not Apply in Practice'," in Reiss (1991), 73–87.

[10] Kant (1996a), 98 [6: 321–2], and 136–7 [6: 371], and Reiss, "Postscript," in Reiss (1991), 267–8, and Kant (1960), 142 n. [6: 154 n.].

positions about when, if ever, disobedience is justified. John Rawls, for example, gives a persuasive argument that, because there will be imperfections in any legal order, justice requires obedience to unjust laws in a more or less just system except in certain conditions, such as those he specifies for civil disobedience.[11]

The air of paradox in Kant's combination of views results from overlooking some necessary distinctions. Once a ruler and set of laws is branded "unjust," this may be seen as a general negative taint, suggesting "bad and void of moral claims," on everything connected with them. But there are separable questions here: "Are the laws made by the legal authority just?" and "If not, what does justice demand and allow in response?" A negative answer to the first question leaves open, for example, the specific questions falling under the second: "What are the duties of officials in various roles subservient to the unjust authorities?" and "What may those mistreated by the unjust laws, and their allies, justly do?" Once the necessary distinctions are made, we can see that it is a consistent and coherent position to say, with Kant, that *state officials* have a duty to make, or remake, their legislative, executive, and judicial decisions in accord with principles of justice, and if state officials fail in their duties of justice, then the duties of the *citizens* include lawful efforts to encourage reform by public criticism of unjust laws and policies, passive refusal to obey orders to do what is intrinsically immoral, but abstention from attempts to overthrow the lawful authorities by force. Whether this combination of claims is in the end justified, or warranted by Kant's own basic principles, can be reasonably doubted, but, absent further premises, there is no real paradox here.

Can There Be a Legal Right to Revolution?

A legal right to revolution would be a legal right of those under a sovereign authority to displace the authority by force, ignoring its orders and proceeding as if there were no sovereign authority or a new one constituted by extralegal procedures. It is crucial to understanding Kant's position to

---

[11] Rawls (1999e), 176–89.

distinguish revolution in this sense from other transfers of political power that are often hailed as morally progressive.

Consider, for example, the widely acclaimed English Glorious Revolution of 1689. Whether this was a revolution in the sense that Kant's principles condemn depends on how we understand what happened. On John Locke's interpretation, this was a case in which a government was removed from its delegated and contractually limited authoritative role by a more basic authority, the body politic formed by an original compact of land-owning males subject only to God's laws of nature. By Locke's theory, this was not a revolution in Kant's sense but withdrawal of legal authority from an unjust government by a prior, duly constituted group, the majority of the body politic, with more fundamental legal authority.[12] Similarly, the American Revolution might be seen, not as the overthrow of the former sovereign authority in the colonies, but as merely a forceful separation of the American people from the British government with which it formerly had looser legal ties. On the first interpretation, the American Revolution would count as a revolution in Kant's sense, but not on the second interpretation.

Kant argues that no legal system, which maintains a juridical condition, can include a permission to ignore or forcibly oppose the laws of the system, even if from a broader ethical point of view doing so would be desirable. Any system of legal rights, good or bad, presupposes that there is a recognized, effective sovereign power to make laws, enforce them, and adjudicate questions about their application. In a state of nature, anarchy, or quasi-legal systems with defective constitutions that fail to meet the essential conditions for a system of laws, rights will be merely provisional. They will be merely what should be enforced in a proper legal system. Again and again, Kant argues that trying to incorporate an alleged right to revolution into a constitution for a legal system would be incoherent because it would purport to be a legal authority to destroy the very source of legal authority.[13] Someone cannot coherently claim legal authorization to defy and overthrow the highest legal authority. This seems undeniable. If we conceive of

---

[12] See Locke (1960).
[13] See Kant, "On the Common Saying: 'This May be True in Theory, but it does not Apply in Practice'," in Reiss (1991), 81–2, and Kant (1996a), 96–7 [6: 320], and 111–12 [6: 339–40].

revolution as Kant did, and so as not including the lawful removal of officials with delegated power, there can be no legal right of revolution.

Does it Follow That Revolution is Always Morally Wrong?

We need not deny that there are important relations between moral and legal wrongdoing to acknowledge that these concepts are not identical. To call something a crime is not the same as saying that it is immoral. It is at least logically possible that crimes in certain circumstances are morally justified; and few philosophers would deny the possibility, even the fact, that some immoral acts are not prohibited by law. Arguments establishing that revolution is always illegal, then, do not by themselves show that engaging in revolution is always morally wrong. Kant's belief that revolution is morally impermissible in all conditions, then, is a substantive moral claim, going beyond his conceptual point that legal systems cannot allow a right to overturn forcibly the ultimate source of legal authority. This must draw its support, if any, from further premises.

There are general presuppositions embedded in the structure of Kant's moral system that might seem to warrant the inference from illegality to immorality. First, Kant classifies the prohibition against revolution as a juridical duty, and juridical duties in his system are classified as perfect duties in contrast with imperfect ethical duties, such as beneficence. These terms require some explanation.

Juridical duties are distinct from ethical duties in that it is possible conceptually and morally to compel people to fulfil juridical duties, but not ethical duties. To avoid theft, for example, is supposed to be a juridical duty. To make it our principle, for moral reasons, to promote the happiness of others is an ethical duty. Juridical duties depend on an external legislator, but ethical duties as such depend only on what Kant calls internal legislation, which refers to the commands of reason within each rational agent. We satisfy juridical duties if we avoid behaving in prohibited ways, such as committing theft, murder, and breach of contract, regardless of the motives behind our restraint. By contrast we satisfy ethical duties, such as gratitude, beneficence, and respect, only if we act for morally good reasons.

The major division between two parts of *The Metaphysics of Morals* is marked by the fact that Part I lays out principles for determining our juridical duties and rights while Part II presents principles for determining our directly ethical duties. All the principles are supposed to be based, in some way, on practical reason, but Part I is concerned with standards of law and justice while Part II is focused on standards for personal decisions beyond what the law can enforce. All duties, however, belong to ethics in a wide sense. Kant classifies juridical duties to others and certain duties to ourself as perfect duties, and classifies ethical duties to others and certain other duties to ourself as imperfect duties. Perfect duties are supposed to give determinate prescriptions of the form "Always . . . " or "Never . . . " This is in contrast to imperfect duties, which typically prescribe adopting certain general ends such as the happiness of others, leaving an indeterminate playroom for choice about when, where, and how much to work toward the end. It follows that perfect juridical duties take precedence over imperfect ethical duties, limiting, for example, the means we can permissibly use in pursuing the ends prescribed by ethical duties. We must first satisfy the determinate juridical duties before considering ways to promote the ends prescribed in our ethical duties of virtue. The ends prescribed in the ethical duties, then, cannot serve as justifying grounds for violating a juridical duty. Therefore, if it is a juridical duty to avoid revolution, we cannot appeal to the directly ethical duties, such as beneficence, to justify making an exception.

Another claim that Kant makes about his classification scheme supports the same conclusion: all juridical duties are indirectly ethical duties.[14] For every juridical duty that prescribes external acts and not motives, such as "Never rebel," there corresponds an ethical duty, resting on inner legislation, that we should fulfill the juridical duty from morally good motives. From a strictly legal point of view, our conformity to the laws of the state is all that is required; but from a broader ethical point of view, we fail to fulfill an indirectly ethical duty if our motives are not good. Assuming that revolution is always contrary to juridical duty, then, we also have an indirectly ethical duty always to avoid it from good motives.

In sum, although the immorality of revolution does not strictly follow from its illegality, Kant sets up his classification scheme to reflect his

---

[14] Kant (1996a), 21–2 [6: 219–20].

presuppositions that we always have an indirect ethical duty to conform to our juridical duties and that our imperfect direct ethical duties cannot justify our violating any perfect juridical duty. Given Kant's classification scheme, then, to assert that revolution is always contrary to a perfect juridical duty implies that it is always immoral.

Does this bridge the gap, giving us adequate reason to infer the immorality of revolutionary activity from the arguments that no legal system can require us to acknowledge revolution as legal? It seems not, for several reasons. First, Kant simply builds into his classification scheme the crucial premises that there is an indirectly ethical duty to fulfill each juridical duty and that the juridical duties are perfect and directly ethical duties only imperfect. If these are substantive moral claims, they require argument which Kant does not provide. If they are merely stipulations about how the terms of the classification scheme are to be used, then independent argument is needed to show that revolution is in fact contrary to a perfect juridical duty in the strong stipulated sense. In either case, crucial argument is missing.

Even if there is an indirectly ethical duty corresponding to each legal duty, it does not follow that the content and stringency of the duties are the same. Perhaps we have some moral obligation with respect to all the requirements that the law places on us, for example, to give it weight in our deliberations and to resist, if we must, respectfully. But it is far less plausible to assume that the indirectly ethical duty must take the same form as the legal duty so that every unqualified legal duty to do something under a set of conditions automatically generates an unconditional moral obligation to do it under the conditions. Given its implausibility, perhaps Kant did not mean to endorse so strong a claim with his remark that juridical duties are indirectly ethical duties.

An Argument From the Publicity Requirement

A thorough critique of Kant's belief that revolution is always immoral would need to have us examine many particular passages to see whether they establish more than the impossibility of a legal right to revolution.

Reasons for doubt may be illustrated by considering briefly exerpts from an argument in *Perpetual Peace*:

[T]he transcendental formula of public right: All actions affecting the rights of other human beings are wrong if their maxim is not compatible with their being made public . . . a purely negative test . . . valid without demonstration . . . easy to apply. This principle should be regarded not only as ethical (i.e. as pertaining to the theory of virtue) but also as juridical (i.e. as affecting the rights of man).

According to [the transcendental formula], the people, before establishing the civil contract, asks itself whether it dares to make public the maxim of its intention to rebel on certain occasions. It is easily seen that if one were to make it a condition of founding a political constitution that force might in certain eventualities be used against the head of state, the people would have to claim rightful authority over its rule. But if this were so, the ruler would not be the head of state; or if *both* parties were given authority as a prior condition of establishing the state, the existence of the state itself, which it was the people's intention to establish, would become impossible. The injustice of rebellion is thus apparent from the fact that if the maxim upon which it would act were publicly acknowledged, it would defeat its own purpose. The maxim therefore would have to be kept secret.[15]

Kant is apparently arguing both that no justifiable, or even coherent, constitution can allow a right to revolution and that the revolutionaries' maxim is ethically wrong. Consider the case for dismissing a right to revolution. When thinking of establishing an initial contract to institute a constitution of a legal and political order, the hypothetical parties to such a contract should first consider whether they could include a clause permitting revolution in certain defined conditions. That, in effect, is what their public maxim would endorse. They cannot publicly include the principle, "People may rebel under these conditions" as part of the constitution or even publicly advocate for their private maxim, "We will rebel under these conditions," as legally permissible consistently with their aim to set up a constitution of a coherent system of law.

Kant's background assumption is that the head of state has undivided sovereignty. There cannot be two supreme powers, executive, judicial, or legislative, although these different functions can, and should, be separated. Furthermore, in a juridical order, and so in a rationally coherent constitution, there cannot be any ultimate indeterminacy about who is to decide on

---

[15] Kant, "Perpetual Peace," in Reiss (1991), 126.

matters of law. Given this, a constitution that allowed coercive removal of a head of state, based on the judgment and force of anyone other than the supreme judicial and executive authority, would both affirm and deny that designated head of state was the highest authority. To grant that an authority is the supreme authority with respect to any power is to deny that any other person or group has the authority to rebel against it. A constitutional right of revolution, even if specified only for conditions that are unlikely to occur, leaves a gap in legal authority that the ideal of a juridical condition abhors. A public claim to legal permission to rebel is incompatible with the hypothesized purpose of having a constitution that maintains a civil order, and this is a purpose that anyone claiming a legal right is presumed to have.

Kant thinks that he has a case for the ethical duty never to rebel as well, but it is not clear that this is so. The principle to which he appeals goes beyond the formula of universal law to require that individual maxims are condemned if they could not be made public without defeating the agent's purposes. This leaves open whether the formula of universal law or the humanity formula could justify revolution in some cases. In addition, Kant probably did not intend to make the empirical, contingent argument that the maxim of revolutionaries to overthrow the ruler, if made public, would always prove to be self-defeating, for example, by leading the ruler to crush the incipient rebellion. In any case, this empirical argument would fail to show that revolution is always wrong, for in some circumstances making their maxim public would not in fact undermine either the revolutionaries' immediate aim to remove the ruler or their more basic aim to move quickly to a new juridical order under a morally more defensible constitution. Unless they claim a legal right to rebel, we have no empirical grounds to attribute to them the aim of maintaining a legal order without any gaps in authority over time. After all, they are avowedly determined to break the continuity of the old order.

Kant's argument against a legal right to rebel might appear to have moral force if presented with crucial terms left ambiguous, as in the following. Suppose we imagine ourselves trying to establish a constitutional order from a state of nature by original contract and yet we consider making it our maxim to rebel if the sovereign power acts oppressively. Making our maxim public in this context amounts to insistence on retaining a legal or moral authority to judge and overthrow the sovereign moral or legal authority. By advocating a constitutional order, we are committed to there being an official sovereign authority whose judgments are legally or morally final; but by publicly declaring the legal or moral permissibility of judging and over-throwing the ruling powers, we imply that they lack sovereign legal or moral authority. Therefore, going public with the maxim of rebelling against oppressive rulers would be self-defeating. Publicly declaring a legal or moral permission to rebel in some conditions undermines our endorse-ment of having a constitutional order in which a designated sovereign has the final right to determine what we may legally or morally do.

The argument, as reconstructed here, is obviously ambiguous because it leaves open whether the permission and authority in question are merely legal or also moral. Its plausibility requires understanding it as concerned with legality, not moral permissibility. It seems to support a moral prohibi-tion on revolution only by conflating legal and moral permissibility. To assume that what is illegal is also immoral is highly implausible. At least this needs to be argued.

Possible Kantian Grounds for Revolution?

If Kant's arguments do not establish an absolute moral prohibition against engaging in revolution, this leaves open the further question whether or not, contrary to Kant himself, basic elements of his moral theory might support a more qualified position on revolution. To pursue this question adequately we would need to identify, interpret, and explain what we take the basic elements to be. Short of that large undertaking, we can at least note some prima facie reasons to expect that Kant's fundamental moral princi-ples, reasonably construed, would allow revolution in some extreme cir-cumstances.[16] Arguably, the various forms of the Categorical Imperative, charitably interpreted, allow applications more sensitive to particular con-texts than Kant seemed to assume. If so, given certain empirical facts, they might allow or even require exceptions to the general prohibition on revolution. Also, since Kant did acknowledge that passive resistance to state orders could sometimes be justified, it is reasonable to conjecture that the Kantian grounds for this limitation on the duty of obedience

---

[16] Hill (1997).

might also provide a basis for arguing that active revolutionary resistance is sometimes justified. Kant himself thought that there is relevant difference between the two cases that is always decisive, but that is far from obvious.

Although Kant presents the principles of *The Metaphysics of Morals* as if they governed all foreseeable human circumstances, he also acknowledges the need for judgment in applying abstract principles. It is only reasonable to suppose that individuals judging their duties in particular circumstances should keep in mind, not only the general principles of *The Metaphysics of Morals*, but also the ideals expressed in the various forms of the Categorical Imperative. For example, the general imperfect duty to promote the happiness of others in *The Metaphysics of Morals* is indefinite with regard to the time, manner, and extent that helping is required, but applying the Categorical Imperative directly to a particular case may reveal a more stringent requirement than would follow from the indefinite principle to promote the happiness of others, taken by itself. Kant says that juridical duties, such as the duty to avoid revolution, are perfect duties, and so, although judgment is required to apply them, they are not supposed to leave the same kinds of latitude for judgment. However, all principles of *The Metaphysics of Morals* are supposed to be consistent with the Categorical Imperative. Thus judgments regarding their application, at least to particular individual choices, can presumably be informed and checked by the Categorical Imperative. If there is a conflict between the requirements of the Categorical Imperative and what the intermediate principles of *The Metaphysics of Morals* seem to imply regarding individual moral responsibility, then something in the system needs to be revised.[17] Kant himself would no doubt have given priority to the Categorical Imperative, even if this meant acknowledging a need to modify the perfect duties listed in *The Metaphysics of Morals*. All the more, contemporary Kantians, especially those doubtful of Kant's rigorism regarding revolution, lying, and sex, would want to revise the system by qualifying the intermediate principles rather than introducing qualifications to the basic standard expressed in the formulas of the Categorical Imperative. It is not inappropriate, or un-Kantian, to ask whether an absolute prohibition on revolution is compatible with judgments directly appealing to the Categorical Imperative.

---

[17] See Kant (1996a), 16–17 [6: 219–24], and Donagan (1993).

Consider first the universal law formula of the Categorical Imperative: act only on maxims that you can will as universal law.[18] Interpretation is controversial, but a key issue on any account is how maxims are to be articulated. If we assume that maxims must be simple and unqualified, like "Whenever I judge the government unjust, I will revolt," then the formula is likely to yield absolute prohibitions. For example, the maxim mentioned presumably cannot be willed as universal law, and so, if we assumed that it is the only possible maxim of a revolutionary, then revolution would always be prohibited. If, more plausibly, we take maxims to be more subtly articulated policy statements, then we can expect the universal law formula to yield more qualified conclusions. For example, arguably someone could will as universal law a maxim such as, "When the ruler is clearly unjust, oppressive, and utterly resistant to reform and revolution is almost certain to be successful, bloodless, and more humane and respectful of human rights, then I will join in the revolution." The more qualified maxim may well express more accurately the policy of revolutionaries in certain situations, and it seems morally arbitrary to suppose that the relevant maxim must always be the simple, unqualified policy stated earlier. Many questions remain, but at least there seems to be initial reason to suspect that appeal to the universal law formula, reasonably construed, will not always condemn participation in revolution.

Kant's formula of humanity as an end in itself also seems to provide presumptive grounds for questioning an absolute prohibition on revolution.[19] Again, interpretations vary widely, but Kant clearly implies an affirmation of human dignity, a prohibition of merely using people, and a concern for promoting the permissible ends of others.[20] What someone "can will as universal law," under the universal law formula, is arguably constrained by these ideas, which also seem presupposed when we consider what laws autonomous rational members of a "kingdom of ends" would legislate. Our policies must be justifiable to others insofar as they share these general values. Taking these ideas seriously requires concern not only for lives and welfare of those potentially injured by revolution, but also for the lives and welfare of those slaughtered or oppressed by tyrannical rulers.

---

[18] Kant (1998a), 16 [4: 403], and 31 [4: 421].
[19] Ibid. 37–8 [4: 428–9].
[20] See Hill (1993).

Admittedly, dignity, as an incomparable value without equivalent, does not allow us to determine our guiding principles simply by doing utility calculations and treating human lives as commodities subject to trade-offs. Nor does the humanity formula provide a simple decision procedure for choices in particular cases. However, human dignity should serve, in any reasonable reconstruction of Kant's basic principles, as an abstract but not merely empty value that must be taken into account in determining what we, as individuals, may, and may not, do. If this is right, then decisions about whether to join a revolution are more complex than Kant leads us to believe. The humanity formula does not simply require us to pay attention to how revolution may affect human dignity in the future, but it also requires us to reflect on how our participation, or refusal to participate, honors and respects the humanity of persons now. Surely, under any reasonable interpretation, the humanity formula will oppose slaughtering innocent people now in hopes of promoting a distant utopian future, but all revolutions are not of this sort. Strictly, there need be only forcible overthrow of the de facto lawful powers without justification in the existing legal system. What means are necessary and available, whether they violate the moral rights of individuals, and much else, can vary from case to case. Given the complexity of the issue, it seems antecedently unlikely that reasonable reflection on humanity as an end in itself would support either an easy encouragement to revolution or an absolute prohibition of it.

Kant grants that it is morally permissible, even obligatory, to disobey laws or legal orders that require us to do something in itself immoral. He mentions this only a few times, almost as an afterthought, and he does not provide any arguments. It seems clear, however, that any Kantian argument for moral disobedience to law must appeal, ultimately, to the Categorical Imperative. The intrinsically immoral acts that he refers to must be acts of a kind that are wrong in all circumstances. In Kant's moral theory only reflection from the Categorical Imperative could ground such claims. It is natural to conjecture that the same sort of considerations that call for passive disobedience to law might justify active attempts to overthrow a tyrant. In some cases, passive disobedience may have worse impact on human rights and welfare than a revolution would have. It is implausible to assume, and Kant does not argue, that in general passively refusing to cooperate with evil is morally better than actively attempting to fight it. Kant evidently thought that there is always a morally relevant and decisive difference between the cases of passive refusal and active rebellion, as no doubt there often is. It is not clear, however, that the supposed difference is anything more than offered in the sort of arguments we have considered, which only show there is no legal right to revolution.

13

Treating Criminals as Ends in Themselves

Few ideas in moral and political philosophy have been as influential or as variously interpreted as Immanuel Kant's version of the Categorical Imperative that is commonly called "the humanity formula." In his *Groundwork for the Metaphysics of Morals*, he states the formula as follows: "Act in such a way that you treat humanity, whether in your own person or in any other person, always at the same time as an end, never merely as a means."[1] Kant later implies that persons, as ends in themselves, have dignity, which is "an unconditional and incomparable worth."[2] In *The Metaphysics of Morals*, he repeatedly appeals to this idea as the ground for various moral principles and judgments. My intention here is to draw from Kant's ideas, and perhaps extend them, in order to raise questions about how criminals should be treated. I think that the main elements of my reconstruction of the idea of humanity as an end can be found in Kant's texts, but my aim is not to give a literal and exact interpretation of Kant's texts. The aim, rather, is to develop a more broadly "Kantian" account of the norms associated with human dignity and then to consider implications for the treatment of those found guilty of offenses under the criminal law.

Kant introduces the humanity formula as a foundational principle of morality, but he later makes a significant distinction between principles of law (*Rechtslehre*) and principles of ethical conduct (*Tugendlehre*).[3] Some of Kant's arguments in the *Rechtslehre* evidently appeal to the humanity formula, at least to the idea that persons must not be treated merely as means,[4]

---

[1] Kant (2002), 230 [4: 429].
[2] Ibid. 236 [4: 436].
[3] Kant (1996a), 20–2 [6: 218–21], 145–7 [6: 379–82], 152–4 [6: 388–91].
[4] e.g. ibid. 62 [6: 278] and 105 [6: 331].

but the extent to which he intended basic ethical principles to be applicable to principles for law remains controversial.[5] Accordingly, in applying my account of the humanity formula to the treatment of criminals, I distinguish several issues.

First, I consider implications for those aspects of the treatment of criminals that are independent of Kant's official principles of law and justice (i.e. the *Rechtslehre*). Those principles are addressed to the central questions about punishment: Who should be punished, how much, in what way, and why? Those principles, however, leave open further questions about the *manner* in which punishment is carried out. Kant's official principles of punishment include a standard for the appropriate *amount* of punishment for various offenses, but they do not determine every aspect of how criminals are to be treated. Even if we provisionally assume that those principles are justifiable, then, we can usefully ask whether ethical considerations urge us to seek reforms in the manner in which just punishments are carried out.

Second, setting aside the provisional acceptance of Kant's official principles of punishment, I consider the implications of the humanity formula regarding the more central questions of punishment: Who should be punished, how much, in what way, and why? What I propose here is an admittedly un-Kantian thought experiment. Suppose that we were to reject or ignore Kant's own theory of just punishment and yet accept my reconstruction of his humanity formula: What sort of practice of punishment, if any, would we as conscientious individuals advocate and support? Would the humanity formula, applied in this context, provide presumptive reasons for urging reforms for our current practices?

Third, I consider the discrepancy between the results of the last section and some of Kant's official principles of punishment. Arguably, the humanity formula, applied independently of Kant's official theory of justice, would endorse policies in conflict with aspects of that official theory. The conflict calls into question his official principles of punishment and the special distinction between law and ethics on which the principles rest. Unless these can be adequately justified on independent grounds, the ideals

---

[5] e.g. in the recent anthology, Timmons (2002), several essays challenge the common view that the *Rechtslehre* is simply the application of Kant's basic moral theory to questions of law and justice. See Marcus Willaschek, "Which Imperatives for Right?: On the Non-Prescriptive Character of Juridical Laws in Kant's *Metaphysics of Morals*," Thomas Pogge, "Is Kant's *Rechtslehre* a "'Comprehensive Liberalism'?" and Allen Wood, "The Final Form of Kant's Practical Philosophy."

encapsulated in the humanity formula would require abandonment or modification of those official principles.

Before turning to these three issues regarding its application, I will summarize some of Kant's basic points about humanity as an end and then mention briefly interpretations that, in my view, pose problems, textual and philosophical. Following this, I will make several suggestions regarding how Kant's idea should be understood or at least how it might be best developed. My ideas here overlap with the interpretations offered by others in some respects, but there are some significant differences.

Preview

My main suggestions drawn from the humanity formula, some old and some new, will be these: (1) There are thinner (more formal) and thicker (more substantive) conceptions of humanity as an end in itself, both in Kant's texts and in contemporary appeals to the humanity formula. (2) In Kantian ethics, value concepts, such as dignity, essentially abbreviate rational prescriptions about our choice of acts and attitudes. (3) Human dignity, the value associated with the humanity formula, encompasses several distinguishable prescriptions; it implies that, in choosing our policies and attitudes, we have compelling reasons to be guided by a cluster of related precepts. (4) Dignity is an inviolable moral status, not a commensurable value, but not all the prescriptions implicit in it are absolute, unqualified prohibitions or demands. (5) The idea is best employed, not as a case by case decision rule, but as a guide and constraint on reasonable reflections about which intermediate level moral principles we should accept, how we should interpret them, and what qualifications we should acknowledge. (6) A Kantian perspective for such reflections can be developed that incorporates basic Kantian moral values; and, if so, reflection on (intermediate) principles from this perspective might appropriately guide us to principled decisions about what to do when, tragically, the various prescriptions implicit in human dignity are apparently in conflict.

Turning to questions of application, my main suggestions are these. (7) The cluster of norms inherent in the humanity formula, as I develop it, provides significant guidelines for the humane and respectful treatment of criminals in the process of punishment. They call for conscientious persons to seek reform of abusive, unhealthy, mentally numbing, and dehumanizing conditions and practices that are not essential aspects of just punishment. (8) If we provisionally were to set aside the special assumptions and principles in Kant's official theory of punishment, arguably these same norms would lead us to conclusions apparently contrary to aspects of Kant's official theory: for example, its exclusive focus on "external acts," protecting external liberty as the sole ground for criminal laws, the principle of retribution (*ius talionis*), and its sanction of capital punishment for murder. (9) This conflict raises anew the question whether Kant's *Rechtslehre* contains adequate grounds for his special distinction between law and ethics and the official principles of punishment that depend on this.

The Humanity Formula: Basic Points[6]

The humanity formula obviously contains two related prescriptions: (1) never treat humanity in any person merely as a means and (2) always treat humanity as an end.[7] The second encompasses the first: if we always treat humanity as an end, we will never treat humanity merely as a means. Also the meaning of the first is apparently dependent on the second: to treat humanity *merely* as a means is just to treat it as a means without also treating it as an end.[8] Kant says both that persons are ends in themselves and that humanity in persons is an end in itself, apparently regarding these as equivalent. Humanity, as something *in* a person, contrasts with a person's animality.[9] Kant identifies it with rational nature in a person. Whether the

---

[6] Here and in the following two sections I review material from previous chapters, esp. ch. 2, as necessary background for my arguments about punishment.

[7] One might suppose that the expression "at the same time" shows that what Kant meant was more limited, i.e. when treating humanity in a person as a means always treat it also as an end. In *The Metaphysics of Morals*, however, Kant explicitly says that indifference to persons fails to treat them as ends in themselves. See (1996a), 157 [6: 395]. The fourth example in *Groundwork* (2002), 231 [4: 430] implies the same. The official statement of the formula uses "end" rather than "end in itself," but the context makes it clear that the latter is intended.

[8] My interpretation here, and subsequent points, are discussed at more length in Hill (1980), 84–90. This is reprinted in my collection of essays (1992a), 38–57.

[9] See also Kant (1998b), 50–2 [6: 29–31]. Here Kant makes a three-way distinction between animality, humanity, and personality, but it seems clear that in the *Groundwork* (Kant 2002) "humanity" includes what he later calls "personality."

idea is expressed by reference to "persons" or "humanity in persons," the point evidently is that we must treat persons, qua rational beings, as having a special value. That they are rational, even if imperfectly so, is a crucial part of *why* we must treat them as ends in themselves, but it also suggests vaguely *how* they should be treated. "An end in itself" is an "objective ground of the will's self-determinating,"[10] or, in other words, it is or implies an objective reason for doing or refraining from various things. It is not, however, an "end" in the sense of a goal to be achieved. It is a reason-giving value or status "that we should never act against" and with which we should also "harmonize" positively (e.g. through beneficence).[11] Kant's illustrations suggest that treating humanity merely as a means is a violation of perfect duty whereas neglecting to treat humanity as an end through indifference, without treating it as a means, is a violation of imperfect duty.

Interpretations of the Humanity Formula and Problems

Beyond these elementary points, interpretation becomes more complicated. For example, do all human beings count as ends in themselves? Some passages seem to suggest that only by virtue of having a good will are we entitled to be treated as ends, and this "moralist" interpretation has been argued with ingenuity by Richard Dean.[12] Arguably, however, both philosophical charity and the weight of textual evidence favor the more common understanding that, no matter how immoral they are, all persons are to be treated as ends in themselves. Even the worst people, according to Kant, have an indistinguishable spark of goodness in them, though here the goodness evidently refers to the rational disposition to morality, not to the agent's operative commitments.[13]

It is only this rational disposition, I think, that is required to qualify a person for treatment as an objective end.

---

[10] Kant (2002), 228 [4: 427].
[11] Ibid. 238 [4: 437] and 231 [4: 430].
[12] Dean (1996), 268–88.
[13] See Kant (1996a), 210 [6: 463–4].

We may still ask, are all human beings persons in the relevant sense? Some feminists have questioned whether Kant counted women as rational persons, and recently several African-American writers have argued that Kant regarded nonwhite people as subhuman. Some of Kant's expressed views on women and nonwhites were in fact deplorable, worse even than some contemporaries whose work Kant read; but arguably these empirical beliefs and objectionable attitudes do not infect what we can identify as more central features of Kant's moral theory.[14] Hard questions arise, as Kant's critics repeatedly remind us, with regard to sociopaths, people who are severely brain-damaged, and even infants. For present purposes, however, I set these questions aside, limiting the discussion to those with sufficient rational competence to be moral agents or persons in Kant's sense.

The question remains: What is it to treat humanity as an end in itself? Several interpretations have some merit but, in my view, are not fully adequate. Some, for example, think that the humanity formula adds nothing practically significant to the universal law formulas. We treat humanity as an end in itself, they suggest, simply by restricting our treatment of persons to maxims that we can will as universal laws.[15] This is one way to accommodate Kant's remark that the formulas express fundamentally the same principle, but it overlooks Kant's several efforts to mark a distinction between the formulas. The interpretation would also impose on the humanity formula all the familiar difficulties of using the universal law formulas as a decision guide, and in my view that is a substantial objection independent of textual considerations.

In his second example Kant says that ends in themselves are beings who must "be able to share in the end of the very same action."[16] Some commentators take this as the key to understanding the humanity formula (at least as applied to perfect duties). Onora O'Neill, who apparently takes this view, argues that coercion and deceit are wrong because no one can consent or aim to being coerced or deceived at the very time that this is happening to them.[17] If they consent to being dragged across the room, it ceases to be coercion. If they beg "Please deceive me now," the would-be deceivers lose the credibility needed for successful deceit. This approach,

---

[14] Bernard Boxill and I review some of these charges in "Kant and Race," Boxill (2001), 448–71.
[15] e.g. Singer (1961), 235.
[16] Kant (2002), 230 [4: 430].
[17] O'Neill (1989), 126–44.

however, seems to prove too much or too little. It proves too much if it is supposed to yield absolute prohibitions on coercion and deceit, for surely coercion and deception are justified in many cases. (Kant was rigid about overt lying, but clearly thought that individuals may exercise coercion when acting as authorized by law.) If, on the contrary, O'Neill's interpretation of "sharing the end" yields only a moral presumption against coercion and deception, then it leaves us with too little to indicate how we should act, all things considered. Given the complexity and range of moral problems to which the humanity formula is supposed to be relevant, there is reason to look for more substance in it than O'Neill's account allows.

Another interpretation that, in my view, is less than adequate is that proposed by David Cummiskey.[18] Drawing from an essay by Christine Korsgaard and an early essay of mine, Cummiskey argues that the humanity formula calls only for a priority of "dignity" over "price" but otherwise treats dignity as a commensurable value, subject to trade-offs in the realm of the things that have dignity.[19] Given that humanity is rational nature in persons, then, we should treat the preservation, development, and exercise of rational capacities as a type of value that is more important than satisfying inclination-based ends, but, respecting that priority, we should do whatever maximally brings about the realization of values associated with our rational capacities. Cummiskey's view has the merit of acknowledging substantive values implicit in the humanity formula (thickly conceived) and also the merit of realizing that these cannot reasonably be translated into absolute prohibitions, such as "Never do anything that impedes or may lead to the cessation of the life of a rational person." Nevertheless, his interpretation makes dignity a commensurable value, which arguably is contrary to the spirit and letter of Kant's texts. More important, his view inherits most (but not all) of the familiar objections to consequentialism.

Alan Donagan was another philosopher who made Kant's humanity formula the centerpiece of his Kantian ethics.[20] Donagan interprets the formula as a universal prescription "to respect every person as a rational creature." Rationality is the feature of persons that ultimately *grounds* moral principles, and the expression "respect . . . as a rational creature" also *indicates*

---

[18] Cummiskey (1996).

[19] Korsgaard (1996a), 106–32, and my "Humanity as an End in Itself" (Hill 1980). Neither Korsgaard nor I, however, treated dignity as a commensurable value.

[20] Donagan (1977).

what morality requires. Donagan does not try to define the phrase but relies on commonsense understandings of it. Applying it intuitively to cases, he purports to derive many specific moral principles, regarding suicide, self-development, coercion, injury, beneficence, truth-telling, property, law, family, and military service. Donagan's principles are more qualified than those in Kant's *The Metaphysics of Morals*, but nevertheless they are quite strict. For example, Donagan would allow lying to a murderer to save a friend because the person threatening murder has forfeited his right to the truth, not because good consequences outweigh the obligation to respect every person.

Donagan's position has several disadvantages. It places the burden of applying the humanity formula entirely on a common understanding of what it is to respect someone as rational. An intuitive requirement to *respect* persons as rational is, of course, an important aspect of Kant's moral theory, but in *The Metaphysics of Morals* respect is only one among many moral requirements that are supposed to follow from the more comprehensive humanity formula.[21] In addition, Donagan invites us to settle complex moral issues by focusing on simple interpersonal exchanges and simply asking ourselves whether the treatment in question is "respectful" in a familiar sense. This procedure unfortunately encourages us to ignore other relevant factors in complex moral situations. It leads to the acceptance of inflexible prohibitions and threatens to generate irresolvable moral dilemmas, for an exchange that appears disrespectful to one person may be seen from a broader perspective as necessary for adequately respecting all persons.[22]

The Value of Humanity as a Guide and Constraint on Deliberation about Principles

My proposal is to think of the humanity formula as providing a cluster of general moral considerations that must be taken into account in our deliberations about how to articulate and interpret more specific moral principles regarding recurring moral situations. In such deliberations we must consider

---

[21] Kant (1996a), 209–13 [6: 462–8].
[22] I discuss these points more fully in "Donagan's Kant," Hill (1993), 22–52.

not merely whether a certain interpersonal exchange was superficially respectful but also whether the principles that would allow, or disallow, the exchange most adequately reflect the value of humanity in each person. We can think of Kantian moral theory as calling for moral thinking at two levels: first, attempts, guided by the basic values and constraints inherent in the Categorical Imperative, to identify or construct more specific moral principles and, second, judgments about how the principles apply in the particular contexts at hand. The proposed procedure is similar in form to the two-tiered thinking recommended by rule-utilitarians, but, of course, Kantians are not attempting to identify the principles (or "rules") that maximize utility. Instead, the cluster of moral considerations inherent in the humanity formula must guide and constrain their deliberations about more specific principles (which are the basis for judgments about particular cases).

In previous work I have suggested how such a two-tiered Kantian model might be drawn from Kant's brief discussion of a "kingdom of ends," but the details of this proposal are not crucial for present purposes.[23] The main idea is to think of an ideal legislature in which every rational person is both a legislator of the laws and (with one exception) subject to the laws.[24] The legislators are conceived as rational and free (in several senses). They have private ends, but in thinking of them we must "abstract from the differences" between the legislators and their private ends. Legislating with autonomy of the will, they set aside parochial concerns, but at some stage they must take into account pervasive facts about the human condition, including human weakness and fallibility. We can imagine that initially they seek to identify or construct principles relevant to all human beings, but most principles will no doubt be "universal" only in the sense that they prescribe conduct for anyone in specified circumstances, though some will never actually be in those circumstances. The basic moral standard for us, analogous to Kant's kingdom of ends formula of the Categorical Imperative, acknowledges that such an ideal legislature is only an ideal: act in conformity to those principles (or "laws") that you, and other rational agents,

---

[23] Hill (1992a), 58–66 and 226–50; (2000), 33–56, 95–114, and 210–31; (2002), 61–95; and chs. 8–11 in this volume.

[24] The exception is that the "head" (a holy will without needs and inclinations) cannot be described as "subject" to the laws merely because such a being necessarily does what is rational and so is not *constrained* or *bound* by rational principles.

would endorse *if* legislating in an ideal kingdom of ends. In attempting to use the model, we would *aim* to find principles that everyone in the deliberative situation would adopt; but, more realistically, it can be understood as saying that the standard for *conscientious* choice is one's best judgment, after due deliberation and consultation, about what there is good and sufficient reason to choose from the legislative perspective. The ideal of moral legislation is, of course, only partially analogous to lawmaking in a legal system. For example, with moral legislation there is no bargaining and voting, the principles are not restricted to "external" actions, coercive threats are not at issue; and the legislators are stipulated to be informed and well-motivated.

Obviously, more needs to be said to give an adequate characterization of a Kantian perspective for deliberating about principles, but the key point for present purposes is that the deliberation would be guided and constrained by the moral considerations inherent in the humanity formula. Before sketching my view of what these considerations are, I should mention two background assumptions that I am making. First, textual considerations suggest that at different points Kant worked both with a thinner (or more formal) and a thicker (or more substantive) conception of humanity as an end in itself.[25] Arguably, as a version of the Categorical Imperative that is supposed to express the same basic principle as the other formulations, the humanity formula may be understood as a variation on the basic theme "conform to universal law," that is, conform to the necessary principles of pure practical reason.[26] We do so by restricting our ends and means to those that anyone affected by us "could share" at least in the sense that they could rationally and reasonably endorse them.[27] This does not yet tell us substantively how to treat others, but, especially in *The Metaphysics of Morals*, Kant appeals to the humanity formula as if certain ways of valuing humanity in persons followed from the basic idea. For example, the idea is supposed to oppose lying, suicide, drunkenness, gluttony, servility, mockery, etc. My suggestions draw from both aspects of Kant's texts, but I make no claim here of strict fidelity to his views.

The second assumption is that judgments about value are to be understood as implicitly judgments about what it is rational and reasonable to

---

[25] This is discussed in Hill (1993), esp. 142–51.

[26] See Kant (2002), 203 [4: 402] and 222 [4: 420–1].

[27] See ibid. 230 [4: 429–30].

choose. Value, or goodness, in Kant's view is the object of rational willing, not something that exists independently.[28] This is the key to the Kantian rejection of consequentialism, for it is a denial that we can first determine what is valuable or good and then treat morality as a requirement to produce as much of what is valuable as possible. The point is relevant to understanding the humanity formula in two ways. First, the humanity formula affirms the unconditional value of humanity but it cannot be "grounded" in an intuition of a value that exists independently of norms of rational choice. Second, the meaning and implications of the idea that humanity has an unconditional value must ultimately be unpacked in terms of precepts about how persons ought to be treated. In effect, an affirmation of the special value of humanity can be seen as an abbreviation for a cluster of related prescriptions.

The cluster of practical precepts associated with the Kantian idea of human dignity, as sketched in chapter 8, is the following.[29] The first three are relatively formal, the rest more substantive.

First, and most formally, we must treat persons only in ways that we could in principle justify to them as well as to all other rational persons who take an appropriately impartial perspective. That is, we respect the dignity of persons by constraining ourselves by the principles we think all would endorse from the Kantian legislative perspective, assuming that this can be adequately defined.

Second, because dignity is not a commensurable value, our deliberations about specific principles must not proceed as if the dignity of a person can be compared and weighed against the dignity of others. We can speak of their "equal dignity" as persons, but, like "equality before the law," this refers to their common standing with rights and duties under moral principles, not "the same amount" of exchangeable value.

Third, we must treat persons as having a significant moral status that restricts how we may treat them even to achieve good ends. This idea acquires full practical import only insofar as the moral restrictions can be specified from the ideal moral legislative perspective. Even apart from the details, however, attributing to each a status honored and protected by

---

[28] Kant (1997b), 50–7 [5: 57–66].

[29] The following is a slightly revised version of what I proposed in ch. 8.

some significant restraints on how he or she may be treated is an important condition on Kantian deliberation about principles. It implies that Kantian legislators must try to find reasonable principles that define these restraints specifically, understanding that ignoring or trivializing them is not an option.[30]

Fourth, and more specifically, the existence of each rational person is an objective end and so something to be valued by all rational persons. This implies a strong presumption against killing persons and for helping them to maintain the conditions necessary for living as rational autonomous persons. Objective ends take precedence over subjective ends, and so we honor human dignity by placing a higher priority on preserving human life than on goods and services whose value depends entirely on nonrational inclinations. Further implications are that we must develop and use our rational capacities and, when possible, communicate and interact with others as rational agents, rather than through deception, coercion, and manipulation.

Fifth, the dignity of humanity calls for avoiding *expressions* of disrespect for persons and for positively expressing respect for them as persons in various appropriate ways. How respect can be expressed depends on the context. Sometimes conventional gestures suffice, but often more is needed, for example willingness to consult, to listen, to allow privacy, and to trust, all in ways suitable to the context.

Finally, as Kant implies, we fully respect human dignity only if we count the personal ends of others to some extent as worthy of our attention and aid, even if the ends are based on morally indifferent preferences rather than basic needs. This is a lower priority than preserving life and avoiding expressions of disrespect, leaving considerable flexibility in practice. What clearly fails to respect dignity, however, are attitudes and policies of indifference to others' personal ends.

My proposed list of precepts associated with the humanity formula includes moral considerations that can conflict with one another in actual cases. The humanity formula itself is supposed to be an absolute requirement, not merely a cluster of prima facie duties. My proposal is to interpret this as

---

[30] Many would now call these restraints "*moral* rights," but to followers of Kant the term might misleadingly suggest legally enforceable restrictions.

follows: what is absolutely required is to conform to those principles that, from the moral legislative perspective, are supported by the best reasons, as determined by reasonable reflection on all the considerations implicit in the humanity formula (and their relative priorities). We avoid treating persons *merely* as means if our treatment of them satisfies this condition, for then the treatment is justifiable *even to them* on grounds that as fully as possible honor the value of humanity in each person. The first formal point, then, must always be satisfied as far as possible, but other points provide strong presumptive considerations that may, in tragic cases, be overridden. For example, there is a strong moral presumption in favor of preserving human life, but reasonable principles in light of the value of humanity in each person may justify killing in certain circumstances. Exceptions must be justifiable from the legislative perspective, and that leaves many matters open to reasonable debate. Like rule-utilitarianism, the Kantian perspective sets the standards for moral debate even when it cannot yield definitive answers; but the Kantian standards are importantly different from utilitarian ones.

Implied Constraints on the Manner of Punishment

As indicated earlier, I want to begin by considering how the precepts associated with the humanity formula might influence what conscientious moral agents would advocate regarding ways in which criminals are to be treated insofar as these not mandated by the principles of just punishment. These applications are for the most part fairly straightforward.

First, the policies relevant to the manner of treatment of criminals must ultimately be justifiable to anyone, including the criminals themselves, if they were to take up the moral deliberative perspective. This prohibits thinking of the value of persons as commensurable, and requires recognition of a moral status to all persons, even the worst, as a significant constraint on how they may be treated. These are relatively formal requirements, but they set the general framework for deliberation. In addition, I suggest, they provide some indirect support for procedures of appeal and complaint that allow offenders to be heard regarding the conditions under which their punishment is carried out. This is not because their actual assent is necessary to justify those conditions: they are not in a position to claim a veto over these matters. Rather, the point is that those who coercively impose the conditions of treatment cannot reasonably claim confidence that their policies are in principle justifiable to all if they refuse to listen to the point of view of those being punished.

More obviously, unless otherwise mandated by just punishment, the manner of punishment should protect the lives and health of the offenders who are being punished.

Most will return to civil society after punishment, and even those imprisoned for life presumably have a valuable capacity for living as rational autonomous agents within the limits imposed by their just sentences. In addition, in most cases both the sentence and reasonable concern for security are compatible with various ways of communicating and interacting with those being punished as rational agents. When the necessary control can be secured by providing rational incentives and disincentives, this is preferable to dragging, pushing, chaining, and caging offenders like wild animals. Expressions of mockery and utter contempt, by guards, officers of the court, and the public, are demeaning to humanity in persons, no matter how serious their crimes are, and it is not plausible to argue that such expressions are mandated by just sentences. Disrespect can be expressed not only in words but also by demeaning physical circumstances and dehumanizing practices. For example, one might question rules that needlessly deprive jail inmates of all privacy, choice of activities, and tokens of individuality in dress, hair, pictures, etc. Also, prison policies can hardly express full respect for the rational capacities of inmates if they deny them reading and educational opportunities (assuming these are not ruled out by the just sentence). Introducing voluntary programs that promote reform by reducing blinding rage and cynicism would presumably express respect for their rational capacities. Finally, a lower priority but still a significant implication is that there is a presumptive reason not to cause the punished to suffer beyond what is mandated by just sentences. They should not be gratuitously deprived of opportunities to set and pursue ends of their own, though just sentences may rightly restrict these opportunities.

Details regarding these matters may vary with the context, but the general message seems clear. We should advocate that criminals be treated well, with respect, and in ways that encourage the exercise and development of their rational capacities—unless principles of justice demand otherwise (a matter to be considered shortly).

Apparent Implications of the Humanity Formula for Central Questions of Punishment

The question now is: What answers to central questions of punishment would the humanity formula recommend if we set aside Kant's official theory of justice? The central questions, I take it, are: Who should be punished, how much, in what way, and why? The main issues here, unlike in the last section, concern guidelines for sentencing and for legislation that determines what is a crime and what punishment is justified. Famously, Kant himself insisted that all and only those convicted of legal offenses should be punished, and the degree and (with exceptions) the kind of punishment should be determined by the law of retribution.[31] At present, however, I set aside Kant's official views on punishment in order to speculate briefly about what, apart from that, the humanity formula would recommend.

Why have judicial punishment at all? The question is too large for adequate treatment here, but a few points seem clear. First, an equal regard for the humanity of all persons gives strong presumptive reasons to maintain social institutions that, in a fair and respectful way, tend to prevent acts that destroy or impair persons' capacity to live as rational autonomous agents. Thus, for example, there is presumptive reason to endorse practices that significantly hinder murder, mayhem, theft of legitimate property, torture, enslavement, and other unjustifiable restrictions on individual liberty. Arguably, criminal law provides a system of coercive threats that, if strictly circumscribed in certain ways, could serve that purpose, not perfectly but as effectively as any morally acceptable alternative.[32] The right to carry out the justified threats, at least in most cases, is an essential part of the practice. Ideally the threats would set out rational incentives for conformity to the law and, compared to having a massive police force ever present to prevent

---

[31] Kant (1996a), 104–10 [6: 331–7]. See also 19–20 [6: 228] regarding the degree of imputation of a deed as culpable.

[32] My suggestions here draw from Sharon B. Byrd's important paper, "Kant's Theory of Punishment: Deterrence in its Threat, Retribution in its Execution," (1989), 151–200. Byrd, however, follows Kant more closely than I do in this section. For example, she does not appeal to the humanity formula for the basic justification of state coercive threats, and she takes for granted that punishments more severe than allowed by Kant's principle of retribution (*ius talionis*) would treat criminals merely as means. My proposed account would agree on the last point only if the principle of retribution could be shown to be an essential requirement of justice that conscientious moral agents should respect and support.

crime, the system trusts each person to be self-constraining, at least on prudential grounds. If the degree and kind of punishment threatened for each offense were justifiable from the moral legislative perspective, in light of all its constraints, then the criminal could have no legitimate complaint because, by hypothesis, he too would endorse the practice if deliberating from the appropriate moral perspective. Using the threats of criminal law to achieve ends (such as happiness) much broader than the preservation of life and basic liberties would at least be suspect because carrying the threats out typically deprives *offenders* of something (e.g. liberty) that, by the humanity formula, has a higher value than happiness. Treating persons as rational agents calls for respecting them (in all normal circumstances) as free and responsible for their choices, and arguably an ideal practice of punishment would do so because it hinders wrongdoing not by terror and irrational manipulation but by a reasonably defined and limited system of public antecedent warnings that all can understand and heed.

These possible grounds for a practice of punishment drawn from the humanity formula differ strikingly from a view held by many and often attributed to Kant, namely that it is intrinsically good that people suffer for their immoral deeds and it is a legitimate aim of the state to bring this about.[33] The humanity formula, as I see it, attributes equal dignity to all persons and does not count our imposing suffering or deprivation on any person as intrinsically good, even though in a complex and imperfect world doing so is at times justified.

What kinds of acts should legislators make punishable by law? Assuming that the relevant aim is to hinder unjustifiable interferences with persons' ability to live as rational autonomous agents, there is *some* reason to consider using the criminal law to protect individuals from any such interference. However, because of the effects of punishment on offenders, who are also persons with dignity, there is also reason to look for alternative means to the end, provided they are equally or more respectful of rational agents. Preventative detention simply based on empirical evidence that a person is "likely" to commit a crime is not a method that respects individual freedom and responsibility. Similarly, it is objectionable to treat all offenses as rooted in illness or unfortunate social conditioning. Not all social and educational

---

[33] I argue that Kant was not committed to this view, despite passages that might suggest it, in my (1999b), 407–41.

practices that encourage respect for law, however, are disrespectful in these ways. It is no denial of freedom and responsibility to try to foster social conditions that reduce the irrational urges that lead to crime and make the good reasons for mutual respect more apparent. The values inherent in the humanity formula surely encourage the use and development of such means at least as supplementary to punishment and, one may hope, for certain kinds of wrongdoing as an alternative to criminalization.

Can the agent's motives and mental states be part of the description of the acts that legislators may forbid under the criminal law? Kant himself insisted that criminal law must be concerned only with the "external acts" of free agents, but scholars do not agree on how this is to be interpreted. The question at hand, however, is what recommendation we could draw from the humanity formula if we set aside Kant's official theory of justice. At least one point seems clear: the state should not presume to forbid and punish rational agents for acts that courts are in no position to judge. Presumably criminal investigations and trials can often discover significant facts about offenders' intentions, motives, and state of mind, but, notoriously, reliable access to these matters is quite limited—especially when the trials and investigations follow respectful and non-invasive procedures. Given this, one might argue from the humanity formula that legislators could allow the adjustment of penalties for motives and mental states only when very high standards of evidence are met and when doing so serves the ends and satisfies the constraints of the precepts associated with the value of humanity. These provide strong reason not to "punish" a person for what cannot confidently be attributed to the person, but arguably they do not insist that the criminal law focus only on external "behavior" without regard to anything else.

How much punishment is appropriate to various offenses? From the Kantian legislative perspective sketched above, this would be a very complex question because there are many potentially relevant factors to consider. However, certain oversimple answers are clearly ruled out. For example, we cannot seek answers by a consequentialist cost/benefit analysis that treats all values as commensurable. Nor can we suppose that offenders have a judicially discernible "inner desert" that can be rated on a scale as proportionate to the severity of various punishments. The relative effectiveness of deterrent threats would be relevant, but it cannot be decisive by itself because this could authorize punishments that are too severe, or too light, from the perspective that reflects the equal dignity of all persons.

Suppose that the credible threat of extremely severe punishment would effectively deter most people from committing some relatively minor offense, but a few of the foolish and weak are not deterred. When the threat is actually carried out on these few, this seems to use the suffering of those few merely as a means to uphold the credibility of the threats. From the moral legislative perspective, we might argue that each person, in advance of the crime, benefits from extra security; but still the practice, as it works out, seems to express a willingness to deprive the few of basic values to confer a minor benefit on the many. Given that foolishness and weakness are all too common, it would be difficult to justify to all who respected the dignity of each person equally.[34] On the other hand, even if a light punishment would have as much deterrent value as a more severe one, to impose only a light penalty for the most severe violations of dignity threatens to convey the disrespectful message that the humanity of some victims and offenders is worth more than that of others.

Fixed mandatory sentences determined by legislation might seem to be a way to express equal regard for all offenders and victims, but they too raise problems. If judges have relevant information about particular cases that undermines the presumptive reasons for a severe punishment, then legislation that denies the judges any flexibility in sentencing threatens to impose unjustifiable deprivations on the offenders. From the moral legislative perspective, a variety of considerations inevitably have a bearing on legislative and sentencing policies. Eliminating judicial flexibility of responses to particular cases may initially seem more even-handed and equally respectful of all, but only on a quite narrow interpretation of the requirements of equal respect.

Finally, let us consider *how* criminals should be punished. Kant famously insisted that punishments must respect human dignity, and on this ground opposed, for example, "quartering a man, having him torn by dogs, cutting off his ears and nose."[35] Nevertheless, Kant called for capital punishment for

---

[34] The considerations offered here admittedly raise further questions. Kantian purists will probably protest that they rely too heavily on empirical considerations. Some complications can be avoided by stipulating that any penalty more than allowed by the law of retribution (roughly, make the offender lose what he made his victim lose) will be treating the offender merely as a means, but this presupposes that the law of retribution has been established as a requirement of justice. One treats offenders as mere means if one punishes them more than justice requires, but it is still at issue what justice (understood as requirements for law that we are morally obligated to maintain and respect) demands.

[35] Kant (1996a), 210 [6: 463]. See also 106 [6: 333].

murder and treason and allowed that an offender may be reduced permanently to "the status of a slave" for [some] lesser crimes. The value of
humanity gives us a strong presumption against judicial killing and also
against sentencing offenders to demeaning and debilitating conditions.
Life, however, is not an absolute value on the account sketched here. The
question is whether in some circumstances there are sufficiently strong
countervailing considerations, such as a clear necessity for capital punishment to protect and express the cluster of values associated with the humanity formula. Given the options in most advanced contemporary states, the
necessity for judicial killing becomes doubtful. Arguably, it tends to undermine the central message of the humanity formula, namely that existence of
rational agents is an unconditional value to be cherished, protected, and
respected. Kant, however, did not see the issue as dependent on potentially
variable contingent circumstances. In the next section I turn to the theory of
justice in which Kant's own views of punishment are embedded.

Kant's Official Theory of Justice and the Relevance of Moral Concerns

If typical English-speaking moral philosophers ask, "What sort of practice of
punishment, if any, is morally justified?" they face a terminological problem
when consulting Kant's texts for advice. Their familiar terms "right,"
"justice," and "ethical" do not fully match Kant's use of the corresponding
terms in German. Their terms may be unclear or ambiguous, but even so it
is evident that in *The Metaphysics of Morals* Kant has narrower, special senses
in mind. For example, Kant restricts "right" and "justice" to suitability for
legally enforceable rules regarding the use of "external freedom," and
"ethics" (conceived as one branch of *The Metaphysics of Morals*) is limited
to unenforceable principles intended for individuals' guidance and self-
restraint. Ethics (in this sense) prescribes "maxims of actions" and moral
motivation; the theory of "right," by contrast, prescribes and prohibits
"actions" with regard to their impact on others' external freedom, not the
moral worth of their motives.[36]

---

[36] Kant (1996a), 152–4 [6: 388–91].

To summarize briefly Kant's theory of justice, as I understand it, the authority of the coercive power of the state stems from the universal principle of right/justice and its corollary, which entitles legal authorities, once established, to use its power to "hinder" those who would "hinder" others exercising their legitimate freedom of conduct as defined by law. Although Kant does not explicitly give us the argument, presumably a system of judicial punishment accords with "right" and "justice" insofar as it is a system designed to "hinder" legal offenses by coercive threats.[37] Thus, presumably, legislators must define crimes in terms of the discernible ways in which they restrict legitimate liberty, as defined by the universal principle of right/justice and interpreted by constituted legal authorities. Judges and enforcement officers, in their official capacities, are required by justice to carry out the laws so defined and interpreted. Their official job, then, is not to assess the moral worth of the motives and character of offenders and to make them suffer according to their moral deserts.[38] Nor is it their place to estimate and impose the penalties they think will best deter *others* from committing similar crimes: their job in the system is to carry out the threats legitimately imposed by law. In fact, officials would be acting contrary to their legal responsibilities in the system if they punished for moral deserts or "to make an example" of the offender. The fact that legal authorities themselves fail to conform to the principles of right does not undermine the legitimacy of their orders or our legal duty to obey them. The system of right or justice provides no authorization for citizens to resist, still less to rebel against, an unjust ruler, even a tyrant.[39]

The best reconstruction of Kant's theory of punishment, arguably, acknowledges a distinction between the principles or policies governing the practice of punishment and the ultimate grounds for the legitimacy and justice of the practice.[40] The practice, Kant argues, should determine the

---

[37] This interpretation is well defended in the article previously cited by Sharon Byrd, but many commentators apparently reject the idea that deterrence is the justifying aim of punishment or even part of the grounds for maintaining it.

[38] The offenders must, however, be "persons" and "free causes" to whom the crimes can be "imputed," and, although the overall moral quality of the offender's motive is not at issue in the law, presumably the offenses must be intentional and committed against laws promulgated in advance. It is not as though *mens rea* is irrelevant to the "external acts" that the law is concerned with.

[39] Ethical considerations, as distinct from the system of justice, may give an individual grounds to resist orders to do what is intrinsically immoral.

[40] See, in addition to Byrd (1989), Scheid (1983), and Hill (2000), 173–99, and (2002), 310–39. Ripstein (2009), 300–24, gives a related but different interpretation.

degree and kind of punishment, so far as possible, by the *ius talionis*. Those who offend against the liberty of others are to be punished proportionately to the illegitimate infringement against others' rights. Thus, with some qualifications, the policy is to arrange sanctions so that it is as if "if you insult [another person], you insult yourself, if you steal from him, you steal from yourself, if you strike him, you strike yourself; if you kill him you kill yourself."[41] Kant qualifies this by prohibiting degrading punishments and acknowledging a need to interpret with some flexibility both the severity of a punishment and the gravity of an offense.[42] The *ius talionis*, however, is only a standard for a just practice of punishment, not the ultimate ground for having punishment. Kant apparently believed that to punish us in accord with our intrinsic moral deserts is appropriate for God, but his theory of justice does not authorize state officials to play God in this respect. The main ground for having a system of punishment as Kant conceives it must be the universal principle of right and its corollary authorizing state coercion to prevent acts of injustice, as interpreted and enforced by the state.[43] Although Kant does not give us the argument explicitly, the aim to prevent infringements of legitimate liberty by a system of coercive threats is the key. So understood, Kant's theory of punishment is not "deeply retributivist" despite its endorsement of *ius talionis*.

Kant draws a sharp distinction between ethics and law, but arguably this does not rule out all moral criticism of legal practices. Although Thomas Pogge may be right that Kant first conceived the doctrine of right as a self-contained "module" independent of his "comprehensive moral theory," Kant does imbed the doctrine in a work entitled *The Metaphysics of Morals*.[44] The general introduction, covering both parts, makes evident the intention to lay out general prescriptions of practical reason conceived as a source (directly or indirectly) of categorical imperatives. In addition, at various points Kant appeals to the ideas in both the universal law and humanity formulas. Furthermore, although the doctrine of right defines "juridical duties" rather than "duties of virtue" (or "ethical duties," in a narrow sense), Kant says that all duties belong to ethics in a more comprehensive sense.[45]

---

[41] Kant (1996a), 105 [6: 332].
[42] Ibid. 106–9 [6: 332–7].
[43] Ibid. 24–5 [6: 230–1].
[44] Thomas Pogge, "Is Kant's *Rechtslehre* Comprehensive?" in Timmons (2002).
[45] Kant (1996a), 21 [6: 219].

Juridical duties are "indirectly" ethical duties, which implies that at least in general everyone has the moral responsibility to obey and uphold the law (from duty). Twice Kant briefly acknowledges an exception: if the state gives us an order to do something intrinsically immoral, we should refuse.[46] Here, in effect, Kant grants that individuals, as moral agents, cannot assume that they are ethically justified in fulfilling their assigned roles in their legal system, even if the system meets Kant's minimal standards for being legitimate under principles of "right." Legal requirements are relevant to conscientious deliberation because most are also indirectly ethical duties, but legal requirements are not always decisive morally. Finally, though relevant texts are complex and controversial, Kant argues that, even though it is not necessary for state legitimacy and legal duties, a republican form of government would be the fullest realization of justice. Here, perhaps, Kant comes closest to using justice (or "right") as (what I would call) a moral standard for law and government; for, given an ethical responsibility to further justice, the republican ideal has moral implications for how legal authorities should govern, what reforms philosophers should advocate, and even how ordinary citizens should behave.

These considerations indicate that, despite his distinction between law and ethics, Kant granted that in principle broadly moral considerations are relevant to the assessment of legal practices, especially to individuals' moral obligations with respect to the law. He himself thought that his principles of punishment were just and that citizens were morally obligated (an "indirectly ethical duty") to maintain and respect them, but his position on this can, of course, be challenged. In the next section I call attention to some points on which the value of humanity, as sketched here, raises questions about his official theory.

Can Morally Conscientious Persons Endorse Kant's Theory of Punishment?

In this final section my aim is merely to call attention to some apparent conflicts between Kant's official theory of punishment and the suggestions

---

[46] Ibid. 136–7 [6: 371]; Kant (1998*b*), 153 n. [6: 154 n.].

regarding punishment drawn earlier from the humanity formula considered in the absence of Kant's official theory. Four points especially deserve mention.

First, although earlier discussion cited reasons for understanding the aim of criminal law narrowly as protecting life and liberty, the complex values associated with the humanity formula also provide reasons to question whether the aim should be more broadly understood. Kant's universal principle of right is often interpreted narrowly as a "libertarian" principle. Whether or not this is accurate on textual grounds, we may question whether there are adequate grounds for endorsing the principle when interpreted in this way. If only some of the complex values associated with the humanity formula are relevant to the system of criminal law that we, as individuals, are morally obliged to uphold, then we need to be quite clear about why this is so. Is it obvious, for example, that promoting the happiness of citizens in circumscribed ways is not even a part of the legitimate aim of government and law?

Second, a basic point in Kant's official theory is that punishment can only be for "external acts." This implies the uncontroversial proposition that criminal law, unlike conscience, cannot demand that citizens act from morally worthy motives. It seems, however, to imply more than this: for example, that both legislators and judges should consider the motives, character, and mental state of the offender as irrelevant to the appropriate degree of punishment.[47] Scholars may differ about how strictly Kant adhered to that idea, but in any case we may question whether we can conscientiously support a system that does not take into account motivational and character factors beyond the "external act." Arguably, the complex considerations associated with the value of humanity suggest a somewhat more qualified and flexible standard.

Third, and more obviously, rigid adherence to the law of retribution (*ius talionis*) seems to conflict in several ways with the recommendations

---

[47] Kant presupposed at least that the criminal acts must be imputed to agents as their "free cause." The "external acts" with which justice is concerned, then, are not bodily movements beyond a person's control. Hence questions about intention, negligence, and mental competence must be relevant to whether there was a punishable criminal act even if other aspects of offenders' mental states, such as the kind and quality of their motives, are considered irrelevant to the kind and degree of punishment because they are not part of the "external act." Note Kant's brief remark at (1996a), 20 [6: 228]: "Hence the state of mind of the subject, whether he committed the deed in a state of agitation or with cool deliberation, makes a difference in imputation, which has results."

drawn from the value of humanity. Even if we set aside the many familiar problems in trying to use the law of retribution as a practical guide, the law seems to prescribe sentences that are too severe in some cases and too light in other cases. Given that limited and respectful law enforcement systems can discover and prosecute only a fraction of actual crimes, often a penalty that "takes back" only what the offender unlawfully "took" is not likely to be an effective deterrent to potential offenders. By liberally interpreting what the offender "took" or endangered (e.g. the security of all) and its equivalent, one might argue in many cases for sterner, more effective deterrents than a superficial application of the law of retribution might suggest. We may doubt, however, how far this defense can plausibly be extended.

In other cases, the penalties prescribed by the law of retribution appear to be too severe, at least when assessed by the aims and constraints associated with the humanity formula. Principled reduction of standard penalties for some cases does not necessarily affect deterrence, convey a message of unequal respect, or deny the offender's freedom and responsibility. In addition, it can positively promote the possibility of rational autonomous living for both the offender and others. In cases where it is clearly discernible that imposition of the full punishment prescribed by the law of retribution would serve none of the values of humanity, then there needs to be convincing argument that we should support the retributive principle nonetheless.

Finally, as I noted earlier, the values associated with humanity raise serious doubts about the justifiability of capital punishment. One might argue, contrary to Kant, there are alternative punishments for murder that should count as "equivalents" under the law of retribution, but the important and prior question is whether that standard is justified. As we noted earlier, the values drawn from the humanity formula provide a strong presumptive case against capital punishment, and so, once again, we are left with the question whether Kant provides any compelling reasons for discounting this. A thorough treatment of the matter would need to consider in detail whether the *Rechtslehre* provides grounds for the law of retribution, for the claim that it requires capital punishment, and for thinking that any countervailing moral considerations that we might draw from the humanity formula are irrelevant to the justification of legal practices, such as punishment. I am skeptical on all three points, but I cannot pursue the matter further here.

14

Kant and Humanitarian Intervention

Act in such a way that you treat humanity, whether in your own person or in any other, always at the same time as an end, never merely as a means.

Immanuel Kant, *Groundwork for the Metaphysics of Morals*, 1785

No state shall forcibly interfere in the constitution and government of another state.

Immanuel Kant, *Perpetual Peace*, 1795

Introduction

Over two hundred years ago Immanuel Kant was deeply concerned, as we are today, about the destruction, misery, and chaos caused by war. In his late work *Perpetual Peace* he attempted to articulate principles to guide heads of state toward a more peaceful world and ultimately, he hoped, to a permanent end to war. There he argued as a moral philosopher and vigorously defended the appropriateness of a broadly moral perspective on issues of international relations.[1] Heads of state, he argued, ought to abide by the

An earlier version of this chapter was presented at a conference on Kant, Justice, and International Law at the University of Oslo in 2004. I am grateful for comments by participants at that conference, especially Thomas Pogge, Sven Arntzen, and Helga Varden, and for discussions with students and faculty at the University of Toronto Law School, the University of Arizona, and the University of North Carolina at Chapel Hill. I am grateful to Adam Cureton for both discussions and editing.

[1] See e.g. Appendices I and II of *Perpetual Peace*, in Kant (2006), 94–111 [8: 370–86]. Bracketed numbers always refer to volume and pages in the standard Prussian Academy edition of Kant's works. Unless otherwise indicated, references will be given by these bracketed numbers, by which passages can be located in most recent translations of Kant's works.

preliminary articles and work toward satisfying the definitive articles that he proposed. Among the preliminary articles was the prohibition (quoted above): "No state shall forcibly interfere with the constitution and govern-ment of another state."[2] Lest cynicism undermine their efforts toward peace, he also offered an argument for believing that an everlasting peace is possible and will come about eventually even if our intentional efforts to end wars fail.[3] This argument, apparently based on moral faith as well as empirical conjecture, was meant to combat debilitating hopelessness as we see tragic wars proliferating, but in no way was it to be an excuse for not fulfilling the duty to seek peace by all legitimate means.

The world has changed immensely since 1795, and we can reasonably wonder whether even the most reasonable prescriptions for peace suitable then are valid today. In particular, I wonder about Kant's preliminary article 5—the prohibition on interference just quoted. What was Kant's rationale for this, and to what extent does it apply in the conditions we face today? Our world has changed in many ways: the technology of war, growing global dependencies, vastly greater populations, experience of the horrors of modern war, the rise of superpowers, the development of the United Nations and elements of international law. Just war theory has been affirmed and developed, but often blatantly ignored and even defiantly rejected. Powerful nations have increasingly attempted to justify invasion of weaker nations, not for self-defense or conquest, but on the grounds that their rulers are oppressing their own people. We need to ask: In our new and ever-changing world, when, if ever, is this "humanitarian" purpose an adequate justification for intervening in the affairs of other states?

The term "humanitarian intervention" has been used to cover a wide variety of cases. Sometimes, no doubt, it serves as a euphemism for the use of force for ulterior purposes having nothing to do with respect for human-ity. In the present discussion, what I mean by a *humanitarian intervention* is roughly the following: a forcible interference in the governance of one legitimate state by another for the primary purpose of protecting the latter's subjects from abuse and oppression by its own government.[4] By "legitimate state" here I do not mean a reasonable and just, or even decent, state, but

---

[2] Kant (2006), 70 [8: 346].
[3] Ibid. [8: 360–8].
[4] "Forcible" here is not necessarily "by violent military action" but includes boycotts and other economic sanctions.

only a state that has a functioning legal order, a more or less effective government in power,[5] and international recognition as an independent state. For now I exclude states in anarchy or deeply divided in civil war.[6] Also I set aside interventions by a nation or federal government in the affairs of its territories, colonies, or subdivisions. These other cases are obviously important, and my remarks may be relevant to them in some respects; but these cases introduce special considerations that would require a fuller discussion. The term "humanitarian," as I use it, refers to a commendably humane *purpose* of an intervention, but it does not imply that the intervention is justified, all things considered. Thus it remains a serious, substantive question: When, *if ever*, is humanitarian intervention, as conceived here, justified? More specifically, I want to explore the implications of Kantian practical philosophy on this issue, both what Kant himself implied and said, and what a critical, modified Kant*ian* ethics might say.

My plan is this: First, I sketch the critical, modified Kantian moral perspective from which my discussion will draw. Next, I argue that Kantian ethical theory provides a strong presumption in favor of humanitarian interventions in certain special conditions though it also opposes such interventions when those conditions are absent.[7] Then, I review some

---

[5] Here I assume that a "government" is more than a band of rogues that enforces its will by arbitrary violence and threats without even the most minimum conditions for rule of law. It is notoriously difficult, however, to draw a line between such regimes and very bad governments. Kant, ever concerned to avoid revolution and anarchy, seems to set the bar low for legitimacy in the sense required for obligations of obedience and recognition by other states even though he has high standards for what is needed for a state to be fully just. His abhorrence of lawlessness, and his belief that the best hope for reform is "top-down," help to explain his position, even if they do not justify it. Several commentators note that Kant apparently distinguishes between *rechtlich* (rightful) and *gerechtmaessig* (lawful or just). This corresponds roughly to what I call "legitimate" and "just," though my term *"fully* just" may suggest a higher standard than *gerechtmaessig*. For references and helpful commentary, see Arntzen (1995); Bernstein (2008); Byrd (1995); Cavallar (1999); Pogge (1988); Ripstein (2009); and Westphal (1992).

[6] Kant ((2006), 70 [8: 346]) refers briefly to such internal conflicts, implying that at some point when a state is (de facto) "divided into two parts," external intervention in the conflict might be justified.

[7] My claim here is about Kantian *ethical* theory, not Kant's official theory of law and justice. Kant distinguishes the realm of law, justice, and "right" (*Recht*) and the realm of virtue (ethics beyond law). The former concerns only "external acts," subject to "external legislation" and enforcement whereas the latter concerns reason's "inner legislation" regarding obligatory ends and moral motivation. See *The Metaphysics of Morals* (1996a). The relationship between Kant's principles for the law and justice (pt. I) and his principles for ethical virtue (pt. II) is controversial in many respects, but he clearly maintained that, with some exceptions, we have an "indirect ethical" duty to conform to "juridical duties" and that virtue requires doing so from a moral motive. The presumptions that I infer from Kant's idea of humanity as an end in itself are drawn from his ethical theory in *The Metaphysics of Morals* pt. II and *Groundwork for the Metaphysics of Morals* (2002). Objections to applying these ethical presumptions to humanitarian interventions come from his theory of law and justice.

features of Kant's political writings that suggest that the presumptive reasons for humanitarian intervention are always defeated by other more stringent considerations. These include (1) the responsibilities of leaders of a sovereign state toward citizens of their own country, (2) the absence of authority to punish the foreign heads of state or to judge that they have forfeited the right to rule, and (3) the rights of the citizens in the country that is targeted for intervention. I conclude that, despite what Kant may have thought, these considerations do not provide decisive arguments against humanitarian intervention *in all cases*. Both moral and practical considerations urge extreme caution, but Kantian grounds for respecting state sovereignty need not, in all circumstances, be an insurmountable obstacle to interventions of the sort that commonsense may endorse.

I. A Critical Kantian Perspective

A. Standards Are Not Drawn from Examples

Kant argued that we do better in moral philosophy when we begin with theory rather than examples. We cannot derive general moral principles from a survey of particular cases, especially controversial cases in which even the facts are in dispute. Instead we need to examine our basic moral ideas in order to articulate the norms that are *relevant* to particular cases.[8] Only then would we be in a position to attempt the complex task of determining what acts are justified in various actual circumstances. I propose to follow Kant here by concentrating on possible theoretical grounds for and against humanitarian interventions rather than focusing on controversial examples. The aim is to consider what it would take to justify a humanitarian intervention. Whether these conditions were satisfied in the actual cases which have been called "humanitarian interventions" is a further question that turns on empirical facts beyond the present philosophical investigation.[9]

---

[8] My proposal is to start with theory, but ultimately, I think, we must examine the implications of our first theoretical efforts for real cases in order to see whether, on reflection, they conflict with our considered judgments. The aim, as I see it, is what John Rawls calls reflective equilibrium.

[9] For other perspectives and discussion of particular cases, see e.g. Holzgrefe and Keohane (2003).

B. Empirical Evidence is Relevant to Mid-level Principles and Applications

That moral judgments on particular cases depend upon empirical facts would be obvious from the point of view of consequentialism. Consequentialism holds that all that ultimately matters is the effectiveness of various means to the most desirable end. We are concerned here, however, with a Kantian perspective, and so it may be thought that the legitimacy of intervention cannot depend in any way on empirical facts, especially not on what we predict the likely consequences of intervention will be. Although unfortunately some passages in Kant's writings encourage this extreme interpretation, it is a dangerous exaggeration of his view. Kant did argue vigorously that the supreme moral principle, expressed in the various formulations of the Categorical Imperative, is valid unconditionally and so independently of the consequences of our conforming to it. More controversially, he held that from this principle, together with presupposed background facts about the human condition, we can derive some quite strict principles expressible in the form "Never do this, whatever the consequences." For example, he held strict principles of this form about adultery, degrading punishments, lying, "unnatural sex," being contemptuous of others, and making it a policy never to help others in need.[10] Kant's arguments to *justify* principles at this level, however, clearly presuppose general facts about the human condition. This is as it should be, and arguably Kant's reasoning at this stage should have taken into account much more empirical information than he did.

Also, whatever Kant himself may suggest, we cannot reasonably expect, when we try to *apply* Kant's fundamental moral principles to the real world, that the resulting intermediate principles and policies would be *free from reference* to empirical conditions. Obviously, we need to know empirical facts about particular cases in order to judge when the intermediate principles apply. Such principles prescribe, explicitly or implicitly, what must be done (or avoided) in certain circumstances. Without specific information we cannot even tell whether a case counts as a rebellion, deceit, broken

---

[10] See Kant (1996a), 62 [6: 278], 130, 210 [6: 362–3, 463], 182 [6: 429], 178–9 [6: 424–6], 209 [6: 463], 153, 199 [6: 390, 450]. Kant's "casuistical questions" suggest that refinements of the definition of what must never be done are needed in some cases, but they do not imply that the prohibitions can be set aside to avoid undesirable consequences.

promise, degradation, or principled refusal to give aid. Moreover, although Kant is no consequentialist, many of his own mid-level principles require that we take *expected consequences* into account. We cannot carry out duties to promote the happiness of others, to work toward perpetual peace, to preserve our health, and so on, without considering what acts are likely to promote the prescribed moral end.[11] Any reasonable development of a Kantian ethics, I think, must acknowledge that empirical information is relevant in these ways. In order to justify intermediate principles and judge how they apply to particular cases, we need *both* basic moral standards and relevant empirical information. To borrow Kant's phrase from another context, the moral law without facts is empty; facts without the moral law are blind.

Kant typically expresses his mid-level moral principles in either of two forms. Paradigm principles of imperfect duties tell us to promote certain good ends (for example, our own perfection and the happiness of others), and paradigm principles of perfect duty tell us to avoid certain acts, whatever the consequences (for example, lying, suicide, adultery, revolution).[12] Kant treats some of his principles, however, as if implicitly qualified, saying in effect "Avoid (or do) this, unless x, y, and z."[13] Arguably, given his basic moral theory, he should have acknowledged that most mid-level principles should take this qualified form. Such principles establish a presumption rooted in deontological considerations, such as respect for humanity, but they allow that the presumption may be cancelled in light of certain facts. Arguably, these relevant facts may include those about the effectiveness, necessity, and costs of adhering to the presumption. In Kantian ethical theory, a deontological presumption could not be cancelled *merely* because "the consequences are very undesirable" but only because they are of a kind and degree that undermines the very rationale for the presumption.[14] In

---

[11] See Kant (2006), 160–3 [7: 91–4], and Kant (1996a), 180–1 [6: 427–8] and 164–95 [6: 445–6].

[12] Kant (1996a), 154–5 [6: 390–4], 176–84 [6: 421–32], 61–4 [6: 276–80], 96–7 [6: 320–3].

[13] An example might be "Murderers must be executed unless it is a case of infanticide or killing in a duel done to avoid dishonor." See ibid. 108–9 [6: 335–7]. Kant held that the ideal form for principles of perfect duty, or at least perfect juridical duties, would be free from qualifications that might seem arbitrary: for example, they should say "Always (or never) do X" rather than "Do (or avoid) X unless, a, b, or c." See Kant (2006), 71–2 n. [8: 348 n.]. Differences of this kind in the form of principles, however, do not necessarily reflect a substantive difference in their context. For example, "Do not intentionally kill human beings except when required in a just war or self-defense or state ordered execution" is approximately equivalent to "Never commit murder."

[14] For more explanation see Hill (1992c), 196–225.

what follows, I propose that there are Kantian principles that establish presumptions both for and against humanitarian intervention but that they are defeasible.[15] They may be set aside if (but only if) certain conditions are met. Assuming for now that there is no decisive argument for an absolute prohibition on humanitarian interventions, to justify a particular humanitarian intervention we would need to take into account, among other things, estimates of the necessity and effectiveness of intervention, the urgency of the primary moral purpose, and the impact on other moral values. This requires well-focused attention to empirical facts about consequences, not to support the basic moral principles, but to apply them.

C. A Kantian Legislative Perspective

As I suggest in previous essays, Kant's ideas about a fundamental perspective for moral deliberation might be reconstructed as follows.[16] Kant's idea of a "kingdom of ends," an all-inclusive moral commonwealth, combines important insights inherent in his several formulations of the Categorical Imperative. The latter is supposed to be the fundamental moral standard, expressed in imperative form appropriate to human beings, who (as imperfectly rational agents) cannot help but acknowledge the standard but often fail to live up to it. If we extend Kant's all-too-brief suggestions, we can view the perspective of the legislators in the ideal "kingdom of ends" as a perspective for assessing, endorsing, and specifying mid-level principles to guide and constrain moral deliberation in recurring problematic situations. Mid-level principles stand between the most basic moral standards inherent in the defining conditions of the moral legislative perspective and the particular moral judgments that must be made in concrete circumstances.

---

[15] By "Kantian" here I mean what is arguably a reasonable modification of Kant's view, not that this was Kant's own position. In his division of *The Metaphysics of Morals* Kant seems to imply that, while even law and justice (*Recht*) must avoid treating persons merely as means, the imperative to treat humanity (positively) as an end belongs to *ethics* independently of law and justice. If so, this suggests that Kant regarded the latter aspect of his humanity formula of the Categorical Imperative [4: 429] to be irrelevant to law and justice—and so irrelevant to humanitarian interventions. My concern here, however, is not so much with the textual question whether Kant himself did draw such a sharp division, but whether he gives *adequate reasons* why ethical individuals, concerned for humanity as an end, should support public policies that take that division for granted.

[16] This perspective, admittedly an extension and modification of Kant's explicit views, is described briefly in Hill (1992a), ch. 11, and developed further in Hill (2000), chs. 2, 4, and 8. Some objections to use of the idea of hypothetical agreement in the legislative model are discussed in Hill (2002), ch. 3. See also chs. 8–11 and 13 of this volume.

The Kantian legislative perspective is that of rational autonomous persons, committed to human dignity and mutual respect, who seek to identify (or construct) standards applicable to all members. As Kant's formula of universal law requires, the legislators are concerned to see that individual maxims conform to universal law. As Kant's formula of humanity requires, they adopt only principles duly respectful of humanity as an end in itself. In accord with Kant's formula of autonomy, they regard themselves, and every other rational legislator, as "making laws," or adopting principles, from a point of view that sets aside private interests and personal bias and focuses on broader human needs, especially the conditions necessary for living with others as rational autonomous agents.

D. The Cluster of Prescriptions Inherent in the Idea of Humanity as an End in Itself

For present purposes, the most important guide and constraint is that legislators must always regard humanity as an end in itself, never merely as a means. Interpretation of this is notoriously controversial, but here I assume some ideas discussed more fully elsewhere.[17] Briefly: Kant's humanity formula cannot reasonably be used as an inflexible principle to be applied intuitively on a case by case basis. Such use results in irresolvable moral dilemmas and inflexible applications that ignore morally relevant considerations. Instead, the humanity formula attributes a special value—dignity—to persons. In Kantian ethics, as I understand it, attributions of *value* are equivalent to prescriptions about how we must treat whatever is said to be valuable. In effect, the idea of human dignity encapsulates a cluster of rational prescriptions. In sum, these are, *negatively*, not to regard persons as having a merely commensurable value and not to violate principles that rational autonomous persons would endorse, all things considered; and, *positively*, to exercise, preserve, and develop one's own rational nature, to respect it in all persons, to count the happiness of others (or, strictly, their permissible ends) as important in our deliberations, but to prioritize the requirements for rational autonomous living over other concerns.[18]

---

[17] e.g. chs. 8 and 13 of this volume.

[18] "Rational" here is not exclusively instrumental rationality or efficiency in choice of means to one's rationally contingent ends. Aspects of what writers now call "reasonable" are incorporated into Kant's idea of "rational."

The proposed Kantian perspective regards the second negative prescription as an inflexible constraint on action: *never* violate the principles that, in one's best judgment, rational autonomous deliberators would endorse, if guided and constrained by the idea of human dignity and mindful of the complexities of the real world for which the principles are intended. The first negative prescription ("*never* regard persons as having a merely commensurable value") and the remaining positive prescriptions are also non-optional demands, but they directly concern our *attitudes* when we deliberate and act.[19] They provide strong presumptive considerations for or against various courses of action, and they are often unequivocal and decisive in particular contexts. In cases of tragic conflict, the prescriptions may pull us toward different courses of action. For example, what is needed to develop the rational capacities of persons is not always what contributes to their happiness, i.e. the achievement of their actual (permissible) ends. What seems from a narrow perspective the most appropriate way to *respect an individual* may turn out, from a broader viewpoint, to be in conflict with what *respect for all persons* requires. What preserves the lives of some persons may endanger others. An important aim of engaging in higher-order deliberation about principles is to find or construct standards that uphold, as best we can in imperfect conditions, these various ideals inherent in regarding humanity as an end in itself.

E. Diversity of Aims and Values Must Be Protected but Constrained through Shared Principles and Institutions

Kant's practical philosophy affirms and defends certain general principles concerned with law, politics, and moral attitudes, maintaining that these *fundamental* principles are rational and universally valid. These principles prescribe a framework of thought for deliberating about practical issues, and they urge us to establish more specific principles, institutions, and rules that are appropriate to guide and constrain everyday choices. The deliberative framework and derivative principles, institutions, and rules, as I understand them, are not meant to dictate answers to all legal, political, and personal

---

[19] They rule out certain *acts* as immoral and show that others are morally required by demanding that our deliberations, choices, and intentions are compatible with the prescribed attitudes. It is not as though one could muster up a motivationally inert and non-reason-giving "inner state of mind," a mere wish or "pure thought," and then anything one does will be permitted.

questions. They are to allow and protect the freedom of individuals to pursue their own projects, to develop their own personal values, and to unite with others to pursue common goals of diverse kinds. At the same time they place rational and moral constraints on the pursuits of individuals and groups when they threaten to undermine the equal status of others. Unlike utilitarianism and perfectionism, Kantianism offers no all-encompassing goal as the standard for individuals and institutions, but instead it proposes constraining principles to protect and regulate the pursuit of diverse values with a framework of mutual respect for all.[20]

Within this sort of theory, the question "Who is to judge?" is important but complex. The answer depends on context. If the question is, who is to judge whether I have a moral obligation to give to famine relief, the answer is that the judgment is primarily my responsibility. This is not to say that my judgment will be correct, no matter what it is; for there are rational and moral standards relevant to the judgment. Other people may, of course, form judgments about what I ought to do, but it is my ethical duty, not theirs, to make the judgment, in an informed and honest way, and then to follow it. But now suppose the question is who is to judge what is strictly legal in my state? The idea of strict legality requires that there be an unequivocal authority with the right and responsibility to make such judgments. Others may have opinions, correct or incorrect, but their determinations do not carry legal force. Again, despite some grey areas, there are standards in any legal system, beyond wishes and conjectures, by which the authorities are supposed to make their judgments.

A third context is when questions are raised about the justifiability of laws from a broadly rational and moral perspective.[21] Are certain particular laws and legal determinations morally and rationally justifiable, first, as requirements that, however imperfect, ought to be obeyed by those subject to them and, second, as requirements that legal authorities should continue to endorse and leave unchanged? Anyone may raise such questions, and often we should, but it is another matter who is morally justified in putting their

---

[20] Rather than a goal to be achieved, human dignity represents a status to be respected, which translates into a cluster of related prescriptions about attitudes and acts. Kant argues these include two obligatory ends—one's own perfection and the happiness of others—but also "perfect duties to oneself," respect for others, and the "indirectly ethical duty" to conform to juridical duties. See Kant (1996a), pt. II, 139–234 [6: 373–493].

[21] These questions are Kant's concern in (1996a), pt. I, 9–138 [6: 211–372].

judgments into effect. These are not simply legal questions, but they are also not questions of moral responsibility that are independent of legal institutions. They concern both how universal rational/moral standards apply to existing legal systems and how individuals in different roles in these systems should act. This last kind of question is what is at issue when we ask whether humanitarian interventions are justifiable. Though anyone can form opinions, the question "Who is to judge?" in this context reminds us that our judgments must be justifiable to others to whom we are related within complex legal and social institutions. What I, or anyone, should advocate and do in these contexts typically depends not only on what *ideal* moral judges *would* say but also on what the *actual* people involved do *in fact* say.[22] The criteria for justifiable decisions in this area are complex and controversial, but at least it should be clear that what we should do, given existing legal and political roles, is neither simply whatever moral decision apart from such roles would dictate nor whatever the existing role-defined responsibilities prescribe.

II. The Presumption for Humanitarian Intervention, Relevant Practical Considerations, and Kant's Apparently Inflexible Opposition

Humanitarian intervention, as defined here, is a state's attempt to protect the citizens of another state from abuse and oppression by its own government. Suppose the perceived "abuse and oppression" includes persistently

---

[22] e.g. suppose that, reasoning privately from general moral principles, you conclude (rightly, let us suppose) that virtually all ideally informed, clear-thinking moral people would agree that certain social constraints should be abandoned as unduly restrictive though not seriously harmful or discriminatory. Suppose that these constraints are still widely accepted and shape actual people's lives and expectations. Then what individuals actually think is surely at least relevant to how one should respond to the constraints—whether to flout them, to mock them, merely to tolerate them, or try to persuade others of the better way. Similarly, suppose a president and a few advisers think that the world would be better if everyone accepted their global policies and even imagine that everyone would agree if unbiased, informed, and right-minded. But suppose that those global policies are seriously opposed, even condemned by most world opinion and more than half of the president's own people. Then, even without changing their own view of the ideal policy for everyone to agree on, surely the president and advisers should take into account the actual opposition of others—not just as "evidence" that they might be mistaken but as crucial facts that (with other facts) determine what ought to be done in the actual situation.

depriving a minority group of life, liberty, or other essential conditions for living as rational autonomous agents. Then the positive prescriptions inherent in the idea of humanity as an end in itself would give everyone a *strong moral reason* to prevent or stop the abuse and oppression by all *permissible* means. This limited thesis, I take it, is uncontroversial. From the Kantian moral legislative perspective, however, we must find and respect principles that adequately respect *all* morally relevant considerations. Many considerations are *apparently* relevant to the justifiability of humanitarian intervention, but it remains a question whether certain decisive considerations trump all others, implying that even after all things are considered, intervention in another state is *never* a permissible means to promote humanitarian ends.

Among the many apparently relevant considerations, some are notoriously difficult to judge in particular cases. For example, is the coercive interference necessary to achieve the humanitarian purpose? Are there viable alternatives? How likely is it that the interference will be effective? Will it have further implications or unintended side-effects that we have moral reason to avoid? For example, will innocent people be killed in the effort to save others? Will interference destroy or destabilize the existing legal order so that, although some are rescued, others' prospects for autonomous living are diminished? These questions require good judgment about degrees of risk often in quite uncertain conditions, but, absent a decisive counter-argument, we cannot respect the cluster of prescriptions inherent in the humanity formula without taking these questions into account. That an intervention would save lives, for example, would be a presumptive reason for it, but that it might also result in unlawful coercion or even death for others would be a presumptive reason against it. The fact that the purpose of an intervention is to liberate oppressed people would be a point in its favor; but if there is no good evidence that the intervention is necessary or likely to be effective for that purpose, then the high-minded purpose cannot justify it.

This is not to suggest that moral deliberation about humanitarian interventions reduces to a calculation of lives lost and saved, the odds of further costs, and so on. A Kantian perspective rejects the idea that we can determine what is right simply by weighing and balancing a set of commensurable values. We cannot treat the worth of persons, or the value of their lives, as a determinable quantity, subject to permissible trade-offs. The opposite extreme, however, i.e. treating the incomparable worth of persons as absolutely forbidding doing anything that harms them, is both unwarranted and impractical. Although its fundamental values are not commensurable, a reasonable Kantian ethics cannot deny that *at some level of duly constrained moral deliberation*, it often matters how many will be killed or rescued. As I have argued elsewhere, by distinguishing levels of moral reflection, a critical Kantian theory can provide a reasonable alternative to both an unduly calculating consequentialism and an unduly rigoristic inter-pretation of the humanity formula as a simple rule to be applied directly to particular cases.[23]

Among those who accept that some humanitarian interventions might be justified, it is not controversial that moral deliberation must consider its necessity, likely effectiveness, and side-effects. My main point so far is just that, *unless good Kantian arguments absolutely forbid all humanitarian interven-tions,* then any reasonable Kantian principles regarding when it might be justified would have to include qualifications regarding these practical matters. That is, arguably the principles would permit humanitarian inter-vention *only so long as it is reasonably certain that intervention is necessary and will be effective without further implications and effects that are morally unacceptable.* This is because unnecessary, inefficient, and morally reckless interventions would be opposed by the same sort of considerations inherent in the humanity formula that presumptively favored the intervention.

The practical questions are admittedly difficult matters to judge in actual cases, even with the best of intentions—and all the more difficult when the judges have mixed motives. Moreover, these questions would be irrelevant *if* there were good principled arguments showing that all humanitarian interventions are unjustified. Are there, then, principled objections to humanitarian interventions that prohibit them regardless of the calculation in particular cases of the degrees of likelihood, necessity, and significant further costs? Several aspects of Kant's political writings may *seem* to rule out humanitarian interventions, regardless of the calculated costs and benefits in particular cases. I turn now to review and comment briefly on some of these issues.

---

[23] I summarize ideas discussed more fully in Hill (1992a), ch. 10, Hill (2000), chs. 2, 5, and 8, and chs. 8–11 and 13 above.

III. Does a Government's Responsibility to its Own Citizens Prohibit Intervention Primarily for the Sake of Citizens of Other Countries?

For many years, at least in the United States, political rhetoric has been based on the assumption that the primary *and overriding* responsibility of our government is to promote the welfare of its own citizens. Aid to other nations, then, must be justified by arguing that it ultimately benefits us at home. Some politicians may regard this merely as pragmatic rhetoric, but others take a principled stand that any aid to others must "pay off" for us. In their view, we can never legitimately intervene in foreign countries for *humanitarian* purposes as defined here—that is, primarily for the sake of citizens of other countries—because a government's sole business is the welfare of its own local citizens. Does Kant endorse and provide support for this attitude?

Several factors might at first lead one to think so. In *The Metaphysics of Morals* (and the Doctrine of Right more specifically) Kant focuses primarily on relations between a government and its own people. He addresses international relations briefly, apparently with each head of state conceived as the representative of the rights and interests of its own citizens.[24] Cosmopolitan right is acknowledged, but it is primarily a weak negative right of peaceful foreigners not to be harmed when they land in one's territory.[25] Kant urges rulers to try to end all war, but this is generally in the interest of their own citizens. Moreover, rulers are not expected to compromise their local sovereignty in order to create a world government, even if it might better guarantee world peace and justice than a voluntary union would.[26] Kant argues that a government's authority presupposes the idea of the united will of the people governed, with no overt reference to the will or interests of outsiders.[27] The social contract theories of Hobbes and Rousseau obviously influenced Kant's political thinking, and, in very different ways,

---

[24] Kant (1996a), 114–24 [6: 343–55].

[25] Ibid. 121–2 [6: 352–3].

[26] Ibid. 114–15 [6: 344], 119 [6: 350–1]; (2006), 78–81 [8: 354–7].

[27] Regarding the necessity and roles of a united will, see e.g. Kant (1996a), 6: 315, 267, 316, 340; (2006) [8: 371, 383].

they present government authority as derived *from* the people governed and *for* their benefit.

None of this, however, commits Kant to the extreme view that a government must act exclusively for the sake of its own people. Kant understandably focused most attention on law and justice within a state. He had a full agenda for domestic justice: for example, to correct errors in previous social contract and natural law theories, to oppose a right to revolution without denying standards of justice for rulers, to justify coercion for the sake of liberty, and to affirm a retributive principle of punishment on secular grounds. His discussions of cosmopolitan right, the goal of world peace, and the preconditions of state sovereignty do not by themselves forbid heads of state from acting for the sake of citizens of other countries. As we know, in his fifth preliminary article (quoted earlier), Kant rejects helping them by forcibly intervening in the governance of their countries. His reason, however, was not that each government must be exclusively concerned with the rights and interests of its own citizens, but that, to the contrary, forcible interference would *violate the rights of the citizens of the other country*.

Whatever the merits of this argument (to which I return shortly), at least it makes clear that Kant thought that heads of state must take into account the rights of citizens of other countries. "By virtue of his humanity," Kant says, every person has an innate right of freedom and equality.[28] This right becomes determinate and enforceable only within a structured legal order, but in that context it grounds and limits what state authorities can permissibly do. It also lies behind Kant's argument that people in anarchy or "a state of nature" can rightly be forced to join and maintain a legal order. The innate right, though not a determinate legal right, would seem as well to provide a broadly justice-based presumption in favor of some humanitarian interventions apart from any more narrowly "ethical" presumption, even though Kant assumed he had further arguments that cancel or override the presumptions.[29]

---

[28] Kant (1996a), 30 [6: 237–8].

[29] A presumption, unlike a "prima facie" duty or reason, can be totally canceled without residue, not just "overridden," when certain conditions are not satisfied. To avoid confusion, we could say that, *absent further argument*, human dignity and the "innate right" create the *reasonable expectation* that Kant's theory would permit humanitarian interventions in certain cases.

Is it then a violation of the state's authority for it to use the resources of its citizens to aid people beyond its borders *whether or not it benefits its own citizens*? A reasonable Kant*ian* theory, in my opinion, would say, "No, we must appropriately respect the right and dignity of humanity everywhere and our government must at least take into account their vital interests for their sake, not just when it proves to be beneficial to us at home." Why? The right and dignity of humanity are necessary moral values for all individuals, citizens as well as government officials. Each citizen should will that, *by all permissible means*, the humanity of all human beings be respected, regardless of national borders. The special responsibility of government officials, arguably, is to respect and carry out, within a just constitutional framework, the will of the citizens, so far as it is reasonable and informed. At least, as Kant says, they should govern in such a way that "the will of the people" *could* accept their laws.[30] The "could" here obviously does not mean "psychologically capable" or "could consistently with their self-interested plans." The question is: Would it be *contrary to practical reason* for the citizens to accept the laws or policies? That is, is there *any sound argument that would prevent reasonable, duly informed citizens from accepting* the laws or government policies? Government officials need not be limited to policies that are endorsed by citizens focused exclusively on their own self-interest. Arguably, reasonable and informed citizens *could* (and should) be willing to make some sacrifices to rescue and extend justice to oppressed people in other countries, assuming it is otherwise permissible. If humanitarian interventions are always forbidden, then, it must be on other grounds.

IV. Does the Case for Humanitarian Intervention Depend on Illegitimate Ideas about the Right to Punish or Forfeiture of the Right to Govern?

Often arguments for intervention in the affairs of another state are based on the contention that the governing powers in the other state have committed such serious moral offenses, injustices, or "crimes against humanity" that they deserve to be punished. Intervention is seen as a way to punish those

---

[30] Kant (1996*a*), 51 [8: 297]; cf. 161 [7: 91].

who have abused their power. The forceful intervention may be seen as itself a form of punishment or merely as a step toward a punishment to take place later. By definition, humanitarian interventions do not have punishment as their primary aim. However, it might be thought that the fact that the governing powers deserve punishment establishes a foreign power's right to interfere even when the primary purpose is to prevent harm to oppressed citizens. Thus, if Kant has sound arguments against a right to punish unjust rulers, then at least a familiar strategy to justify humanitarian interventions would fail.

Kant's views on punishment are notoriously harsh, but his position is often misunderstood and exaggerated.[31] He maintains that judicial punishment within a state should be meted out to all and only criminal offenders in accord with the law of retribution (*lex talionis*) and that, with some limits, the punishment ought to be equivalent in degree and kind to the offense. Sentences should not be reduced for pragmatic or humanitarian reasons, and criminals are almost never to be pardoned. Even those who resist an oppressive tyrant may be justly punished.[32]

Kant insists, however, that there are strict conditions for the just imposition of judicial punishment. We may expect that God will ultimately punish the wicked according to their inner deserts, but it is not the task or right of the state to assess inner worthiness of persons.[33] What criminals "deserve" from the judicial system is not divine retribution, but rather the proportionate penalties antecedently threatened in clear, accessible criminal laws that give citizens a fair opportunity to avoid crime. The justification of the practice of punishment, arguably, is "to hinder hindrances to freedom." Extra-legal attempts to punish adults are unjust. The head of state, Kant argues, cannot legitimately be punished even by his own people, while in power or afterwards, because the conditions for just legal punishment are absent. Just punishment presupposes a lawful condition in which it is unambiguously determinate who has the ultimate authority and power to make and enforce laws within a given jurisdiction.

We may question Kant's theory of punishment, but for now let us focus on its implications regarding intervention. Clearly, intervention *for punitive*

---

[31] Kant (1996a), 104–13 [6: 331–42].

[32] Kant (2006), 105 [8: 382]. A possible exception would be when state officials order one to do something "intrinsically immoral," Kant (1996a) [6: 371].

[33] For references and support of this interpretation, see Hill (2000), ch. 7, and Hill (2002), ch. 10.

purposes would be forbidden in the absence of an international legal system that approximated in relevant respects Kant's conception of the juridical condition of a state.[34] Although skeptical about world government, Kant urged the development of a world federation that mirrors in some respects subsequent development of international law. It is unclear, I think, whether the international order now satisfies reasonable Kantian conditions for the just punishment of oppressive rulers, but for present purposes we can bypass that issue. The primary purpose of humanitarian intervention, as I have defined it, is not punishment but rescue. Let us stipulate, for now, that punishment cannot even be a secondary purpose. The question remains, however, does an outside power have the *right* to pursue its humanitarian aim by forceful intervention? The accusation that a government is wrongfully oppressing its citizens may be relevant to this question, even if punishment is not an option. A long tradition of political philosophy maintains that by extreme wrongdoing rulers can *forfeit their right* to govern. This is a modest residue of the claim that the rulers deserve to be punished: at least, it is argued, they cease to have any right to continue to rule.

Natural law theorists, such as Thomas Aquinas and John Locke, have no qualms about the idea of a *forfeitable right* to govern because they presuppose a nonsecular legal order headed by God. Rousseau does not appeal to the idea of forfeit in this sort of quasi-legal framework, but nevertheless he insists that governments that ignore the general will of the people are merely imposing their own will by *might*, not right. Although he rejects other features of Hobbes's philosophy, Kant follows Hobbes in denying that a government can forfeit its right to govern by wrongdoing. At least this is so within limits necessary for it to be a "government" as opposed to a rogue regime that uses force but has no authority. Kant holds that, although there are reason-based standards of justice that rulers *should* respect, so long as they retain their *power* to govern they do not lose their *rightful authority* to govern even if they are despotisms that, within some minimal limits, govern very badly.[35] Kant's underlying reason, apparently, is that (strictly) the ideas of *rights* and *rightful authority to govern* make sense only in a system that has and *enforces* rules that unambiguously determine the members' responsibilities

---

[34] For Kant's explicit opposition to punitive wars see e.g. his (1996a), 117 [6: 347]. Kant also opposes "the moral annihilation of a state," e.g. by merger or reducing the people to servitude, but humanitarian interventions need not take this form. Ibid.

[35] See n. 5.

and say who is to prevail in case of conflict.[36] Moral complaints by individuals against their rulers may be correct, but they are complaints outside the framework of determinate adjudication and enforcement that Kant thought necessary to establish or undermine (full-fledged) claims of *right*.

For these reasons, it *seems* that (with qualifications noted) Kant must reject the argument that *because the government's mistreatment of its subjects has undermined its right to rule*, forceful intervention is a legitimate means to further humanitarian aims. Those of us who, despite Kant's arguments, think that humanitarian intervention *is* sometimes justified have several possible responses. First, we can question whether Kant has adequate grounds for his extreme premises: namely, (*a*) that (full-fledged) rights claims make sense only in a framework of determinate adjudication and enforcement and (*b*) that traditional appeals to natural law, the common good, the general will, and other widely acknowledged moral standards for government must only be guides that ruling powers should voluntarily consult, never grounds for extra-legal interference with a de facto government.

A second line of response would be to develop and extend Kant's suggestion in *Perpetual Peace* that we must establish, so far as possible, international organizations and agreements that serve for many purposes as a moral surrogate for world government. As these continue to develop, they might satisfy some of Kant's concerns for determinacy, general acceptance, and enforcement as preconditions for claims of right and authority. Moreover, arguably, some indeterminacy and irregularities of enforcement must be tolerated in the early stages of an emerging international order just as, one imagines, these imperfections would need to have been tolerated in the early stages of transition from a lawless "state of nature" to the legal order of a nation-state. Despite the fictions of social contract theorists, the move from a lawless to a lawful condition is rarely, if ever, an all-at-once seamless transition. Kant conceded that the ideal of justice could be fully realized only in a republic, but he argued that governments that fell short of this ideal must nevertheless be tolerated and obeyed in the transitional periods in which subjects hope and work for gradual reform. Kant acknowledged,

---

[36] Kant does write of "rights" prior to the existence of a legal order, but he treats these in effect as "ought-to-be-legal-rights" or claims grounded in practical reason that can and should become full-fledged rights within a legal system.

then, the rational necessity in some circumstances to respect and conform to imperfectly just systems. He himself had more tolerance for imperfections in the form of government than for ambiguities in the power structure and irregularities of enforcement, but his preference here may well be questioned.

A third response would be to explore a possible gap in Kant's argument that a ruler's mistreatment of his subjects never undermines his right and authority to rule. We can distinguish a ruler's rights with respect to his subjects from his rights with respect to those outside his jurisdiction. Kant's discussions of the right to govern (and the specific rights of the governing authorities) concentrate almost exclusively on their rights with respect to the citizens over whom they have authority. His reason for this limited focus, I assume, is that, absent world government and enforceable treaties, the relations between the governing powers in different states cannot be *full-fledged legal rights*, that is, matters of right (*Recht*) in the strictest sense. In *Perpetual Peace* Kant proposes articles for international relations that he regards as rational and reasonable, but apparently in Kant's view, they remain want-to-be-rights and counsels for prudent and wise statecraft. The relevant point for present purposes is that, *absent further argument*, a ruler's right to govern his subjects does not entail that he has a right against foreign powers that they not interfere with his governance. Even if, as Kant says, citizens have an almost unlimited juridical duty to obey the laws of their ruler, this does not by itself imply that those outside his jurisdiction must respect his right to rule.[37] Thus, without further argument, Kant provides no sufficient reason why foreign governments may not forcefully intervene if this, on balance, would further a significant humanitarian purpose. Without claiming the legal authority to punish the oppressive ruler or even contending that he has forfeited his legal rights with respect to his subjects, the foreign governments may nevertheless consider the gross

---

[37] Assuming the absence of world government and binding international treaties, then Kant must (like Hobbes) view the head of one state as in a state of nature with respect to the head of another state—apart from considerations of the cosmopolitan rights of outsiders and proto-rights (or ought-to-be-rights) reason requires one to consider even in a state of nature. The latter, I take it, might ground an argument that the head of state should seek, by coercion if necessary, to enter into lawful, or law-like relations, with all outsiders, unless the prior organization of the outsiders into a state of their own somehow makes this impermissible. The next section considers an argument to support the latter, i.e. that once the outsiders are within a state of their own they may not be coerced into a different (e.g. more comprehensive) legal order.

injustice of the ruler as a moral consideration relevant to the justification of their humanitarian intervention.

Kant does in fact have a supplementary argument that, if sound, would block this last response. This supplementary argument, to which I turn next, is that intervention in the governance of a state by foreign powers violates the rights of the citizens of that state. The question remains whether this final argument is sound and decisive in all cases.

For present purposes, then, I want to concede that a ruler's oppressive behavior toward his own citizens may not justify foreign powers' efforts to *punish* him and that he has not *forfeited* his rights with respect to his subjects. This, however, does not mean that humanitarian interventions, as defined here, are always unwarranted. A punitive purpose is ruled out, and the right to intervene is not established by the idea that "the wicked deserve punishment." But the intervention might still violate the *rights of the people* in the state that is targeted for intervention.

V. Does Forceful Intervention in the Governance of Another State Necessarily Violate the Rights of the Citizens of that State?

In *Perpetual Peace* Kant argues very briefly for the fifth preliminary article, that "no state shall by force intervene with the constitution or government of another state."[38] He focuses on interference, not in a civil war or anarchy, but in a state suffering from "internal dissention," which is in fact the usual condition when the issue of humanitarian intervention arises. His basic argument is implicit in the question, "What is here to authorize [the intervention]?" More positively, he argues, "Intervention would infringe on the rights of an independent people struggling with its internal disease; hence it would itself be an offense and would render the autonomy of states insecure."[39] Further he asserts something never at issue, namely that "the evil into which the state has fallen" (through "lawlessness") does not violate the rights of "free" people in other states, and from this he infers something

38 Kant (2006), 70 [8: 346].
39 Ibid.

that may seem to us rather callous, namely that the evil in the foreign state should simply serve as a scandalous example and warning to free people elsewhere.[40]

The background assumption is that the intervention is not authorized by a world government, by binding treaties, or even by the limited "right of nations" to go to war, for example in response to unwarranted aggression or threat.[41] The so-called "right of nations" and its limits are not, of course, full-fledged juridical rights, assuming there is no sufficiently determinate system of international lawmaking, adjudication, and enforcement. Instead, these "rights" and their limits are supposed to be what practical reason prescribes for national self-protection constrained by the need to seek perpetual peace. In any case, Kant insinuates that nothing *authorizes* interventions. But what, we may ask, is supposed to *prohibit* them?

A tempting, but ultimately confused, response might seem to follow from a combination of Kant's contentions. To summarize briefly, he holds, first, that we must presume a united will of the people in favor of the government in power (so long as it maintains a juridical condition) because ambiguity of authority is incompatible with a legal order; further, that the ultimate source of authority must be the will of the people subject to the laws; and finally, that allowing extra-legal determinations of the united will of the people would yield ambiguity and conflicting judgments. From these premises one might argue that interference in the lawful governance of a state by outsiders always disrespects the will of the people in the country in which the interference takes place. This might be said to violate those citizens' "rights" to authorize their own government, at least in a broad sense of "rights."

Perhaps if duly qualified an argument of this sort might have some force, but it seems to me utterly implausible that it could ground an absolute

---

[40] The impression of callousness would be warranted if the attitude expressed were "Because they did not strictly violate *our* rights we should just let them suffer *in order to* serve as a warning to others to avoid dissension and lawlessness." This suggests that letting them suffer is justified simply as a means to the moral/political instruction of others. This would be both callous and un-Kantian, I think, especially if the suffering is obvious, very great, and consists in deprivation of basic necessities of life as rational autonomous agents. Kant's remark, however, would not be callous in the way suggested if he had, as he thought, a decisive reason against the interference quite apart from its utility as a warning to others. Then the utility of non-intervention as a warning is merely a consolation, a foreseen good side-effect, of refraining from what would be wrong and unjust independently of such consequences.

[41] See Kant (1996a), 116–17 [6: 346–7].

prohibition on interventions, humanitarian or otherwise. The reason is that when a ruling government seriously and persistently mistreats its people, the presumption that it is backed by the united will of the people is either false or without normative force. On the one hand, it is *false* if we understand the "united will" in the normative sense that Rousseau typically uses, for this holds that a necessary condition of there being a united or general will in favor or laws is that these are for the common good, not a consequentialist aggregated good, but the good of each and all as citizens. The appeal to the united will is *without normative force*, on the other hand, if it is simply a stipulation for political and legal purposes that whatever (minimally legitimate) government exercises the power to make, adjudicate, and enforce laws is backed by the "united will." The argument in question tries to have it both ways. It stipulates that we must regard the powers that be as representing the united will of the people, and then it tries to borrow the normative force of the idea of a "united will" that depends on a condition that is absent—the government's genuinely serving the common good.

I conclude this preliminary inquiry with these suggestions: (1) Kant's ethics rightly indicates that there is a presumption in favor of humanitarian interventions in some cases; (2) it wisely points to grounds for caution, avoiding punitive motives, and respecting the reasonable will of the citizens in other states; but, absent further arguments, (3) it fails to provide adequate reasons for an absolute prohibition of humanitarian interventions in all cases.

15

Moral Responsibilities of Bystanders

My aim here is, first, to frame my question about the responsibility to resist oppression, second, to describe briefly three second-order responsibilities especially pertinent to "bystanders," third, to note some connections to often overlooked aspects of Kant's ethics, and, finally, to suggest very briefly how we might see neglect of these responsibilities as failures to respect both oneself and others. My main question is about *forward-looking*, preparatory moral responsibilities of those who take the role of bystanders in situations of oppression.[1] The three special responsibilities are second-order responsibilities to exercise due care in deliberation, to scrutinize one's motives for passivity, and to try to develop virtue conceived as strength of will to do what is right despite obstacles. The three responsibilities are drawn from Kant's later writings on ethics and religion, where Kant seems to take more seriously the problem that many moral failures are due to negligence rather than intentional wrongdoing. By neglect of the special second-order duties, we contribute to the ongoing oppression of others, but we also fail to respect ourselves properly insofar as we do not do what we can to implement our basic moral commitments.

---

[1] Most discussions of oppression, quite understandably, focus on first-order responsibilities, that is, how and when *to act* to resist oppression, to change the social conditions that feed it, and to ameliorate its effects. Here, instead, I discuss several second-order responsibilities regarding how we should make ourselves ready to fulfill these first-order responsibilities—through proper deliberation, self-understanding, and self-discipline. These are actually moral responsibilities that everyone has but are especially important for, and commonly neglected by those I call "bystanders." A more specific but unwieldy title for this chapter, then, might have been "Certain preparatory, second-order moral responsibilities especially pertinent to bystanders disinclined to resist oppression." Thanks are due to anonymous reviewers and to Bernard Boxill, Sarah Buss, Ann E. Cudd, Jean Harvey, Anita Superson, and other participants at the American Philosophical Association, Central Division, session on "Responsibility for Resisting Oppression," 19 April 2008.

Roles in Oppression: Primary Agents, Bystanders, and Victims

Oppression, I assume, is a systematic, persistent, and damaging mistreatment of members of a group of people identified, for example, by race, religion, gender, or ethnicity.[2] It takes many forms including slavery, physical abuse, political domination, social castes, demeaning stereotypes, and more subtle cultural norms. Paradigm examples are the treatment of Jews in Hitler's Germany, of blacks under apartheid South Africa, and of women in Taliban-controlled Afghanistan. Our own history, of course, provides familiar examples closer to home. In all these cases oppression is maintained through an ideological framework that enables the oppressors to regard themselves as justified in their behavior and encourages the oppressed to accept their inferior status as natural and fitting.

Our task, however, is not so much to explain the nature of oppression as to discuss the responsibility to resist oppression. For this purpose, we can take for granted our rough understanding of what oppression is. We can also assume that it is a bad thing that should be opposed, resisted, and eliminated, so far as possible, by legitimate and effective means. To say in general *why* oppression is wrong we might appeal to human rights and their ground in fundamental moral ideals of equality, freedom, and humanity, but details would depend on the examples and context. But again, our task here is not to make the case that oppression is immoral but rather to discuss our responsibility to resist oppression. Within a system of oppression our responsibility will vary (to some extent) depending on our place in the system. The *primary agents of oppression*, for example, typically bear a different and greater responsibility than *bystanders*, and both the primary oppressor and the bystander normally have more responsibility than the *victims*. Details of what each is responsible *for doing* depend, of course, on what legitimate means of resistance are available, the moral costs of resistance in the context, and so on. My main focus will be on certain second-order responsibilities of those I call "bystanders," but my conclusions have broader implications.

These distinctions—*primary oppressor, bystander,* and *victim*—are admittedly somewhat artificial and imprecise, but I hope they will be clear enough

---

[2] For a thorough analysis see Cudd (2006), esp. ch. 7 regarding responsibility to resist Marilyn Frye's classic account of oppression is the essay "Oppression," in her (1983), 1–16.

for present purposes. We might argue that, in a sense, any nonresisting bystander is also guilty of oppression and that everyone, even the primary oppressor, is ultimately a victim of an oppressive system. Such arguments have a point, but here I think it may be useful to focus attention initially on somewhat simplified paradigms.

Forward-Looking Responsibility versus Culpability

My main interest here, and in moral theory generally, is with what I call *forward-looking moral responsibility* as opposed to mere *causal responsibility* or *backward-looking moral responsibility* for past misdeeds. We can ask what was responsible for something in a purely causal sense: for example, what was responsible for the extinction of the dinosaurs?[3] The (more literal) responsibility we are interested in here, however, is a *moral* responsibility. So our question is not: "What were the acts, events, forces, and circumstances that brought about the system we now regard as oppressive?" Rather it is: "What is the *moral* responsibility of those who have various roles within an oppressive system?" Our question is also forward-looking, not essentially tied to blame or punishment. The forward-looking normative question is not "Who is to blame (or even liable) for having initiated, practiced, or tolerated oppression?" but rather "Given their place in a context of oppression, what are those in each position *now* morally responsible *for doing* to change or resist the system and its particular manifestations?"

The main idea here, I trust, is familiar. Normally when I take a job, commit to a partnership, or otherwise willingly participate in a more or less just association, I take on certain responsibilities. That is, given my position, it is my responsibility to bring about certain desirable future occurrences and to prevent others. At least I must try. This is not only because convention says so, but because (and so far as) living up to the conventional expectations or "responsibilities" of my position is required by the principles and values of a broader moral perspective. I also have forward-looking responsibilities because of social relations I did not choose, for example being a son, a brother, or a white man in a racist and sexist world. Our forward-looking

---

[3] We may even speak of human acts as responsible for consequences in the same morally neutral causal sense: for example, Jim's eating toxic wild berries, not a heart attack, was responsible for his death.

responsibilities are often clear when we voluntarily take a job in a just social system; but when we find ourselves within a system of oppression, we take on roles defined by that system, whether we like it or not. Setting aside questions of blame, the pertinent question becomes "What is it my responsibility to do now, given my position in this deplorable social scheme?"

As I have said, the issue here is moral responsibility, which should not be confused with merely being a salient link in a causal chain of conditions and forces that result in an outcome. The questions are "What is the range of things that it is my *moral job*, as it were, to take charge of—to promote and to protect, or, when necessary, to fix or reform?" and so "What must I do now?" and not "What have I done to cause this situation?" It is easy to be confused here because, like the word "responsible," the word "cause" can be used in different ways. As others have noted, in moral and legal contexts the question who is (or would be) *the cause* of an undesirable event is partly determined by our normative judgments.[4] Typically when we ask "Who caused these riots?" we are not merely interested in tracing all the complex forces that explain an event in a neutral sociological sense. Sometimes we are interested in who was the blameworthy or morally liable cause, but not always. We may be primarily concerned to identify whose moral task it is (was and will be) to prevent such occurrences. This is often a question of backward-looking accountability and blame, but at each present moment we also face the forward-looking moral question, "If certain bad events occur or bad conditions persist, would I then be rightly regarded as (morally speaking) the cause?" In other words, "Is it my responsibility to prevent them?"

These distinctions are important to how we see the purpose and method of moral philosophy. For some, such as Kant, the primary question is: "What ought *I* to do?" This leads us to focus directly on the *moral reasons for doing or refraining* from doing various things. What to do (or avoid) in response to others' wrongdoing (or one's own) is a secondary and derivative matter. For others, such as Hume, the primary question is: "What acts and traits of character appropriately prompt our approval and disapproval, admiration and contempt?" This leads us to focus directly on our reactive attitudes rather than the reasons, from a moral point of view, for making one

---

⁴ See Hart and Honoré (1959), 62–84; Donagan (1977), 37–52; and Hitchcock and Knobe (2009), 11: 587–612.

choice or another. The merits of these different approaches can be debated, but the difference, I think, matters. I mention it here just to emphasize that the reason for setting aside questions of blame, at least initially, in our discussions of responsibility to resist oppression need not be a soft-hearted or too accepting or forgiving attitude toward those who perpetuate oppression. The point, rather, is to focus attention where it is most needed, on each person's moral task to identify and take whatever steps he or she can to oppose and eliminate oppression. Just as in my earlier essay "Servility and Self-Respect," it was not my purpose "to blame the victim," in this discussion my aim is not to blame the bystanders (even if they are probably more culpable than the victims) but to reflect on what we who stand somewhere between the primary oppressors and victims should be doing.

The Bystander: A Paradigm

For purposes of discussion, as I have said, I want to focus attention on a certain kind of person who plays a certain role in situations of oppression. At first I point to some examples to indicate roughly the main differences between bystanders, primary oppressors, and victims. Then I narrow the characterization of bystanders by simply stipulating that those I call *bystanders* here have certain features.[5] I hope that the type is recognizable, but I make no claims about how often the paradigm is instantiated or by whom. The stipulations of bystanders' situations and attitudes are helpful by exposing clearly the need for the second-order responsibilities to be discussed, but in other respects the distinction between primary oppressors, bystanders, and victims can be left rough, intuitive, and indicated by examples. Although perhaps important in other contexts, a more fine-grained distinction is not needed for my purposes here. The aim here is to focus on bystanders in order to draw attention to three preparatory responsibilities that directly concern moral needs that are especially clear in bystanders but are shared to some extent by everyone.

---

[5] My conception of bystanders here is narrower than the term may initially suggest and includes only a subclass of examples that are well discussed by others. See e.g. Howard McGary's "Psychological Violence and Institutional Racism: The Moral Responsibility of Bystanders," in Thomas (2008), ch. 19.

Examples of bystanders, provided they have the features stipulated below, would be the "ordinary" German people during the Nazi era who were not in the SS, did not vote for Hitler, and were not aware of "the final solution," but saw Jews being humiliated and having property confiscated and yet did not protest or try to stop it. Another example might be my Southern Presbyterian ancestors who tolerated segregation and Jim Crow in the South with only mild moral discomfort. They had some compassion for minority individuals, for example their maids and nannies, but did not notice systematic oppression inconsistent with their own fundamental principles. Further examples might include men who see themselves as "enlightened" about sexism, who do not beat their wives or deliberately discriminate against women in hiring but still remain insensitive to subtle offenses to women and treat systemic sexism as not their fault or their problem. The bystanders in these cases contrast with primary oppressors, for example Hitler, Himmler, the SS, the KKK, Bull Connor, racist lynch mobs, or men who beat their wives, commit rape, preach that women must obey their husbands, and so on. Bystanders, nevertheless, can be enablers of oppression in ways that amount to complicity. They may be regarded as oppressing or adding to the oppression of the victims through their omissions and passivity.

In order to focus on certain moral defects, we can stipulate that those regarded as being *bystanders* here also have these features: (1) they do not *intend* to harm, exploit, or oppress anyone; (2) they are either unaware of the wrongful oppression or they think that they have no responsibility to do anything about it; (3) there is in fact serious oppression in the situation all around them; (4) they do have at least forward-looking (first-order) responsibilities to try to eliminate, oppose, diminish, and/or ameliorate the effects of the oppression; (5) they see themselves as basically people of good will, well-meaning people who would not tolerate atrocities, gross injustices, or systems of abuse in their communities, at least not if they had any legitimate and effective way to prevent or stop them; (6) for the most part, they are in fact fundamentally people of good will who would not knowingly and entirely willingly[6] tolerate preventable atrocities, gross injustices, and

---

[6] I am supposing here that failures due primarily to moral weakness, ignorance, and some kinds of self-deception are not "entirely willing" in the way that intentional, fully aware, and whole-hearted wrongdoing is willing. But separating cases becomes very difficult. Moral weakness of will, as I see it, is not a disability like physical weakness but more like having a will that is less than fully effective because

systems of abuse in their communities; and (7) among the things that keep them from a more realistic, painful, and effective awareness of their actual situation and first-order responsibilities are reluctance to disturb a familiar way of life, aversion to effort and risk, habits of making excuses and blaming others, a public culture that masks oppression, the influence of primary oppressors who intentionally put a favorable "spin" on its symptoms, the support of other self-justifying bystanders, and other social conditions that promote conformity and undermine confidence in one's ability to think for oneself.

These stipulated features would not be sufficient by themselves to distinguish bystanders from primary oppressors or even victims, but the rough distinction should be familiar enough from examples. Intuitively "primary oppressors" actively oppress by overt wrongdoing; "bystanders" passively let this happen by standing idly by; and "victims" are those wronged by the others. The clearest examples of bystanders are cases of basically good but weak and excuse-making people who quietly observe others' overt acts of sexist or racist abuse but do not intervene. More subtle examples, however, would include cases of well-meaning husbands and employers who avoid overt sexist and racist offenses but contribute indirectly to an oppressive system by their passive acceptance of its supporting social norms.

Three Second-Order Moral Responsibilities

Suppose we focus our attention on the moral failings of the (potentially not-so-innocent) bystander that I have described, not to assign blame but to see more clearly what we, bystanders to oppression, have a moral responsibility to do. Now our primary (first-order) responsibility is clear *in general*, though its applications to specific circumstances are often hard to determine. Most obviously, we *must* do what we can to oppose and eliminate oppression, by all morally *legitimate* means consistent with other equal or stronger obligations (acknowledging possible limits on the sacrifices each individual must

---

it is divided against itself, as it were. Moral ignorance and relevant self-deception may be due to neglect of the second-order responsibilities that I consider here, even if it is not entirely willing and whether or not the agent is blameworthy for it.

bear).[7] What means are available, and which are morally permissible to use, and which are strictly required must be determined for (and perhaps in) each context. Should we use violence, civil disobedience, or only lawful protests? Can we change the system by these or other means? Is symbolic protest called for even if there are no effective means to change the system or block its application to a particular case?[8] These are important questions, but I want to raise a question about the *second-order responsibilities* of all bystanders, regardless of their special circumstances. That is, what must we *do to understand and implement* our primary responsibility to oppose and try to eliminate oppression? More specifically, what are our responsibilities to make ourselves ready of mind and will to see what we must do and to follow through on our best judgment?

A reason for attending to these questions, at least initially, is that they concern responsibilities of deliberation that are prior to and to some extent independent of the special circumstances of each case of oppression. We cannot expect moral philosophy to articulate more than general principles and values relevant to varying situations. Although general principles and prior abstract reflection can be helpful, what we should do specifically in each case (our particular first-order responsibility) must be judged by each person in the particular oppressive circumstance.[9] For this reason we need to reflect not only on the principles about what to do on the ground or in the streets, as it were, but also on how to be ready to make good judgments when faced with particular oppressive situations.

Another reason for focusing on the second-order responsibilities of the bystander is that neglect of these seems an especially characteristic and damaging defect in bystanders (as conceived here). My suggestion that this

---

[7] A possible qualification to the idea that we should do "*whatever* we legitimately can" is that, in addition to the constraint that we must not use immoral means, our moral duty to sacrifice our personal interests for the cause may be limited to some extent. Our duty to work for the elimination of injustice and other wrongdoing in the world must be compatible with our other duties and, in addition, it may be limited by the idea that, although we each have a moral responsibility to do our fair share to solve these problems, doing substantially more may be above and beyond duty—morally commendable but not strictly required. How much each is responsible for doing, arguably, depends on circumstances: the seriousness of the evil, one's relations to it, one's ability to help, the moral side-effects, and so on. Thanks to Sarah Buss for emphasizing this point in discussion.

[8] Hill (1991) is concerned with possible reasons one might have for protesting in these circumstances.

[9] This is not to say, of course, that there are no criteria for the individual's judgment, that she must be correct whatever she judges, or that the judgment should be without advice and consultation with others.

neglect is *especially characteristic* of bystanders, however, is not essential here because primary oppressors and victims share the same second-order responsibilities even if neglect of them is not their most evident problem.

Consider again my paradigm bystanders. Although I stipulated that they intend the (primary) victim no harm, there are things they could legitimately do to fight oppression that they do not do. They fail to see the problem, or make self-deceptive excuses and blame others, or fail through weakness of will to follow through on their fundamental moral commitments. My suggestion is that these failings point to three distinguishable second-order responsibilities: a duty of *due care* in moral deliberation, a duty of *moral self-scrutiny*, and a duty to *develop moral virtue*. These are responsibilities articulated in Kant's later ethical writings, but arguably they should be acknowledged in any moral theory. They are responsibilities that everyone has, but responsibilities that seem especially important for (basically) well-meaning bystanders to reflect on.[10] Their moral failings may be more open to self-correction than those of the primary oppressors, and their failings seem more in need of attention than those of the primary victims.[11]

Before we consider these responsibilities in more detail, it may be worth noting that they are responsibilities often thought to be missing from Kant's moral theory. This may be because Kant's famous examples in the *Groundwork for the Metaphysics of Morals* concern people who are aware of the morally relevant facts, prepared to formulate and test their maxims, and are easily able to identify and avoid the wrongdoing. This is most obvious in the cases of intentional lying, false promising, and suicide, but Kant presents even the failures to develop talents and help others as cases in which the agents know their maxims, question them morally, and easily see that they

---

[10] One might suppose that primary oppressors, who intentionally and willingly mistreat others, most obviously and characteristically fail in these second-order responsibilities, but I am imagining that primary oppressors either lack genuine moral commitment (for Kant, "a good will") or else have a deep misunderstanding or distorted view of what morality requires. It is not weakness of moral will, for example, that causes them to oppress others, for their moral will is deficient to start with. Due care in moral thinking now might be a good beginning toward change, but it is not a matter of clearing away minor confusions and factual errors in order to "see" what they must do. Kant may have thought that the Inquisitors had the clear "moral law" within them so that they only needed to consult and apply it "with due care," but I doubt this is how it was for Eichmann and Himmler.

[11] My thought here is that primary oppressors, such as Hitler, Bull Connor, and self-justifying wife-beaters, may have deeply distorted "moral" ideas and/or psychological disorders that would block any path to reform through reflection, self-scrutiny, and developing a stronger will to do what they think is right. And primary victims may rightly be more concerned with survival and self-protection than improving their character, motives, or deliberations.

should (and presumably can) avoid acting on them.[12] The characteristic failings of the bystander, I suggest, are due to negligence of a different kind—that is, wrongdoing resulting from failure to exercise due care in deliberation, to scrutinize one's motives and excuses honestly, and to make oneself ready to stand up and act on one's moral beliefs.[13] These are duties that Kant includes in his later ethical writings, *The Metaphysics of Morals* and *Religion within the Limits of Mere Reason.* No one, I imagine, sets out *deliberately* to remain blind to morally relevant reasons, to indulge a self-righteous opinion of his motives, or to live in serious conflict with his basic moral beliefs. But it is our responsibility to avoid these failings insofar as we can. We can act, of course, only within the limits of our awareness and understanding, and so arguably one task of moral philosophy is to highlight and explain the relevant second-order responsibilities in order to encourage and help people who are basically good to see the problem. Once we see our second-order responsibilities clearly, it is up to us to resolve (or "will the maxim") to fulfill these responsibilities. Together, they are an important part of seriously trying to do what is right (which for Kant is the essence of "a good will").

The Duty of Due Care in Moral Deliberation

In *Religion* Kant considers the Inquisitors who burned people at the stake for heresy.[14] He does not deny that they were generally conscientious men

---

[12] Kant (2002), 222–4 [4: 421–3], 230–1 [4: 429–30].

[13] The second-order duties I describe may be (or seem) hard to fit into Kant's system of moral thought. For example, Kant suggests that ordinary people, apparently without much effort to reflect carefully on moral questions, can readily know what their (primary) moral duties are. He only rarely (though sometimes) admits that serious moral errors are possible. If what is the right thing to do is always obvious without much reflection, it seems that there should be no need for a duty of due care in moral reflection. Second, regarding the duty of moral self-scrutiny, it might seem to be undermined by Kant's repeated insistence that we cannot know or judge with any confidence what are our deep motives. If these are really deeply hidden or inaccessible, what is the point of self-scrutiny, one might ask? Third, weakness of will is a puzzling concept for Kant because it does not (fully) excuse wrongdoing (and so cannot be an inability to do right, strictly speaking), and yet it is supposed to be a kind of "weakness" in the agent's good "will" to do right that leads somehow to acting on a bad maxim. If all free acts are interpreted as acting on a maxim, wrongdoing from weak will must be willing to act on a bad maxim. But how is that compatible with the agent at the same time willing (too weakly?) a good maxim to do what is right, as seems needed for a genuine case of moral weakness of will? (I discuss this in ch. 5 above). These are problems I will leave aside for now.

[14] See Kant (1998b), 178–80 [6: 184–7]. Although a duty of due care is acknowledged by others, I cite Kant here to credit a source of influence and to note for those who might think otherwise that Kant did not altogether neglect moral negligence.

who did what they thought was right—saving souls from eternal damnation. But they were gravely mistaken due to their failure to exercise due care when they formed and maintained their opinion that the horrible killings were justified. The Inquisitors were not bystanders to this evil but many others were bystanders who neglected their responsibilities. They watched the burnings without protesting, continued to accept the authority of perpetrators, and did not question the Inquisitors' assumptions or reasoning. Their passivity contributed to the harm and helped to perpetuate an oppressive system. They were "standing idly by" in their minds as well as their behavior. It would not have helped simply to say to them "Stop your abuse of (alleged) heretics" because they saw the burnings as justified or in any case someone else's responsibility. Given their situation, perhaps they could not by themselves come to a better understanding of the situation, or even think it their right to question it. There is no guarantee that their best efforts to assess the morality of the burnings (and their relation to it) would have changed their views, but if they had been aware of the responsibility to think for themselves morally,[15] they might have to some extent seen their place in the system. Similar thoughts apply to the "ordinary" German citizens who passively accepted Hitler's rule, my Presbyterian ancestors who rationalized racial segregation, and many of us today who do not bother to question the social structures that are most familiar to us.

The duty of due care in moral deliberation, as I understand it, calls for us to be sensitive to potentially relevant moral considerations, to check our facts, to make sure that our particular moral opinions follow from our basic moral commitments, and so on. It is a requirement to be conscientious in moral judgment and its recognition presupposes, among other things, some degree of commitment to morality and awareness of its basic values.[16] But

---

[15] See Kant (1996b), 11–22 [8: 35–42].

[16] In *The Metaphysics of Morals* the duty of due care is implicit in "a human being's duty to himself as his own innate judge," Kant (1996a), 188–91 [6: 437–40]. In this section Kant discusses conscience conceived metaphorically as an inner forum analogous to a criminal court. In it one must think of oneself as different persons, by turns the accuser, the defender, and the judge. As judge one hears and assesses evidence that one is failing to fulfill one's responsibilities. Conscience is also seen as warning us unbidden and calling us to court, and it is one's duty to "sharpen one's attentiveness to the voice of the inner judge" (ibid. 161 [6: 401]). The metaphor of courtroom activity, however, also suggests that the duty is to take on seriously the active role of the judge, using reason to weigh evidence scrupulously before exonerating the defendant or rightfully imputing an act or omission as a violation of moral law. For further discussion, see Hill (1998), 13–52. All three second-order preparatory responsibilities are discussed further in ch. 7 of this volume.

our bystanders' neglect of their first-order responsibilities to oppose oppression is not all traceable to cognitive failings, moral or otherwise. The next two sections concern other sources of neglect and second-order responsibilities to counteract them.

The Duty of Moral Self-Scrutiny

The neglect is often due to defects of motivation—sometimes moral weakness (to be considered shortly) but also due to letting our baser inclinations rule us through *self-deception, special pleading, and other ways of representing our motivations to ourselves as better than they are*. The problem here is not straightforward cognitive failure of moral judgment, such as *simply* overlooking relevant facts, making false inferences, or not thinking about the implications of one's moral commitment, though failings of these kinds could be partially due to self-deception and other motivational deficiencies. Instead, the problem now is a motivated tendency that allows us to continue to *act for bad reasons* because *we see them as good reasons*—or simply assume that our motives are good, whatever they are. Misrepresentation of our motives and reasons may be motivated in ways difficult to understand, and our capacity to change may be limited even with a better understanding. But arguably, at least questioning our own motivations for passive toleration of oppression is a necessary starting point if we take seriously our commitment to having good reasons for what we do—and do not do. Our problem as bystanders is that by misrepresenting to ourselves our real reasons for passivity in the face of oppression, we mute the cognitive dissonance and moral distress signals that might motivate us, as basically well-meaning people, to act as we should.

In *The Metaphysics of Morals* Kant sketches his idea of our ethical responsibilities (duties) to others and to ourselves. In a brief section he says that "the first command of all duties to oneself" is "to know (scrutinize, fathom) yourself...in terms of your moral perfection in relation to your duty."[17] This includes a responsibility to guard against a natural tendency to self-deception and excuse-making that keeps us from facing squarely our real motives. Although Kant often notes that our inner motives remain difficult, if not impossible, to see clearly, he writes that self-scrutiny can result in

[17] Kant (1996a), 191 [6: 441–2].

awareness "that will counteract that egotistical self-esteem which takes mere wishes . . . empty of deeds" as "proof of a good heart."[18] Kant's message was partly that we should expose our impure motives without cynically denying "the noble predisposition to the good in us," which makes us worthy of respect despite our faults.[19] But the message most relevant here was that a person of good will, who has a serious overriding commitment to respect human dignity in every person, should take all steps necessary to implement this commitment. This includes scrutinizing one's motives for acting or for remaining passive—for example, standing idly by while oppression continues.

A Duty to Develop Moral Virtue

Sometimes as bystanders we fail to do what we should. This is not because we deliberate carelessly or deceive ourselves about our motives, but because we are morally weak. Although philosophers have long been puzzled about how to understand the idea, common sense acknowledges that, in some important sense, even if we are fundamentally committed to doing what is right, when confronted with obstacles and temptations, sometimes we intentionally do what we know is wrong. Our heart was right, we say, but our will was weak. To say we did wrong because we were weak-willed may partially mitigate culpability, but the relevant *forward-looking* responsibilities here are to anticipate the problem and try to develop ways to overcome or circumvent it. Various ways of getting around the problem have been suggested. For example, an ancient prescription is to develop through practice, by emulating paragons of virtue, good habits and desires until they are "second nature" so that we always will do what is right easily and gladly no matter how difficult the circumstances.[20] Seeing this ideal as not feasible for most of us, indirect means of self-control are often recommended, for example manipulating our environment so that temptations do not arise or external forces keep us from following them.[21] In a context of oppression, however, the bystander already faces formidable external

---

[18] Ibid.

[19] Ibid.

[20] This is more or less Aristotle's view, though Aristotle also emphasizes that we must strive to develop practical wisdom and intellectual capacities that require the use of reason.

[21] Ulysses having himself tied to the mast is a classic example of the use of external forces. Weight Watchers' recommendations for weight control emphasize changes in one's environment.

pressures to remain passive and conform to the status quo norms. There may be relatively little opportunity to change one's environment to reinforce one's general commitment to do what is right.[22] A natural suggestion, then, is that in anticipation we ought to try to develop more strength of will, if we can, so that we can overcome pressures and temptations to remain passive when we realize that we should resist oppression.

Virtue, as Kant conceives it, is strength of moral will, not merely "a good will" (basic commitment to acting rightly), but the developed capacity and disposition to overcome obstacles to carrying out this commitment.[23] Among the main obstacles are temptations of various kinds—fear of negative reactions from others, a desire to please, and wanting to maintain a comfortable way of life. I imagine that few readers are tempted to steal, murder, or intentionally oppress others, but many of us are tempted to stand idly by when we know, or half-know, that others are suffering unjustly. Unlike those who are (negligently) blind to relevant facts or their true motives, as *morally weak* persons we sometimes understand what needs to be done and half-realize how hollow our excuses are for not doing it. Our problem is that we lack *virtue* in Kant's sense—that is, although we are basically committed to morality, we are not ready, not "strong enough" as we say, to resist even mundane everyday temptations to continue along the easier path. Whether or not we are to blame for our weakness of (moral) will, arguably it is something that all of us who are, or might become, bystanders to oppression have a forward-looking responsibility to avoid insofar as we can. In Kantian terms, this is a duty to develop virtue as moral fortitude or strength of will to overcome obstacles to fulfilling one's first-order duties.

The Second-Order Responsibilities as General Requirements of Self-Respect

My focus has been on bystanders, but it becomes obvious on reflection that everyone in a context of oppression (and other morally problematic situa-

---

[22] This is probably an exaggeration. Sometimes a start would be going to meetings and listening to the voices of people who are oppressed instead of always hanging out with fellow bystanders who reinforce one's temptation to remain passive.

[23] Kant's conception of virtue and the duty to develop it are presented in Part II of *The Metaphysics of Morals*. For specific discussions, see Betzler (2008).

tions) has the responsibilities of due care in deliberation, self-scrutiny regarding one's motives, and doing what one can to strengthen one's will to do what is right. Primary oppressors, bystanders, and victims all have these responsibilities even if neglect of them is more characteristic of bystanders. By neglecting them everyone contributes to oppression to some extent. The line between the primary agents of oppression, bystanders, and victims, as I said, is somewhat blurred.

Nevertheless, to continue the focus on the role of bystander, it is easy to see that continuing to be a bystander when one can protest and do something about oppression would be *to fail to respect its victims*.[24] Insofar as this failure to respect others stems from neglect of the three second-order responsibilities, arguably it would *fail to show proper self-respect* as well. Why? At least in broadly Kantian theory, we are rational moral agents deeply disposed to respect moral requirements, not as externally imposed, but as an essential aspect of our humanity. Beyond this, as bystanders (as conceived here), we are basically people of good will who have accepted (or "willed") on some level that serious moral considerations should constrain and override our personal preferences. We show this when we try to put a good face on our passivity by lazy conventional moral thinking, hiding from our true motives, and masking our culpable moral weakness as a genuine inability to help.[25] Thus, in the Kantian view, as bystanders it is our own nature and personal commitment that we fail to respect when we do not do what is right to the extent that we can. A serious will to do what is right includes a will to implement that commitment as best one can. Arguably, this requires due care in moral deliberation, scrutiny of one's motivations, and strength of will to act well, especially in a context of oppression. It seems, then, attention to these responsibilities is required for us to fully respect ourselves as moral agents and as the basically well-meaning people we take ourselves to be. I have expressed the idea here in Kantian terms that some may find uncongenial, but I suspect that the point would still have resonance if re-expressed in other ways.

---

[24] An exception, as Sarah Buss has noted, is when the cost to oneself and one's loved ones of engaging in protest is excessive relative to the reasons for doing it. For further discussion of self-respect, see my "Servility and Self-Respect" and "Self-Respect Reconsidered" in Hill (1991), 1–18 and 19–24.

[25] "Hypocrisy is the tribute that vice pays to virtue" (La Rochefoucauld).

References

Primary Sources

Kant, Immanuel (1960) [1793], *Religion within the Limits of Reason Alone*, trans. Theodore M. Green and Hoyt H. Hudson (New York: Harper & Row).

——(1964) [1785], *Groundwork of the Metaphysics of Morals*, trans. and ed. H. J. Paton (New York: Harper & Row).

——(1965) [1781, 1787], *Critique of Pure Reason*, trans. Norman Kemp Smith (New York: St Martin's Press). Translated from *Kritik der reinen Vernunft* in *Kants gesammelte Schriften*, and cited by A/B pagination.

——(1996a) [1797–8], *The Metaphysics of Morals*, trans. and ed. M. J. Gregor (Cambridge: Cambridge University Press).

——(1996b), *Practical Philosophy: Cambridge Edition of the Works of Immanuel Kant*, trans. and ed. Mary Gregor (Cambridge: Cambridge University Press).

——(1997a) [1788], *Kants gesammelte Schriften*, ed. Königlich Deutsche Akademie der Wissenschaften (Berlin: de Gruyter, 1902–).

——(1997b) [1788], *Critique of Practical Reason*, trans. and ed. Mary Gregor (Cambridge: Cambridge University Press).

——(1998a) [1785], *Groundwork of the Metaphysics of Morals*, trans. and ed. Mary Gregor (Cambridge: Cambridge University Press).

——(1998b) [1793], *Religion within the Boundaries of Mere Reason*, trans. and ed. A. Wood and G. Di Giovanni (Cambridge: Cambridge University Press).

——(2002) [1785], *Groundwork for the Metaphysics of Morals*, ed. and trans. T. Hill and A. Zweig (Oxford: Oxford University Press).

——(2006) [1784–98], *Toward Perpetual Peace and Other Writings on Politics, Peace, and History*, ed. Pauline Kleingeld, trans. David L. Colclasure (New Haven: Yale University Press).

Secondary Sources

Allison, Henry J. (1990), *Kant's Theory of Freedom* (Cambridge: Cambridge University Press).

Arntzen, Sven (1995), "Kant's Denial of Absolute Sovereignty," *Pacific Philosophical Quarterly* 76: 1–16.

Baron, Marcia (1995), *Kantian Ethics (Almost) without Apology* (Ithaca, NY: Cornell University Press).

——and Fahmy, Melissa Seymour (2009), "Beneficence and Other Duties of Love in *The Metaphysics of Morals*," in Thomas E. Hill, Jr. (ed.), *The Blackwell Guide to Kant's Ethics* (Oxford: Wiley-Blackwell).

Beck, Lewis White (1971), "Kant and the Right of Revolution," *Journal of the History of Ideas* 32.

Bernstein, Alyssa R. (2008), "Kant on Rights and Coercion in International Law: Implications for Humanitarian Military Intervention," *Jahrbuch für Recht und Ethik* 16 (Berlin: Duncker & Humblot), 57–100.

Betzler, Monika (ed.) (2008), *Kant's Ethics of Virtue* (Berlin: de Gruyter).

Boxill, Bernard (2001), *Race and Racism* (Oxford: Oxford University Press).

——and Hill, Thomas E., Jr. (2001), "Kant and Race," in Boxill (2001).

Brandt, Richard (1959), *Ethical Theory* (Englewood Cliffs, NJ: Prentice Hall).

——(1979), *A Theory of the Good and the Right* (Oxford: Clarendon).

Byrd, B. Sharon (1989), "Kant's Theory of Punishment: Deterrence in its Threat, Retribution in its Execution," *Law and Philosophy* 8/2: 151–200.

——(1995), "The State as a 'Moral Person'," in Hoke Robinson (ed.), *Proceedings of the Eighth International Kant Congress* (Milwaukee: Marquette University Press), i/1. 171–89.

Cavallar, Georg (1999), *Kant and the Theory and Practice of International Right* (Cardiff: University of Wales Press).

Crisp, Roger, and Slote, Michael (eds.) (1997), *Virtue Ethics* (Oxford: Oxford University Press).

Cudd, Ann E. (2006), *Analyzing Oppression* (Oxford: Oxford University Press).

Cummiskey, David (1996), *Kantian Consequentialism* (New York: Oxford University Press).

Dancy, Jonathan (2004), *Ethics without Principles* (Oxford: Oxford University Press).

Darwall, Stephen (ed.) (2002), *Virtue Ethics* (Oxford: Blackwell).

Dean, Richard (1996), "What Should We Treat as an End-in-Itself?" *Pacific Philosophical Quarterly* 77: 266–88.

——(2006), *The Value of Humanity in Kant's Moral Theory* (Oxford: Oxford University Press).

Denis, Lara (2001), *Moral Self-Regard: Duties to Oneself in Kant's Moral Theory* (New York: Garland).

——(ed.) (2010), *Kant's 'Metaphysics of Morals': A Critical Guide* (Cambridge: Cambridge University Press).

Donagan, Alan (1977), *The Theory of Morality* (Chicago: Chicago University Press).

Donagan, Alan (1984), "Consistency in Rationalist Moral Systems," *Journal of Philosophy* 81: 291–309.

——(1991), "Symbolic Protest and Calculated Silence," in Hill (1991), 52–66.

——(1993), "Moral Dilemmas, Genuine and Spurious: A Comparative Anatomy," *Ethics* 104: 7–21.

Duns Scotus (1986), *Opus Oxoniense*, ed. Allan B. Wolter, in *Duns Scotus on the Will and Morality* (Washington, DC: Catholic University of America Press).

Engstrom, Stephen (2009), *The Form of Practical Knowledge: A Study of the Categorical Imperative* (Cambridge, Mass.: Harvard University Press).

Epictetus (1925), *Arrian's Discourses of Epictetus*, 1. 12 and 1. 15, Loeb Classical Library 131 (Cambridge, Mass.: Harvard University Press; London: William Heinemann).

Fahmy, Melissa Seymour (with Marcia Baron) (2009), "Beneficence and Other Duties of Love in *The Metaphysics of Morals*," in Hill (2009).

Foot, Philippa (2003), *Natural Goodness* (Oxford: Oxford University Press).

Frankena, William (1973), *Ethics* (Englewood Cliffs, NJ: Prentice Hall).

Frye, Marilyn (1983), "Oppression," in *The Politics of Reality* (Freedom, Calif.: The Crossings Press), 1–16.

Gert, Bernard (2005), *Morality: Its Nature and Justification*, rev. edn. (Oxford: Clarendon).

Gibbard, A. (1990), *Wise Choices, Apt Feeling* (Oxford: Clarendon).

Gregor, Mary J. (1963), *Laws of Freedom* (Oxford: Blackwell).

Guyer, Paul (ed.) (1998), *Kant's Groundwork of the Metaphysics of Morals: Critical Essays* (Lanham, Md.: Rowman & Littlefield).

——(2000), *Kant on Freedom, Law, and Happiness* (Cambridge: Cambridge University Press).

Hare, R. M. (1981), *Moral Thinking* (Oxford: Oxford University Press).

Hart, H. L. A. (1961), *The Concept of Law* (Oxford: Clarendon).

——and Honoré, Tony (1959), *Causation in the Law* (Oxford: Oxford University Press; 2nd edn., 1985).

Henry of Ghent (1979), *Quodlibet* 1. 16, ed. Raymond Macken, Opera omnia 5 (Leuven: University Press; Leiden: E. J. Brill).

Herman, Barbara (1984), "Mutual Aid and Respect for Persons," *Ethics* 94: 577–602. Repr. in Herman (1993), 45–72.

——(1993), *The Practice of Moral Judgment* (Cambridge, Mass.: Harvard University Press).

——(2007), "Making Room for Character," *Moral Literacy* (Cambridge, Mass.: Harvard University Press), 1–28.

Hill, Thomas E., Jr. (1961), "Intrinsic and Non-intrinsic Senses of 'Good'," B.Phil. Thesis, Oxford University.

——(1979), "A Review of *Acting on Principle* by Onora Nell," *Ethics* 89: 306–11.

——(1980), "Humanity as an End in Itself," *Ethics* 91: 84–90. Repr. in Hill (1992a), 38–57.

——(1983), "Ideals of Human Excellence and Preserving Natural Environments," *Environmental Ethics* 5/3: 211–24. Repr. in Hill (1991), 104–17.

——(1991), *Autonomy and Self Respect* (Cambridge: Cambridge University Press).

——(1992a), *Dignity and Practical Reason in Kant's Moral Theory* (Ithaca, NY: Cornell University Press).

——(1992b), "A Kantian Perspective on Moral Rules," in *Philosophical Perspectives*, vi. *Ethics*, ed. James E. Tomberlin (Atascadero, Calif.: Ridgeview), 285–304. Repr. in Hill (2000), 33–56.

——(1992c), "Making Exceptions without Abandoning the Principle: Or How a Kantian Might Think about Terrorism," in Hill (1992a), 196–225.

——(1992d), "Kant's Anti-Moralistic Strain," in Hill (1992a), 176–95.

——(1993), "Donagan's Kant," *Ethics* 104: 22–52. Repr. in Hill (2000), 119–52.

——(1997), "A Kantian Perspective on Political Violence," *Journal of Ethics* 1: 105–40. Repr. in Hill (2000), 200–36.

——(1998), "Four Conceptions of Conscience," *Nomos* 40, 13–52. Repr. in Hill (2002), 277–309.

——(1999a), "Happiness and Human Flourishing in Kant's Ethics," *Social Philosophy and Policy* 16: 143–75. Repr. in Hill (2002), 164–200.

——(1999b), "Kant on Wrongdoing, Desert, and Punishment," *Law and Philosophy* 18/1: 407–41. Repr. in Hill (2002), 310–39.

——(2000), *Respect, Pluralism, and Justice: Kantian Perspectives* (Oxford: Oxford University Press).

——(2001a), "Comments on Franz and Cafaro," *Philosophy in the Contemporary World* 8/2: 59–62.

——(2001b), "Hypothetical Consent in Kantian Constructivism," *Social Philosophy and Policy* 18: 300–29. Repr. in Hill (2002), 61–98.

——(2002), *Human Welfare and Moral Worth: Kantian Perspectives* (Oxford: Oxford University Press).

——(2003), "Treating Criminals as Ends in Themselves," in *Annual Review of Law and Ethics* 11: 17–36.

——(2006), "The Importance of Moral Rules and Principles," *Annual Lindlay Lecture* (Kansas: University of Kansas Press).

Hill, Thomas E., Jr. (2008*a*), "Kant on Weakness of Will," in Tobias Hoffmann (ed.), *Weakness of Will from Plato to the Present* (Washington DC: Catholic University of America Press), 210–30.

——(2008*b*), "Moral Construction as a Task: Sources and Limits," *Social Philosophy and Policy* 25: 214–36.

——(2008*c*), "Legislating the Moral Law and Taking One's Choices to be Good," *Philosophical Books* 49/2: 97–106.

——(ed.) (2009), *The Blackwell Guide to Kant's Ethics* (Oxford: Wiley-Blackwell).

——(2010), "Kant's *Tugendlehre* as Normative Ethics," in Denis (2010).

——(2011, forthcoming), "Varieties of Constructivism," in David Archard, Monique Deveaux, Neil Manson, and Daniel Weinstock (eds.), *Reading Onora O'Neill* (London: Routledge).

——(2012, forthcoming), "Practical Reason, the Moral Law, and Choice," *Analytical Philosophy*.

——(forthcoming), "Kantian Perspectives on the Rational Basis of Human Dignity," in Marcus Düwell, Jens Braarvig, Roger Brownsword, and Dietmar Mieth (eds.), *The Cambridge Handbook of Human Dignity* (Cambridge: Cambridge University Press).

Hitchcock, Christopher, and Knobe, Joshua (2009), "Cause and Norm," *Journal of Philosophy* 11: 587–612.

Hobbes, Thomas (1994), *Leviathan*, 1. 6, ed. Edwin Curley (Indianapolis: Hackett).

Holzgrefe, J. L., and Keohane, Robert O. (eds.) (2003), *Humanitarian Intervention: Ethical, Legal, and Political Dilemmas* (Cambridge: Cambridge University Press).

Hooker, B. (2000), *Ideal Code, Real World* (Oxford: Clarendon).

Hume, David (1978), *A Treatise of Human Nature*, 2nd edn. P. H. Nidditch, analytical index L. A. Selby-Bigge (Oxford: Clarendon).

Hursthouse, Rosalind (1999), *On Virtue Ethics* (Oxford: Oxford University Press).

Johnson, Robert (1998), "Weakness Incorporated," *History of Philosophy Quarterly* 15.

Korsgaard, Christine (1996*a*), *Creating the Kingdom of Ends* (Cambridge: Cambridge University Press).

——(1996*b*), "Kant's Formula of Universal Law," in Korsgaard (1996*a*), 77–105. Originally pub. in *Pacific Philosophical Quarterly* 66: 24–47.

——(1997), "Kant on the Right of Revolution," in *Reclaiming the History of Ethics: Essays for John Rawls* (Cambridge: Cambridge University Press).

——(2009), *Self-Constitution: Agency, Integrity, and Autonomy* (New York: Oxford University Press).

Locke, John (1960) [1689], *Second Treatise of Government*, in Peter Laslett (ed.), *Two Treatises of Government* (Cambridge: Cambridge University Press).

Luscombe, D. E. (1982), "Natural Morality and Natural Law," in *The Cambridge History of Later Medieval Philosophy*, ed. Norman Kretzmann et al. (Cambridge: Cambridge University Press).

Malpas, J. E. (ed.) (1994), *Philosophical Papers of Alan Donagan*, 2 vols. (Chicago: University of Chicago Press).

Mill, J. S. (1976), *Utilitarianism* (Indianapolis: Bobbs Merrill).

Moore, G. E. (1903), *Principia Ethica* (Cambridge: Cambridge University Press).

——(1912), *Ethics* (Oxford: Oxford University Press).

Morgan, Michael L. (ed.) (2005), *Classics of Moral and Political Theory*, 4th edn. (Indianapolis: Hackett).

Nell, Onora (O'Neill) (1975), *Acting on Principle* (New York: Columbia University Press).

Nicholson, Peter P. (1992), "Kant, Revolution, and History," in Howard Lloyd Williams (ed.), *Essays on Kant's Political Philosophy* (Chicago: University of Chicago Press).

O'Neill, Onora (1989), *Constructions of Reason* (Cambridge: Cambridge University Press).

——(1996), *Towards Virtue and Justice* (Cambridge: Cambridge University Press).

——(2000), *Bounds of Justice* (Cambridge: Cambridge University Press).

——(2003*a*), "Constructivism in Rawls and Kant," in Samuel Freeman (ed.), *The Cambridge Companion to Rawls* (Cambridge: Cambridge University Press), 347–67.

——(2003*b*), "Constructivism vs. Contractualism," *Ratio* 16/4: 319–31.

——*see also* Nell, Onora.

Paton, H. J. (1958), *The Categorical Imperative* (London: Hutchison).

Pogge, Thomas (1988), "Kant's Theory of Justice," *Kant-Studien* 4/79: 407–33. Repr. in Richard Arneson (ed.) (1992), *Liberalism* (Cheltenham: Edward Elgar), 586–612.

——(1998), "The Categorical Imperative," in Guyer (1998), 189–214.

——(2002), "Is Kant's *Rechtsiehre* a 'Comprehensive Liberalism'?" in Timmons (ed.) (2002).

Potts, Timothy C. (1982), "Conscience," in *The Cambridge History of Later Medieval Philosophy*, ed. Norman Kretzmann et al. (Cambridge: Cambridge University Press).

Rawls, John (1955), "Two Concepts of Rules," *Philosophical Review*, 64/1: 3–32.

——(1971/99), *A Theory of Justice* (Cambridge, Mass.: Harvard University Press).

——(1996), *Political Liberalism* (New York: Columbia University Press).

——(1999*a*), "Outline of a Decision Procedure for Ethics," in *Collected Papers*, ed. S. Freeman (Cambridge, Mass.: Harvard University Press), 1–19.

——(1999*b*), "Kantian Constructivism in Moral Theory," in *Collected Papers*, ed. S. Freeman (Cambridge, Mass.: Harvard University Press), 303–58.

——(1999*c*), *A Theory of Justice*, rev. edn. (Cambridge, Mass.: Harvard University Press).

——(1999*d*), "Themes in Kant's Moral Philosophy," in *Collected Papers*, ed. S. Freeman (Cambridge, Mass.: Harvard University Press), 497–528.

Rawls, John (1999e), "The Justification of Civil Disobedience," in Samuel Freeman (ed.), *Collected Papers* (Cambridge, Mass.: Harvard University Press).

——(2000), *Lectures on the History of Moral Philosophy*, ed. B. Herman (Cambridge, Mass.: Harvard University Press).

——(2007), *Lectures on the History of Political Philosophy*, ed. S. Freeman (Cambridge, Mass.: Harvard University Press).

Reath, Andrews (2006), *Agency and Autonomy in Kant's Moral Theory* (Oxford: Oxford University Press).

Reiss, Hans (ed.) (1991), *Kant: Political Writings* (Cambridge: Cambridge University Press).

Ripstein, Arthur (2009), *Force and Freedom: Kant's Legal and Political Philosophy* (Cambridge, Mass.: Harvard University Press).

Ross, W. D. (1930), *The Right and the Good* (Oxford: Clarendon).

Scanlon, T. M. (1998), *What We Owe Each Other* (Cambridge, Mass.: Harvard University Press).

Scheffler, Samuel (1982), *The Rejection of Consequentialism* (Oxford: Clarendon).

Scheid, Donald E. (1989), "Kant's Retributivism," *Ethics* 92: 262–82.

Sensen, Oliver (2009), "Kant's Conception of Human Dignity," *Kant-Studien* 100: 309–31.

Sidgwick, Henry (1981), *Methods of Ethics*, 7th edn. (Indianapolis: Hackett).

Singer, Marcus G. (1961), *Generalization in Ethics* (New York: Knopf).

Slote, Michael (1992), *From Morality to Virtue* (Oxford: Oxford University Press).

Smart, J. J. C. and Williams, Bernard (1973), *Utilitarianism: For and Against* (Cambridge: Cambridge University Press).

Stocker, Michael (1976), "The Schizophrenia of Modern Moral Theories," *Journal of Philosophy* 73: 453–66.

Swanton, Christine (2005), *Virtue Ethics: A Pluralistic Approach* (Oxford: Oxford University Press).

Thomas, Laurence (ed.) (2008), *Contemporary Debates in Social Philosophy* (Oxford: Blackwell).

Timmons, M. (ed.) (2002), *Kant's Metaphysics of Morals: Interpretative Essays* (Oxford: Oxford University Press).

Westphal, Kenneth R. (1992), "Kant on State, Law, Obedience to Authority in the Alleged 'Anti-Revolutionary' Writings," *Journal of Philosophical Research* 17: 383–426.

William of Ockham (1980), *Quodlibet* 1. 16, ed. J. C. Wey, Opera Theologica 9 (St Bonaventure, NY: St Bonaventure University).

Williams, Bernard (1973), "A Critique of Utilitarianism," in Smart and Williams (1973), 77–155.

——and Smart, J. J. C. (1973), *Utilitarianism: For and Against* (Cambridge: Cambridge University Press).

Williams, Howard Lloyd (ed.) (1992), *Essays on Kant's Political Philosophy* (Chicago: University of Chicago Press).

Wittgenstein, Ludwig (1958), *Philosophical Investigations*, ed. and trans. G. E. M. Anscombe and R. Rhees (Oxford: Blackwell).

Wolff, Robert Paul (1973), *The Autonomy of Reason* (New York: Harper & Row).

Wood, Allen W. (1999), *Kant's Ethical Thought* (Cambridge: Cambridge University Press).

——(2002), "The Final Form of Kant's Practical Philosophy," in Timmons (ed.) (2002), 1–21.

——(2008), *Kantian Ethics* (Cambridge: Cambridge University Press).

Index